SAMUEL BUTLER AND THE MEANING OF CHIASMUS

SAMUEL BUTLER AND THE MEANING OF CHIASMUS

Ralf Norrman

M
MACMILLAN

First published in 1986

Published by
THE MACMILLAN PRESS LTD
Houndmills, Basingstoke, Hampshire RG21 2XS
and London
Companies and representatives
throughout the world

Printed in Hong Kong

British Library Cataloguing in Publication Data
Norrman, Ralf, *1946–*
Samuel Butler and the meaning of chiasmus.
1. Butler, Samuel, *1835–1902* – Criticism and
interpretation
I. Title
823'.8   PR4349.B7Z/
ISBN 0–333–38861–5

306310

Contents

Preface

The subject of this study is *symmetry*, and in particular those of its manifestations in language and literature which are connected with the rhetorical figure of *chiasmus*.

Certain uses of chiasmus may signal – on the part of the user or users – a state of mind which will here be called *ambilateralism*. 'Ambilateralism' means an unwillingness or inability to distinguish between left and right (hence also between beginning and end, before and after, subject and object, active and passive) and a general preference for symmetry over asymmetry.

Ambilateralism, and especially its manifestations in language and literature, is an important and neglected topic. Very little has been published on chiasmus, and nothing, so far as I am aware, on those implications which will be the theme here.

My own interest in chiasmus, symmetry and ambilateralism grew out of my studies of Henry James. I put some of my ideas into the fifth chapter of *The Insecure World of Henry James's Fiction* (London: Macmillan, 1982). I very much recommend that chapter as a companion-piece to the present work. During my attempts to get a clear view of James's mentality I became convinced that one cannot properly understand the 'psychomorphology' of James's thought unless one becomes aware of the existence, in some individuals, of an excessive, or even obsessive, love of symmetry. It seemed obvious that a book-length study of ambilateralism (as revealed through the use of the figure chiasmus) was called for.

After one has been alerted to the importance of ambilateralism the question still remains how the phenomenon can most profitably be approached. Should it be studied in relation to individuals? Are there, in other words, persons particularly addicted to this pattern of thought? Or should it perhaps be studied in relation to periods of history, geographical areas, genres, levels of style, and so on?

While realizing that several, perhaps all, of these alternatives could legitimately claim some attention, I nevertheless decided that for the present the most rewarding approach would be to deal with a particular individual – an author. I also decided that it would be desirable to choose an author whose obsession with symmetry is as extreme as possible. That way the mental mechanisms of ambilateralism would be revealed with maximum clarity and simplicity.

The nineteenth-century Samuel Butler – author of *Erewhon* – seemed an ideal choice. He is extremely obsessed with symmetry, and this can easily be proved. It would be wise, I felt, to begin the investigation of ambilateralism with a study of a clear-cut and obvious case.

Choosing Samuel Butler, however, created what one might call a marketing-problem. A study of symmetry in a particular author may be expected to attract on the one hand readers interested in symmetry, and, on the other, readers interested in that author. But *is* anyone interested in Samuel Butler today?

Butler is usually regarded as a minor classic, but it seems that many people think the emphasis should be on 'minor' rather than on 'classic'. Most people have read *The Way of All Flesh*, and perhaps *Erewhon*, but few people today are interested in Butler's other works, which are in many respects more typical of him than *The Way of All Flesh*. These works also, unfortunately, reveal Butler's ambilateralism far more clearly than *The Way of All Flesh*.

As a compromise I have decided to stick to Butler as my source of examples, even though a choice of a more popular author could have ensured a larger audience. But for the convenience of my readers I shall, in this study, concentrate on those of Butler's works which are most likely to be read today, i.e. *Erewhon*, *The Way of All Flesh* and *Erewhon Revisited*. In addition I shall devote one section of a chapter to Butler's early works, since this may give some indication of whether his obsessive love of symmetry was a lifelong affair or not.

I hope to be able to give some attention to Butler's remaining works elsewhere, in a separate publication.

It must be emphasized that the subject of the following chapters is *symmetry in Butler's works*, and that the two main elements (symmetry and Butler) are equally important and inseparably linked. Thus – emphatically – this is neither just another book on Butler (one in which such terms as 'symmetry' have been introduced without sufficient justification), nor merely a book on symmetry (in which Butler happens to be the randomly chosen source of examples). The connection is organic, and the book is an attempt to describe the mind of a person to whom the love of symmetry had become an obsession and to whom symmetric patterns of thought had become compulsive.

Acknowledgements

I wish to thank Ruth Gounelas for comments on an early version of the manuscript and for permission to quote from her dissertation. It was also she who brought Butler to my attention at a time when I had not yet decided which author to choose for this study.

To my friends at Linacre College, particularly John Bamborough, I am grateful for stimulating discussions and generous encouragement.

I am indebted to Linacre College, Oxford, and to Harvard University for academic hospitality; and to the Finnish Academy and the H. W. Donner fund for financial assistance. Except for the final draft, this book was written in the winter of 1980–1 while I was at Linacre. Now, in the autumn of 1983, I have been able to resume my investigations of symmetry, and to extend them to the works of some American authors. For this opportunity I am very grateful to the American Council of Learned Societies, the United States Educational Foundation in Finland, the Ford Foundation, and the Andrew W. Mellon Foundation.

Finally I wish to thank my wife, Eva-Liisa, whose help has, as usual, been invaluable.

Cambridge, Massachusetts   Ralf Norrman

1 Chiasmus and Samuel Butler: an Introductory Sketch

The word *chiasmus* is the Latin form of χιασμός, from χιάξειν, to order in the shape of the letter χ. The term will be used here to denote a two-part structure, of which the second half repeats the two main elements of the first half, and inverts their order – thus: *ab–ba*.[1]

In principle chiastic structuring can be found on all linguistic levels. Sounds or letters, syllables, words, phrases, sentences – and even larger units of texts, such as paragraphs or chapters – can be arranged chiastically. But in literature one also often finds thematic chiastic structuring, as when, for instance, two characters exchange roles and positions in the plot, so that the character who was the villain at the beginning of the work is the hero at the end, and the character who was the hero at the beginning is the villain at the end.[2]

To illustrate chiasmus on the sentence level the traditional example, since Quintilian, is the statement 'Non ut edam vivo, sed ut vivam edo' (*Institutio oratoria*, IX.3.85). The sentence is a good example of chiasmus, but Quintilian unfortunately had little to say about chiasmus (which he called ἀντιμεταβολή). Moreover, what he did say is mostly irrelevant from the point of view of the present inquiry. The same is true of the other ancient authors who commented on chiasmus: Galen, Hermogenes (from whom we have the word, see 4.3: περὶ περιόδου), and even of Aristotle (in the sense that he did not write anything directly useful on the subject, though he did make highly relevant observations on neighbouring topics that also deal in some sense with symmetry, such as the idea of the *via media,* and was in general much better informed on questions of symmetry and asymmetry than, for example, Plato).

The views of the ancient authors on chiasmus are no longer sufficient or satisfactory today, in countries such as Britain and the

United States, because the role of chiasmus in English is radically different from its role in Greek or Latin. The function of chiasmus in a so-called *analytical* language (such as English) is different from its function in a so-called *synthetic* language (such as Greek or Latin). Chiasmus is all about *order,* in the sense of sequential order, i.e. what comes first and what comes after, and sequential order is vastly more important in the analytical languages than in the synthetic. The synthetic languages indicate what is subject and what is object in the sentence mainly through case; the analytical languages again mainly through word-order. Thus, in English, what is left in the sentence is normally subject and what is right is object (except in the passive)[3]. Therefore, if we say 'Jack loves Jill', we know that Jack is the one doing the loving (subject), and Jill the one being loved (object), because 'Jack' occurs left and 'Jill' right in the sentence (when it is written; or before and after, respectively, if the sentence is spoken – 'left and right' being the spatial equivalents of 'before and after', since English script is read from left to right). If we want to say that Jill is the one doing the loving and Jack the one being loved we have to reverse the order, thus: 'Jill loves Jack.' And if we wish to imply reciprocity or mutuality of loving we use chiasmus: 'Jack loves Jill, and Jill Jack.'[4]

Sequential order being important in chiasmus, it follows that the role of chiasmus in the analytical languages is bound to be different from its role in the synthetic languages. In the synthetic languages chiasmus may affect only form; in the analytical languages it inevitably affects both form and content, since the mechanism is such that one specific thing within form, i.e. word-order, *determines* an important kind of content, i.e. the subject- and object-functions.

In the synthetic languages, then, chiasmus is likely to be something primarily ornamental or decorative; in the analytical languages something philosophical or psychological.

This fundamental distinction has not been obvious to modern writers on rhetoric. No one, it seems, will face up to the consequences of the increased importance of word-order. In modern comments on chiasmus the figure is usually treated very much as it always has been treated by rhetoricians for the last two thousand years.

There are probably two reasons for this unsatisfactory state of affairs. First, the study of rhetoric is still heavily influenced by antiquity. In the case of chiasmus, as we have seen, this influence leads astray. Second, scholars still persist in traditional, misguided attempts to study rhetorical figures as if they were a phenomenon of form only. In the case of chiasmus such an approach does not lead very far. In the study of chiasmus one cannot successfully separate form from content and study either in isolation. Both have to be taken into account simultaneously.

We must not regard rhetorical figures as something exclusively or primarily ornamental. Rhetorical figures do not get into texts as an afterthought. It is not the case that first authors perceive; then they think; then they decide what to write on; then they formulate it; and finally – for decorative and ornamental purposes – they throw in a certain amount of rhetorical figures, the way one puts icing on a cake after it has been finished in every other respect.

Such a 'decorativist' view of the nature and function of rhetorical figures is largely false. It is certainly false in the case of chiasmus and those authors who use it most. In the case of these authors one must rather conclude that not only their style is influenced by chiasmus, but so are their thoughts, and even their perception.

During the last two decades it has been generally recognized that the 'ornamental' or 'decorative' theory of rhetorical figures was insufficient in the case of at least one specific figure, i.e. metaphor. The 'decorativist' line of thought has now been largely abandoned in the general view of metaphor. I should like to see a similar shift in our view of chiasmus, and I hope that the present work may contribute to such a shift of emphasis.

Naturally there does exist a decorative or ornamental dimension to the use of chiasmus, but that is not the most important aspect. The chiastic structure is not there only in some insignificant superficial ornamental or decorative level of style. In the case of the authors who are most obsessed with chiasmus, and make the most frequent use of it, chiasmus determines what they see, what they think, what they write, and finally, of course, *how* they write.

There are some authors whose fondness for chiasmus is so extreme that it deserves to be called obsession. I shall call these authors *chiasticists,* and their state of mind *chiasticism.* Thus, in the following, in contrast to the term 'chiastic', which will quite neutrally and objectively denote something structured according to the *ab–ba* pattern, the term 'chiasticistic' will imply a habitual use of chiasmus which has become a psychological necessity to the user.

In the case of these authors it is easy to see the truth of Count Buffon's famous dictum 'le style est l'homme même'. Even with the least mannered writer one can sense that there is a grain of truth in Buffon's view, and the more mannered a writer is the easier it is to see the connection between 'le style' and 'l'homme'. In the case of a chiasticist such as Butler it is eminently true – and eminently demonstrable – that 'le style est l'homme'.

Rhetorical figures do not get into authors' texts by chance. Most authors probably have a command of most rhetorical figures. But some authors use certain figures more often than other figures, and they use these figures more often than other authors use them. An understanding of the psyche of an author can explain why he favours certain figures; conversely, by observing which figures he favours, one may learn something about the psyche of an author.

The ambition of the present work is to help chart what we may call the 'psychomorphology' of chiasticistic thinking. It is not likely that the psychomorphological profile of every chiasmus-addict will be exactly the same. But probably a case-study of one chiasticist will reveal features that are characteristic not only of him, but also, to a varying degree, of other individuals of the species.

There are many authors with a well-known love of symmetry whom one could choose for a study such as the present one. Lewis Carroll, for instance, with his constant preoccupation with mirror-phenomena, would be worth consideration. As could be expected, chiasmus is a fairly prominent feature of his style.

The best choice for the moment, however, must surely be Samuel Butler (1835–1902). It is difficult to find any author, from any period or country, who is so extraordinarily obsessed with chiasmus as Butler. He uses chiasmus constantly. His texts abound in chiastic sentences. His thought is dominated by chiastic structuring. He fits whatever he can into the chiastic pattern and usually denies the existence of other patterns. The leading ideas of practically all his books have their origin in the chiastic formula. *All* his scientific doctrines derive from his obsession with chiasmus. It is hardly an exaggeration to say that everything he observed went through a chiastic filter, so that he took in only what chiasmus let through. Once the pattern emerges it becomes easy to go even further than this, and see the influence of chiasmus also in the biographical material.

It may seem here that some very large claims are being made, and that 'psychomorphology' is a pompous word. This is all quite deliberate. The facts of the case are so extraordinary that these kinds of claims, and this kind of term, both seem called for. I believe that a knowledge of the way the mechanism of chiasmus functions can be used as a map to Butler's mental landscape. And I believe that, without exaggeration, one can argue that whoever understands chiasmus will also understand Butler.

The complete pattern of chiasmus is made up of a number of abstract principles that all have to be present before one can properly speak of 'chiasticism'. Let us take a brief look at some of these principles straightaway here, since they all work together in the mechanisms of chiasticism, all influencing one another, so that the function of one cannot be understood except in conjunction with the others. These constituent parts of chiasmus will be returned to later and gone through more fully. But first let us familiarize ourselves with the general idea of how they might work as a team.

First and foremost of these constituent principles of chiasmus is *dualism,* or, more generally, the use of the number two. A chiasmus is made up of two halves, which are each other's mirror-image – each other's *enantiomorph*. Each half further contains two main elements. Since the number two plays such an important role in chiasmus it is to be expected in literature that dualism and chiasmus should go together. We may conclude that only a strict dualist will become a strict chiasticist.

Another important element in chiasmus is the principle of *antithesis*. In a chiasmus the two halves, on each side of the break in the middle, are somehow perceived as being 'turned against one another'. Chiasmus is therefore seen as a particularly suitable vehicle for the expression of opposition – of antithetical relationships. Since the number two – which, in addition to the principle of opposition, is the structural backbone of antithesis – occurs in chiasmus not only in the major division of the chiasmus into two halves, but also in the further division of each half into two subdivisions, antithesis predictably enough often invades the halves of a chiasmus rather than the chiasmus as a whole, and sometimes both the halves and the whole.

Let us now briefly consider some of the consequences of the interplay of the two principles mentioned so far.

For anyone addicted to the number two there are two categorical imperatives: one, to reduce all numbers larger than two to two; the other, to split the number one if it should threaten to come into existence.

Butler was a master at both of these activities. As to the first, he would always try to arrange things in such a way that he could structure reality dualistically. If there was more than two of something he would see this larger number as forming two groups (usually in opposition to each other). Another strategy was simply not to take notice of more than two of anything. Butler did not feel comfortable with any other patterns of thought than binary or dualistic ones.

As an example we may take Butler's numerous attempts to restore forgotten, but in his view deserving, artists to fame. Butler's strategy for rehabilitation was normally to take his favourite, say Tabachetti, and put him up in opposition to some generally recognized master, such as Raphael, and then to extol the virtues of the former and denigrate the latter. Butler was normally incapable of visualizing a hierarchy of more than two artists and giving his favourite a position among these. The way he preferred to visualize anything was to take a particular thing and put it in relation to another particular thing, and usually in an antithetical relation.

Another method of fulfilling the desire for dualism is to stay within that part of reality which is intrinsically dualistic. Butler embraced this possibility with great enthusiasm. Little that he came across would escape his attention if it was in itself dualistic.

He was, accordingly, very fond of reading such authors as Homer – since there are *two* works, the *Iliad* and the *Odyssey*! But, as we know, if there are two of anything, the principle of antithesis demands that they should also preferably be in opposition to one another. Therefore Butler's happiness over the *Iliad* and the *Odyssey* was to begin with only half complete. There *was* dualism, sure enough, but where was the antithesis? Such incomplete symmetry as this must have been a thorn in Butler's chiasticist flesh.

The solution, however, was near at hand. In his introduction to volume XII of the Shrewsbury Edition of Butler's works, Henry Festing Jones reports how Butler as early as his school days used to say that 'the Odyssey was the Iliad's wife'.[5] This is symptomatic of what was to come. To ordinary people a dichotomy such as male–female is faintly antithetical. Indubitably man and woman are different, yet they are similar too, both being human. But to a chiasticist such a relation as male–female appears overwhelmingly antithetical. Gradually and inevitably, therefore, Butler's theory ripened – the *Odyssey* was written by a woman!

After many tentative articles Butler finally presented his theory at length in his book *The Authoress of the Odyssey* (1897), in which he maintains that the *Odyssey* was written by a Sicilian princess from Trapani. Butler had now restored the universe to the order in which he loved to see it: two parts, in antithetical opposition to one another.

The two halves of a chiasmus are each other's mirror images. Chiasmus is therefore likely to be typical of narcissistic people, who have problems with their relations to others, and most of all wish to see in others a reflection of themselves. It therefore seems that it was not by chance that Butler, in collaboration with his friend Henry Festing Jones, wrote an opera with the title *Narcissus*.

Butler hardly ever had a completely successful relationship with anyone. With Jones things went well for a long time, primarily because to begin with he was content to be merely a copy of Butler – an echo or a reflection.

In the Narcissus-myth, we recall, the name of the nymph who loves Narcissus is 'Echo'. An echo is a repetition that returns to its source. A mirror image – as from the surface of a well – is likewise a repetition that returns to its source. In a chiasmus the second half is a repetition of the first, but with the order of the two main elements inverted, so that the meaning returns to its source in the first half. A chiasticist is likely to be a self-centred person, since chiasmus is a self-sufficient thing, self-generating and self-perpetuating.

Not even Jones, however, was capable of being a perfect mirror image of Butler. The only perfect partner for a chiasticist is really his own self. Fortunately it is easy to split the ego – chiasticists are trained in that, since one of the demands of dualism is that the number one must be split if it threatens to appear. In 1879 Butler published a series of articles on God, later brought together in a volume and published as a book with the title *God the Known and God the Unknown* in 1909. By splitting God into two aspects Butler managed to avoid the number one. This example is typical; this is how he always behaved.

If we assume that the only really perfect partner for a chiasticist is his own self, this will explain a lot of Butler's strangely schizoid behavior on many occasions. When he lived in New Zealand at the middle of the nineteenth century, for instance, he wrote a series of articles for the journal *The Press* expressing a variety of views on the then hotly debated subject of Darwinism. An even better example is a series of letters to *The Examiner* in 1871. Butler wrote under various pseudonyms and his technique is first to defend a view in one article; then later to attack his own defence in another article (under a different pseudonym); then to attack his own attack; and so on and so forth. This is typical chiasticistic dialectics; views are forever reflected back and forth between the two halves of the chiasticistic mind, without anything ever leading anywhere.

In his first contribution to *The Press* Butler made use of the dialogue form. The use of this genre is again symptomatic: in a dialogue the dialectic exists within one and the same text.

Butler presented to posterity a gift of a large number of notebooks, neatly bound. A striking feature of the innumerable notes is the importance Butler places on his own changes of opinion. Having changed his mind about something was always something that Butler considered important and worth noting down. The notes, with their dated additions of second thoughts, show us Butler-now carrying on a conversation with Butler-then.

In addition to the two principles mentioned so far, i.e. dualism and antithesis, let us now introduce a third of the principles involved in chiasmus: *inversion*. In a chiasmus the second part not only repeats the two main elements of the first half but also inverts their order. Thus the second half of a chiasmus is an inversion of the first half, or rather both halves are each other's inversions, since it is debatable whether there is, strictly speaking, a 'first' and a 'second' in a chiasmus.

To invert things was Butler's favourite pastime. All the words derived from, or related to, Latin *vertere* are highly frequent and significant in Butler: 'perversion', 'conversion', 'aversion', 'subversion', and – of course – the word 'inversion' itself. Likewise the word 'turn', English for *vertere*, occurs again and again in his prose. (Since Butler's universe is relativistic, not absolute, the word 'turn' is often found in conjunction with its own near-antonym 'straight' – compare for example, the 'straighteners' in Butler's utopian novel *Erewhon*. In Butler's philosophy nothing has an existence of its own. Everything exists only in relation to its opposite. Only relations are real.)

In chapter 50 of Butler's novel *The Way of All Flesh* (published in 1903 though written several decades earlier) we learn that the protagonist, Ernest Pontifex, had 'been lately ... getting into an odious habit of turning proverbs upside down' (Shrewsbury, xvii 228[6]). *The Way of All Flesh*, like many of Butler's other works, is heavily autobiographical in content, and Ernest was not the only person who had got into the habit of turning proverbs upside down. Butler, too, throughout his career, suffered from a compulsion to turn everything he came into contact with upside down, inside out, back to front, topsy-turvy; and particularly proverbs. In the light of the dictates of chiasticism it is easy to see why. In a perfectly chiasticistic world nothing ever exists on its own; everything must be complemented with its own inversion.

That Butler should have singled out proverbs in particular for his attacks also fits the pattern perfectly. What a chiasticist strives for is balance and lability. Proverbs, on the contrary, represent imbalance and stability. When Butler comes across such a saying as 'God is love', he is never content until he has turned it around and complemented it with its own mirror image, as the following note in his *Notebooks* shows: '"*God is love*": I like "Love is God" better.'[7]

Butler was a great controversialist (note the word and its connection with *vertere*)[8] and he loved to fight for the underdog. He travelled around Europe looking for neglected artists whom he could rehabilitate. He often turned against the established view; he felt a compulsion to be a rebel. His attitude to proverbs falls neatly into place against the background of his anti-authoritarianism.

Fighting for the underdog is a fight that must not be won – only fought. Should the chiasticst win such a fight, that would upset the balance again. Then of course he would have to change sides. There are some patterns in Butler's changes of allegiance that may not be accidental. As long as Darwin was the underdog, during the 1860s, Butler tended to be friendly towards him and defend his views. But, when, in the 1870s, it had become obvious that Darwin would win, we find Butler on the other side, sharply attacking Darwin in his pamphlets and articles, and in his four books on evolution: *Life and Habit* (1877), *Evolution, Old and New* (1879), *Unconscious Memory* (1880), and *Luck, or Cunning?* (1886). Butler's reasons for aligning himself with one or the other side in the controversy were various, but, whatever the ostensible reasons in each case, Butler's decisions coincide with what the demands of chiasticism lead one to expect. Butler's choice of sides is often connected with his longing for balance.

As to the question itself, Butler's views on evolution were also determined by the same chiasticistic mechanism. Darwin's theory is based on two main theses: first, that there is always in nature an amount of chance variation; and, second, that natural selection allows the most suitable among the variants to survive.

It is, then, a question of two factors, of which one influences the other. Given that starting-point, Butler's behaviour is entirely predictable. Whichever factor is stressed by the (Darwinian) establishment, Butler must, of course, stress the other. Of the two factors, the variant and the environment, Darwin and the scientific establishment said that environment is primary and the variant secondary; accordingly Butler had to say that the variant is primary and environment secondary.

To be able to do this Butler developed his teleological theory of evolution – i.e. that species change because they want to, not because natural selection favours those among variants who happen to be best suited. This, of course, was a view similar to those that the early evolutionists Lamarck, Buffon and Erasmus Darwin had held, in varying degrees. Butler now, therefore, had the additional gratifying chance of defending the views of the palaeo-Darwinians (the underdogs) against the attacks and neglect of the neo-Darwininians.

In the same way that Butler sought balance by supporting the side which he saw as weaker in the debate on evolution he strove for balance in most of his debates, and in the ideas he adopted. Thus one may understand why he developed a system of thought which is parallel to the philosophy which was later given the name 'pragmatism' and largely ascribed to William James. During Butler's lifetime William James had not yet published the most important of his works on pragmatism, but Butler and William James were kindred spirits, and Butler had read some minor things by James, and naturally picked out any chiastic thoughts he happened to come across. Thus he enthusiastically notes down William James's allegation that 'we do not cry because we are sorry; but are sorry because we cry'.[9] In everything that Butler read – which was a great deal, since he spent a considerable number of his waking hours in the British Museum – he was sure to notice all chiastic thoughts.

In creating the philosophy of pragmatism William James was doing something similar to what Butler had done in the debate on evolution. In the division of the world into the subjective and the objective, the self and the other, if philosophy had hitherto stressed the latter William James would stress the former. Accordingly he creates his pragmatistic philosophy according to which truth and reality are not primarily something that the environment imposes on the individual but something that the individual imposes on the environment.[10]

Butler's attacks on proverbs should be seen as one manifestation of his attacks on authority. Among the elements of language, proverbs play the role of the establishment. They express truths that in the opinion of mankind are so important that they have had to be codified in a stable form for ready reference. To a chiasticist such an implied stability is like a red rag to a bull.

Proverbs were not the only elements of language that Butler attacked. Other petrified elements also attracted his displeasure. He constantly tried to destroy such things as the myths of antiquity, and in general anything that very definitely has come to symbolize something. Jeremiah, for instance, has come to epitomize unhappiness and misery. Therefore Butler inverts this in his *Notebooks*: '*Jeremiah*: In private life he was very likely a person of the most playful humour, brimful of fun and merriment' (p. 27).

For a chiasticist there must always exist an *alternative* (and please note that this word again reminds us of the number two). Of two alternatives, moreover, both should be equally possible. We may be sure that Butler was rather irritated that men such as Galileo had proved that the earth goes round the sun, rather than the sun round the earth. A pleasing chiasticistic uncertainty had been destroyed. But at least Butler dutifully and delightedly reports the *bons mots* of uneducated people on the subject; i.e. people for whom the question is still open.

Sun going round the earth: A child asked the same old lady whether the earth went round the sun or the sun round the earth. 'Lor, child,' she said, 'what questions you ask, to be sure. I thought it all over yesterday and I can't think it all over again to-day; what I thought then I think now; sometimes one and sometimes the other.' (*Note-books*, pp. 107–8)

And in his utopias *Erewhon* and *Erewhon Revisited* Butler gives free rein to his chiasticism and pleases himself. In Erewhon many things go sometimes one way, and sometimes the other.

What a chiasticist thus strives for is balance. In a chiasmus the two halves are exactly balanced: there are two main elements on each side, and as to their sequential order each is a mirror image of the other.

Chiasmus is an example of *bilateral symmetry*, and relativism and symmetry go together. In a chiasmus the distinction disappears between left and right, beginning and end, subject and object, active and passive. A chiasticistic universe is *incurvatus in se*; relativistic and self-sufficient.

We shall shortly look at some examples of the consequences of this. First, however, let us note the sheer overwhelming magnitude of the phenomenon. In Butler's books there are thousands and thousands of sentences in which he consciously (as opposed to unconsciously, which also comes into the picture) inverts the order of some linguistic elements – usually words. He does this in order to achieve the effect he aims for, but also because sequential order (the question of precedence) is something problematical for him – so problematical, in fact, that his inability to distinguish between left and right sometimes borders on the pathological.

In this study I shall define *ambilateralism* as an unwillingness or inability to distinguish between left and right, and a preference for symmetry over asymmetry. This is of course different from the use of the term in clinical psychology. In psychology only inability would count. Psychologists are interested in the literal inability to distinguish between left and right; its causes (insufficient cerebral lateralization) and effects (various kinds of handicaps).

It is not practical to draw a sharp distinction here between Butler's unwillingness and his inability, since the end-product of both is the same. It is obvious that the pathological dimension should not be overemphasized. Thus it is clear, for instance, that Butler was not a dyslexic. In some severe cases of dyslexia it would seem that the inability of the patients to distinguish between left and right is relevant.[11] There are few instances of inversion of sounds or letters, or syllables, in Butler that could be interpreted as pathological. Instead, where these occur, they are rather to be seen as evidence of the keen aesthetic pleasure that Butler always derived from any inversion – inversion being a prerequisite for the completion of symmetry. Butler occasionally reports cases of metathesis. In his book *Alps and Sanctuaries* (1881) he relates how a little boy and the boy's younger sister came to watch him while he was making a drawing of a landscape in Ticino. Butler asked the girl's name. The boy answered, 'Forolinda.' Butler concludes that the name must have been 'Florinda' – the boy metathetically inverting the order of the 'l' and the 'r'. Butler was so amused by this episode that he included it in his book.[12]

Another type of inversion on the level of sounds and letters that Butler showed a predilection for was anagrams. These usually occur in their pure form, going from the end to the beginning – though other types are used occasionally. Anagrams are found in particular in *Erewhon*, where the title itself is an example.

But it is usually on the level of the sentence, or the level of ideas (the thematic level), that Butler's blindness to the distinction between left and right is most striking, and it is on the level of the sentence that those examples are found that could most obviously be described as cases of pure inability rather than unwillingness. Very revealing is, for instance, a letter from Francis Darwin (son of Charles Darwin) to Butler, in which he says that he found Butler's polemical book interesting, but wonders why Butler calls his father's book *Plants and Animals* when in fact its title was *Animals and Plants*.[13]

It is obvious from this episode, and from others like it, that Butler lived in a world characterized by left–right inversion to such an extent that he was not aware of having inverted the order. Butler writes a comment and a reply to Francis Darwin saying that he had been tired ('brain fag'), and he had not observed the slip. But Butler was usually 'tired' whenever he had to distinguish between left and right, beginning and end, subject and object, active and passive. He was, in some sense of the word, constitutionally unable to choose, and thus, although to say that Butler was unwilling to distinguish between left and right is a safe way of stating the case, it is also certainly no exaggeration to claim that at times he is not only unwilling but unable.

At least Butler continually *worried* about questions of sequential order. It is therefore again symptomatic that he wrote a book on Shakespeare's sonnets, *Shakespeare's Sonnets Reconsidered, and in Part Rearranged* (1889), in which he puts a lot of time and effort into an attempt to sort out the sequential relations of the sonnets – their order. To be sure, Butler is not the only critic to have done this; many other Shakespearean scholars have occupied themselves with the order of the sonnets. Nevertheless it seems that the various pieces of the puzzle do fall neatly into place, one after another.

In Butler's works there are many thousands of examples of inversion and chiastic structuring on the sentence level. But equally important are the examples of inversion and chiastic structuring found on the thematic level. Practically all of Butler's books can be explained with the aid of these.

To start with a case in which inversion determines the birth of an entire work, let us take *The Fair Haven* (1873), a book which gradually grew out of earlier material, such as the pamphlet *The Evidence for the Resurrection of Jesus Christ as Given by the Four Evangelists Critically Examined* (1865). The subject of these works is the resurrection.

As we have seen, Butler felt a compulsion to invert anything which was commonly accepted as having a certain established sequential order. If public opinion said *a–b*; then out came Butler, and said *b–a*. So far so good.

The trouble is that public opinion is not always consistent. Sometimes it says *a–b* in ninety-nine cases out of a hundred, and *b–a* in the remaining one. As could be expected, such exceptions caused Butler great problems. What was he to do? Should he invert the inversion and say *a–b*? Or should he go along with it, and say *b–a*, since it *was*, after all, an inversion?

Public opinion says that the order of life and death is life-to-death. First people live, and then they die; in that order. This made Butler uncomfortable; he felt that the sequence 'life–death' – if it was ever to become pleasingly chiasticistic – ought to be complemented by its inversion, i.e. the sequence 'death–life'. In his writings Butler searches world literature and the accumulated traditions of mankind, dragging forth any rare instances of the sequence 'death-to-life' that he can find. He is thus, for instance, very fond of the Orpheus-myth. Orpheus, we recall, was allowed to bring his wife Eurydice back from the realm of the dead, on condition that he did not turn around. (The last element, as we should by now realize, is pregnantly symbolic – 'turning', 'not turning', is precisely what this sort of thing is all about. In the Orpheus-myth there are other features too that fit the picture; thus we again meet the phenomenon *echo*, and so on.)

Butler sifted forth such things as the Orpheus-myth, and in general whatever examples he could find of a death-to-life sequence. Failing to find enough cases to satisfy his craving he would invent his own. In Butler's utopias *Erewhon* and *Erewhon Revisited* there are numerous variations on the theme 'death-to-life'. In *Erewhon*, for instance, people are 'drawn through life backwards'. The Erewhonians also believe in the sentence, 'To grow old is to grow young and to grow young is to grow old.'

In these cases Butler was allowed to keep his role as the rebel who points out the complementary inversion of that order which is commonly accepted by public opinion. One thing, however, created enormous problems for him – the resurrection of Jesus Christ. Christ rose from the dead; in other words he went through the sequence 'death-to-life'; not only 'life-to-death'. This, of course, was fine in itself, but the annoying thing was that public opinion was on the side of the inversion; on the side of *b–a*, rather than *a–b*. Public opinion cheated Butler out of his triumph; by believing, for once, in an inversion. What should have been a daring minority-view, was in fact the belief of the majority.

Butler meditated for years on the question of the resurrection. He read the New Testament in Greek till he knew it by heart. He studied modern (continental) biblical criticism. Gradually he began to see a way out, and was able to start formulating his own compromise theory. Jesus had not died on the cross; he had only swooned. He had been saved from the grave by Joseph of Arimathaea. In other words, he had in a sense risen from the dead; yet in another had not. With this theory, presented at length in *The Fair Haven*, Butler was able to satisfy all his emotional needs. On the one hand he could keep the sequence 'death-to-life' which he wanted so desperately; on the other he could also keep his position as a rebel. Public opinion was still wrong, and he, Butler, was alone right.

In order to understand why chiasmus mixes up the chiasticist's view of the relation between symmetry and asymmetry we must take a closer look at one particular variety of chiasmus, and what it does to one's sense of distinctions.

At the beginning of *Erewhon Revisited* (1901) the narrator, who is the son of Higgs, the protagonist of *Erewhon* (1872), says that he had never read his father's book, but after an important conversation with his father he got hold of the book and read it eagerly 'from end to end' (Shrewsbury, XVI 8–9).[14]

Consider this choice of phrase and its implications: Normally one would say, in English, that one has read a book 'from *beginning* to end'. But a chiasticist does not want an asymmetrical universe. There should be no beginning and end, only two ends.

Why should a chiasticist choose such a phrase as 'end to end' rather than 'beginning to end'? Why should a chiasticist always feel he has to choose a behaviour which will negate the difference between left and right and assert symmetry rather than asymmetry? Why can he never tolerate the existence of distinctions and differences?

Probably this negation of asymmetry is connected with the nature of the most important of all varieties of chiasmus: the type which I shall here term *existential chiasmus*. An existential chiasmus is a chiasmus which makes use of the verb 'to be'. As a famous example we may take Shakespeare's line from the beginning of *Macbeth:* 'Fair is foul and foul is fair'.

In an existential chiasmus there exists a problematical relationship between the two principles of similarity and difference. How could 'fair' be 'foul', or 'foul' be 'fair'? 'Fair' should be 'fair' and 'foul' should be 'foul' (there should be stability in the world; including semantic stability). If 'fair' and 'foul' are at all separate entities to begin with, they should be different; yet the chiastic existential formula implies that they are the same or similar, partly because they are capable of taking each other's places and roles, and partly because the verb 'to be' expresses identity or identicality. Existential chiasmus creates conceptual chaos, which in the line from *Macbeth* is a linguistic parallel to the political and emotional chaos in the play.

It is above all existential chiasmus that shatters the stability – most of all the semantic stability – of Butler's world. 'The beginning is the end and the end is the beginning' seems to be the formula in question here, making beginning and end the same thing. Therefore in Butler's world one reads books from 'end to end'. If end and beginning are the same thing anyway (i.e. in meaning), why should they not then be referred to by the same word?, argues the chiasticist.

Before moving on to a fourth principle, i.e. *reciprocity,* which together with the three principles already mentioned – dualism, antithesis and inversion – determines most of the nature and function of chiasticism, let us investigate a few more effects of existential chiasmus.

We remember that in the utopian society of Erewhon it is customary to punish the sick. They are brought to trial, thrown in jail, and they are condemned morally. On the other hand it is customary to try to cure criminals. These are given medical care by a profession known as 'straighteners', and they are the object of tolerance and compassion. In other (chiastic) words, illness is treated as crime and crime as illness. The existential formula underlying this is of course, 'Crime is illness and illness is crime'.

One could speculate over the question which of the two halves of this formula came first to Butler's mind (knowing as we do that, once *one* had come, the appearance of the other was automatic). If we consider carefully the demands of chiasticism, and the consequences which habitual chiastic thinking brings with it, it may be possible to make an informed guess.

Critics in search of programmatic literature could easily be tempted to try to read a social, political or moral message into *Erewhon*. Behind the chiastic structuring 'crime–illness; illness–crime' there is – they would argue – a prescriptive sentence saying approximately the following: 'In England we ought to treat criminals as if they were ill'. The other half of the chiastic structure could then be read as a satire on hypochondria. No matter how appealing such a view may seem, I nevertheless fear that any critics who stick to it misread Butler, at least partly.

What we have to take into account – no matter how reluctantly – is Butler's enormous capacity to accommodate cruelty in his attitudes and his periodic indifference to suffering. Butler was capable of great emotional involvement from time to time (every now and then; periodically), but chiasticism dictates that no emotion exists on its own, only in relation to, and in conjunction with, its own opposite. Moreover, chiasticism decrees that nothing is for ever; everything must be periodically inverted. If there are two of something, and you are supposed to distribute something to these two, a chiasticist must never wholeheartedly give all to one for a long period of time. That would imply an acceptance of asymmetry. The chiasticist instead must either give equal shares to both; or else alternate, so that he favours now one, now the other.

Our life as humans is largely built on asymmetry. Our morals, for instance, enjoin us to take sides, asymmetrically, *for* the tortured, *against* the torturer. But, since chiasmus negates and annihilates the difference between subject and object, a chiasticist is not capable of a sustained asymmetrical, moral attitude of this kind. To him, on the contrary, the truth is a sentence of the following type: 'To pain is to be pained, and to be pained is to pain.' The perpetrator and the victim of a wrong are equally culpable.

In his distribution of sympathy and antipathy to such a duality as 'torturer–tortured' a chiasticist either gives half of both sympathy and antipathy to each, or else, if he gives all his sympathy to one and all his antipathy to the other, there is constant alternation, through periodic inversion, so that each sometimes receives sympathy, sometimes antipathy. The cruel truth is, therefore, that Butler, at least periodically (in accordance with the demands of chiasticism), thought that the sick and unfortunate have themselves to blame.

The thematic structure of *Erewhon* therefore probably started off with the sentence 'illness is crime.' Once this is a given, the complementary inversion, 'crime is illness', then automatically follows, completing the chiastic existential formula: 'Illness is crime and crime is illness.'[15]

Let us now call to mind the chapters on machinery in *Erewhon* – how machines take over the role of humans, and men become slaves to machines. These chapters are also easily explained as deriving from the rules of chiasticism. Butler's contemporaries had a mechanistic view of the world and of man. In Darwin's theory, Butler thought, there is no room for mind, for the living, for the non-mechanical. What contemporary science was in fact arguing, Butler thought, was the sentence 'Man is a machine.' The machine chapters in *Erewhon* are naturally Butler's obligatory inversion of this, 'Machines are human.'[16]

An existential chiastic formula, such as 'The mechanical is the living and the living is the mechanical', is, however, somehow rather strange and problematical – this was obvious even to Butler. How can *a* be *b*, and *b* be *a*, if they are at all *a* and *b* to begin with? All his life Butler incessantly racked his brains over this problem.[17]

One of his answers was that it is impossible to define limits; that in *b* there is always a little quantity of *a*, and that in *a* there is always a little quantity of *b*. There is some life in machines, and there is a little bit of the mechanical in the living. We may call this pattern of thought 'Butler's yin-and-yang philosophy'. Just as in the yin-and-yang symbol of the Orient there is a little spot of white[18] in the black, and a little spot of black in the white, so Butler thought that in everything there is at least a small quantity of its opposite. Butler loved metaphors making use of the word 'alloy'. The noblest metals have to be mixed with something baser to be useful – gold has to be mixed with a small quantity of a baser metal. In Butler's works one finds numerous 'alloy' metaphors, and numerous metaphors that are closely related, or reveal the same thought-pattern.

Chiasticism, however, also demands extremism. In the universe of a chiasticist it is not only the case that only opposites exist; it is moreover the case that only extreme opposites exist. If something is a little true, then it must be very true. If something has gone a little way, then it must go all the way. Another very revealing favourite metaphor in Butler is that of 'wedges'. 'To let in the thin end of the wedge' is one of Butler's favourite expressions. The implied rule is that, if something has gone a little way, it must go all the way.

'Wedges' and 'alloys' together give Butler *carte blanche*. Using these two he can take any pair of opposites – 'the animal kingdom – the vegetable kingdom', 'the organic – the inorganic', and so forth – and always prove that the one is the other and the other the one, if only he can find the least little evidence of a blurring of the border-line.

In the later editions of *Erewhon* there are two chapters in which a philosopher extends the vegetarianism of the Erewhonians to a ban on eating plants as well. This is the extremism, the 'wedge philosophy', created by underlying existential chiasmus. If you do not eat animals, then you should not eat plants, because 'Animals are plants and plants are animals' (the border-line, you see, is blurred; some plants, for instance, have a habit which is characteristic of animals, i.e. that of movement!). In his writings, both in *Erewhon* and elsewhere, Butler invents never-ending variations on this theme: 'The inorganic lives' (for example, bacteria in stones) and 'The living is inorganic' (hair, fingernails, and so on, are dead material), and so on and so forth *ad infinitum*. One of his favourite themes was that God is human and humanity divine. In general one need not scratch the surface for very long to reveal the existential chiastic formula underlying anything that Butler wrote.

It may seem strangely inconsistent that Butler should have believed in extremism and alloys at the same time. Indeed it *is* inconsistent, and this is far from being the only inconsistency of its kind in Butler. Butler is not only occasionally inconsistent; he is habitually and programmatically inconsistent, and has to be so, because inconsistency is part of chiasticism. After any statement that a critic makes on Butler's thought the critic ought to add, 'The opposite is also true.' In the present study I shall henceforth assume that this goes without saying.

Butler's opinions come in disjunctive pairs, the halves mutually exclusive.[19]

Our own type of consistency is worthless as a tool in trying to grasp Butler's habits of thought. Instead we must try to submit, and get under Butler's skin, and see the internal consistency of his system – which, I repeat, has nothing to do with our type of consistency. The process is rather like trying to learn one of those systems of geometry which are not based on Euclid's premises. It is a great effort; and the system demands to be dealt with on its own terms. It has an internal consistency; but one touch of Euclid and the whole thing crumbles. The two are incompatible; but each is consistent within itself.

Butler's consistency builds on symmetry; not on asymmetry. When we have said one thing it is inconsistent to say the opposite. To Butler, on the contrary, it follows that if a statement is true its inversion must also be true, and the statement is not even complete without its inversion.

The enormously important role of chiasmus in Butler's thinking is indicated by the nature of the epigraphs of the twenty-odd volumes he wrote. An epigraph is meant to distil the essence of the work that it is a motto for, and practically all of Butler's important books have a motto which is directly or indirectly chiastic in nature. Of those that are indirectly related we may mention those on *balance* (for instance, the motto of *Erewhon* or of *Ex Voto*). Of those that are directly chiastic in structure we may take as example the motto of *Alps and Sanctuaries,* which goes as follows:

> Sicut vos estis nos fuimus,
> Et sicut nos sumus vos eritis.

The two lines form the caption to a picture of a crypt. On the stairs of the crypt some small children are playing. The chiastic thought is accordingly that 'Such as you [the children] are, we [the dead] were; and such as we [the dead] are, you [the children] will become.'

As one of his mottoes for *Luck, or Cunning?* Butler chose a chorus from his own and Jones's opera *Narcissus,* which goes as follows:

> Oh, wondrous scheme decreed of old on high
>> At once to take and give,
>> He that is born begins to die,
>> And he that dies to live:

> For life is death, and death is life,
> A harmony of endless strife,
> And mode of universal growth
> Is seen alike in both.

Here we see a flowering of many chiastic ideas: to take and to give are the same (opposites are always in the end the same; the ostensible reason in this case being that the two activities are simultaneous); life is never pure but mixed (cf. 'alloys') with its opposite, death, even from the very start at birth, and, conversely, death is never pure (one mutation of this was Butler's hobby-horse idea that authors, for instance, live on through their works). Further we may note the phrase 'A harmony of endless strife' – it is a typical chiasticist idea that 'endless strife' should be seen as 'harmony'. The motto ends with a favourite chiasticist word, 'both', testifying to the underlying dualism of the conceptual frame.

We may also note how both these epigraphs, like so much else in the universe of a chiasticist, are on the subject of death. The world of a chiasticist tends to be one of death, sterility, negation, unhappiness and destruction.[20] Ernest, it is true, is said to reach a form of happiness at the end of *The Way of All Flesh*. But it is a happiness through negation: Ernest rids himself of his parents, of his wife, his children, his profession, his friends, his religion, and so on. The most dramatic word in the whole novel, the word that really excites Ernest, is the word 'no' – see, for instance, chapter 57.[21] In another context Butler jokingly, but maybe in the end not all that jokingly after all, grumbles about things as they are, and longs for some real progress when such good things as divorce, infanticide and suicide will become common.[22]

The equivalent of the Ernest character in the opening part of *The Fair Haven*, John Pickard Owen, also, like Ernest, travels in a zigzagging line from extreme to extreme. When at the end he reaches 'the fair haven' of a compromise he dies from a brain fever.[23]

In *The Way of All Flesh*, at the end of chapter 45, a metaphor is used about Ernest's career which likens it to the flight of a snipe: 'when he rose he flew like a snipe, darting several times in various directions before he settled down to a steady straight flight, but when he had once got into this he would keep to it' (199). A snipe flies in a zigzag line and the snipe-metaphor therefore fits chiasticist thinking perfectly. But as to the ultimate synthesis – 'a steady straight flight' – it is conspicuous through its absence in the rest of the narrative. Interestingly enough, the snipe-metaphor recurs, but only to denote the dialectical switches of direction hither and thither, not to denote any final synthesis of a steady straight flight – or even a hope of one.

For Butler, no less than for many another dialectician, the creative and imaginative energy lies in the constant alternation between thesis and antithesis, not in the ultimate synthesis, which – in a vague manner – *is* dreamt of, but never materializes. In fact this ultimate synthesis at times seems so much of a mirage that Butler hardly believes in it at all – not to mention the poor reader.

In the way a chiasticist visualizes the world the number two plays an important role. But often it is a question not only of the number two on its own, but of the number two *plus one* – the chiasticist imagining two bilaterally symmetrical halves (2), with a dividing line between them (+1). In a chiasmus there are two halves, but between the halves there is also a dividing-element which the chiasticist perceives as constituting a third entity. This leads to a way of thinking which seeks out the pattern *aba;* a pattern in which a central entity is flanked by two symmetrical wings, as in Palladian architecture, or in a sonata, or in the facial form of, for instance, mammals (two similar eyes on each side of a nose).

In the theory of symmetry, the dividing entity between the two halves in pure cases of bilateral symmetry (this dividing entity is called the *centre of symmetry* in a one-dimensional world, the *axis of symmetry* in a two-dimensional world, and *the plane of symmetry* in a three-dimensional world) is not thought of as having any substance. Butler seems confused about this, or allows himself a liberal interpretation, so that the middle part in his 'palladian' three-part structures does not seem to be the plane (without substance) dividing the middle third of the building or whatever, but rather the middle third itself. Looking at a human face then, for instance, Butler does not, apparently, perceive it as two symmetrical halves, divided by a plane of symmetry going down the middle, but rather as a structure with a middle (a nose, a mouth) and symmetrical additions on each side (eyes, eyebrows, ears, and so on).

Butler was much given to 'palladian' thinking. Looking, for instance, at the geography of his novels we find numerous traces of this. The complete title of *Erewhon* was *Erewhon: Or, Over the Range.*[24] There is then, in this palladian geography, a separating range of mountains in the middle; on one side is European culture and on the other Erewhonian culture, which are both each other's inversions. All his life Butler strove to achieve the structure *aba* (or

aba_1). After *Erewhon Revisited* had just appeared, when Butler was lying very ill on what he thought was his death-bed, he got annoyed when one day he discovered that he felt better. As an author he had begun his career with *Erewhon* (stage *a*), then he had done different things in between (stage *b*), and now he had returned to the point of departure with *Erewhon Revisited* (stage *a* or a_1). Now it was appropriate to die.[25] (Butler recovered temporarily. But in his books, where he is in command of events himself, he arranges things differently, so that the *aba*-structure can always be achieved).

We know from the existential formula that what is on either side of the central dividing-element in a chiasmus seems *the same,* or *similar.* This is the basis of 'palladian' chiasticist thought. But *aba* happens to fit in perfectly with other constituent elements of chiasmus as well, which means that these elements, one after the other, mutually or reciprocally all influence and reinforce one another. What we have in the *aba*-structure is the beginning (the minimal unit) of *alternation;* in its extended form *ababab ... (ad infinitum).*

Here, then, we find the origin of Butler's belief that the different and the similar alternate. For something to return to its starting-point in a chiasticistic universe it need not even turn – if you continue far enough, even in the same direction, you will ultimately come to the same again, since same and other – similar and different – alternate. When Butler sends out his boomerang-thoughts he is thus doubly sure of their return. Whether they turn or not, the result will always be the same, because beyond the different the similar takes over again.

This idea recurs again and again in Butler. He uses different terms for it; most commonly he calls it 'extremes meeting'. He makes, for instance, the following observation. Some people receive little or no pay (stage *a*). As you rise in the social hierarchy you are paid more (stage *b*). But when you reach the top and become an MP you are not paid at all (stage *a* again, or a_1).

> *When a thing:* is old, broken, and useless, we throw it on the dust-heap, but when it is sufficiently old, sufficiently broken, and sufficiently useless, we give money for it, put it into a museum, and read papers over it which people come long distances to hear. (*Notebooks,* p. 311)

Nothing continues for ever in one and the same direction; if you go far enough everything ultimately returns to its original state. In Butler's universe everything in the end returns to its origin.

Butler's thinking normally follows a dialectical zigzag line. *One* inversion is not enough; every turn in turn contains within itself the seeds of *its* own inversion. Maybe, in view of this, a zigzag line is the wrong image, and maybe 'dialectics' is the wrong term. Perhaps the movement of a pendulum (one of Butler's own favourite images) would be a better metaphor, and perhaps the word 'dialectics' should be forgotten. Thesis and antithesis are never fused in Butler's logic.

In a chiasmus there does somehow exist a middle, but the middle has no substance. Butler longs violently, with an aching heart, for synthesis, compromise, *via media,* mixture, melting-together, fusion, union. But with equally obstinate, tantalizing regularity his longing is frustrated. This seems to be the nature of chiasticism – i.e. both to create the longing for union and to frustrate that same longing. In a chiasmus the 'direction' of each half is towards the middle, and chiasmus is therefore a perfect symbol of the desire of two to meet and unite. If the desire were fulfilled, however, there would perhaps no longer be the same need for chiasmus.

In fact it may not seem too far-fetched to guess that the type of chiasmus which expresses reciprocity is mostly used in cases where mutuality or reciprocity is felt to be lacking. In that case the presence and frequency of this type of chiasmus in Butler's style can be taken to reflect his loneliness. Conversely, if we know from other sources about Butler's loneliness, his frequent use of this type of chiasmus will come as no surprise to us. A frequent use of this kind of chiasmus in an author's style can be interpreted as the tell-tale sign of unresolved and unresolvable conflicts within the psyche of that author.

Chiasmus both creates and frustrates the longing for fusion. A middle, in the chiasticist's way of visualizing reality, exists only in relation to two extremes, one on each side. Thus the very idea of a middle (middle representing union, compromise, fusion) for a chiasticist at the same time presupposes the poles, and the chiasticist, imprisoned within his system of thought, is forever back where he started. Since he did not avoid dualism in his initial structuring of reality he will never be rid of it, no matter how much he uses chiasmus to bring one half of the duality into contact with the other, and the other with the one. This futile exercise is self-defeating.

Sometimes Butler's yearning for union can be quite moving and full of pathos. There are in particular two passages in his works which I think may be quoted here, since these two vignettes seem to have been written with blood rather than ink.

The first is a scene from the opening chapter of *Erewhon*. Butler describes the life of a sheep-farmer, above all the loneliness. Doing so he slips into chiasmus – fairly predictably, we may say, since, if loneliness comes, chiasmus is seldom far behind.

> Never shall I forget the utter loneliness of the prospect – only the little far-away homestead giving sign of human handiwork; – the vastness of mountain and plain, of river and sky; the marvellous atmospheric effects – sometimes black mountains against a white sky, and then again, after cold weather, white mountains against a black sky – sometimes seen through breaks and swirls of cloud – and sometimes, which was best of all, I went up my mountain in a fog, and then got above the mist; going higher and higher, I would look down upon a sea of whiteness, through which would be thrust innumerable mountain tops that looked like islands.   (Shrewsbury, II 5)

The narrator begins with the idea of loneliness – the number one. This leads him to a longing for the number two. He now begins to structure reality dualistically: 'mountain and plain'; 'river and sky'; 'black and white'. He then tries desperately to bring the separate halves of these dualities into contact or relation with one another, with the aid of the principle of reciprocity inherent in chiasmus – chiasmus being a pregnant symbol of the desire of two to unite: 'sometimes black mountains against a white sky, and then again, after cold weather, white mountains against a black sky'. Nevertheless, Butler does not seem to trust the reality of the reciprocity in chiasmus, and the way the text continues strongly reveals Butler's feeling of frustration:

> I am there now, as I write; I fancy that I can see the downs, the huts, the plain, and the river-bed – that torrent pathway of desolation, with its distant roar of waters. Oh, wonderful! wonderful! so lonely and solemn, with the sad grey clouds above, and no sound save a lost lamb bleating upon the mountain side, as though its little heart were breaking. Then there comes some lean and withered old ewe, with deep gruff voice and unlovely aspect, trotting back from the seductive pasture; now she examines this gully, and now that, and now she stands listening with uplifted head, that she may hear the distant wailing and obey it. Aha! they see, and rush towards each other. Alas! they are both mistaken; the ewe is not the lamb's ewe, they are neither kin nor kind to one another, and part in coldness. Each must cry louder, and wander

farther yet; may luck be with them both that they may find their own at nightfall. But this is mere dreaming, and I must proceed.   (Ibid.)

The symbolic significance of this passage can hardly be overestimated. The lush, emotional rhetoric of the prose is uncharacteristic of Butler's style. We may assume that what is dealt with in these lines is enormously important to him. His pathos (however overdone it may seem to the admirers of a more sober style of prose) is genuine, because this scene expresses what Butler all his life kept longing for but could never attain: a union of separates.

That it should be a question of a 'parent–child' relationship (ewe–lamb) is highly symptomatic. Many critics have here seen the key to Butler's entire personality. His unhappy relationship with his parents (especially his father) during his childhood left a lifelong impression on his character, they maintain.

Let us now look at the other passage, a parallel example, from *The Way of All Flesh,* in which we are told about Ernest's reaction to the dining-room in his home:

> Over the chimney-piece there was a veritable old master, one of the few original pictures which Mr George Pontifex had brought from Italy. It was supposed to be a Salvator Rosa, and had been bought at a great bargain. The subject was Elijah or Elisha (whichever it was) being fed by the ravens in the desert. There were the ravens in the upper right-hand corner with bread and meat in their beaks and claws, and there was the prophet in question in the lower left-hand corner looking longingly up towards them. When Ernest was a very small boy it had been a constant matter of regret to him that the food which the ravens carried never actually reached the prophet; he did not understand the limitation of the painter's art, and wanted the meat and the prophet to be brought into direct contact. One day, with the help of some steps which had been left in the room, he had clambered up to the picture and with a piece of bread and butter traced a greasy line right across it from the ravens to Elisha's mouth, after which he had felt more comfortable.   (Ch. 41, p. 176)[26]

Again we have the painful longing for a union of two separates, and again the same frustration. It is important to consider the context. The passage occurs immediately before yet another confrontation between Ernest and his father.[27]

Butler's chiasticism worked havoc with his attempts to enter into normal relationships with other people. Chiasmus expresses reciprocity; therefore to a chiasticist a relationship should be strictly mutual in nature. Moreover, the chiasticist strives for balance and equilibrium. Against this background it is easy to realize that there are a thousand things that can go wrong in the relationship between a chiasticist and the world around him.

A chiasticist cannot love someone until this someone loves *him*. Moreover, if someone *hates* a chiasticist, the chiasticist has to hate that someone. These two rules are dictated by the principle of reciprocity.

Further rules follow from the chiasticist's belief that only antitheses exist. Accordingly, if someone is not one thing he must be 'the other', i.e. the (extreme) opposite. If, then, the chiasticist does not detect any signs of somebody loving him, it must mean that the somebody hates him, because if you do not do the one you are bound to do the other (and not do it by halves either). From this follows (the rule of reciprocity) that, if somebody hates the chiasticist, why then the chiasticist must hate this somebody (and not by halves either).

If somebody sets the whole merry-go-round in motion by initiating the relationship and loving the chiasticist, everything goes well – Butler never forgot a kindness nor anyone who did him a good turn. If only the chiasticist is given a chance, through the outside world *starting* a positive relationship, everything will be all right, but if the chiasticist has to take the initiative himself there is every chance that it will all end in disaster. The chiasticist cannot decide on a role; after all, 'Subject is object and object subject', is it not? Hater is hated, and hated is hater. Every once in a while the chiasticist chooses to start the hate-relationship himself, out of fear that perhaps hate was the feeling his partner-to-be would have chosen in any case, and a desire to anticipate a mutuality that is thus imagined as possible or inevitable.

Despite the fact that the second half of a chiasmus negates the first, still the first is objectively there *as* the first, and a residue of lopsidedness remains. Butler occasionally tries to combat this by repeating not only the first half of the chiasmus in the second half, but the chiasmus as a whole, according to the following pattern: *ab, ba; ba, ab*. These double occurrences of chiasmus naturally reduce further the distinction between left and right, or beginning and end, but even here there remains a trace of asymmetry. No matter how many inversions you employ, the fact remains that you always have to begin with something, and the choice of what to begin with will always in itself favour that half of the duality. This minimal residue of asymmetry rankled in Butler's mind, and some of the minutely precise niceties of his relationships with others may be traced back to his quest for what remained ultimately elusive – a perfect balance.

The chiasticistic rule that only antitheses exist, and that if you are not one thing you are bound to be its extreme opposite, deserves some further comment. A number of variants in a relationship between two are missing from the logic of a chiasticist. It may be useful here to recall the distinction traditionally made in philosophy between *contraries* and *contradictories*. Of two contrary propositions both cannot be true; but both *can* be false. If one is true, the other must be false. But if one is false it does not follow that the other is true. In the case of two contradictory propositions both cannot be true and both cannot be false; therefore from the truth of one the falsehood of the other can be inferred, and from the falsehood of one the truth of the other can be inferred.

In the logic of a chiasticist there tend to be no contraries, only contradictories. Contraries allow for the possibility of *irreversibility*, and this the chiasticist is not willing to consider since it would imply an acceptance of asymmetry. Contraries also belong to a world in which dualism is not obligatory, and this is equally undesirable to a chiasticist. Contraries therefore are usually not found among the logical tools of the chiasticist. His rules instead include the following set of two:

(1) everything has a complement, which is a contradictory;
(2) if something is not one thing it must be the other (the opposite) and *vice versa*.

Butler realized that this logic led him up a cul-de-sac. He therefore went on from these rules to a corollary that, of any two, both are both things (for example, true and false) at the same time.[28]

If my readers have by now accepted that such a phenomenon as chiasticism may exist, I expect that many will be asking what it is that *causes* such a phenomenon. How does one turn into a chiasticist? What is it that causes such an obsessive love of symmetry in an individual? Unfortunately this is a very difficult question. I cannot claim to know the answer in Butler's case. One may speculate, but it is difficult to reach any certainty.

One might try a cultural explanation, and investigate whether Butler was influenced by occurrences of chiastic structuring in those things with which he came into contact. It is easy to see that this was so. Butler, sponge-like, would absorb any chiastic structuring with which he came into contact, when reading the works of other authors, for instance. But then the question arises of why he picked on these elements rather than others. There were other things he could have borrowed. Other authors, who were influenced by the same works, borrowed other things.

There are naturally things that fit the 'cultural' model of explanation perfectly, such as Butler's stay in New Zealand. To go to the Antipodes is likely to make a person aware of chiastic structures, since in the Southern Hemisphere winter is summer and summer winter, spring is autumn and autumn spring. Also, north is south and south north (in the sense that, whereas in the Southern Hemisphere the climate gets warmer if you go north but colder if you go south, in the Northern Hemisphere it gets colder if you go north and warmer if you go south). But even this sort of material is in the end not entirely satisfying. It helps explain the growth and continuing existence of Butler's chiasticism, but not its origins. Since other people went to New Zealand without turning into chiasticists, Butler's affliction looks like a pre-existing condition. As an *ad hoc* explanation in Butler's case, the Southern Hemisphere experience might have a value, but it has no general predictive value. In general, one is forced to conclude that the 'cultural' model of explanation (i.e. *influence*) can account for some things but not for all.

We must then consider the possibility that chiasticism is caused by neurophysiological irregularities. Here I must tread carefully, because the clinical study of left–right confusion, insufficient cerebral laterali- zation, and laterality is better left to the experts. A physiological cause of Butler's excessive love of symmetry cannot, however, be ruled out. It should be remembered that Butler had a tumour in the neck. However, in the end it is difficult to say whether such things are relevant. It is clear that Butler's chiasticist and ambilateralist habits were fully formed long before he began to complain about the tumour and the strange 'noises' in his head. Also, there were periods later on when he does not seem to have suffered very much from the tumour and the noises, and yet his chiasticism continued unabated. Probably there is not a neat and simple reason for Butler's ambilateralism.

It is possible that the question of the reasons for chiasticism and ambilateralism in Butler is connected with something so fundamental in the way our brain (not to say our entire universe) is constructed that the mind boggles. I suspect that the study of chiasmus ought to be complemented by a general study of the relationship between symmetry and asymmetry. People are interested in the relationship between symmetry and asymmetry in astronomy, physics, biology, chemistry, pictorial art and neurophysiology – the study of symmetry cuts across many disciplines. If one had more exact knowledge of the manifestations of symmetry and asymmetry in language, and how these relate to questions of symmetry and asymmetry in general, one might be in a better position to understand chiasmus.

If Butler's love of symmetry was neither culturally nor physiologically conditioned, what other possibilities are there?

I think that, as yet, the explanatory model which comes most easily to mind is a psychological one. Perhaps we should search for an explanation of Butler's chiasticism in his childhood experience, and his unhappy relationship with his parents, particularly his father.

Many of our asymmetric preferences are acquired, and are not found in children. Young children will often, for instance, when beginning to learn to write, form letters the wrong way round. They are gradually taught by parents, teachers and society in general to accept what is the ruling convention, in this respect as in others (i.e. in the case of script, left-to-right in, for instance, the languages of Europe, or right-to-left in, for example, the Hebrew and Arab world[29]). In innumerable, separate, small instances we learn in childhood which out of two asymmetries to favour, through instruction.

If, then, instruction is tyrannical and despotic – as it seems to have been in the case of Butler and his parents – the trainee will resent it; hence resent whichever asymmetry common convention favours, and will develop a passionate longing for its enantiomorph; an enantiomorphic variant of anything always becoming *per se* a symbol of the childhood integrity of self and individuality that was repressed so ruthlessly. In other words, the individual emotionally asks something like the following questions: 'Why was *I* never allowed to have anything *my* way? Why should I not have it my way *now,* since I was not allowed to *then!*' – and then proceeds to satisfy the impulse, by emphasizing the enantiomorph to whatever is at the moment under consideration. Thus a rebel attitude and a love of inversion would go together, according to this theory.

I am not suggesting any specific technical explanation here, but rather a kind of general idea of where an explanation should be sought. Since the years of childhood are so important to the individual's acquisition of technical and specific left–right habits and preferences, may not these formative years have been equally important for the development of Butler's 'emotional' ambilateralism, i.e. his compulsion to 'set himself the other way'?

Nearly everything that Butler wrote was in one way or another autobiographical, but the most autobiographical of all his works is *The Way of All Flesh*. Of the thirty-odd occasions in that work when chiasmus, on the sentence-level, is used to express a reciprocity of feeling between parents and offspring, about two thirds express a mutual feeling of hate. The facts of the case seem to confirm that Butler's father really did treat him very badly. At any rate there can be no doubt that Butler all his life felt this to have been the case.[30]

Many important asymmetric preferences, and many of the specific skills involved in distinguishing left from right, are acquired before the age of seven. If the childhood years are so important for the development of technical and specific left–right habits, perhaps they are equally important in the development of general emotional attitudes towards symmetry and asymmetry. What were Samuel Butler's childhood years like? Ernest Pontifex in *The Way of All Flesh* is a picture of Butler himself as a child, and in chapter 20 we learn what Ernest's childhood was like:

> Before Ernest could well crawl he was taught to kneel; before he could well speak he was taught to lisp the Lord's prayer, and the general confession. How was it possible that these things could be taught too early? If his attention flagged or his memory failed him, here was an ill weed which would grow apace, unless it were plucked out immediately, and the only way to pluck it out was to whip him, or shut him in a cupboard, or dock him of some of the small pleasures of childhood. Before he was three years old he could read and, after a fashion, write. Before he was four he was learning Latin, and could do rule of three sums.   (p. 88)

It is possible that Butler's 'emotional' ambilateralism was thrashed into him in childhood – if his childhood was similar to Ernest's, we have it on his own authority that he was brutally whipped more or less every day, year after year.[31]

At this point I should perhaps add a few words about terminology and definitions. The concept 'emotional ambilateralism' may seem imprecise to psychologists and physicians, who prefer to reserve terms such as 'ambilateralism' for narrowly defined and easily measured phenomena.

Many of my terms in this study, such as 'ambilateralism',

'symmetry', 'asymmetry', 'enantiomorph' and 'inversion', will not have as precise and closely circumscribed meanings as in the natural sciences. This is deliberate. To a psychologist, studying well-defined, precise, clinical forms of ambilateralism – such as mirror writing – it is helpful to use a strict definition and stick to things that can be measured. But these restrictions are not necessarily a virtue in linguistic and literary scholarship. On the contrary. If we want to find out what made Butler tick, it is not our own definition of symmetry that matters, but Butler's. We must submit to the dictates of the task in hand, and try, temporarily, to see the world as it appeared to Butler. If an impure form of symmetry counted as symmetry to Butler, then we had better choose a definition which will include it. Practicality must come first and dainty delicacy second.

Despite the variation in the degree of preciseness, however, terms such as 'symmetry', 'asymmetry' and 'ambilateralism' mean essentially the same wherever they are used. The study of symmetry cuts across disciplines, and I wish to emphasize here, most strongly, that the significance of chiasmus should be seen against the background of the entire question of the relationship between symmetry and asymmetry.

In my experience people are, on average, not very aware of left-right questions. It is fairly unusual for people to realize what a complex phenomenon laterality is, for instance. Not everybody has a clear view of what 'symmetry' means. Sometimes, when information on left-right questions is disseminated, the information is unreliable. This is particularly the case with the deluge of books on brain-hemisphere functions that has flooded the world's bookshelves in recent years.

For reasons of space I cannot here add a chapter on general questions of left and right, as I ought to. Nevertheless it is important that the question of chiasmus should be seen in its context of general questions of left and right. I should therefore like to recommend (to those who have not already read them) a couple of books which will be found useful as a first introduction to symmetry, and which will provide references for further reading.

As an amusing start I recommend Martin Gardner's *The Ambidextrous Universe*.[32] This delightful volume – symmetry without tears, we may call it – will put the layman in the right, expectant mood on questions of left and right, symmetry and asymmetry. Gardner deals with symmetry and the dimensions; symmetry in the arts; symmetry and cosmology (galaxies, suns, and planets); symmetry and asymmetry in plants and animals; in the human body (with a chapter on left-handers); symmetry and asymmetry in crystals and molecules. He then goes on to carbon, the asymmetry of life, and the origins of that asymmetry; symmetry and asymmetry in theoretical physics; and finally to such questions as symmetry and asymmetry in relation to entropy and time. For the reader who had not previously realized what fundamental questions the subject of left and right touches upon, Gardner's book will be a useful stimulant.

An absolutely indispensable guide to questions of left and right on a more prosaic level is *The Psychology of Left and Right,* by Michael C. Corballis and Ivan L. Beale. I warmly recommend this work. Particularly relevant are chapters 11 and 12 (pp. 160–89) on 'Left–Right Confusion, Laterality, and Reading Disability' and 'The Pathology of Left and Right: Some Further Twists'; but all the chapters are highly interesting, and there is an extensive bibliography.

A classic work on the subject is the short study by Hermann Weyl, *Symmetry.* [33] Inversion is one of the important constituent principles of chiasmus, and a work on inversion which I highly recommend is *The Reversible World: Symbolic Inversion in Art and Society,* a collection of essays edited by Barbara A. Babcock. [34]

The question 'Why did Butler become an ambilateralist?' postulates that Butler did become an ambilateralist, and that there is such a thing as ambilateralism in the sense that I use the term here. One should perhaps not only look for an answer, but also try to see whether the question has been formulated in the right way. Is the concept 'ambilateralism' justified? If symmetry appealed to Butler, does it not appeal to everyone?

Certainly there is an enormous aesthetic appeal in symmetry. That human beings are so fascinated by bilateral symmetry is usually explained as resulting from the bilateral symmetry of the human body. We want to create the world in our image, and we want to see in our environment a reflection of ourselves, it is argued.

The enjoyment that human beings derive from symmetry need not only be of an aesthetic nature, but can also be, for instance, religious. Symmetry is found to play an important role in many kinds of religious thought. In the same way as man creates art in his own image, making extensive use of symmetry, he also creates God, Heaven and Paradise in his own image, making use of symmetry in his attempts to visualize Divine Perfection. In *The Reversible World,* Barbara G. Myerhoff, in an essay entitled 'Return to Wirikuta: Ritual Reversal and Symbolic Continuity on the Peyote Hunt of the Huichol Indians' (pp. 225–39), relates how the Huichol Indians on their annual expedition to Wirikuta invert whatever they can invert. Apparently the idea is that by supplying a missing enantiomorph a symmetry which is divine or sacred in character will be achieved.

The state of harmony and rest which is a feature of many attempts to visualize Paradise or Heaven is often connected with ideas involving symmetry. And man's longing for Heaven is sometimes seen as his wish to be united with a missing half so that a symmetric, perfect whole can be achieved. (Plato's theory of love is based on a similar idea.)

In so far as symmetry plays a role in religious thought, it is predictable that the principles necessary for its creation (such as inversion) will become important. It is further predictable that various symmetric phenomena will be important. In Christianity chiasmus itself was at one time given a particular significance, ostensibly because the letter χ (from which chiasmus derives its name) is shaped like a cross, but in reality, one suspects, because of the appeal of symmetry. Chiasmus was known as the *figura crucis* and associated with Christ.[35]

The love of symmetry varies in intensity, not only from person to person, but from culture to culture and period to period. There are variations between one ideology and another and between one religion and another. In literature there are variations between genres. Two genres in which symmetry makes its presence felt very strongly are aphorisms and jokes. A large proportion, with some aphorists even a majority, of aphorisms are chiastic in structure, and many jokes depend on some kind of 'switch' pattern. Therefore the appeal of aphorisms and jokes may to a large extent depend on the appeal of symmetry.

There are, then, variations of degree, and accordingly there is not a sharp difference between Butler and other chiasticists, on the one hand, and ordinary, non-chiasticistic people, on the other. Some involuntary inversionary phenomena are found in the language of us all (spoonerisms, metatheses), and we all to some extent enjoy the various manifestations of symmetry in language, including chiasmus.

But, when love of symmetry becomes so extraordinarily prono-unced as in Butler's case, I think that we are justified in giving it a name, and looking for a cause, even though there are intermediate forms of symmetry-obsession between Butler and the human average.

What can safely be said in the end about the origins of Butler's ambilateralism is that the question is exceedingly difficult. Certainly cultural influence played a role, but that is hardly an exhaustive explanation. Possibly there was a physiological cause; but that is hard to prove. Most likely, however, is the explanation that the origin of Butler's desire for symmetry was emotional starvation in childhood.

Be that as it may. Whether chiasticism was a burden that Butler himself acquired by picking up here one bit and there another; whether it was the dubious gift of cruel nature, making him constitutionally incapable of accepting distinctions that are taken for granted by other people; or whether (as seems most likely) it was a legacy from a tyrannical home and an unhappy childhood – whatever the case may have been, it is certain that chiasmus became a dictator governing Butler's entire existence: what he saw, what he thought, what he wrote, and – finally – *how* he wrote.

2 The Psychomorphology of Chiasticism

I INVERSION

(a) Why did Butler invert proverbs?

Butler's inveterate habit of turning proverbs upside down follows logically from his love of symmetry. Butler wanted everything to come in pairs, of which each half was to be the other's enantiomorph. His inversions of well-known sayings are his way of supplying the half which he sees as missing from a symmetric whole.

Note that chiasticism is at work whether the inversion results in an actual chiasmus on the page or not. Whether the inverted version is added to the uninverted version, so that both together (on the page) form a chiasmus, or whether the inversion is given on its own does not matter in principle. We should not restrict ourselves to a surface definition of chiasmus if we wish to understand Butler's psycho-morphology. In addition to actual, manifested examples of chiasmus (when the figure is there on the page) there are those passages in which a chiasmus is *implied,* in an inversion of a well-known saying. We may regard these inversions of well-known sayings as cases of *hidden chiasmus.*

The aesthetic appeal of inverting well-known sayings depends on symmetry. When Oscar Wilde says, 'Work is the ruin of the drinking classes', everyone knows that this inversion is a travesty of the slogan, 'Drink is the ruin of the working classes.' The aesthetic appeal of symmetry is there even though in Wilde's travesty only one half of the symmetrical whole actually surfaces. There is no need for the target of the inversion to be mentioned explicitly, since everyone is familiar with the cliché that Wilde is inverting. Indeed, the success of inversionary epigrammatic wit often depends on the target *not* being mentioned explicitly, since it gives the audience a pleasurable sense of belonging to an in-group if explicit mention of the target is suppressed. It is a test of cleverness and of knowledge, and one of the first operations that the audience automatically employ as a means of decoding a puzzling and, as they suspect, witty message is inversion.

Butler's love of symmetry is thus in evidence not only when he presents an inversion and its target so that together they form a chiasmus, but also when inversions of famous sayings occur on their own, since these can be regarded as examples of hidden chiasmus.

The narrator's remark on Ernest's habit of inverting proverbs in *The Way of All Flesh* (ch. 50, p. 228) is as usual autodiagnostic. Butler's compulsive habit of inverting proverbs is one of his most characteristic mannerisms, as anyone familiar with his works, and in particular his *Notebooks*, will have noted. Butler acquired the habit early and retained it throughout his career.

There are a number of ways in which proverbs can be inverted in Butler; he has a number of favourite ways of attacking them. Let us botanize briefly among the most common of these.

The easiest method of turning a proverb upside down – a method that Butler regularly resorted to – is simply negation. Sometimes this involves the creation of neologisms. These may be negative complements of existing positive words, as when Butler in *Erewhon* (ch. 3, pp. 13–14), in a comment on Virgil's *Georgics*, ll. 458, complements the word *fortunatos* with its negative variant *infortunatos*. (The word *infortuniam*, however, Butler had to get rid of – see Preface to second edition.)

Conversely, these neologisms may be positive complements of existing negative words, in which case they are often somewhat eccentric. I am told that in England there exists a 'Society for the Restoration of Suppressed Positives', whose aim is to further the cause of such neglected positive variants of negative words as 'couth' from 'uncouth', and 'gruntled' from 'disgruntled' – the latter one of P. G. Wodehouse's favourites. If there is indeed such a society, or if one is formed, I sincerely hope that Butler will be posthumously elected an honorary member. The cause of Suppressed Positives was dear to him, and he did what he could for it. He often complains about missing positive variants of negative words, as in the following note: *'On the art of "covery": This is as important and interesting as "dis-covery". Surely the glory of finally getting rid of and burying a long and troublesome matter should be as great as that of making a great discovery ...'* (*Notebooks*, p. 252).

These neologisms, in which either a negative complement of a positive word or a positive complement of a negative word is supplied, reveal an essential aspect of Butler's attitude to language. The final authority – the ultimate idol – for Butler is always symmetry, and he feels that language, like everything else, should be under the obligation to create and uphold symmetry.

Butler's inversions of proverbs and attacks on well-established sayings should be seen as part of his rebellion against authority. We may also learn something about the nature of Butler's rebelliousness and anti-authoritarianism by considering his attacks on proverbs. In attacking proverbs Butler feels that he can defy authority all the better because he is appealing to a higher authority – to symmetry. Symmetry, for Butler, makes any cause just, any scientific theory true, any joke witty, and so on. Symmetry is always the ultimate redeemer.

Coining complementary negative variants of positive words, or complementary positive variants of negative words, was a safe kind of rebellion against language, because to Butler this rebellion meant the introduction of a better and more perfect order rather than the introduction of chaos. We may imagine that when Butler coined a complementary word he felt that he had caught language out in a glaring shortcoming. Bilateral symmetry demands that every pheno-menon should have a mirror-image complement, and Butler notices that language is not true to its own ideal order.

Butler was for ever attacking people, but he did so with a heavy heart. He was seldom sure about his own position. Therefore he always felt relief when he could show that his opponents were not even true to their own standards. In his polemical works Butler is most at ease when he is able to show that Darwin, the classicist, or whoever it might be, is not living up to his own standards.

Butler's temperament is a curious mixture of courage and cowar-dice. Somehow this is evident in his attacks on proverbs too. In one sense he probably chose these as he chose his other objects of attack –for the challenge. One cannot really accuse Butler of not picking worthy opponents. His opponents were formidable: the Church, the Darwinians, the classicists, and so on. As Butler instinctively hurried to fight *for* the underdog, he complementarily hurried to fight *against* the 'overdog' – if such a Butlerian coinage may be excused. In Butler's logic, of course, fighting for the underdog and fighting against the overdog come to the same thing. Butler saw proverbs as the overdog in language. The culmination of the authority of language is in proverbs; they represent established wisdom.

It is important to realize that the motivating force behind Butler's rebelliousness and belligerence is a longing for symmetry. Even when he is not analysing the inconsistencies in his opponent's view, but simply attacking, he is engaged in an activity that for him means the introduction of a desirable and superior pattern – symmetry.

Several biographers, particularly Malcolm Muggeridge in *The Earnest Atheist,* have suggested that the strongest motivating force in Butler's psyche was hate. There is a good deal of truth in this suggestion. But, as Muggeridge perceptively puts it, it was 'hate at its worst, because love gone rancid'.[1] In other words Butler shows his love by hating.

When Butler inverts a proverb he is putting himself in relation to it; he is trying to translate the demands of his symmetry-addiction into a role in a relationship, and the relation he chooses is antithesis or opposition. Butler cannot accept a proverb at face-value: that would create an imbalance between the self and the other, between his passive receptivity and his active creativity, and it would imply monism rather than dualism. No, in order to appropriate the proverb he must first put himself in relation to it (and thereby it in relation to him) and the relation that most easily comes to his mind is opposition; antithesis; hate.

In her study 'Some Influences on the Work of Samuel Butler (1835–1902)' Ruth Gounelas shows, particularly in her final section (Part III: 'The 1890s: Butler as Controversialist', pp. 185–232), that Butler always had to put himself in opposition to someone or something, even when he was writing on subjects that one might have thought very uncontroversial, such as the life and letters of his grandfather. Butler had to have a cause. Unless he felt convinced that by setting himself up in opposition to someone or something he was supplying the missing enantiomorph (to complete a symmetric structure), he thought his effort wasted, and did not bother.

The very word *controversialist,* through its semantic kinship with *inversion,* should alert us to the obvious reason for Butler's controversialism. Normally turning away – *aversion* – is a symbol of displeasure; turning (especially one's face) towards, a symbol of favour. But in Butler aversion finds little manifestation. Instead of aversion there is *controversion,* a strange pseudo-hostile turning-towards, which in fact should be seen as a cry for love via hate.

It is important to realize that the basic unit in a Butlerian controversy is not Butler (one unit) or his opponent (another unit). The basic unit is 'Butler-plus-his-opponent'. These together form a symmetric whole, with the halves turned against one another.

Butler shows his fascination with sayings, sententiae, maxims, aphorisms and proverbs by inverting them. The more 'authoritative' a formula was, the more likely it was to be attacked. The following, from *Erewhon Revisited,* involves the well-known legal oath: 'It almost seemed, so George told my father, as though he had resolved that he would speak lies, all lies, and nothing but lies' (ch. 22, p. 202).

It will be seen here that I use the term 'inversion' in a wide sense. I regard as inversion not only the cases in which the sequential order of two previously mentioned elements is inverted, but also all cases of the replacement of a word with its conventional opposite, as in the case of 'truth' and 'lies' above. All these cases, and many more, counted as inversion to Butler, and are therefore relevant.

Butler's love of inversion *for its own sake,* can perhaps most clearly be seen in the dullest and least witty of his notes. When the notes are brilliant the inversion could have come from the pen of any gifted author. But to Butler an inversion did not have to result in a brilliant new insight to be valuable. Inversion had a value *as such.*

Butler therefore mechanically replaced one half of any conventional dualistic pair with its opposite: for instance, 'evil' with 'good' in 'Resist good, and it will fly from you' (*Erewhon Revisited,* ch. 13, p. 123) or 'part' with 'meet' in '*The best of friends must:* meet' (*Notebooks,* p. 118).[2]

Butler's doctoring of proverbs and quotations often involves simply misquotation, particularly if there are two outstanding elements in the first part of the quote, one of which is repeated in a second part. Butler's technique in such cases is invariably to repeat the wrong one. The following famous example from *The Way of All Flesh* is typical: 'Perhaps; but is it not Tennyson who has said: "Tis better to have loved and lost, than never to have lost at all"?' (ch. 77, p. 341). If he cannot misquote in any other way, Butler will invert the keyword by adding a morphological element that makes it negative, or the sentence ambiguous, as in the following *Notebooks* entry: '*The better part of valour:* is indiscretion' (p. 165).

Many of these inversions are fairly witty and really do open the reader's eyes to things he may not have seen before. But inversion was compulsive for Butler and there is often something forced in these passages, as in:

He will visit the virtues: of the fathers upon the children, etc. to the: third and fourth generations. How often do we not see children ruined through the virtues, real or supposed, of their fathers and mothers? The most that can be truly said for virtue is that there is a considerable balance in its favour, and that it is a good deal better to be for it than against it, but it lets people in very badly sometimes.

(*Notebooks,* p. 235).

Butler expected that by the mere substitution of 'virtue' for its antonym 'sin' (or 'vice'), a wonderful, neat and sudden new insight would be produced, and when this does not materialize he cannot let go of the idea but brings in some rather feeble explanation to support it. Epigrammatic wit depends on the neatness, unexpectedness and suddenness of the new insight. Butler knew how to achieve all of these, but his love of inversion was so strong that he tended to keep his tentative inversions even when they did not really produce any spectacular new insights. If they failed to do so he would construct elaborate systems of thought to justify the inversion anyway, so that at least in his private world of ideas the inversion would be brilliantly meaningful.

If the proverb Butler wants to invert is in itself already structured around two visible conventional antonyms, this means that he only needs to change their order. In the following example the antonymic pair is 'God–man': '*God:* Let man be true and every god a liar' (*Notebooks,* p. 277). Such inversions as these may be regarded as a kind of deliberate spoonerism on the sentence level. They involve a pleasurable abandonment of order in favour of chaos, and aesthetic delight if it is discovered that the result is not nonsense after all, but a new order, with a new meaning.

The connection between Butler's 'unhealing wound' and his habit of inverting proverbs can sometimes be seen directly. It is a fairly reliable indication of his hatred of clichés that he puts some of the worst in the mouth of father characters in his fiction. In *The Way of All Flesh,* we find Theobald Pontifex repeatedly using the same odious cliché: 'one could not wish it prolonged' (ch. 83, p. 385). This is immediately followed by one of the most memorable felicities of formulation in the novel: 'and he buried his face in his handkerchief to conceal his want of emotion' (ibid.). Here is authority doubled: the authority of the father and the authority of the cliché.

Even though Butler attacks proverbs and wants to destroy them, nevertheless even the attack itself puts him in relation with them and testifies to the fascination he felt for them. Butler was both repelled and attracted by authority. If Butler had been only repelled by authority he could have chosen to ignore it rather than attack it. His feelings were always ambivalent; they came in antithetical pairs. It is impossible to talk about repulsion in Butler without also talking about attraction, and *vice-versa*.

In *The Way of All Flesh*, we are told that for Ernest the Simeonites had 'a repellant attraction' (ch. 47, p. 208). This oxymoronic phrase epitomizes not only Ernest's but also Butler's reaction to everything. To be attracted is at the same time to be repelled, and to be repelled is at the same time to be attracted. Opposites coexist.

The rhetorical figure of *oxymoron* is highly frequent in Butler's style. Oxymoron is a natural consequence of chiasticism. If opposites are really in the end the same, there is no reason why you should not put them next to one another as in the figure of oxymoron. A rebel attitude is also likely to result in a frequent use of this figure. A rebel sets himself up in opposition to conventional standards (for example, of morality or political opinion). What is good to public opinion is bad to him; what is bad to public opinion is good to him. Inevitably, then, he will begin to talk about the bad in terms of the good, and about the good in terms of the bad. Thus it is likely that he will combine opposites oxymoronically in his style; to make neighbours of a negative adjective and a positive noun, or *vice-versa*, for instance.

Butler could not ignore proverbs and sayings. Instead he endlessly pored over them, listening to their sound, inverted their sense, brooded over the sentiments they expressed or could be made to express. A typical example of his habitual scrutiny of petrified expressions is his comments on the formula 'peace in our time': *"Give peace in our time, o Lord":* Is this indifference to what may befall the next generation, or does it proceed from a feeling that peace for a longer period is past praying for?' (*Notebooks*, p. 279).

A spectacular consequence of Butler's ambilateralism is his great talent for revitalizing clichés. This talent is a predictable result of chiasticism. People normally use clichés unthinkingly, without reflection. When clichés are used, we may say that people's thoughts go in one direction only: *from* the cliché *to* something else. The cliché is the starting-point, which is taken for granted.

Thanks to chiasmus, Butler's thinking was never a one-way street. His thoughts went with equal ease from the abstract to the concrete and from the concrete to the abstract. His thoughts also as easily turned back in on the cliché itself as they went *from* a cliché *to* something else – in fact rather more easily so.

Butler, like Henry James, was a master in the art of revitalizing clichés and breathing new life into dead expressions. Sometimes his technique is to ambiguate the most important word in a saying, or amphibolize the sentence, rather than openly invert it. Often it is sufficient for Butler merely to draw our attention to a saying in the wrong context to make us see more meanings than we are used to. In *The Way of All Flesh* Overton reflects,

> I thought how the Psalmist had exclaimed with quiet irony, 'One day in thy courts is better than a thousand', and I thought that I could utter a very similar sentiment in respect of the Courts in which Towneley and I were compelled to loiter.   (Ch. 62, p. 271)[3]

A similar example is, *'Lord, I do not believe:* help thou mine unbelief' (*Notebooks,* p. 284), which we would not take to be ambiguous in an author less given to vacillation and ambivalence, but which in Butler is immediately recognized as ambiguous.

If Butler could not get at proverbs through direct attacks such as negation or inversion, he would try to wreck their cause by joining it, taking the meaning beyond its original application until he was able to upset the balance that way. The following *Notebooks* entry is typical: *'The vanity of human wishes:* There is only one thing vainer than this, and that is the having no wishes' (p. 179). To wreck a cause by joining it is of course the characteristic strategy of the parodist and satirist, and the basic mechanism of irony.

Proverbs represent stereotype on the sentence-level. On the level of textual narrative their equivalents are standard episodes, stock descriptions, topoi of various kinds. In characterization the corresponding phenomena are flat characters, archetypal mythical beings, and so on. Butler reacted to these in the same way as he reacted to their cousins on the sentence-level, the proverbs. In particular he had it in for the myths of the ancients. The ancients used mythical characters to epitomize particular aspects of human existence. Thus Tantalus and Sisyphus, for instance, are concretizations of the abstract idea of *frustration* (we have the word; the ancients expressed the idea through myths). Butler was furious over the patent truth that such myths expressed. Whenever he could, he tried to reinterpret them, to take the sting out of their truth. In a long note (*Notebooks,* pp. 241–5), he argues that it was Sisyphus himself who *liked* to let his stone roll back downhill; that Tantalus was quite happy and would have been annoyed if his condition had changed (he drank dew and got apples 'when the

wind was napping'), and that to Tityus the bird eating his liver was not
an eternal torment but 'a gentle stimulant'.[4]

This is the familiar Butlerian habit of blaming the victim rather than
the victimizer, which should also be seen as a variety of inversion.
Roles must be freely interchangeable, and if stereotype has created
asymmetry, i.e. a set distribution of roles, this inevitably triggers
inversion in Butler.

'Change of roles' is accordingly one of his favourite ways of
attacking stereotype episodes. In chapter 81 of *The Way of All Flesh*, it
is the episode of Abraham's near-sacrifice of Isaac which is inverted
this way: ' "No, no, no," said he, "it would be too cruel; it would be
like Isaac offering up Abraham and no thicket with a ram in it near at
hand" ' (p. 365).[5] Roles, Butler felt, should be interchangeable.
Solomon pontificating on the lilies should be complemented by the
lilies pontificating on Solomon:

> What would the lilies of the field say if they heard one of us declaring
> that they neither toil nor spin? They would say, I take it, much what
> we should if we were to hear of their preaching humility on the text
> of Solomons, and saying, 'Consider the Solomons in all their glory,
> they toil not neither do they spin.'   (*Erewhon*, ch. 27, p. 220)[6]

The roles of judge and judged should be interchangeable as in the
following *Notebooks* entry: '*God:* He might begin the Day of
Judgment, but he would probably find himself in the dock long before
it was over' (p. 191). God laying down the law for the world should be
complemented by the world laying down the law for God: ' "The world
thy world is a jealous world, and thou shalt have none other worlds but
it" ' (ibid., p. 212). Again and again Butler asserts, with an insistence
that betrays his anxiety, that every principle has its antithetical
complement: '*There is such a thing:* as doing good that evil may come'
(ibid., p. 282).

The extent of Butler's inversionary mania can be gauged from his
inveterate habit of 'tasting' the inverted variant of any saying that
involves two main elements. Even in using those standard binomials
that have become 'part and parcel' of the language – to put it in a way
that makes use of one of them – Butler would in passing sometimes
invert their order. (Many of these binomials have a traditional order in
English; often a word with fewer syllables precedes a longer one.)
Butler's mania for inversion is half asleep at such moments, but still
sufficiently awake to take a few desultory pot-shots at stability while

waiting to get to a suitable context in which to engage in more serious linguistic guerrilla warfare against the establishment.

When Butler invents antithetical alternatives there is a glory in the act itself, a delight in setting oneself up against something else. Common morality and Christianity say one should visit the sick, therefore Butler thinks the other way: '*I was sick & ye visited me:* I should say, "I was sick, and you were kind enough to leave me quite alone" ' (*Notebooks,* p. 13). The gods of conventional religions ask men to believe in them. If Butler were a god, or a prophet (the megalomania of some people is content to stop at Napoleon; not so Butler's), he would ask men *not* to believe in him:

> *Gods and prophets:* It is the manner of gods and prophets to begin: 'Thou shalt have none other God or Prophet but me.' If I were to start as a God or a prophet I think I should take the line: 'Thou shalt not believe in me. Thou shalt not have me for a God. Thou shalt worship any d——d thing thou likest except me.'   (Ibid., pp. 88–9)

Butler took a perverse delight in opposing, and in being opposed. There was no word he loved so well as the word 'no' – the sign *par excellence* of opposition. It did not matter whether he was the person saying, or the person hearing, the word.[7] Neither does the specific result or the direction of a negation matter very much in his fiction in comparison with the intensity of effect when a 'no' occurs. Consider the extraordinary dramatic force of Towneley's 'no' in *The Way of All Flesh*, chapter 57, when Ernest asks Towneley whether he does not like poor people. Ernest at this point is ready to turn, and Towneley's frank 'no' transforms him completely. The scales fall from his eyes. Opposition brings about a complete reversal.

As to opposing and being opposed, Butler naturally had control over the former. But one of his regular sorrows was that his hoped-for opponents did not always oppose his polemical works. This was an attempt to suffocate him, to deny him the oxygen of controversy. He tried to shock, and they were not always shocked. Or maybe they were? Sometimes Butler is convinced that he has been successful and notes down some episode of inversionary shock-tactics in the *Notebooks:* ' "*Cleanse thou me from my secret sins*": I heard a man moralizing on this, and shocked him by saying demurely that I did not mind these so much, if I could get rid of those that were obvious to other people' (p. 101).

When Butler tried to create symmetry by turning against others and making others turn against him his attempts were sometimes frustrated when people ignored him. Fortunately language, unlike the humans, could not avoid or ignore him or refuse to be put into relation with him. And so, after each successive failure to engage the mighties of the world in verbal combat, Butler returned to the British Museum, read some more, found some more self-satisfied, smug, authoritative-sounding proverbs that he could invert, stand on their heads, turn inside out or back to front, ambiguate, amphibolize, and in general put himself in antithetical relation with; and some more myths, archetypes, clichés, topoi, and so on, that he could deal with in similar fashion. To *their* self-satisfied babble of received, conventional wisdom, and their pernicious assumption that things are *one* way, rather than either of *two* ways, he could at least react in an ideal way. *They* could not refuse to interact. In their case Butler was allowed to add his inverted variants and achieve symmetry.[8]

(b) Inversion serves the principle of complementariness

As we have seen, Butler felt that there was always 'another side' to everything. Nothing is ever complete on its own; everything has to have a companion piece in the form of its own inversion.

We should realize that ultimately Butler's inversions are not meant to *cancel out* what is inverted. On the contrary, whatever is the target of the inversion is felt to come fully into existence only after it has been complemented with its enantiomorph. Thus many of Butler's inversionary musings in his *Notebooks* begin with the word 'Yes' (or 'Yes, but...'), followed by the inversion. An inversion is in other words an affirmation and a negation at the same time. If a statement seems true to Butler, this automatically means that its opposite must be true as well, as in *'The importance of little things:* This is all very true but so also is the unimportance even of great things – sooner or later' (*Notebooks*, p. 79).

His inversions quite regularly begin with explicit assent to the target-statement which he is just about to invert:

The peace that passeth understanding: Yes. But as there is a peace more comfortable than any understanding so also there is an understanding more covetable than any peace.   (Ibid., p. 219)

'Woe unto you when all men speak well of you': Yes, and 'Woe unto you when you speak well of all men.'   (Ibid., p. 260)

Similarly, many of his inversions begin with the phrase 'it might be added', as in *'The world's greatest men:* It is said the world knows nothing (or little?) of its greatest men; it might be added that its greatest men have known very little of the world' (ibid., p. 218). Butler's inversions are thus additions at the same time as they are negations.

Usually the inversions exist to assert the belief that anything you can say of any two existing things works both ways: from the one to the other, and *vice-versa.* Thus with the ridiculous and the sublime: *'The ridiculous and the sublime:* As there is but one step from the sublime to the ridiculous, so also there is but one from the ridiculous to the sublime' (ibid., p. 220); and with men and women:

> *Women sometimes say:* that they have had no offers, and only wish that some one had ever proposed to them. This is not the right way to put it. What they should say is that though, like all women, they have been proposing to men all their lives, yet they grieve to remember that they have been invariably refused.   (Ibid., p. 287)

A variant of this rule is that, if anything is impossible *one way,* it must be impossible *both ways:*

> *The chatter of men and monkeys:* In his latest article (Feb. 1892) Prof. Garner says that the chatter of monkeys is not meaningless but that they are conveying ideas to one another. This seems to me hazardous. The monkeys might with equal justice conclude that in our magazine articles or literary and artistic criticisms, we are not chattering idly but are conveying ideas to one another.   (Ibid., p. 248)

Whether anything is a matter of presence or absence does not matter as long as it is *the same* both ways.

It is not only in the ambidirectionality of interrelations between recognized pairs, however, that Butler's passion for complementariness is found. His entire vision of the world and reality presupposes that whatever exists ought to exist in complementarily antithetical pairs. When he thinks that he sees a case in which one half of such a pair is lacking he tries to supply it.

This applies to language. 'Hypocrisy' is a fine term, but where is its antithetical mate? 'That vice pays homage to virtue is notorious; we call this hypocrisy; there should be a word found for the homage which virtue not unfrequently pays, or at any rate would be wise in paying, to vice' (*The Way of All Flesh*, ch. 19, p. 84). It also applies to social institutions. There should be an antithetical complement to orphanages: 'There are orphanages,' he exclaimed to himself, 'for children who have lost their parents – oh! why, why, why, are there no harbours of refuge for grown men who have not yet lost them?' (ibid., ch. 67, p. 295).

Hate in Butler is ultimately internal; warfare internecine. Butler's strange eagerness to set himself up in opposition can be understood when we realize that, in his groping for a method to realize emotional enantiomorphism, he had come to regard antithetical opposition as a way of complementing and making symmetrically whole an unfinished, asymmetric half.

(c) 'Toppling-over': unidirectionalism causes a growing strain until it triggers a catastrophic reversal

'Toppling-over' imagery came easily to Butler. In *The Way of All Flesh*, chapter 19, the narrator philosophizes on virtues, 'A system which cannot stand without a better foundation than this must have something so unstable within itself that it will topple over on whatever pedestal we place it' (p. 82). There is a return to 'toppling-over' imagery in chapter 83 (p. 384), and in chapter 69 a similar image is again used, though this time in the more 'active'-sounding form of 'knocking-over':

> The trouble is that in the end we shall be driven to admit the unity of the universe so completely as to be compelled to deny that there is either an external or an internal, but must see everything both as external and internal at one and the same time, subject and object – external and internal – being unified as much as everything else. This will knock our whole system over, but then every system has got to be knocked over by something. (p. 304)

The last sentence formulates Butler's chiasticistic 'toppling-over' credo very well. Nothing is for ever. Nothing can go on in the same direction forever; sooner or later it must turn and double back in on itself. A process of change cannot go on indefinitely; at some point – the 'toppling-over' moment – it has to reverse its direction.

Obviously Butler's fascination with the 'toppling-over' image stems from chiasticism, but precisely how is difficult to determine. If we imagine a movement from either side towards and beyond the middle of a chiasmus, turning is inevitable, since the middle is a turning-point. But probably it is unnecessary to seek the explanation of the 'toppling-over' philosophy in specific visualization of this kind. Rather, an explanation should be sought in the fundamental chiasticist rule that nothing must be allowed to exist on its own without its inversionary complement. Unidirectionalism implies asymmetry and can therefore not be tolerated. The 'toppling-over' philosophy asserts ambidirectionalism and thereby indirectly symmetry.

A chiasticist believes that unidirectionalism causes a strain which keeps growing until it triggers a sudden and total reversal. The theory which is nowadays known as *catastrophe-theory* is relevant to chiastic thinking. According to catastrophe-theory, changes in nature are of different kinds. One type of change is common, slow, minimal and continuous, while another is rare, sudden, maximal and periodic – i.e. catastrophic. These catastrophes often involve a complete reshaping of an existing structure: for instance, the inversion of a hierarchy.

At this point let us remind ourselves of some basic facts relating to the nature of inversion as a principle. We must remember that inversion is impossible without hierarchical or sequential order. Inversion presupposes such principles as directionality; it is hierarchy that gives inversion meaning. Unless there is a preferred order between units, the term 'inversion' has no meaning. In a completely egalitarian society, such as the Greenland Eskimo cultures, the word 'revolution' is meaningless. You cannot 'subvert' when there is nothing to subvert. The more hierarchical a society becomes, the more the word 'revolution' acquires a meaning – or 'its' meaning.

In order to have symmetry you must have inversion, and in order to have inversion – as we have just seen – you must have hierarchies, sequential order, preferentiality. The attitude of the chiasticist towards the principle of hierarchical or preferential ordering, therefore, must of necessity be ambivalent. On the one hand he is bound to attack (with an inversion) any existing case of hierarchical order; yet he cannot quarrel with the principle of preferential ordering *itself,* since it is indirectly needed for symmetry. *Which one* of any unequal *a* and *b* pair should be on top he will concern himself with endlessly, but he cannot take a course which would do away with the difference between *a* and *b* altogether.

Symmetry also causes another important restriction in the way the chiasticist understands and uses the concept of inversion. To a chiasticist inversion should ideally be inversion of extremes. Therefore, if we imagine a scale 1-to-5, the chiasticist likes a 5-to-1 (or

1-to-5) switch better than, say, a 4-to-3 switch or a 5-to-4 switch, although broadly used the term 'inversion' might be argued to take in all of these cases. To a chiasticist some cases of inversion are better than others.

In addition to the rule that inversion should ideally be of extremes, there is also a rule favouring exact mirror-image inversion. This could be visualized in the following way. If you have an existing scale 5-to-1,

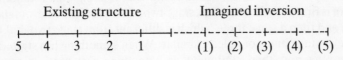

and the chiasticist has to imagine or create an inversionary variant of a position (on the existing scale), he will prefer the exact mirror-image position, on the imagined complementary scale, of the point (on the existing scale) for which he is creating a complement. Thus, for 3 he will choose (3) rather than (1), (2), (4) or (5); and so on. Best of all he will like to complement 5 with (5).

To sum up, on any scale the chiasticist is likely to focus on a point at either extreme. For inversionary or exchange-purposes the ideal mate for this point is, then, the opposite extreme of the existing structure, or a mirror-image position in an imagined structure. Against this background one can understand why catastrophic rather than gradual change appealed to Butler's imagination.

Butler was well aware of different kinds of change – at least of *two* kinds, as is evident from the following passage, in which he structures a description of different kinds of change precisely around a dualist division into slow, continuous and minimal, on the one hand, and sudden, periodic and catastrophic, on the other:

> Under these circumstances an organism must act in one of two ways; it must either change slowly and continuously with the surroundings, paying cash for everything, meeting the smallest charge with a corresponding modification so far as is found convenient; or it must put off change as long as possible and then make larger and more sweeping changes.   (Jones, II 97–8)

Butler's preference for catastrophic change, rather than any other kind (or, to put it in Butlerian language, *the* other kind), results from the combination of dualism and extremism. Dualism dictates that of all imaginable units on a continuum one is allowed to take notice of only two. Extremism dictates that of all units the most extreme are the ideal ones, preferable to all others. Together the principles of dualism, extremism and inversion ensure that inversion will be inversion of extremes, and change catastrophic rather than minimal.

Extremism does not make a chiasticist more hesitant to accept inversion. The reason may be the idea inherent in chiasticism that extremes are not dissimilar but the same. Thus the love of catastrophism should be seen in connection with Butler's 'palladian' thinking. There is first a stage one; then a stage two, which is different from stage one; and then a stage three, which is different from stage two, but the same as stage one – or at least similar. When something has started as something and then continued as something different, it cannot continue different for ever; there must come a moment when it reverts to what it was originally.

Butler, groping around for terms, calls this either 'contradiction in terms' or 'extremes meeting': '*Contradiction in terms*: (or perhaps extremes meeting). So we pay higher and higher in proportion to the service rendered till we get to the highest services, such as becoming a Member of Parliament, and this must not be paid at all' (*Notebooks*, p. 249).

When Butler seeks out or invents boomerang patterns and images of resilience, the main metaphoric thrust is simply against unidirectionalism. What these images primarily assert is that nothing can go in one direction for ever – there must be a turn. In some of these patterns it is not specifically stressed that the turn has to be sudden, only that it is obligatory. One of Butler's favourite verbs is 'to pitchfork': '*Colour*: is like nature; you may pitchfork it out as you will, but it will always find its way back. I mean, cover a building with Portland cement, and it will, ere long, get lichen-grown and in good colour again' (ibid., p. 194). 'Pitchfork', we recall, is an illusion to Horace: 'Naturam expellas furca, tamen usque recurret' (*Epigrams*, I.10.24) – a famous assertion of the futility of attempts to achieve a going without return. A movement, in Butler, is attached by strong elastic to its starting-point. The elastic may stretch and stretch but finally the backward pull overcomes the forward thrust and the direction of the movement is reversed.

Though it is not always stressed that the change from stage *b* back to stage *a* (or stage a_1) must be sudden, this nevertheless is normally implied. The change from *a* to *b* causes a gradual build-up of tension so that when the change to stage *a* or a_1 eventually occurs it will not be a smooth change but a catastrophic toppling-over.

In an increase of pain there are three stages – the first when we feel little pain, the second when we feel progressively more, and the third when toppling-over ensures a reversal to something like stage one:

> *The art of feeling*: If there is truth in my lecture on the genesis of feeling, people cannot feel unless they know how to feel – i.e. what to feel under what circumstances. When, then, a position becomes too horribly novel for us to have had any experience that can guide us in knowing how to feel about it, the probability is that we cannot feel at all. Hence we may hope that the most horrible apparent suffering is not felt beyond a certain point, but is performed under a natural automatic anaesthetic. (*Notebooks*, p. 255)

Butler made use of this idea in chapter 42 of *The Way of All Flesh*, where Ernest's parents are torturing him to find out about his misdemeanours at school. When Ernest's pain becomes unbearable, he is relieved by a fainting fit:

> Theobald was resolved that this time Ernest should, as he called it, take him into his confidence without reserve, so the school list which went with Dr Skinner's half-yearly bills was brought out, and the most secret character of each boy was gone through *seriatim* by Mr and Mrs Pontifex, so far as it was in Ernest's power to give information concerning it, and yet Theobald had on the preceding Sunday preached a less feeble sermon than he commonly preached, upon the horrors of the Inquisition. No matter how awful was the depravity revealed to them, the pair never flinched, but probed and probed, till they were on the point of reaching subjects more delicate than they had yet touched upon. Here Ernest's unconscious self took the matter up and made a resistance to which his conscious self was unequal, by tumbling him off his chair in a fit of fainting. (pp. 184–5)

Butler even literalizes the toppling-over idea in this passage by having Ernest 'tumbl[e]' down from his chair. Butler was fond of the word 'tumble' (see, for example, *Notebooks*, p. 273 or p. 100) and the concept sometimes seems to have had a special value to him. Knowing how to 'tumble' well is as important a skill to a chiasticist as is always landing on one's feet to a cat.

The image of top-heaviness also came particularly easily to Butler:

It is here, moreover, that effort is most remunerative. For when we feel that a painter has made simplicity and subordination of importances his first aim, it is surprising how much shortcoming we will condone as regards actual execution. Whereas let the execution be perfect if the details given be ill-chosen in respect of relative importance the whole effect is lost; it becomes top-heavy, as it were, and collapses. (*Notebooks*, p. 69)

Top-heaviness is a necessary prerequisite for toppling-over. A top-heavy structure is one which will soon topple over.

Many different kinds of structures get top-heavy in Butler's works. The Anglican Church does so in *The Way of All Flesh* (ch. 83, p. 384). The idea recurs in chapter 25 of *Erewhon Revisited*, where the religion in question is Sunchildism:

'Do you think we shall ever get rid of Sunchildism altogether?'

'If they stick to the cock-and-bull stories they are telling now, and rub them in, as Hanky did on Sunday, it may go, and go soon. It has taken root too quickly and easily; and its top is too heavy for its roots; still, there are so many chances in its favour that it may last a long time.' (p. 227)

Political systems also become top-heavy – the idea of toppling over in the form of revolution is far from foreign to Butler. In the development of Erewhonian society there are a number of toppling-over inversions in the form of revolutions. In chapter 13 of *Erewhon* it is recounted how the proliferation of bad statues reaches such proportions that it causes a backlash:

At last the evil reached such a pitch that the people rose, and with indiscriminate fury destroyed good and bad alike. Most of what was destroyed was bad, but some few works were good, and the sculptors of to-day wring their hands over some of the fragments that have been preserved in museums up and down the country. (p. 100)

A similar pattern is found in the chapters dealing with Erewhonian attitudes to animals and vegetables. The dietary rules become more and more extreme; one source of food after another is forbidden, until eventually, in chapter 27, the sudden reversal comes; the system of rules topples over and the Erewhonians revert to a normal diet.

Another revolution in *Erewhon* is the destruction of the machines, and in *Erewhon Revisited* their reintroduction. History in *Erewhon* and *Erewhon Revisited* is a rushing from one extreme to another, a turn, and endless repetition.

Another nineteenth-century habitué of the British Museum also sat there speculating on future toppling-over scenarios. Capital would be concentrated in fewer and fewer hands, he predicted. The system would become increasingly top-heavy, until in the end a violent reversal would usher in the dictatorship of the proletariat, when the slaves become masters. Whereas this theorist was in earnest, and claimed a connection between the patterns he envisaged and reality, Butler was content to let *his* inversionary visions take place in utopias that were professedly fictional.[9]

But there are questions of symmetry and asymmetry that may plague a political thinker whether his political thinking is in earnest or in jest. For instance: What attitude should a revolutionary take to reformism? Is it wise to support piecemeal improvement if this postpones the revolution?

On the whole, however, the revolutionary can contemplate ambilateralist possibilities with greater peace of mind than the reformist. In one sense the revolutionary can never lose. If conditions improve, that is good. If, on the other hand, they deteriorate, that is good too, since it hastens the revolution.

The reformist cannot trust the latter half of this sanguine ambilateralist view, because he thinks asymmetry may be possible. 'What guarantees *are* there that a bottom exists, so that once you hit it there will be a rebound?' the reformist asks himself uneasily. Maybe there are no limits to unidirectionalism? Maybe conditions can just go on deteriorating for ever? Faced with this unidirectionalist possibility the reformist feels compelled to take an asymmetric attitude. He decides that any change for the better is welcome and any change for the worse unwelcome.[10]

The ambilateralist idea of aiding the wrong side, so as to help make the system more top-heavy and bring nearer an ultimate inevitable toppling-over inversion, is often found in Butler's characters. The professor who writes on the rights of vegetables in *Erewhon*, chapter 27, does so with the intent of wrecking a cause by joining it.

The tactics of joining a cause to wreck it are, as already noted, the strategy adopted in parodies and satires, and Butler was attracted to these genres. But he never became a good parodist or satirist in the conventional sense. Those who join a cause to wreck it should have a stable purpose. Once they have joined it they should stay with it. There should be one inversion, but one only. Butler was seldom content with one inversion, and, since he could not keep to one perspective in his parodies and satires, these works are not pure products of the genre.

Once an inversion has taken place, the inverted state will not prove permanent either. In due time it will itself be inverted by a toppling-over incident. Images of series of multiple toppling-over inversions are found, as in the following passage from *Life and Habit*:

> The so-called man of science, on the other hand, seems now generally inclined to make light of all knowledge, save of the pioneer character. His ideal is in self-conscious knowledge. Let us have no more Lo, here, with the professor; he very rarely knows what he says he knows; no sooner has he misled the world for a sufficient time with a great flourish of trumpets than he is toppled over by one more plausible than himself.   (Shrewsbury, IV 34-5)

The 'toppling-over' images indicate a preference for sudden, total and periodic change over regular, minimal and continuous change. When a development has gone as far as it can in one direction and the turning-point is reached, the change is not a small but a maximal one; a wild rushing all the way to the other extreme.[11]

Again one is tempted to compare Butler to the James brothers. The typical pattern of thought for many of Henry James's fictional characters is a wild rushing from one extreme to another, and a horror of the middle ground. It is as if, once they decide that a certain position is untenable, the only possible alternative is an extreme mirror-image opposite view. Their insecurity also periodically manifests itself as its opposite – self-assurance.

Is not self-assertion also the message preached in William James's pragmatist philosophy? William James advocates self-reliance, much like Emerson and many other Americans, though William James's self-reliance concerns such basic things as epistemology and cognition. He employs an instrumentalist criterion of truth: if something works it is true; and this enables him to argue in favour of the provisional acceptance of hypotheses – in other words that until they have proved themselves false we should regard them as true.

Whether William James meant it or not, his critics have understood him as speaking in favour of postponement of verification; as speaking in favour of letting reality actively bring the falsification of your theory to *you* (if it is false) rather than of anxiously going out to reality to test the theory for yourself; and also as speaking in favour of an ultimate violent moment of revelation of the truth (whether falsification or verification) rather than a continuing series of repeated small tests that result not in one, single, violent swing (or non-swing) of falsification (or verification), but in small, continuous adjustments. If this view of his philosophy is accurate to any extent at all, it is possible that William James's complacent attitude towards catastrophic falsification suggests that he is influenced by chiasticist attitudes.

Butler's thinking, despite his cult of the mean tended to extremism. Every reader of Butler is familiar with his 'cult of the mean': his love of the average, his search for the *via media*, his praise of 'common sense' and his general longing for a meeting of extremes. But, like everything else in Butler, this cult of the mean existed only in paradoxical conjunction with its own opposite, which is horror of the middle ground, i.e. a preference not only for antithetical juxtaposition but for antithetical juxtaposition of extremes.

At this point it may be convenient to trace further the connection between dualism and extremism. Faced with a multiplicity of units of anything, Butler always had to pick out *two* from the many. After that he would then try to bring the one in contact with the other, and *vice-versa*, with the aid of chiasmus. In the *Notebooks* (pp. 121–3) there is a long note on 'Tools' which Butler characteristically ends with the following reflection: 'It seems to me that all tools resolve themselves into the hammer and the lever, and that the lever is only an inverted hammer or the hammer only an inverted lever whichever one wills... .' There exist in reality a great number of different tools. It is not true that only two tools exist. Thus reality is in this respect not intrinsically dualistic. In his mania for dualism Butler is therefore compelled to *impose* dualism on reality rather than *find* it. The overall situation is, then, that, though sometimes dualism is intrinsic to nature or reality, it is more often adduced by Butler.

It is the process of creating artificial dualism, in those areas where nature or reality does not provide it, that affords much scope for a marriage between dualism and extremism. When Butler had to pick two out of many he would try to pick two antithetical extremes.

There is also a connection between dualism and catastrophism. Whenever there existed a scale with infinite gradations, Butler's instinct was to dualize it, and some of his methods of making language dualistic reveal the connection between dualism and the toppling-over idea. A case in point is Butler's predilection for composite words beginning 'over-'. Butler, as he would have said himself, 'overused' these. He used those that existed frequently, and in cases where none existed he coined neologisms. The following are conventional examples from the *Notebooks*:

> *Prudence*: There is nothing so imprudent or so improvident as over-prudence or over-providence. (p. 224)

> *Not to over-breed*: will be one day recognized as not less essential for national well-being than breeding is. (p. 281)

> This indeed is what one of the wisest men who ever lived – the author of the book of *Ecclesiastes* – definitely concludes to be the case, when he tells his readers that they had better not overdo either their virtue or their wisdom (*Ecc.* vii, 16). (p. 251)

Butler's most famous passage of this kind, however, is found in one of the cruel sonnets he wrote about Miss Savage: 'For she was plain and lame and fat and short'/Forty and over-kind, (Shrewsbury, xx 424). Kindness, we learn, is not for the compulsive dualist a phenomenon of infinite gradations. There is only 'kind' and 'over-kind'. Miss Savage's kindness had catastrophically toppled over.

When human beings observe nature they do not perceive uniformly what exists, but bring to their observation their inclinations and preferences. Of the various forms of change that exist in nature and reality, a chiasticist is most likely to take note of catastrophic change, because he is mentally preconditioned for it.

(d) Butler's mind like the amphisbaena: goes with equal ease in either of two opposite directions

Reading Butler's ambilateralist and ambidirectionalist passages, one is reminded of the snake that the ancients called the 'amphisbaena' (ἀμφίσβαινα).[12] This snake had a head at each end, and could go in either direction. Aelian (AD 170–235) comments:

ἡ δὲ ἀμφίσβαινα ὄφις δικέφαλός ἐστι, καὶ τὰ ἄνω καὶ ὅσα ἐς τὸ οὐραῖον. προϊοῦσα δέ, ὅπως ἂν ἐς τὴν ὁρμὴν ἐπαγάγῃ τῆς προόδου ἡ χρεία αὐτήν, τὴν μὲν ἀπέλιπεν οὐρὰν εἶναι, τὴν δὲ ἀπέφηνε κεφαλήν. καὶ μέντοι καὶ πάλιν εἰ δεηθείη τὴν ὀπίσω ἰέναι, κέχρηται ταῖς κεφαλαῖς ἐς τὸ ἐναντίον ἢ τὸ πρόσθεν ἐχρήσατο.[13]

This is neutral and merely descriptive. Other ancient authors take more evaluative attitudes. Pliny waxes quite indignant against this snake which has two heads, as if it were not enough to spew out poison from one mouth ('geminum caput amphisbaenae, hoc est et a cauda, tamquam parum esset uno ore fundi venenum').[14] Some ancient authors were deeply suspicious of the snake and its ambidirectionalism. Lucan calls it 'gravis', whatever that may mean ('Et gravis in geminum vergens caput amphisbaena'); and in Aeschylus the word ἀμφίσβαινα, as denoting an odious monster, is even used as an epithet of abuse: 'τί νιν καλοῦσα δυσφιλὲς δάκος τύχοιμ' ἄν; ἀμφίσβαιναν'. Most ancient authors, however, simply mention the fact that the snake has two heads, one at each end, and can go in either direction.[15]

The amphisbaena is a perfect symbol of emotional ambilateralism; of the ever-ready willingness to go in either of two opposite directions. Butler's mind was exactly like the amphisbaena. It had a head at each end, and it could go with equal ease in either direction. Part of the lore of the amphisbaena – though apparently not in antiquity – was that, while one half of the snake sleeps, the other wakes. Again, the image suits Butler's mind. The enantiomorphic other half was always latently there, ready to wake up and take over at a moment's notice.[16]

In addition there is, with Butler, the missionary impulse: the urge not only to accept ambilateralism in one's self, but to try to make as much as possible of the outside world ambilateralist as well. We may say that *Butler's ideal was an amphisbaena at rest*. To achieve such a state of relativistic equilibrium was the motive behind most of his behaviour, and his favourite principles of thought serve his attempts to reach this ideal state. Thus the *raison d'être* of inversion is to help restore relativistic equilibrium, in cases where the balance has been upset.

It is important to realize that in those instances in which Butler definitely and strongly advocates one particular sequential order –usually end-to-beginning – he does so only because he sees this as the weaker of two alternatives. His advocacy of one particular sequential order should not be seen as something on its own, but as the enantiomorph to an already existing order.

In chapter 6 of *Ex Voto,* Butler recommends visitors to the Sacro Monte at Varallo to see the chapels in the wrong order, starting from the end and going towards the beginning:

> I have glanced at some of the wealth in store for those who will explore it, but at the same time I cannot pretend that even the greater number of the chapels on the Sacro Monte are above criticism; and unfortunately some of the best do not come till the visitor, if he takes them in the prescribed order, has already seen a good many, and is beginning to be tired. There is not a little to be said in favour of taking them in the reverse order.   (Shrewsbury, IX 63)

The reason Butler gives is that some of the best statues and paintings are to be found in the chapels at the end of the series, and the visitor should not tire his senses by looking at worse works of art at the beginning, when there are better ones later on. Naturally it may be true that the works of art on the Sacro Monte really *are* better at the end of the series of chapels, but, as we know, Butler did not really need an objective reason for inversion. If an objective reason could be found, then so much the better; if not he would invent one.

Butler feels that movement should be equally possible and likely both ways. But convention and tradition have upset the balance and made people take a certain sequential order for granted. At the Sacro Monte they have got into the habit of starting at the beginning and going through to the end. To redress the balance Butler feels he must recommend the inverted order. If his recommended order were to gain universal acceptance the balance would of course be upset again, and then he would have to change sides. At the moment, however, the balance is clearly upset the other way and Butler feels it is his duty to redress it.

The invertibility of real-world objects varies. Some tools can be inverted; some not so easily. Some that cannot be inverted in reality can be inverted metaphorically. This is the case with the telescope; it cannot be inverted in reality (i.e. used the wrong way around), but in chapter 1 of *Erewhon,* Butler inverts it metaphorically when he describes 'the yards and wool-sheds on the flat below; all seen as through the wrong end of a telescope' (p. 4). Tools or implements with two ends different from one another were worrying and problematical to Butler, because he could not see his way to inverting them. (Metaphor extends the possibilities only to a limited degree.) Quite simple, on the other hand, are cases in which the usage is intrinsically invertible and convention comes down strongly on one side. In such cases Butler delightedly comes down on the other.

Equally easy are the cases where Butler is dealing with pairs. Then he invariably makes the two halves of the pair complementary and antithetical, thus satisfying his thirst for balance and symmetry. Hanky and Panky in *Erewhon Revisited* are such a pair. Throughout the book Butler puts them in antithetical relation to each other, and in the matter of dress he predictably makes one of them, Panky, wear his European costume reversed, while the other, Hanky, wears his clothes the normal European way:

> They were not in the Erewhonian costume. The one was dressed like an Englishman or would-be Englishman, while the other was wearing the same kind of clothes but turned the wrong way round, so that when his face was towards my father his body seemed to have its back towards him, and *vice versa*.   (Ch. 3, p. 23)[17]

Butler's treatment of pairs proves that his primary goal was relativism, not inversion *per se*.

Inversion on its own was all right when conventional usage was an uninverted one; then conventional uninverted usage, strong as it usually is, provided the other half with which Butler's inverted usage could be balanced. But when Butler had two of something, and was thus free to please himself, he regularly made one an example of an uninverted state and the other one of an inverted.

Worrying about order, Butler sometimes, in desperation, tried to bring some sort of logic or rationality to bear on the question. Thus he devised various dogmatic rules, such as doing things in the order 'better-to-worse' or 'important-to-unimportant'.[18] Such attempts to bring the problem of sequential order under rational control are the basis for a number of well-known Butlerisms, such as the doctrine of 'eating grapes downwards':

> *Eating grapes downwards:* Always eat the best first. For so every grape will be good. This is why spring seems longer and drearier than autumn: in autumn we are eating the days downwards, in spring each one is 'still very bad'.   (*Notebooks*, p. 62)

A similar attempt at rationalism dictated his New Zealand doctrine of order in washing up:

Myself and washing up in New Zealand: In New Zealand for a long time I had to do the washing up after each meal. I used to do the knives first, for it might please God to take me before I came to the forks, and then what a sell it would have been to have done the forks rather than the knives.   (Ibid., p. 112)

But there is always something forced and frantic about such attempts at stability as these. The true Butler did not want stability of order – his normal instinct was towards lability and relativism. Reluctant as we may be to face yet another *salto mortale* of logic in tracing the strange course of chiasticist zigzagging, we must conclude that these dogmatic endorsements of asymmetry are only Butler's concern with symmetry coming out in an inverted form.

In the distribution of emphasis to the two members of a pair Butler was always willing to give equal shares, or to redress any real or imagined imbalance. Thus he insisted that portraits tell us more about the painter than about the sitter:

Portrait: A great portrait is always as much a portrait of the painter as of the painted. When we look at a portrait by Holbein or Rembrandt it is of Holbein or Rembrandt we think more than of the subject of their picture. Even a portrait of Shakespeare by Holbein or Rembrandt could tell us very little about Shakespeare. It tells us a great deal, however, about Holbein and Rembrandt.

(Ibid., p. 152)

Behind a portrait is a relation between a painter and a sitter. Lazy thought would stress the connection between the sitter and the portrait, not the painter and the portrait. Usually it is not their own likeness artists aim for when they paint a portrait. This, however, is the result, chiasticists argue, because with them – thanks to their ambilateralism – a critical scrutiny of conventional distribution of emphasis is automatic.[19]

A parallel case is the relation between an author and his subject. Does a literary work depict the subject or the author? Butler's answer is, 'the author':

Every man's work, whether it be literature or music or pictures or architecture or anything else, is always a portrait of himself, and the more he tries to conceal himself the more clearly will his character appear in spite of him. I may very likely be condemning myself, all the time that I am writing this book, for I know that whether I like it or no I am portraying myself more surely than I am portraying any of the characters whom I set before the reader. I am sorry that it is so, but I cannot help it – after which sop to Nemesis I will say that Battersby church in its amended form has always struck me as a better portrait of Theobald than any sculptor or painter short of a great master would be able to produce. (*The Way of All Flesh,* ch. 14, p. 62)

There may be some substance in these observations. Doubtless Butler is also often right in his musings on relativism. In the following example the relativism concerns morality:

> *Morality:* turns on whether the pleasure precedes the pain or follows it (provided it is sufficient). Thus it is immoral to get drunk because the headache comes after the drinking, but if the headache came first and the drunkenness afterwards, it would be moral to get drunk. (*Notebooks,* p. 101)

Relativism is again asserted in a *Notebooks* entry on 'Happiness and misery', in which Butler argues that direction of movement, rather than absolute position, is what counts: '*Happiness and misery:* consist in a progression towards better or worse; it does not matter how high up or low down you are, it depends not on this, but on the direction in which you are tending' (p. 230).

As evidence of Butler's mental habits, however, such 'good' or 'interesting' examples are, in a sense, less valuable than spurious and flippant ones, since with these 'good' examples one is, as it were, distracted by truth and reality from a detached and dispassionate understanding of Butler's psychomorphology; i.e. from a view in which the value or truth of any particular Butlerian statement is a secondary question compared to its similarity to or difference from other elements, its frequency, and its relative importance among Butler's patterns of thought. Therefore Butler's more eccentric inversionary cavortings must be paraded here, even though it goes against one's instinct to choose less valuable passages from an author's work, when better ones could be found. For the sake of analysis, if not for appreciation, let us note such Butlerisms as his 'divorce novelette'. Far too much attention, Butler felt, is paid to the process of getting married. What about its complementary mate, the process of getting divorced? That has been unduly neglected.

The divorce novelette: The hero and heroine are engaged against their wishes. They like each other very well but are each in love with some one else; nevertheless under an uncle's will they forfeit large property unless they marry, so they get married, making no secret to one another that they dislike it very much.

On the evening of their wedding day they broach to one another the subject that has long been nearest to the heart of each – the possibility of their being divorced.

They discuss the subject tearfully, but the obstacles to their divorce seem insuperable. Nevertheless they agree that faint heart never yet got rid of fair lady. 'None but the brave', they exclaim, 'deserve to lose the fair', and they plight each other their most solemn vows that they will henceforth live but for the object of getting divorced from one another.

But the course of true divorce never did run smooth, and the plot turns upon the difficulties that meet them and how they try to overcome them. At one time they seem almost certain of success, but the cup is dashed from their lips and is farther off than ever.

At last an opportunity occurs in an unlooked-for manner. They are divorced, and live happily apart ever afterwards. (Ibid., pp. 56–7)

The Victorian period paid great attention to 'progress'. This clearly upsets the balance of directional relativity. What about the claims and needs of 'regress'? Butler asked himself. These had been neglected. But in his utopia, *Erewhon*, he could redress the balance. A fair proportion of the narrative of *Erewhon* is therefore devoted to scientific and artistic retrogression. The word 'retrogression' itself is used (for instance, in ch. 9, p. 64), and so is the word 'reversion' (ch. 25, p. 192).

If there exists a process of canonization within the Church, there should also exist its complementary inversion, a process of uncanonization, and equal attention should be paid to the necessities of each. If the second has been neglected, it should temporarily be given special priority:

Saint Cosimo and Saint Damiano at Siena: Sano di Pietro shows us a heartless practical joke played by these two very naughty saints, both medical men, who should be uncanonized immediately. It seems they laid their heads together and for some reason, best known to themselves, resolved to cut a leg off a dead negro and put it on to a white man. In the one compartment they are seen in high glee cutting the negro's leg off. In the next they have gone to the white man who is in bed, obviously asleep, and are substituting the black leg for his own. Then, no doubt, they will stand behind the door and see what he does when he wakes. They must be saints because they have glories on, but it looks as though a glory is not much more to be relied on than a gig as a test of respectability. (1889.)   (*Notebooks*, p. 314)

In the same way as it is instructive to pay attention to Butler's frivolous and eccentric passages, it is also important to consider his dull or inconclusive passages. These show how Butler could not let go of certain subjects, even when they did not lead anywhere. A *Notebooks* entry on shepherds shows how Butler endlessly turned questions of direction over in his mind:

'*Pastor ignavus dormit supinus*': This was translated in the old Eton grammar, 'The idle shepherd sleeps with his face upwards.' I took this, when a child, as an interesting fact in natural history, and believed I could always now distinguish an idle from an industrious shepherd by observing whether he slept with his face downwards or upwards. I was sure that Frick, Mr Vincent Hall's shepherd, always slept with his face downwards, but if you really wanted to know about a shepherd you must watch.   (p. 219)[20]

We may even go a step further and note that *not knowing,* or *not being sure,* was something Butler felt to be important and worthy of being put on record, if it had to do with direction or order. In fact we may conclude that Butler regretted any introduction of definite knowledge, if such knowledge settled a question of order or direction. Apparently he thought that one method whereby relativistic equilibrium – an amphisbaena at rest – might be achieved, was *ignorance.* Butler probably thought it a pity that the question of whether the earth goes round the sun, or the sun round the earth, had been settled (cf. Ch. 1, *supra*). Emotionally he hankered after the paradisiacal ambilateralist innocence of uneducated people for whom the question is still open. Butler returns to the subject repeatedly in the *Notebooks:*

Wisdom and knowledge are, like a bad reputation, more easily won than lost; we got on fairly well without knowing that the earth went round the sun; we thought the sun went round the earth until we

found it makes us uncomfortable to think so any longer – then we altered our opinion; it was not very easy to alter it, but it was easier than it would be to alter it back again. *Vestigia nulla retrorsum.*
(p. 251)

Such musings are only the by-products of Butler's longing for a state of restored ambilateralism. If we wish to see what Butler really wanted, we must turn to his fiction. In *Erewhon* there was no need to take any notice of received scientific opinion. Butler accordingly reintroduces ambilateralism – at least partly:

The Erewhonians say it was by chance only that the earth and stars and all the heavenly worlds began to roll from east to west, and not from west to east, and in like manner they say it is by chance that man is drawn through life with his face to the past instead of to the future.   (Ch. 19, pp. 141–2)

The Erewhonians believe 'that we are drawn through life backwards; or again, that we go onwards into the future as into a dark corridor' (p. 141). When this idea is elaborated at the end of chapter 19, Butler, as usual, brings in the myth of Orpheus and Eurydice: ' "... we say in such a moment, when you clutch at the dream but it eludes your grasp, and you watch it, as Orpheus watched Eurydice, gliding back again into the twilight kingdom ..." ' (p. 147). A little earlier the Erewhonian writer argues that no one would voluntarily relive his life:

'Remember, too, that there never yet was a man of forty who would not come back into the world of the unborn if he could do so with decency and honour. Being in the world he will as a general rule stay till he is forced to go; but do you think that he would consent to be born again, and re-live his life, if he had the offer of doing so? Do not think it. If he could so alter the past as that he should never have come into being at all, do you not think that he would do it very gladly?'   (pp. 146–7)

This, we know, is not endorsed by Butler. He introduces the passage only in order to focus his target more clearly. In his own voice he advocates all possible variants of chronological progression and retrogression.

One of the variants of 'living one's life backwards' was the idea of 'returning to the womb'. Butler comes back to this idea again and again, in a number of variations. In *The Way of All Flesh*, the narrator sees not *one* return to the womb, but an infinite series of returns:

> As it was, the case was hopeless; it would be no use their even entering into their mothers' wombs and being born again. They must not only be born again but they must be born again each one of them of a new father and of a new mother and of a different line of ancestry for many generations before their minds could become supple enough to learn anew.   (Ch. 63, p. 275)

In *Erewhon Revisited,* a denial of the possibility of re-entering the womb is put into the mouth of a biased speaker – typical testimony of Butler's ambivalence on any question that concerns relativity of direction:

> 'Who has ever partaken of this life you speak of, and re-entered into the womb to tell us of it? Granted that some few have pretended to have done this, but how completely have their stories broken down when subjected to the tests of sober criticism. No. When we are born we are born, and there is an end of us.'   (Ch. 15, p. 153)

That the wish for complementariness, i.e. the restoration to strength of the weaker of two antithetical but complementary halves, is really the psychological basis for Butler's interest in the idea of return to the womb can be seen with particular clarity in a *Notebooks* entry in which he simultaneously brings in another complementary idea:

> *Erewhon Revisited:* They live their lives backwards, beginning as old men and women, with little more knowledge of the past than we have of the future, and foreseeing the future about as clearly as we do the past, winding up by entering into the womb as though it were being buried. But delicacy forbids me to pursue this subject further: the upshot being that it comes to much the same thing, provided one is used to it.
>
> Let a criminal make a speech to a judge much as the judge's speech to the criminal in *Erewhon*.   (p. 274)

Erewhon and *Erewhon Revisited* make a pair; therefore they should be put in chiastic relation to each other. If a judge has made a speech to a criminal in *Erewhon*, then it is desirable that a criminal should make a speech to a judge in *Erewhon Revisited*. People are born, leave the womb and go forth through life. But where is the other half of the chiastic truth? Obviously people should also go back through life and re-enter the womb, finally dying, which is the same as being born, according to the existential chiastic formula, 'Birth is death; death is birth.'

Butler's particular opinion on any question concerning order does not ultimately matter. What matters is the sum of two opinions. Butler's interest in any phenomenon of inversion is predictable, but what specific attitude he will take in each case – positive or negative, for instance – is not predictable. That Butler cannot help being fascinated by such a phenomenon as the nineteenth-century practice of translating modern English poetry into Latin or Greek is predictable, but what his views of it will be cannot be predicted – or rather it can be predicted that they will vary. In *Erewhon* the practice is half-heartedly condemned by the narrator:

> I have now said enough to give English readers some idea of the strange views which the Erewhonians hold concerning unreason, hypothetics, and education generally. In many respects they were sensible enough, but I could not get over the hypothetics, especially the turning their own good poetry into the hypothetical language.   (Ch. 22, pp. 167–8)

But the very fascination that Butler felt for such a phenomenon in itself sufficiently guarantees that his conviction remains shallow and his attitude ambivalent.

It may seem strange to argue that Butler did not believe strongly in any particular sequential doctrines at all (except ambilateralism itself) when it is well known how ardently he defended his theories of teleological evolution, on the resurrection, and on Shakespeare's sonnets; and how vehemently he stuck to them once he had become convinced. Yet Butler's convulsive adherence to these should be seen in the same light as his fidelity to the doctrine of eating grapes downwards or the set order of washing-up in New Zealand –micro-level parallels already mentioned. The stability is only a deceptive chiasticist mutation of lability. In addition Butler was helped by the stability of his opponents. Had *they* wavered *he* would have wavered too. As it is, Butler thinks he serves ambilateralism and symmetry best by sticking to his views as fanatically as his opponents stick to theirs.

How uncertain Butler nevertheless was, even on these questions, is revealed as soon as one begins to collocate his scattered statements on any of them. Mutually contradictory views are regularly found within Butler's own works. Whatever he says in one place can usually be found contradicted in some other place or even in the same place.[21] On the question of the resurrection of Jesus Christ, for instance, all varieties of opinion are expressed by Butler himself somewhere or other in his writings. Sometimes, in his comments, Butler totaly repudiates resurrection, as in the following *Notebooks* entry:

> *The resurrection:* When I die at any rate I shall do so in the full and certain hope that there will be no resurrection, but that death will give me quittance in full (p. 57).

And in *Erewhon* there is some mild satire on the belief in resurrection:

> and that even the most blessed rising would be but the disturbing of a still more blessed slumber.
> To all which I could only say that the thing had been actually known to happen, and that there were several well-authenticated instances of people having died and come to life again – instances which no man in his senses could doubt.   (Ch. 17, p. 134)

Yet this is the same man who spent the greater part of his scientific books trying to blur the line of division between life and death, the living and the dead, the organic and the inorganic; also the same man who devised elaborate theories of 'life-in-death' – for instance, of authors living through their books, and of people living on in the memory of others. For one who declares, in the quoted *Notebooks* entry, that death is final, Butler spent an inordinate amount of time and effort undermining his own position. It is certainly fair to say that he was of Christ's party without knowing it; but it is actually doubtful whether he was even totally ignorant of the fact.

The Fair Haven is by far the most ambivalent, self-contradictory, self-erasing and self-destructive of Butler's works. There is no consistency either of perspective or tone, and it is all too clear that the author does not hand the reader the solutiuon to his problems, but rather the process of his own grappling with them.[22]

The truth is that, for all his rebelliousness, Butler wanted ideally to include even his target of attack within himself. He stops his attacks halfway if he can. He reinterprets the *Odyssey,* but leaves the *Iliad* intact. He draws attention to teleological evolution, but does not deny the importance of natural selection, and so on. We must remember that attack and hatred do not mean quite the same to a chiasticist as to other people. A chiasticist believes in the possibility of wrecking a cause by joining it. Symmetrically, he also believes in the feasibility of helping a cause by attacking it. Therefore when Butler attacked something he thought he was doing it a favour. By supplying a complementary antithetical half he made possible symmetry, which he thought was the ideal that everyone and everything should strive for.

(e) Can an inversion be made permanent?

Can the state resulting from one inversion, and one only, be made permanent in Butler's world? Briefly the answer is no. Butler successfully resisted all attempts of stability to sneak in through the back door which we might call 'permanent invertedness'.

The definition of ambilateralism excludes permanence, whether the permanence of being always right or its mirror-image of being always wrong. As Corballis and Beale stress repeatedly in their book, an individual who consistently mistakes left for right and right for left must be regarded as capable of distinguishing between left and right. Stability versus lability is the main issue. Whether stability means being constantly right or constantly wrong is secondary.

Material quoted in the earlier sections of this chapter has already made it obvious that permanent inversion was not a real option for Butler. Let us nevertheless look briefly at his behaviour when he toyed with various playful forms of the idea.

The possibility of an easily interpretable code of permanent inversion usually occurs to Butler when he feels reality to be stubbornly in opposition. We may imagine Butler in a situation similar to that of a mule-driver trying to deal with an obstinate mule. The mule-driver wants the animal to proceed; the mule wants to regress. The man urges the mule to go forward; the mule resists and tries to retreat backward. There is a clash of wills between the mule and the man. They are turned against one another in purpose and intention.

To the man it soon begins to look as if there was a general pattern to the whole affair: in other words, that the mule acts on a principle –namely, that of perpetual opposition to his own will. If he tries to make the mule go forward it will try to retreat; symmetrically, then, if he tries to make it retreat maybe it will try to go forward – if it always wants to be in opposition to him.

The course of action now seems obvious. The man wants to make the mule go forward; therefore he must try to make it retreat. It will then oppose him and go forward, and his objective will be achieved. A new code of behaviour will become established on the principle of permanent inversion and the universe will again be stable.

Our normal code (making an animal go forward by trying to make it go forward) is a form of stability. Lack of success brings in lability and inversion. If, however, inversion could be made permanent, there would be stability again, based on the new code of permanent inversion.

The characters in Butler's books do not deal with mules, but they certainly deal with individuals whose opposition creates a clash of wills sufficiently strong for them to start toying with ideas of a new code of permanent inversion. To Ernest in *The Way of All Flesh,* it seems that his failure to live up to his mother's expectations, in the matter of choosing his company, is too consistent not to be part of a chiastic system. He therefore hits upon the idea of inverting his behaviour so as to achieve the right by aiming for the wrong:

> From time to time an actual live boy had been thrown to her, either by being caught and brought to Battersby, or by being asked to meet her if at any time she came to Roughborough. She had generally made herself agreeable, or fairly agreeable, as long as the boy was present, but as soon as she got Ernest to herself again she changed her note. Into whatever form she might throw her criticisms it came always in the end to this, that his friend was no good, that Ernest was not much better, and that he should have brought her someone else, for this one would not do at all.
>
> The more intimate the boy had been or was supposed to be with Ernest the more he was declared to be naught, till in the end he had hit upon the plan of saying, concerning any boy whom he particularly liked, that he was not one of his especial chums, and that indeed he hardly knew why he had asked him; but he found he only fell on Scylla in trying to avoid Charybdis, for though the boy was declared to be more successful it was Ernest who was naught for not thinking more highly of him.   (Ch. 48, pp. 211–12)

We may conclude, with the narrator, that the 'mule-driver' strategy was a good try, but it did not work with Ernest's mother.

It is doubtful whether it in fact works any better with mules. Mules and mothers, and in general all those terrible forces of opposition in the world, have a killer instinct that makes them sense a mule-driver inversion-trick immediately, and they respond with an inversion of their own, so as to send you back to square one.

The mule-driver ruse generally occurs in the form of a humorous speculation in Butler's works. In his *Notebooks* Butler complains that his notes grow longer if he tries to shorten them. He then begins to wonder, complementarily, whether they would grow shorter if he tried to lengthen them:

> *My notes:* They always grow longer if I shorten them. I mean the process of compression makes them more pregnant and they breed new notes. I never try to lengthen them, so I do not know whether they would grow shorter if I did. Perhaps that might be a good way of getting them shorter.   (pp. 226–7)

In real life, as we all know, inverting one's purpose for the sake of achieving it seldom works. *The Way of All Flesh* is meant to be a fairly realistic picture of life, and therefore, in the example above, Butler makes Ernest realize that in trying to avoid Charybdis he has only fallen on Scylla (a typical Butlerian dualistic image, by the way). But in *Erewhon* and *Erewhon Revisited* Butler has more freedom, since these are not 'realistic' in the same way as *The Way of All Flesh*. In *Erewhon* and *Erewhon Revisited* there are therefore a number of passages in which the idea of a new code of permanent inversion is treated fairly seriously. In the *Notebooks* Butler wrote down his idea for this:

> *Examinations and professorships:* We can only examine in respect of the more superficial qualities or acquisitions. We cannot examine for temper, patience, sagacity, daring or any of the more vital and deeper characteristics. And so with professorships. Fancy a professorship of any one of these things. If one wanted to encourage vice one should found a professorship of virtue.   (p. 282)

Another entry expresses the same idea:

> *Erewhon Revisited:* They have a Professor or Mischief. They found that people always did harm when they meant well and all the professorships founded with an avowedly laudable object failed, so they aim at mischief in the hope that they may go wrong here as when they aimed at what they thought advantageous and curiously enough they find it much less easy to do mischief than they expected. They thought they would do any amount in no time, but it all seemed

to come to nothing when they tried.   (p. 239)

Note that the outcome is similar to Ernest's experience.

In *Erewhon,* and particularly in *Erewhon Revisited,* these and similar ideas are often worked out in great detail, particularly in the chapters on the deformatory in *Erewhon Revisited* and in the chapters on the colleges of unreason in both books.

There are also other interesting manifestations of the idea of a new code of permanent inversion. Perhaps the most interesting are those in which Butler anticipates Ferdinand de Saussure's principle of the arbitrariness of the linguistic sign.

> Even when, wriggle as they may, they find themselves pinned down to some expression of definite opinion, as often as not they will argue in support of what they perfectly well know to be untrue. I repeatedly met with reviews and articles even in their best journals, between the lines of which I had little difficulty in detecting a sense exactly contrary to the one ostensibly put forward. So well is this understood that a man must be a mere tyro in the arts of Erewhonian polite society, unless he instinctively suspects a hidden 'yea' in every 'nay' that meets him. Granted that it comes to much the same in the end, for it does not matter whether 'yea' is called 'yea' or 'nay', so long as it is understood which it is to be; but our own more direct way of calling a spade a spade, rather than a rake, with the intention that every one should understand it as a spade, seems more satisfactory. On the other hand, the Erewhonian system lends itself better to the suppression of that downrightness which it seems the express aim of Erewhonian philosophy to discountenance. (*Erewhon,* ch. 22, pp. 171–2)

It is natural that a chiasticist should discover the principle of the arbitrariness of the linguistic sign easily. Probably he is awakened to the idea by the existential chiastic formula, and his problems in coming to terms with that. Contemplating the power of a chiastic existential formula to destroy semantic stability, the chiasticist discovers that it is only stability and convention that count. It does not matter intrinsically whether we call a spade a 'spade' or a 'rake', as long as there is agreement. Inversion is destructive of stability and order, but if it could be made permanent there would be a return to stability and intelligibility. Butler's most exhaustive treatment of the subject of the *arbitraire* was his lecture 'Thought and Language', delivered at the Working Men's College in Great Ormond Street on 15 March, 1890.[23]

Permanent inversion forms the basis for a number of linguistic examples of inversionary codes. Automatic inversion of words, as in Marowskyism, or in certain varieties of 'back-slang' in Cockney English, creates a new code which is no more difficult than the old one, once its governing principle of permanent inversion is mastered. Butler liked one such linguistic phenomenon in particular, namely anagrams, especially anagrams in the pure inversionary form, in which, instead of starting at the beginning of a word and going through to the end, you start at the end and go through to the beginning.

Sometimes Butler reinforced anagrams with other forms of inversion. The full blasphemous implications of the name 'Yram' from *Erewhon* is revealed only in *Erewhon Revisited,* where we learn that Yram had not quite lived up to the role of her name in the matter of immaculate conception. Sometimes the semic connotations of names are inversionary; Miss Snow's moral character in *The Way of All Flesh* is not as white as her name would suggest.

The names Hanky and Panky carry semic connotations of inversion even in that European form. This is further strengthened in their Erewhonian forms Sukoh and Sukop (Hocus Pocus – a formula which is also indirectly concerned with inversion). As testimony of Butler's love of multiple inversions rather than single ones we may note that St Panky's son (*Erewhon Revisited,* ch. 28, postscript), carries the uninverted name 'Pokus' – a reversal in keeping with the general change to European culture in Erewhonian society at that point.

Butler was not enthusiastic about any consistent working-out of a state of permanency as regards inversion. Even in *Erewhon Revisited* it is only in the case of Hanky as a habitual liar, and in the humorous description of the relationship between Hanky and Panky, that the idea of permanent inversion comes out strongly.

In chapter 8 the clever Mayoress, Yram, realizes that all of Hanky's answers are to be inverted, since his lying is habitual. She asks whether her son had let the professors eat any quail.

'And did not this heartless wretch, knowing how hungry you must both be, let you have a quail or two as an act of pardonable charity?'
'My dear Mayoress, how can you ask such a question? We knew you would want all you could get; moreover, our permit threatened us with all sorts of horrors if we so much as ate a single quail. I assure

you we never even allowed a thought of eating one of them to cross
our minds.'

'Then', said Yram to herself, 'they gorged upon them.'   (p. 76)

The mule-driving syndrome in the relationship between Panky and
Hanky is of an easily recognized character. Hanky and Panky, as a
pair, must be put in antithetical opposition to each other; therefore
Panky's attempts to check Hanky's outspokenness are bound to have
the opposite effect: 'Panky, who had been growing more and more
restive at his friend's outspokenness, but who had encouraged it more
than once by vainly trying to check it, was relieved at hearing his
hostess do for him what he could not do for himself' (p. 78).

Though Butler repeatedly toyed with the idea of permanent
inversion he never really showed the mule-driver philsophy as actually
working. It remained an interesting speculation, usually meant to be
humorous or startling. Butler could not sympathize fully with the
mule-driver idea, partly because it would have reintroduced stability
instead of lability, and partly because half his sympathies were with the
'mule' anyway. In the distribution of empathy to either member of a
pair, Butler could never sympathize fully with one. He often cast
himself in the role of the mule, so to speak, obstinately reserving the
right to think for himself, and not letting himself be hoodwinked by
any scheme of deceptive inversion of purpose either.

Butler liked to invert his behaviour periodically. He did not go to
church for seven years, he claims. But this inversion (not going), of the
habits of most of his contemporaries (going), was, after seven years,
threatening to take on the stability of a new code of permanent
inversion. He therefore inverted the inversion and went to church out
of pure cussedness, to show that he still reserved the right to think for
himself:

At Mrs. Salter's: Last week (Oct. 27th, 1883) I went to Basingstoke
and met Mrs Thiselton Dyer. She is a daughter of Sir Joseph Hooker
and is very advanced. I said I should go to church in the evening. I
said this, partly because I knew she would not like it, and partly to
please Miss Burd, who I knew would. Mrs Dyer did her best to
dissuade me. 'Didn't it bore me? And, holding my opinions, ought I
not to let people see what I thought?' etc. I said that, having given up
Christianity, I was not going to be hampered by its principles. It was
the substance of Christianity, and not its accessories of external
worship, that I so objected to; and I would be unprincipled

whenever and in whatever way I thought convenient. So I went to church out of pure cussedness. She could not make it out at all. But I won't go again, not just yet awhile if I can help it, for it *did* bore me. I had not been for more than seven years.   (*Notebooks*, p. 120)

From the evidence of this and countless similar episodes and passages in Butler's life and works we may conclude that Butler only flirted with the idea of permanent inversion. Once he had been able to destroy stability and certainty by using inversion as a tool, to upset a conventional code, he was not going to spoil his achievement by letting the inversion itself become permanent, and thereby develop into a stable new code. His ideal of relativistic equilibrium – the amphisbaena at rest – would not have been served by permanent inversion.

(f) Butler and Buridan's ass: paralysis resulting from vacillation

Somehow symmetry and stasis, and asymmetry and dynamism, go together.

The paralysis potentially resulting from perfect symmetry has fired the imagination of poets and thinkers through the ages, and has been expressed in fascinating images and parables. In particular, thinkers have been attracted to the problems of a situation in which someone faces a choice between absolutely equal alternatives. The alternatives may be both bad (pest and cholera) or both good, as long as they are equal. If they are perfectly equal then symmetry will paralyse the chooser.

One of the most suggestive images ever on this theme was put by Chaucer into the twenty-second stanza of *The Parlement of Foulys*, where he likens the protagonist faced with a choice between equal alternatives to a piece of iron suspended between two magnets of equal strength:

> Right as betwixsyn adamauntis two
> Of euenė myȝt a pece of yryn set
> Ne hath no myȝt to meuė too ne fro –
> For what that on may hale, that othir let –
> Ferde I, that nystė whethir me was bet
> To entre or leue, til Affrycan, myn gide,
> Me hente, & shof in at the gatis wide....[24]

However, beautiful as the image undoubtedly is, it is also bad physics.

It is not possible, in practice, to suspend a piece of iron midway between two equal magnets. This fact may perhaps teach us something else about these images, and the relationship between asymmetry and symmetry.

If it is true – with a terrible generalization – that symmetry and stasis, and asymmetry and dynamism, go together, then – with another terrible generalization – it is perhaps also true that the ideal and symmetry, and the practical and asymmetry, go together. At least these generalizations have a definite heuristic value.

Take a look at the interplay of the ideal and the practical in the Chaucer stanza! Caught in vacillation caused by inability to choose between two contradictory but equal alternatives, the protagonist is paralysed – paralysed by the 'ideal', by theory and by symmetry. 'The practical' is represented, in the last two lines of the stanza, by the narrator's guide, Scipio Africanus, who, without further ado, unceremoniously shoves the narrator in through the gates: 'til Affrycan, myn gide,/Me hente, & shof in at the gatis wide'. The 'practical' does not tolerate symmetry-induced paralysis. In the view of the practical, if such paralysis occurs there should be a spontaneous breaking of symmetry. If you are faced with an *embarras du choix*, i.e. a choice between two equal alternatives, you should go for one or the other immediately, no matter which. The longing, in human nature, for the ideal, makes us prone to all kinds of speculations about perfect symmetry, but the practical, which rules our lives, tends to make short shrift of all of that.[25]

In physics there is no end to the amount of theoretical sophistry that one could invent with the aid of an assumed perfect symmetry. Imagine a perfectly symmetrical cylinder, for example, of a weak material, stood on end upon an unyielding floor, and an enormous weight pressing down on top of it. If the cylinder is perfectly symmetrical there is no reason why it should bend and break in any particular direction. Yet bend and break it most assuredly will – we all know that. In fact common sense makes us take a rather contemptuous view of anybody who is fascinated for too long by ideal symmetry, or lets himself be paralysed by a choice between two equally good alternatives.

Such a person is said to be 'like a donkey between two equal bundles of hay'. This proverbial donkey, we remember, starved to death. Note that the donkey, in the animal symbolism of human thought, is a stupid animal. This is the main semiotic significance of the word 'donkey' (or 'ass') in this context – to signal stupidity.

That the animal faced with an impossible choice between two equal alternatives should be a stupid animal is highly significant. The choice of a stupid animal is intended to reinforce the propagandistic anti-symmetry (and pro-asymmetry) message of the image. Anyone who lets himself be paralysed by perfect symmetry is stupid, as stupid as an ass. Clever people spontaneously break the symmetry. They let practice override-theory and go for one of the alternatives without delay.

The proverbial donkey between two bundles of hay has an interesting history – or rather lack of history! It is popularly known as 'Buridan's ass', but though there are plenty of asses in Buridan's writings I have not been able to find this particular ass anywhere. Other people do not seem to have found the illustrious animal either. One modern editor states categorically that the whole thing is now thought to be a myth or a legend, with no foundation in reality.[26] The *New Encyclopaedia Britannica* (15th ed., 1977) claims that Buridan's ass was really a dog, and that the dog is mentioned in Buridan's commentary on Aristotle's *De Caelo*.[27] However, I have not been able to find any such dog in Buridan's commentary on *De Caelo*, and I am not going to look any further.

It is unnecessary to look any further because the factual origin (whatever it may be, if it exists at all) is unimportant in comparison with the semiotics of animal symbolism. There was an intrinsic probability that this topos of folk-wisdom would develop the way it has.

In the opinion of practical people, to let oneself become victimized by a situation of choice between two perfectly equal (particularly in the case of equally good) alternatives is stupid. Therefore the animal faced with the choice between two equal alternatives should ideally be a stupid animal; therefore a donkey. If the animal was originally a dog, as the *Encyclopaedia Britannica* claims, then it was an improvement if it was changed to a donkey. If there was no animal at all to begin with, it was likely that in their choice of animal the inventors of the proverb would settle for a symbolically stupid animal, such as a donkey.[28]

The man in the street is usually not particularly bothered by questions of symmetry and asymmetry, and to him the 'Buridan's ass' syndrome is no more than an absurd intellectual speculation. But with a chiasticist the case is entirely different. Though it is clear that the syndrome may kill off action, development, change, and in general many of those principles that are necessary for a normal life, a chiasticist cannot let go of the dream of perfect symmetry and relativistic equilibrium, despite the dangers inherent in the Buridan's-ass aspect. Therefore Butler was tempted to take a positive view of a number of phenomena that by the ordinary asymmetry-oriented world are both condemned and avoided. Such phenomena are: vacillation, zigzagging and fascination with 'which-one' ambiguities.

Apparently, in his search for various ways in which the ideal state of relativistic equilibrium could be achieved, Butler considered all of these real options. The lability manifested in vacillation and zigzagging Butler apparently perceived as a form of balance or equilibrium. The amphisbaena of Butler's thought starts to go in one direction, but does not go very far; reverses and goes in the opposite direction, but not very far. Though admittedly there is unidirectional movement for short periods of time, the fact that every move cancels out the previous one makes movement acceptable.

Superficially Butler's attitudes towards multiple inversions run the whole gamut of variation from extreme dislike to uncritical acceptance. As always, however, these variations count for little in comparison with the one factor that does not vary, i.e. Butler's fascination with the subject.

Butler clearly viewed vacillation as a form of balance or equilibrium. Despite movement, vacillation seemed to him a form of stasis, since each movement (being an inversion of the preceding and the following one) cancels out the preceding and the following, and thus any real progress. Vacillation thus represents stability-in-lability, or lability-in-stability; it is dynamic stasis, or static dynamism – to put it in an oxymoronic way that Butler would have loved. To the chiasticist vacillation is perfect, since it gives a feeling of movement despite real stagnation, and a feeling of rest despite the fact that there is really movement. In vacillation we have come as close to a fusion of the contrary principles of movement and rest as we can.[29]

In the *Notebooks* Butler observes his cat unable to make up its mind whether to steal Butler's dinner or not:

My cat: I saw my cat undecided in his mind whether he should get up on to the table and steal the remains of my dinner or no; the chair was some eighteen inches from the table, and the back was next to the table, so it was a little troublesome for him to get his feet on the bar and then get on the table. He was not at all hungry so he tried, saw it would not be quite easy and gave it up; then he thought better of it and tried again, and again saw that it was not all perfectly plain sailing, and so backwards and forwards with the first-he-would-

and-then-he-wouldn'tism of a mind so nearly in equilibrium that a hair's weight would turn the scale one way or the other.	(p. 124)

A similar to-ing and fro-ing is depicted in chapter 14 of *Erewhon,* the chapter on Mahaina. The women in the Nosnibor household discuss their friend Mahaina (who pretends to be a tippler but is really suffering from indigestion) and vacillate between charitable hypocrisy and ruthless realism:

> And so they went on for half an hour and more, bandying about the question as to how far their late visitor's intemperance was real or no. Every now and then they would join in some charitable commonplace, and would pretend to be all of one mind that Mahaina was a person whose bodily health would be excellent if it were not for her unfortunate inability to refrain from excessive drinking; but as soon as this appeared to be fairly settled they began to be uncomfortable until they had undone their work and left some serious imputation upon her constitution. At last, seeing that the debate had assumed the character of a cyclone or circular storm, going round and round and round and round till one could never say where it began nor where it ended, I made some apology for an abrupt departure and retired to my own room.	(p. 106)

A little earlier the narrator has described the conversation between Mahaina and the Nosnibor women as 'ingenious perversity' (p. 104) and again we may note how perfectly this oxymoronic combination of a predominantly positive adjective ('ingenious') with a predominantly negative noun ('perversity') expresses the attitude of the narrator (and Butler). In the conversational vacillation there may be perversity, but it is ingenious perversity; there may be ingenuity, but the ingenuity is perverse. As movement and rest qualify each other in vacillation, so do the two halves in the figure of oxymoron.

In chapter 8 of *Erewhon Revisited,* Dr Downie, 'the most subtle dialectician in Erewhon', is half-heartedly satirized:

> He could say nothing in more words than any man of his generation. His text-book 'On the Art of Obscuring Issues' had passed through ten or twelve editions, and was in the hands of all aspirants for academic distinction. He had earned a high reputation for sobriety of judgement by resolutely refusing to have definite views on any subject; so safe a man was he considered, that while still quite young

he had been appointed to the lucrative post of Thinker in Ordinary to the Royal Family. (p. 70)

There is no real sting in the satire and it is merely transient in the scheme of *Erewhon Revisited*. In his heart Butler was not sure whether it was not a commendable thing never to have definite views on any subject. Is not 'sitting on the fence' an ideal 'symmetric' position? Butler regarded a readiness to 'turn', i.e. to be convinced by an opponent and change one's mind, as a highly positive thing. In his *Notebooks* he often denounces various forms of permanency, such as the permanency of attitude of those who refuse to know when they are beaten:

> *On not knowing when one is beaten:* This is all very well, but one of
> the first businesses of a sensible man is to know when he is beaten,
> and to leave off fighting at once. Not to know when one is beaten is
> made an excuse for some of the most unjustifiable conduct that can
> be imagined, as, for example, in the case of the Liberal party at the
> present moment. (p. 186)

Butler was far from unaware of the ridiculous and humorous side to vacilliation. Take for instance the following passage in a letter from Butler to Miss Savage dated 16 June 1872:

> How about this for a subject?
> A hero, young, harum-scarum, with a keen sense of fun and few
> scruples, allows himself to be converted and reconverted at intervals
> of six months or so, for the sum of £100 on each occasion, from the
> Church of Rome to Methodism and back again by each of two
> elderly maiden relatives who have a deep 'interest in the soul of the
> hero and the confusion of one another'. (Jones, I 160)

But the object of derision here is not really vacillation. The butt of the scorn is not so much the shuttlecock hero as the two well-meaning relatives.[30]

The dialectics of vacillation lead nowhere. In Butlerian dialectics, thesis and antithesis are clear enough – ubiquitous and intrusive – but any ultimate synthesis remains a weak and hazy speculation. Instead of the idea of fusion there is the idea of endless vacillation.

Actually Butler often seems to prefer images that do not even hold out any promise of eventual fusion. The pendulum-image, for instance, suggests only endless back-and-forth movement and is thus typically Butlerian:

> *God:* In the eternal pendulum swing of thought we make God in our own image, and then make him make us, and then find it out and cry because we have no God and so on over and over again, as a child has new toys given to it, tires of them, breaks them and is disconsolate till it gets new ones which it will again tire of and break. If the man who first made God in his own image had been a good model, all might have been well; but he was impressed with an undue sense of his own importance and, as a natural consequence, he had no sense of humour. Both these imperfections he has fully and faithfully reproduced in the God of the Old and New Testaments. (*Notebooks*, p. 281)

That inversion cannot create a new permanency but must instead in turn itself be inverted we learn again and again in Butler:

> *Christianity:* was only a very strong and singularly well-timed Salvation Army movement that happened to receive help from an unusual and highly dramatic incident. It was a Puritan reaction in an age when, no doubt, a Puritan reaction was much wanted; but like all sudden violent reactions, it soon wanted reacting against. (Ibid., p. 186)

Butler was capable of visualizing ascent in a hierarchy, but only if every alternate move involved a reversal. Thus in another *Notebooks* entry he introduces the image of a hierarchy of courts, each one by necessity reversing the verdict of the preceding (lower) court:

> *Reason:* is the penultimate test of truth, but not the ultimate of truth nor is it the court of first instance.
> For example: A man questions his own existence; he applies first to the court of mother-wit and is promptly told that he exists; he appeals to reason and, after some wrangling, is told that the matter is very doubtful; he proceeds to the equity of that reasonable faith which inspires and transcends reason, and the judgement of the court of first instance is upheld while that of reason is reversed. (p. 226)

In such images it may seem that Butler is half-convinced of the possibility of some final verdict, i.e. of a dialectical process leading up to somewhere. But actually the quotation is only another example of Butler's 'palladian' thinking. The last verdict is the same as the first. Doubtless the zigzagging of the plot in *The Way of All Flesh* does in the end lead somewhere, but the energy of the book lies in the zigzagging of trial-and-error itself rather than in the reaching of a final destination. Ernest's ultimate landing in the fair haven of wealthy bachelorhood, with his controversialist intellect at that point about to take over the snipe-like changes of flight that he has until then undertaken in person in the history of his career, seems a bleak ending compared to the convincing and compelling force of what went before. Similarly, in the biographical sketch at the beginning of *The Fair Haven*, the zigzagging is vigorously depicted, but when the ultimate synthesis is due, the protagonist dies of a brain-fever. There seems to be a connection between fusion and death in chiasticism.

In describing Ernest's snipe-like changes of flight, Butler was on familiar ground, i.e. the endless vacillation between thesis and antithesis. The use of the snipe-image itself is revealing. It is only when the image is first introduced (cf. Ch. 1, *supra*) that the hope of a 'steady straight flight' is held out. In the remaining occurrences of the snipe-image in *The Way of All Flesh,* as in chapter 59, we are only told about the dartings hither and thither:

As a matter of fact, however, it was not so. Ernest's faith in Pryer had been too great to be shaken down all in a moment, but it had been weakened lately more than once. Ernest had fought hard against allowing himself to see this, nevertheless any third person who knew the pair would have been able to see that the connection between the two might end at any moment, for when the time for one of Ernest's snipe-like changes of flight came, he was quick in making it; the time, however, was not yet come, and the intimacy between the two was apparently all that it had ever been. It was only that horrid money business (so said Ernest to himself) that caused any unpleasantness between them, and no doubt Pryer was right, and he, Ernest, much too nervous. However, that might stand over for the present.   (p. 262)

Another very powerful example in *The Way of All Flesh* is the image of bees going up and down a wall because of the pictures of roses in the pattern of the wall-paper:

It happened that some years previously, a swarm of bees had taken up their abode in the roof of the house under the slates, and had multiplied so that the drawing-room was a good deal frequented by these bees during the summer, when the windows were open. The drawing-room paper was of a pattern which consisted of bunches of red and white roses, and I saw several bees at different times fly up to these bunches and try them, under the impression that they were real flowers; having tried one bunch, they tried the next, and the next, and the next, till they reached the one that was nearest the ceiling, then they went down bunch by bunch as they had ascended, till they were stopped by the back of the sofa; on this they ascended bunch by bunch to the ceiling again; and so on, and so on till I was tired of watching them. As I thought of the family prayers being repeated night and morning, week by week, month by month, and year by year, I could not help thinking how like it was to the way in which the bees went up the wall and down the wall, bunch by bunch, without ever suspecting that so many of the associated ideas could be present, and yet the main idea be wanting hopelessly, and for ever.   (Ch. 23, p. 98)

The origins of vacillation and hesitation in Butler are various, but among the most important of those things that give rise to vacillation are 'which-one' ambiguities of the type, 'Which came first: the chicken or the egg?' This question about *initiality* is naturally also a question about sequential order and a question about direction, and hence irresistible to a chiasticist.

From a practical point of view, debating such questions of initiality is highly futile. Practical people know from experience that a debate over a 'chicken-and-egg' question usually leads nowhere, or results in a paralysis of hesitation. But that state was precisely what Butler perversely wished to achieve, and he enthusiastically debated any question of initiality, including the chicken-and-egg question itself, in the literal sense.

Hens and eggs perpetually alternate. Therefore you can break into the chain at any point, and take out a palladian structure 'hen-egg-hen'; i.e. a hen reproduces *via* an egg. But Butler complementarily took out also the palladian structure 'egg-hen-egg' and never tired of pointing out that a hen is merely an egg's way of making another egg.

A study of Butler's use of vacillation and zigzagging seems to warrant the following conclusions:

To a chiasticist, movement, as such, is problematical, because it will be in a direction, and hence imply unidirectionalism and therefore indirectly asymmetry. If movement, particularly when it goes straight somewhere, is bad, then the less there is of it the better. If movement does not go very far in its direction then that is good, and it is even better if it regularly reverses its direction and retraces its steps, because this gives a sense that directionalism has been cancelled out or neutralized.

That the negation, or semi-negation, of movement implied in vacillation may result in the Buridan's-ass syndrome of hesitation, inability to act and passivity, is something that the chiasticist is aware of but still willing to accept, because, though negative in the eyes of the world, these things nevertheless remind him of the restful, relativistic equilibrium of perfect symmetry.[31]

(g) Butler and *mundus inversus* phenomena: the safety-valve aspect of temporary inversion

Social customs involving temporary inversion are a well-recognized phenomenon and an established object of study in anthropology and ethnology (see Babcock). These customs are either chiastic through implication (one-sided inversion) or directly chiastic (double-sided inversion). In some British regiments (to take an example at random), during one special day of the year there is an inversionary exchange of roles, so that those who are normally waited upon (the officers) become servants instead, and those who are normally servants (the men) are waited upon.

It is obvious that *mundus inversus* phenomena are in one way or another connected with symmetry, and they are highly relevant to a study of chiasticism. I suspect that a full understanding of the mechanisms of chiasticism would definitely shed some light on these inversionary institutions. But, since I have restricted the present investigation to a study of chiasticism in relation to an individual (Butler), rather than chiasticism in relation to society, customs, collective thought and collective mentality, I shall refrain from going into details. I should, however, like to draw attention once again to Barbara Babcock's *Reversible World,* and recommend it both for the essays themselves and for the extensive lists of further references.

What *does* come within the scope of this investigation, on the other hand, is of course Butler's attitude to *mundus inversus* phenomena. As a chiasticist he was bound to take notice of them and react to them.

Butler's interpretation of these phenomena is fairly predictable. One function of these inversions that he stresses is that they create and uphold difference. This is the familiar theory of contrast in Butler, i.e.

that things acquire meaning through antithetical juxtaposition with other things and above all with their opposites. This can be enlarged to relativism, i.e. the thought that nothing exists absolutely on its own, or has any absolute position by itself; that, on the contrary, everything exists only in relation to something else, and particularly in relation to its own opposite.

Most important to Butler, however, in his interpretation of *mundus inversus* phenomena, is the *relief* aspect. Through periodic inversion people get a rest from the normal state of affairs, Butler argues.

In one of his most important comments on the subject, in chapter 5 of *Alps and Sanctuaries,* Butler greatly stresses the view that things are seen more clearly if they are complemented with their inversion. But above all he emphasizes the 'safety-valve' aspect, i.e. the idea that occasional inversion is necessary as a temporary relief and escape from permanency. This notion is related to the 'toppling-over' ideas – the feeling that nothing can (or should) go on for ever in the same way or in the same direction; that sooner or later there should come a point when the existing state of affairs is replaced by its own inversion, and preferably by its absolute or extreme inversion.

I think it may be best to quote this example at length and forgo others, since it shows so clearly the anatomy of Butler's thought. The section begins with Butler relating how he met the *curato* of Calonico, who was very kind to him. The *curato* was anxious to be assured that Butler was not a proselytizing Protestant; the sort of Englishman who goes around distributing tracts. Butler reassured him on this point. He then goes on to reflect, 'All the time I was with him I felt how much I wished I could be a Catholic in Catholic countries, and a Protestant in Protestant ones' (*Alps and Sanctuaries,* p. 47). The wording of this sentence, as we perfectly recognize by now, implies a negation of chiasticism. Small wonder then that it triggers a typical Butlerian automatic reaction and sends him into chiasticist speculations for the next six pages. With the most extreme responses in Butler one is inevitably reminded of Pavlov's dogs, the sound of the bell and the production of saliva – so automatic is Butler's response. His chiasticism had conditioned him to react to any *aa–bb* formula.

The formula 'Catholic, Catholic – Protestant, Protestant' has a ring of permanency to it. The proper chiastic formula is 'Protestant–Catholic; Catholic–Protestant', or 'Catholic–Protestant; Protestant–Catholic'. The *aa–bb* formula causes an uneasiness that Butler spends the next few pages working off.

There is an obvious starting-point for his attack on this particular *aa–bb* formula. Since he was himself a Protestant, even the very idea of his being a Catholic in Catholic countries in itself contained some assumption of interchange. In other words, there was a discrepancy between the form and the content of the formula. The form 'Catholic, Catholic – Protestant, Protestant' seemingly suggests that Catholicism is Catholicism and Protestantism Protestantism (in other words, permanency and difference); but since he – a Protestant – would have to change in order to be a Catholic in Catholic countries, the contents of the formula suggests that Protestantism is Catholicism, which is one half of the ideal chiastic state of 'Protestantism is Catholicism and Catholicism is Protestantism'. Obviously then, in the next few pages Butler must speak in favour of at least occasional change so as to come to the aid of inversion against permanency. Before starting his attack, however, Butler gives permanency yet another say – doubtless so as to focus the target more clearly. People, he says, have told him that he flirts a trifle too much with *il partito nero*. His friends warn him that the priests are not as nice as they seem; that 'Il prete ... è sempre prete.'

What better word to suggest permanency than *sempre*? Anathema to a chiasticist! The red rag is out, and here comes the charge:

In old times people gave their spiritual and intellectual sop to Nemesis. Even when most positive, they admitted a percentage of doubt. Mr Tennyson has said well, 'There lives more doubt' – I quote from memory – 'in honest faith, believe me, than in half the systems of philosophy', or words to that effect. The victor had a slave at his ear during his triumph; the slaves during the Roman Saturnalia dressed in their master's clothes, sat at meat with them, told them of their faults, and blacked their faces for them. They made their masters wait upon them. In the ages of faith, an ass dressed in sacerdotal robes was gravely conducted to the cathedral choir at a certain season, and mass was said before him, and hymns chanted discordantly. The elder D'Israeli, from whom I am quoting, writes: 'On other occasions, they put burnt old shoes to fume in the censers; ran about the church leaping, singing, dancing, and playing at dice upon the altar, while a *boy bishop* or *pope of fools* burlesqued the divine service': and later on he says: 'So late as 1645, a pupil of Gassendi, writing to his master what he himself witnessed at Aix on the Feast of Innocents, says – 'I have seen in some monasteries in this province extravagances solemnized, which pagans would not have practised. Neither the clergy nor the guardians indeed go to the choir on this day, but all is given up to the lay brethren, the cabbage

cutters, errand boys, cooks, scullions, and gardeners; in a word, all
the menials fill their places in the church, and insist that they
perform the offices proper for the day. They dress themselves with
all the sacerdotal ornaments, but torn to rags, or wear them inside
out; they hold in their hands the books reversed or sideways, which
they pretend to read with large spectacles without glasses, and to
which they fix the rinds of scooped oranges.... Particularly while
dangling the censers they keep shaking them in derision, and letting
the ashes fly about their heads and faces, one against the other. In
this equipage they neither sing hymns nor psalms nor masses, but
mumble a certain gibberish as shrill and squeaking as a herd of pigs
whipped on to market. The nonsense verses they chant are
singularly barbarous:

> Haec est clara dies, clararum clara dierum,
> Haec est festa dies festarum festa dierum.'

Faith was far more assured in the times when the spiritual
saturnalia were allowed than now. The irreverence which was not
dangerous then, is now intolerable. It is a bad sign for a man's peace
in his own convictions when he cannot stand turning the canvas of
his life occasionally upside down, or reversing it in a mirror, as
painters do with their pictures that they may judge the better
concerning them. I would persuade all Jews, Mohammedans,
Comtists, and freethinkers to turn high Anglicans, or better still,
downright Catholics for a week in every year, and I would send
people like Mr Gladstone to attend Mr Bradlaugh's lectures in the
forenoon, and the Grecian pantomime in the evening, two or three
times every winter. I should perhaps tell them that the Grecian
pantomime has nothing to do with Greek plays.   (Ibid., pp. 48–50)

So far the main emphasis has been on relief and rest – the 'safety-valve'
aspect. Permanency is a strain; inversion would give a well-earned
rest. As Butler goes on, he touches on the idea which is the other main
reason for inversion, i.e. that through the inversion the non-inverted
state of affairs would be seen all the more clearly. After hinting at this
idea he returns to the 'safety-valve' aspect, regretting that he cannot
have a truce with the Darwinians and all his other opponents.

They little know how much more keenly they would relish their
normal opinions during the rest of the year for the little spiritual

outing which I would prescribe for them, which after all, is but another phase of the wise saying – *Surtout point de zèle*. St Paul attempted an obviously hopeless task (as the Church of Rome very well understands) when he tried to put down seasonarianism. People must and will go to church to be a little better, to the theatre to be a little naughtier, to the Royal Institution to be a little more scientific, than they are in actual life. It is only by pulsations of goodness, naughtiness, and whatever else we affect that we can get on at all. I grant that when in his office, a man should be exact and precise, but our holidays are our garden, and too much precision here is a mistake.

Surely truces, without even an *arrière pensée* of difference of opinion, between those who are compelled to take widely different sides during the greater part of their lives, must be of infinite service to those who can enter on them. There are few merely spiritual pleasures comparable to that derived from the temporary laying down of a quarrel, even though we may know that it must be renewed shortly. It is a great grief to me that there is no place where I can go among Mr Darwin, Professors Huxley, Tyndale and Ray Lankester, Miss Buckley, Mr Romanes, Mr Grant Allen and others whom I cannot call to mind at this moment, as I can go among the Italian priests. (Ibid., pp. 50–1)

With his reflections on truces and temporary inversions Butler feels he has – at least for the time being – exorcised the devil of permanency and stability and the text returns to its usual subject in *Alps and Sanctuaries,* i.e. the description and enumeration of tourist attractions in Piedmont and the canton of Ticino. Temporary inversions and truces would ensure an unstable world where everything is partly or temporarily its own opposite and where the existential chiastic formula would therefore be this: 'Protestants are Catholics (i.e. when they go to Catholic countries); and Catholics are Protestants (by implication, when *they* go to *Protestant* countries).'

Butler's views on *mundus inversus* phenomena fall neatly into place and combine well with the elements of chiasticism already dealt with. The idea of 'relief', in truces, provides him with yet another reason why things should temporarily or periodically 'topple over'.

(h) Butler and Lot's wife: turning, non-turning, obligatory turning and ban on turning

What further mutations of the 'turning' concept are there in Butler?

Butler's inventiveness in finding new variations on the theme of inversion is inexhaustible. But, despite differences on the surface, there are some basic underlying patterns that stay the same, and, since I expect that these have become sufficiently familiar to the reader by now, we may, after this section, leave the principle of inversion and proceed to two of the other main constituent principles of chiasmus, i.e. *dualism* and *reciprocity*. But first let us cast a parting glance at some of those uses of inversion which, although peripheral to a study of Butler's psychomorphology, may be of interest for other reasons – for instance, in explaining the nature and effect of Butler's prose style.

An important member of the turning and non-turning family is the species that we may call *a ban on turning*. I have already repeatedly alluded to one such case of a ban on turning which was a Butlerian favourite – the Orpheus-myth. Orpheus is allowed to bring back his wife Eurydice from the realm of the dead on condition that he does not turn around.

This element of non-turning enhances and enriches the suggestiveness of the myth. Human beings know all too well that the sequential order between life and death is life-to-death – a one-way movement. On the path of life towards death there is no turning-back. When Orpheus – quite exceptionally – is allowed to reverse the process, and bring an individual back from death, it is only fitting that there should be a ban on turning, so that the journey from death to life becomes symmetrical to that from life to death, in the matter of permanency of direction.

The main semiotic reason for the occurrence of a ban on turning in stories, legends, myths, and so on, is obvious. It is meant to goad on those who are infirm of purpose. A ban on turning, and stories about it, indoctrinates the weak into permanency of resolution. Human beings are fickle, inconstant and weak of purpose. Therefore with them, unidirectionalism has to be bolstered up in various kinds of ways. If you land on an unknown shore, resolved to stay, it helps if you burn your ships. Less drastic methods to reinforce unidirectionalist resolution are warnings which threaten with dire consequences anyone who might have second thoughts about a decision. In your purposefulness you must not turn, and to remind yourself of this, and create a parallel symbol on the level of concrete action, there must be a ban on literal turning. If you flee the sinful cities of Sodom and Gomorrah, when they are about to be destroyed, you should keep going and not turn to look behind you. If you break the ban on turning you are liable to be turned into a pillar of salt (Genesis 19:17, 26).

Such is the fate of those who cannot stick to a resolution once it has been made!

Predictably Butler's interest in narratives with a ban on turning centred on those in which the ban is broken, as in the Orpheus-myth. When a ban on turning is introduced in his fiction, then, regularly, it is introduced only to be broken. In *Erewhon Revisited* a ban on turning and looking back is introduced under cover of sentimentality, and in a spirit of sentimentality it is also broken. At the end of chapter 15, Higgs and George are about to part and the idea of turning is meant to suggest the difficulty of parting:

> They then re-packed all that could be taken away; my father rolled his rug to his liking, slung it over his shoulder, gripped George's hand and said, 'My dearest boy, when we have each turned our backs upon one another, let us walk our several ways as fast as we can, and try not to look behind us.'
>
> So saying he loosed his grip of George's hand, bared his head, lowered it, and turned away.
>
> George burst into tears, and followed him after he had gone two paces; he threw his arms round him, hugged him, kissed him on his lips, cheeks, and forehead, and then turning round, strode full speed towards Sunch'ston. My father never took his eyes off him till he was out of sight, but the boy did not look round. When he could see him no more, my father with faltering gait, and feeling as though a prop had suddenly been taken from under him, began to follow the stream down towards his old camp.   (p. 233)

Apart from Butler's wish to first establish and then destroy the ban on turning, there is another explanation of the asymmetrical pattern of behaviour in this scene. As P. N. Furbank has pointed out, in an excellent chapter of his study, a persistent theme in *Erewhon Revisited* is the childishness of adults.[32]

In fact we may add a complement to this excellent observation. The theme of the childishness of adults in *Erewhon Revisited* is highly important, but so is the complementary theme of the adulthood of the young. Thus *Erewhon Revisited* is in fact to some extent structured on a basic chiastic formula 'Young is old, and old is young.' This chiastic double inversion dictates the behaviour of many people in the book: the childish behaviour of Professor Panky and the comparatively weak behaviour of Higgs (at times at least – he is mothered by George much of the time), as well as the adult behaviour of George and the other youths. Behaviour in the scene of parting quoted above is in keeping with the general pattern. George, who is young (i.e. therefore old), energetic and firm of purpose, does not turn; while Higgs, who is old (i.e. therefore infantile), sentimental and weak of purpose, turns; thus breaking the agreement – which, in fact, he has introduced with no intention of not breaking.

But, even without the pattern 'old, young – young, old' in *Erewhon Revisited,* Butler would have been likely to make his character disobey a ban on turning, since his mind could not stand permanency.

Butler's ambivalence on the question of a ban on turning is demonstrated by the fact that he often puts an injunction against 'looking back' into the mouth of dislikable characters, such as the preacher Mr Hawke in *The Way of All Flesh:*

> 'Oh! my young friends, turn, turn, turn, now while it is called to-day – now from this hour, from this instant; stay not even to gird up your loins; look not behind you for a second, but fly into the bosom of that Christ who is to be found of all who seek him, and from that fearful wrath of God which lieth in wait for those who know not the things belonging to their peace.'   (Ch. 49, p. 222)

As Furbank very rightly remarks, '*The Way of All Flesh* belongs essentially to the literature of Conversion' (*Samuel Butler (1835–1902),* p. 11). Mr Hawke in his sermon urges his listeners to 'turn, turn, turn' and not to look back, i.e. to be converted. Ernest, like Butler, is certainly always willing and ready to turn, but as to the 'not look[ing] back', he reserves his judgement. *The Way of All Flesh* is certainly about conversion, but about multiple conversions – repeated turnings and re-turnings.

So ardent is Butler's desire for multiple turns that he sacrifices even some of his most cherished beliefs to facilitate multiple turns. In chapter 78 of *The Way of All Flesh* the narrator has just drawn up a scheme according to which adolescents would learn how to handle the stock-market by having a miniature stock-exchange set up among themselves in which pence would stand for pounds. This is the familiar Butlerian idea of 'learning by doing' – a doctrine that reappears again and again in Butler's works. ('Do to learn rather than learn to do', is the underlying chiasticist inversion.) At this point Butler is still fairly sincere. But he then goes on to say that 'If Universities were not the worst teachers in the world I should like to see professorships of speculation established at Oxford and Cambridge' (pp. 347–8).

Mentioning Oxford and Cambridge then automatically gets him on to another chiastic hobby-horse: the idea that one *does* learn what one is *not* taught, and *does not* learn what one *is* taught.

> When I reflect, however, that the only things worth doing which Oxford and Cambridge can do well are cooking, cricket, rowing, and games, of which there is no professorship, I fear that the etablishment of a professorial chair would end in teaching young men neither how to speculate, nor how not to speculate, but would simply turn them out as bad speculators.   (p. 348)

In this chiastic doctrine there is a fairly strong taste of the stability of permanent inversion. The variant in this case is that of the liability of the irony of fate always to work against one, so that any scheme is likely to produce a result which is the opposite of what was intended. By aiming for the wrong result it should then be possible to achieve the right one (the 'mule-driver' ruse; cf. section (e), *supra*). However, Butler's sympathy does not lie with the instigator of any such scheme; his sympathy lies instead with the irony of fate, which will always frustrate any such scheme, no matter how many inversions, and inversions of inversions, it may take. In the next paragraph, when he proceeds to give an example by relating an anecdote, he therefore makes the instigator of the scheme the most hateful figure he could imagine – a father – so that a maximum of *Schadenfreude* can be directed against him when he fails. The father wants to achieve the right result (prudence in investment) by aiming for the wrong (a loss of £500). His scheme backfires:

> I heard of one case in which a father actually carried my idea into practice. He wanted his son to learn how little confidence was to be placed in glowing prospectuses and flaming articles, and found him five hundred pounds which he was to invest according to his lights. The father expected he would lose the money; but it did not turn out so in practice, for the boy took so much pains and played so cautiously that the money kept growing and growing till the father took it away again, increment and all – as he was pleased to say, in self-defence.   (Ibid.)

Thus, with a genuine chiasticist, any turn initiates yet another turn, rather than any permanency of direction. Ambilateralism is the goal.

Let us pause here and take stock of the situation. If we have now discovered the psychomorphological basis for Butler's behaviour, how did it influence his works? How does it explain the nature and the effect of his fiction, for instance?

If we begin with the structure of narrative and plot, it is obvious that a mania for inversion will result in what we may call the 'turning-of-the-tables' exchange, a well-known standard element in literature and drama. On the level of plot the chiastic switch can involve any two agents, or parties of agents, but preferably those that already have an established relationship with one another, such as hero and villain, lover and beloved, pursuer and pursued. In the novels of Henry James, plot-inversions of this kind are extremely frequent.[33]

Butler wrote only three works that can properly be labelled novels, *Erewhon*, *Erewhon Revisited* and *The Way of All Flesh*. Two of these being utopias, and the third veiled autobiography, plot cannot be expected to play a very important role in any of them. But it is worth noting that, as soon as plot *does* become important, it predictably evolves into patterns of chiastic switches of roles. In *Erewhon Revisited* Hanky and his party temporarily seem to have the upper hand in the conflict between them and Higgs's party. But in chapter 19 the roles are reversed, the professors being caught in their own trap. The tables are turned. In the chapter-heading the phrase itself occurs: 'A council is held at the Mayor's, in the course of which George turns the tables on the Professors' (p. 179).

In *The Way of All Flesh* there is little scope for chiastic switches of roles since there is in reality only one important actor – Ernest. But at least Butler makes use of the phrase, as in chapter 18: 'About a year and a half afterwards the tables were turned on Battersby – for Mrs John Pontifex was safely delivered of a boy' (p. 80).

'Turning-the-tables' inversion in plots appeals to us because we love symmetry. It is important to realize this, and to realize in general to what an extraordinary extent all kinds of devices in literary and dramatic art depend on the appeal of symmetry. The force of the περιπέτεια (cf. Aristotle, *Poetics,* ch. 11) depends on symmetry. The irony of fate appeals to us because of symmetry. All kinds of plot-development depend for their effect on our love of symmetry, but sometimes it takes a trained eye to detect this. A study of chiasticism, however, opens one's eyes to the significance and role of symmetry in verbal art to an amazing extent.

A love of symmetry is at work not only on the macro-level of plot, but also on the micro-level of sentence and paragraph, in many kinds of literary devices, such as jokes and irony. Consider *comedy* and *the humorous*. There is a well-attested connection between chiastic switches and humour and in general a very close connection indeed between symmetry and humour. Let us trace some of the connections.

There is a kinship between inversions of all kinds: metathesis on the level of sound, anagrams on the level of words, spoonerisms and 'lexical spoonerisms' on the level of the sentence, exchange of roles between two characters on the level of plot, and so on. Obviously Butler's fascination with all of these stems from his unconscious realization that inversion is needed for symmetry.

From the seemingly gratuitously reported metathesis in the 'Forolinda' episode mentioned in Chapter 1 –

> I was sketching at Primadengo, and a little girl of about three years came up with her brother, a boy of perhaps eight. Before long the smaller child began to set her cap at me, smiling, ogling, and showing all her tricks like an accomplished little flirt. Her brother said, 'She always goes on like that to strangers.' I said, 'What's her name?' 'Forolinda.' The name being new to me, I made the boy write it, and here it is. [Butler gives the autograph a little earlier in the text.] He has forgotten to cross his F, but the writing is wonderfully good for a boy of his age. The child's name, doubtless, is Florinda.   (*Alps and Sanctuaries*, p. 29)

– to the kind of incongruous behaviour that implies a chiastic switch of roles, such as an exchange of roles between master and servant, Butler's interest is the same. An example of the latter is an episode recorded in the *Notebooks* in which Alfred, Butler's servant, uses the tone and cliché that should properly be reserved for the employer:

> *Alfred and the stars:* A few nights ago there were two large bright stars quite near a new moon where no other stars had yet come out. Alfred did not like it and said, 'Do you think, sir, that that is quite right?' I said I thought it was and the matter dropped. Next night he said about the same time, 'There, sir, you see those stars are not near the moon now.' I said the moon rose an hour or so later every night and therefore it could not be near those stars for another hour. This was becoming a little difficult, so he said, 'Very well, sir, I forgive you this time, but never allude to the subject in my presence again.' (pp. 34–5)

A love of symmetry is at the basis of such humour. The inverted behaviour of the servant is one half, and the standard convention, of which it is the inversion, the other half of the symmetric whole.

Some theories of the comic stress the principle of *incongruity*. According to this theory a cripple may or may not be funny as such, but is properly funny only if he boasts of being a great athlete. This theory argues that incongruities, such as that between the actual and the fancied, make us laugh.

If we wish to argue that a love of symmetry is an important explanation of humour, the theory that stresses incongruity does not greatly contradict the view. Neither does another theory, which stresses the 'release of aggression' inherent in humour. We shall return to that in a moment; let us first explicate a typical example of a symmetric, chiastic switch which reveals the role of symmetric double-sided incongruity as a generator of humour in a particularly obvious way.

In chapter 8 of *Erewhon Revisited,* the Mayoress, Yram, is giving a dinner-party. In the middle of the chapter Butler reports a number of fragments of conversation. Not all of these bits and pieces of talk are relevant for the story; some are quite gratuitous, and must therefore have an intrinsic value of their own, since Butler decided to include them. It is easy to see why he included this: 'Miss Bawl to Mr Principal Crank: ... "The Manager was so tall, you know, and then there was that little mite of an assistant manager – it *was* so funny. For the assistant manager's voice was ever so much louder than the..." ' (pp. 77–8). This is a typical example of chiastic humour generated through a case of double incongruity. A small voice should go with a small man, and a big voice with a big man – that would be congruous and proportionate. However, Butler could not stand such a formula as 'small, small – big, big'. What *he* wanted was 'small, big–big, small', or 'big, small–small, big'. Whenever Butler had several dualities, as in the present passage, in which there are the three dichotomies of body and voice, manager and assistant, and big and small, he would always try to arrange two of them cross-wise so as to create a chiastic pattern of incongruity. Doubtless humour plays an important role here, and the humour depends on the pleasure of symmetry – there is not only the incongruity between one man and his voice, but a mirror-image inverted incongruity between another man and *his* voice.

Such patterns as that of chiastic double incongruity are irresistible to a chiasticist. Having three dual oppositions at his command enables him to make the chiastic pattern absolutely ideal. If we imagine the pair manager–assistant to be the starting-point, the addition of an antithesis big-small and its application to size of body will create a lopsidedness or imbalance. But an added application of the big–small antithesis to voice, plus a chiastic switch, will perfect the ideal pattern –in which either man is both big (either in voice or in body) and small (either in voice or in body). Big-small is a dualism and as such invites the relativizing influence of the existential formula, i.e. 'Big is small, and small is big.' In the pattern of double incongruity, bigness and smallness are characteristic of both men, either through voice or body. This means that, when they are antithetically contrasted, either man can take either role in the antithesis.

A chiasticist must not tolerate any other number than two, and his normal ways of dealing with the number one is to make it Janus-faced or to split it up into two aspects: in this case, small and big. One man is small (in voice), but at the same time big (in body); the other is small (in body), but at the same time big (in voice). Either half of a pair should always be able to take either role in any relationship.[34]

The psychoanalytic Freudian theory that humour involves a release of aggression is not entirely incompatible with a view that stresses the importance of symmetry. There is much overlapping. Humour allows us to say what is normally unsayable, and to think what is normally unthinkable. Thus humour allows us to deal with delicate and taboo subjects, such as sex, but perhaps also to bring out, in jest or under cover of humour, antithetical, outlawed symmetric complements to our 'official' views.

It is noteworthy that, when Butler does speak of delicate or taboo subjects humorously, the humour is often reinforced with symmetry, through inversion. In Butler the full incongruous pattern of a chiastic switch is sufficiently funny on its own. But when that kind of pleasing and satisfying *full* complementariness is lacking and there is only the substitution of one thing for another – rather than a swap – the form alone is not always sufficient to generate humour. But, if the subject is a delicate one, then Butler is often content to leave the inversions as simple inversions, without any other chiastic complement than an implied one (i.e. the implied conventional uninverted variant of the same thing). The mildly delicate taboo subject of the following two notes is alcohol:

Habitual teetotallers: There should be asylums for such people. But they would probably relapse into teetotalism as soon as they came out. (*Notebooks,* p. 79)

A drunkard: would not give money to sober people. He said they would only eat it, and buy clothes and send their children to school with it.   (Ibid., p. 107)

A far more delicate subject than alcohol during the Victorian period was sex. In another *Notebooks* entry there is a comic inversion when two children would like to put clothes on, rather than take clothes off, two figures, in order to ascertain their sex:

Adam and Eve: A little boy and a little girl were looking at a picture of Adam and Eve.
    'Which is Adam and which Eve?' said one.
    'I do not know,' said the other, 'but I should know if they had their clothes on.'   (p. 74)

One feature of the chiasticity of switches deserves special attention. What I have in mind is the fact that complementariness in these patterns sometimes seems to be thought of as obligatory. If *a* is not *x*, then it *must be y*, and *in that case b must be x*. The latter half of this rule is the result of the application of strict dualism; the exclusion of a third possibility (or any further number of possibilities) and the exclusion of the possibility of one-sided inversion (*a* cannot be *y* without *b* at the same time being *x* – there is only one role left for *b* to have, and a role it *must* have). This is related to the way in which a chiasticist, in the terminology of traditional logic, avoids contraries in his thinking, and relies mainly or only on contradictories (cf. Ch. 1, *supra*).

An underlying rule of obligatory complementariness makes chiastic switches very useful for the generation of humour if we look at it from the point of view of the receiver. Much humour is dependent on implication. Something that would hardly be funny at all stated in a straightforward manner may become funny if left as implied. The implied meaning becomes a riddle that the listener or reader is invited to solve. In attempting to understand the implication the listener or reader has a number of standard keys to try. One of these is a chiastic switch, with the rule of obligatory complementariness taken for granted. The picture of the absent-minded professor who stands by his stove cooking his alarm clock while holding an egg in his hand is meaningful and funny when the implication is grasped with the aid of the rule of obligatory chiastic interchange. A picture of the professor merely cooking his clock would be neither meaningful nor funny, only absurd. Neither would a picture of the professor holding an egg in his hand be meaningful on its own. But together, uninverted, they are meaningful. And together, inverted, they are meaningful and funny.

Freud himself in his essay on the comic has the following example:

> Chamfort tells a story of a Marquis at the court of Louis XIV who, on entering his wife's boudoir and finding her in the arms of a Bishop, walked calmly to the window and went through the motions of blessing the people in the street.
>
> 'What are you doing?' cried the anguished wife.
>
> 'Monseigneur is performing my functions,' replied the Marquis, 'so I am performing his.'

But, if this joke illustrates 'release of aggression', it seems to me that even more it illustrates love of symmetry, in the chiastic switch of roles, and this aspect has been stressed by Arthur Koestler.[35]

This does not mean, however, that we should let go of the idea of 'release of aggression' as an important element in humour. It is an idea which we feel intuitively to be true. There must be connections between a love of symmetry and release of aggression, and I think that it is precisely in the context of a study of turning, non-turning, obligatory turning and ban on turning that one should go hunting for the connections.

Butler's readiness to turn; his ambilateralism; the whole complex of his ideas on turning, non-turning, obligatory turning and ban on turning – these give him a special relationship to the dynamics of narrative prose. When we write there are innumerable conventions and traditions that influence our behaviour as regards turning and non-turning. Butler's frequent rebellion against these gives his style its particular character, and accounts for a lot of humorous (and sometimes not quite so humorous) 'release of aggression'. A special kind of Butlerian inversion (or rather non-inversion) – namely, the technique of frustrating the reader's expectations – plays a very important role in Butler's creation of humour.

There are a few turns of phrase that probably stand out more clearly than anything else in one's memory after a reading of *The Way of All Flesh*. The most famous passage of all, often quoted by critics, is the end of chapter 20:

> Christina did not remonstrate with Theobald concerning the severity of the tasks imposed upon their boy, nor yet as to the continual whippings that were found necessary at lesson times.

Indeed, when during any absence of Theobald's the lessons were entrusted to her, she found to her sorrow that it was the only thing to do, and she did it no less effectually than Theobald himself, nevertheless she was fond of her boy, which Theobald never was, and it was long before she could destroy all affection for herself in the mind of her first-born. But she persevered.   (p. 89)

The savagery of that final sentence, 'But she persevered', seems to express the essence of Butler's world better than anything else in his writings. The reader follows the course of the highly charged text, expecting, or at least half-expecting, a retraction or qualification, until the final short sentence drives home the original sense after all, nailing it fast in our consciousness.

The particularly Butlerian quality of savagery in such passages as this has its origins in the function of inversion. Butler was for ever ready to play with inversion in *any* possible form – to invert when others do; *not* to invert when others do not either; to invert when others do *not;* and *not* to invert when others do. In the same number of ways he could also naturally go against the conventional expectations of readers.

It is the last of these categories that is in use in the passage quoted. Butler's habit of frustrating expectations by *not* providing a turn, when a turn would conventionally be expected, is probably the variety of inversion most important in connection with the kind of humour that involves a release of aggression. In Butler's world there is no definite rule against kicking your opponent when he is down. On the contrary, this is usually when Butler delivers the most savage kick of all. In fact there is more or less a rule *in favour* of kicking your opponent when he is down, since this inverts conventional morality, which says that you should not. Conventional morality dictates that, when one has continued to behave aggressively for some time, if there is a change of circumstances (if one is about to win the fight), there should be a *turn* in one's behaviour so that aggressiveness and vindictiveness are replaced by magnanimity and reasonableness. But, among all the varieties of 'turns' in Butler, a very significant variety is the non-materialization of an expected turn.

Cruelty is important in Butler's world, and inversion through the non-occurrence of an expected inversion probably contributes more than anything else to cruelty. For an example let us not take any of those well-known passages and scenes in *Erewhon* (such as the trial of the consumptive) that regularly cause such acute uneasiness to the reader who expects a commitment to positive values. Let us instead take a passage from chapter 80 of *The Way of All Flesh* which shows the technique more clearly, even though it is not disturbing in the same way as some of the most barbarous passages of *Erewhon* are:

> I could see that Ernest felt much as I has felt myself. He said little, but noted everything. Once only did he frighten me. He called me to his bedside just as it was getting dusk and said in a grave, quiet manner that he should like to speak to me.
>
> 'I have been thinking', he said, 'that I may perhaps never recover from this illness, and in case I do not I should like you to know that there is only one thing which weighs upon me. I refer', he continued after a slight pause, 'to my conduct towards my father and mother. I have been much too good to them. I treated them much too considerately', on which he broke into a smile which assured me that there was nothing seriously amiss with him.
>
> (p. 356)

In this paragraph the trappings of the technique of frustrating the expectation of a turn are clearly visible – down to the pause. But, though the machinery is not as clearly visible in certain other passages, in which the cruelty has more effect on the reader, there can be little doubt that the non-materialization of an expected turn is the basic mechanism behind these passages too. No inhibitions and no sense of propriety could prevent Butler from yielding to the temptation to use every kind of inversion. His judgement on this point was completely eroded. In the *Notebooks* there is one instance in which the narrator (Butler?) records having used comic inversion during a death-bed scene:

> *Spiritualism:* 'Promise me solemnly,' I said to her as she lay on what I believed to be her death bed, 'if you find in the world beyond the grave that you can communicate with me – that there is some way in which you can make me aware of your continued existence – promise me solemnly that you will never, never avail yourself of it.' She recovered and never, never forgave me.
>
> (pp. 16–17)

No matter what the factual background of such anecdotes may be, the note surely indicates the extent to which Butler was a slave under the habit of inversion.

'Excusing oneself' is a behaviour involving the idea of a turn. Butler often, on such occasions, envisages not a turn but a further insult:

> Writing to Miss Savage in March 1893 (shortly before the publication of the book), he said: 'I should hope that attacks on *The Fair Haven* will give me an opportunity of excusing myself, and if so I shall endeavour that the excuse may be worse than the fault it is intended to excuse.' (*Fair Haven*, p. xii; cf. also Jones, I 175–6)

Of all the negative qualities in Butler his callousness is often thought of as the worst, and it is particularly unpleasant in its most ghastly variety – when intermixed with humour.

Many critics have commented on this. As Richard Hoggart says in his introduction to the Penguin edition of *The Way of All Flesh*, after commenting on the ending of chapter 20,

> Years later, immediately after Christina's death, a paragraph about Theobald's response ends: 'And he buried his face in his hand-kerchief to conceal his want of emotion.' Those, or any three or four similar touches, might pass unnoticed. But touches like them come so often, and are so exactly placed to make their full deflating effect, that they give the impression of cruelly gratuitous flicks. The reader enjoys them because they are, after all, funny. But it is a slightly guilty pleasure.[36]

Our guilt stems from our realization that we are laughing at a victim, and we are ashamed of enjoying cruelty.

The tightrope act of the ambilateralist ironist, who balances so precisely and symmetrically between fear and rejection of cruelty, on the one hand, and fascination with it (and approval of it), on the other, that we never know which way he will tilt over, gives such works as those of Butler their tone of clever bitterness. A similar tone is cultivated to its utmost in the earlier works of Evelyn Waugh. We find it in Mark Twain, and others; and of course the 'dark element' in the personality of many humorists is a commonplace in literary criticism.

There are definite connections between humour and cruelty. In Butler's case his love of symmetry explains much of the connection.

II DUALISM

(a) 'Having things both ways'

Dualism is a hierarchically higher concept than chiasticism. In order to become a chiasticist you have to be a dualist, but a dualist need not necessarily become a chiasticist.

It is not practical to make a taxonomy of Butler's dualist habits of thought in the same way as of his inversionary ones. Dualistic structuring is so frequent in his works, and permeates his thinking to such an extent, that it seems unnecessary to draw special attention to it. To any reader who is not a dualist himself, a glance at a few pages of Butler's *Notebooks* – or even a glance at the note-headings – will provide sufficient evidence of Butler's dualism.[37] Again, for anyone who is himself a dualist, no amount of evidence will suffice, since one dualist cannot see the dualism created by another dualist, but thinks it intrinsic to reality. Though some dualism is intrinsic to reality and some imposed on reality, to dualists themselves only the former variety is visible, and they think that all dualism is *found*, none *made*.

Partly because Butler's dualistic habits of thought are self-evident; partly for reasons of space; and partly because dualism will be referred to in passing in other chapters – I shall, in this section, ignore all other aspects of Butler's dualism except one: his inconsistency.

Among all the effects of dualism on Butler's thinking this is the one which is perhaps most difficult to grasp; or rather, the one which we are by inclination most reluctant to grasp, since it demands such a radical adjustment of one's normal vision and logic. You cannot, however, understand Butler at all without understanding his capacity for 'having things both ways'. Since he regarded an antithetical statement as the enantiomorphic complement which completes a whole – by adding a missing half – he developed a capacity for believing in two contradictory things at one and the same time.

This capacity for 'having it both ways' is sometimes satirized in his fiction, but just as often defended or applauded; and always there is, at the very least, a high degree of ambivalence. In *The Way of All Flesh,* chapter 41, a capacity for believing in two contradictory views at once is attributed to Christina; but even Christina is to some extent a portrait of Butler himself, as critics have pointed out.

The episode, in chapters 38–42, concerns the serving-girl Ellen, who is dismissed for being pregnant. Ernest gets into disgrace for having given his watch to Ellen, but at times he is suspected of a worse crime – of being the father of Ellen's child. This accusation the narrator refutes oxymoronically in chapter 38: 'his affection though hearty was quite Platonic. He was not only innocent, but deplorably – I might even say guiltily – innocent' (p. 162). The narrator's oxymoronic bringing together of two antithetical verdicts prepares the way for the attitude of Christina in chapter 41, who is able to see her son as both a Joseph and a Don Juan at the same time:

> As regards Ernest the suspicions which had already crossed her
> mind were deepened, but she thought it better to leave the matter
> where it was. At present she was in a very strong position. Ernest's
> official purity was firmly established, but at the same time he had
> shown himself so susceptible that she was able to fuse two
> contradictory impressions concerning him into a single idea, and
> consider him as a kind of Joseph and Don Juan in one.   (p. 181)

This might be taken as a fairly straightforward satire of Christina's
attitude, particularly by those who read *The Way of All Flesh* in the
most common versions, i.e. those edited by Streatfeild. In fact we
learn how ambivalent this passage is not only if we compare it with
other passages on the same theme in Butler's other works, but also if
we restore the text to its original form. Immediately after the
paragraph just quoted came one which Streatfeild omitted when he
prepared Butler's manuscript for publication:

> Let me say in passing that this power of cutting logical Gordian
> knots and fusing two contradictory or conflicting statements into a
> harmonious whole – is one without which no living being whether
> animal or plant could continue to live for a single day, or indeed
> could ever have come into existence. This holds good concerning all
> things that have a reproductive system, but it is most easily seen in
> the case of those forms that are reproduced by parents of different
> sexes. The first thing which the male and female elements must do
> when they unite to form offspring is to fuse the conflicting memories
> and inconsistent renderings of their two parents into a single
> consistent story. But to return.[38]

Butler could not really satirize the capacity for believing in two
contradictory things at once, since this was one of his own most
inveterate mental habits. All his life he tried to eat his cake and have it
too. There are passages in which he seems to take a negative view of
the capacity for 'having it both ways'; for instance, the following
interior monologue attributed to Christina in *The Way of All Flesh*:

> I do not know exactly what Christina expected, but I should imagine
> it was something like this: 'My children ought to be all geniuses,
> because they are mine and Theobald's, and it is naughty of them not
> to be; but, of course, they cannot be so good and clever as Theobald
> and I were, and if they show signs of being so it will be naughty of

them. Happily, however, they are not this, and yet it is very dreadful that they are not. As for genius – hoity-toity, indeed – why, a genius should turn intellectual somersaults as soon as it is born, and none of my children have yet been able to get into the newspapers. I will not have children of mine give themselves airs – it is enough for them that Theobald and I should do so.'   (Ch. 22, p. 94)

But if such passages are not neutralized by contradiction in the immediate context they can always be found contradicted somewhere else in Butler's writings.

Butler was inconsistent, and proud of it. His inconsistency was programmatic; he cultivated it and regarded it with affection. There is no shortage of eulogies on inconsistency in Butler's explicit comments on the subject. Often he allows himself to become quite lyrical in his praise of the 'blessed inconsistency', 'whereby we can be blind and see at one and the same moment':

When the offence is over and done with, it is condoned by the common want of logic; for this merciful provision of nature, this buffer against collisions, this friction which upsets our calculations but without which existence would be intolerable, this crowning glory of human invention whereby we can be blind and see at one and the same moment, this blessed inconsistency, exists here as elsewhere; and though the strictest writers on morality have maintained that it is wicked for a woman to have children at all, inasmuch as it is wrong to be out of health that good may come, yet the necessity of the case has caused a general feeling in favour of passing over such events in silence, and of assuming their non-existence except in such flagrant cases as force themselves on the public notice.   (*Erewhon,* ch. 13, p. 103)

In his Preface to the second edition Butler blames the inconsistencies in the book on the Erewhonians:

For the inconsistencies in the book, and I am aware that there are not a few, I must ask the indulgence of the reader. The blame, however, lies chiefly with the Erewhonians themselves, for they were really a very difficult people to understand. The most glaring anomalies seemed to afford them no intellectual inconvenience; neither, provided they did not actually see the money dropping out of their pockets, nor suffer immediate physical pain, would they listen to any arguments as to the waste of money and happiness which their folly caused them. But this had an effect of which I have little reason to complain, for I was allowed almost to call them lifelong self-deceivers to their faces, and they said it was quite true, but that it did not matter.   (p. xxi)

The phrase 'having it both ways' occurs in many of Butler's works. We find it, for instance, in *Erewhon Revisited*: '*so they please themselves by having the thing both ways*' (Ch. 9, p. 88). The repeated occurrence of the phrase reflects the repeated occurrence of the idea.

In his private life Butler emulated his characters and cultivated his capacity for believing in two contradictory things at once. In one of her letters to Butler, Miss Savage had written that she wished he 'did not know right from wrong'. This was clearly an allusion to Butler's over-scrupulous honesty in a business transaction, i.e. his behaviour in connection with the bankruptcy of the companies in which he had invested on the advice of his friend Henry Hoare. But Butler chose to take the words in another sense when he wrote one of his sonnets on Miss Savage. Jones comments,

He had just shown, in *Erewhon Revisited*, that although the ascent of Mr Higgs was not miraculous, nevertheless the assumption that it was gave it strength to support a religion; so here, with the poet's ability to see a thing in two senses at once, he assumed a meaning for her words in which he did not believe, and thus gave them strength to support a poem. I suppose that he was taking advantage of their ambiguity to develop in verse this passionate cry of penitence: 'If she really intended that, my God, what a brute I was!'   (Jones, II 351–2)

Jones here remarks that it is part of a poet's talent to see a thing in two senses at once, and naturally there is truth in that. A talent for metaphor, to take the most obvious example, involves some sort of capacity to see two separate things simultaneously. And not only the poet, but also the scientist, or in general any adventurous mind, may need the capacity to accept – provisionally at least – the coexistence of mutually contradictory elements. Scientists and scholars have spoken in favour of the heuristic value of certain kinds of inconsistency.[39]

Butler's inconsistency, however, is far more fundamental. Chiastic-ism made him structure reality dualistically, by seeing two antithetical halves. Then it made him try to fuse these two halves, without success.

Being unable to fuse the antithetical halves, and equally unable to give up the attempt, Butler settled for what he saw as a compromise – a belief in inconsistency.[40] Having asked himself whether one thing is true or the opposite true, his answer was that neither is true and both are true. He developed a philosophy in which opinions come in pairs, as mutually contradictory halves of an inconsistent whole. A rule in this philosophy is that contradiction does not falsify, and therefore Butler never hesitated any more if he felt like contradicting himself than he hesitated if he felt like contradicting others.

This, like dualism in general, is self-evident, but let us refresh our memories with just one example. Butler constantly preached that good luck is the only fit object of human veneration.

> No one with any sense of self-respect will place himself on an equality in the matter of affection with those who are less lucky than himself in birth, health, money, good looks, capacity, or anything else. Indeed, that dislike and even disgust should be felt by the fortunate for the unfortunate, or at any rate for those who have been discovered to have met with any of the more serious and less familiar misfortunes, is not only natural, but desirable for any society, whether of man or brute. (*Erewhon,* ch. 10, p. 72; cf. also *The Way of All Flesh,* p. 296)

This is fairly straightforward. Straightforward also are the comments of the judge in the next chapter:

> 'We shall have', said the judge, 'these crude and subversionary books from time to time until it is recognized as an axiom of morality that luck is the only fit object of human veneration. How far a man has any right to be more lucky and hence more venerable than his neighbours, is a point that always has been, and always will be, settled proximately by a kind of higgling and haggling of the market, and ultimately by brute force; but however this may be, it stands to reason that no man should be allowed to be unlucky to more than a very moderate extent.'   (pp. 81–2)

But here, already, the comments are put into the mouth of a character whom we do not know whether to dislike or not, and thus the ambivalence is there. But above all, when we read the passages in which Butler speaks positively of luck, let us remember that Butler wrote four entire books *against* luck – i.e. his books on evolution! He even named one of them *Luck, or Cunning?* – a 'which-one' dual choice in which he comes down in favour of cunning and against luck.

Given Butler's capacity for 'having things both ways', his attitude to consistency follows. He repeatedly warns the reader against consistency. Sometimes his defence is attributed to the Erewhonians or other unreliable characters, but even then more often than not he is sincere rather than ironic:

> Hence their professorships of Inconsistency and Evasion, in both of which studies the youths are examined before being allowed to proceed to their degree in hypothetics. The more earnest and conscientious students attain to a proficiency in these subjects which is quite surprising; there is hardly any inconsistency so glaring but they soon learn to defend it, or injunction so clear that they cannot find some pretext for disregarding it.
>
> Life, they urge, would be intolerable if men were to be guided in all they did by reason and reason only. Reason betrays men into the drawing of hard and fast lines, and to the defining by language – language being like the sun, which rears and then scorches. Extremes are alone logical, but they are always absurd; the mean is illogical, but an illogical mean is better than the sheer absurdity of an extreme. (*Erewhon*, ch. 21, pp. 163–4)

Butler played around humorously with inconsistency. In chapter 22 of *Erewhon,* for instance, the Professors of Inconsistency implore the anti-machinists to use machines in their fight against the machinists:

> The wonder was that they allowed any mechanical appliances to remain in the kingdom, neither do I believe that they would have done so, had not the Professors of Inconsistency and Evasion made a stand against the carrying of the new principles to their legitimate conclusions. These Professors, moreover, insisted that during the struggle the anti-machinists should use every known improvement in the art of war, and several new weapons, offensive and defensive, were invented, while it was in progress. (p. 173)

Butler is particularly pleased when he can bring consistency and inconsistency together in nonsensical combinations, or in intricate patterns of oxymoronic vacillation, as in *The Way of All Flesh,* chapter 68: 'the privileges which the post involved, made him see excellent reasons for not riding consistency to death. Having, then, once introduced an element of inconsistency into his system, he was far too consistent not to be inconsistent consistently...' (p. 300). In chapter 50 Ernest (and Butler) deals in similar fashion with moderation: 'There should be moderation he felt in all things, even in virtue; so for that night he smoked immoderately' (p. 226).

It is easy to see how Butler's oxymora are a natural consequence of his capacity for believing in two mutually antithetical things at one and the same time. The rhetorical figure of oxymoron, in which two contradictory words are put next to each other, follows logically from Butler's acceptance of inconsistency. Two very different words are so often put next to each other in Butler's texts because two very different ideas are so often put next to each other in his thought. The two contradictory elements in the figure of oxymoron qualify one another as Butler's pet ideas qualify one another.

A case of oxymoron makes the reader pause and reflect, as Butler paused and reflected in front of the contradictions that he saw in life and the world. A case of oxymoron makes the reader vacillate between one half and the other, just as Butler always vacillated. Finally, the combination of two opposites in the figure of oxymoron is somehow 'self-erasing', and therefore a true reflection in style of the self-destructiveness of Butler's world. Oxymoron is the stylistic end-product of Butler's willingness to have things both ways, and accept mutually contradictory things. If you accept them, why should they not be put next to one another?

Butler's oxymora are often witty and memorable. Who, for instance, does not remember the phrases 'tame wild animals' (*The Way of All Flesh*, ch. 12, p. 52), 'guiltily-innocent' (ibid., ch. 38, p. 162) and 'repellant attraction' (ibid., ch. 47, p. 208)? But, oxymoron having a value *as such* in Butler, many oxymora are not witty at all, only contradictory or puzzling. Some of these yield some sort of meaning, if we care to sort it out, the context giving a basis for some kind of interpretation. But sometimes there is no context at all. In chapter 85 of *The Way of All Flesh* the oxymoronic combination 'Irrational Rationalism' (p. 393) is given without any context at all; it is merely reported as the title of one of Ernest's essays. In *Erewhon Revisited,* the first of the Sunchild's sayings contains the phrase 'baseless basis': '1. God is the baseless basis of all thoughts, things, and deeds' (ch. 15, p. 150). If we ponder such phrases sufficiently long, we may construe some meanings, such as God being the baseless basis because he is the first principle; i.e. that which itself has no base. But it would be wrong to try too hard to establish a meaning, and particularly *one* meaning. The role of oxymoron is to puzzle and paralyse and create ambilateralist hesitation between two possibilities, out of which neither is more plausible than the other, so that no choice can be made, although a choice is demanded.

Because of the rule of 'extremes meeting', Butler is convinced that opposites are *of nature* always close together. If something comes, its opposite cannot be far behind. At the end of chapter 40 of *The Way of All Flesh,* Ernest is sure that a storm will break since there is at the moment an unusual calm:

> Altogether the day had proved an unusually tranquil one, but, alas! it was not to close as it had begun; the fickle atmosphere in which he lived was never more likely to breed a storm than after such an interval of brilliant calm, and when Theobald returned Ernest had only to look in his face to see that a hurricane was approaching.   (p. 175)

The presence of one thing for Butler automatically heralds the copresence of its opposite. Therefore Butler feels he is only activating what is latently the truth anyway when he immediately adds the opposite to anything he has written down. Adding an opposite does no damage to the original proposition. In the phrase, 'to see the rooms bereft of every familiar feature, and made so unfamiliar in spite of their familiarity' (*The Way of All Flesh,* ch. 36, p. 153), the addition of 'unfamiliar' does not do away with the 'familiarity'. There is a factual reason in this instance, but there is also the general reason inherent in chiasticism.

Butler's readiness to change his mind, or to accept contradictory opinions, comes from his belief that opposites only complement one another. The proper attitude to a world in which opposites come to the same thing is *indifference;* and indifference in many forms, and under many disguises, is what we often meet in Butler's world.

III   RECIPROCITY

(a) *The Way of All Flesh* and *Erewhon Revisited* compared

The various manifestations of the principle of reciprocity, in chiastic passages in Butler's works, do not lend themselves easily to neat taxonomization. It is not practical, therefore, to botanize among varieties of reciprocal passages in the same way as among inversionary ones. Let us instead apply directly our knowledge that reciprocity is one of the main constituent principles of chiasticism, and see how it works in practice.

The most interesting works for a study of reciprocity in personal relationships, as expressed through chiasmus, should be *The Way of All Flesh* and *Erewhon Revisited,* since these two are the most autobiographical of all of Butler's works. If we begin our studies of reciprocity (in chiastic constructions depicting personal relationships) with a perusal of these two works, some further light may be shed on the theory that Butler's chiasticism may have been caused (or at least nurtured) by an unhappy childhood. If the reason for Butler's development into a chiasticist is to be sought primarily in his childhood experiences – above all in his relationship with his family (particularly his father) – then this ought to show in his use of reciprocal constructions, more than in any of the other constituent principles of chiasmus.

A considerable portion of *The Way of All Flesh* deals specifically with father–son relationships – not only the relationship between Theobald and Ernest but also that between George Pontifex and Theobald (and even between Ernest and his own children by Ellen). In *Erewhon Revisited* again, in Butler's own words, one of the themes is 'the story of a father trying to win the love of a hitherto unknown son'; compare his letter to *The Daily News* published on 31 October 1901:

> Moreover, this after-thought [that Yram should have had a son by Higgs] gave occasion for the second leading idea of the book, which so far no reviewer has noticed. I mean the story of a father trying to win the love of a hitherto unknown son, by risking his life in order to show himself worthy of it – and succeeding.   (Jones, II 357)

Although *The Way of All Flesh* was published only in 1903, it had been started thirty years earlier, and was finished in the form we know it by 1884. *Erewhon Revisited* came out in 1901, very soon after it had been written. The two works are therefore almost twenty years apart in time. In content they are also far apart. Although both are on the theme of parent–offspring relations, they present a widely differing picture.[41]

All of Butler's feelings being mixed, he accordingly depicts the feelings between parents and offspring as a mixture of love and hate. But between *The Way of All Flesh* and *Erewhon Revisited* there is a rather clear-cut division of labour: in the main it is fair to say that *The Way of All Flesh* gives us the hate-side, and *Erewhon Revisited* the love-side, of the same coin. When Butler wrote *The Way of All Flesh* his father was still alive, and Butler was bubbling over with resentment – much of which found its way into the book. When he wrote *Erewhon Revisited* his father was dead, and so were most of Butler's friends and enemies. Butler had mellowed and had begun to brood over his life and the son he had never had. The love that had been repressed during most of his life now surfaced full-scale, in the form of sentimentality.

The Way of All Flesh depicts parent–offspring relations as Butler feels convinced they really are in practice – i.e. characterized by a reciprocity of hate. *Erewhon Revisited* depicts them as Butler felt they should have been ideally – i.e. characterized by a reciprocity of love.

(b) Chiastic reciprocity in *The Way of All Flesh:* the reciprocity of hate

Even simply a rapid survey of the passages in *The Way of All Flesh* in which chiastic constructions imply a reciprocity or mutuality of feeling is rather devastating, but if one begins to look closely at the context of each chiastic construction the picture becomes very negative indeed. If the chiastic constructions do not express hate directly they are usually ironic. Let us go systematically through the most important chiastic passages expressing reciprocity in *The Way of All Flesh,* starting from the beginning.

The first passage worthy of more detailed scrutiny occurs in chapter 9. Butler is philosophizing on the family and therefore begins to comment on family relationships.

> And this, even though your wife has been so good a woman that you have not grown tired of her, and has not fallen into such ill-health as lowers your own health in sympathy; and though your family has grown up vigorous, amiable, and blessed with common sense. I know many old men and women who are reputed moral, but who are living with partners whom they have long ceased to love, or who have ugly disagreeable maiden daughters for whom they have never been able to find husbands – *daughters whom they loathe and by whom they are loathed in secret.* ...　　(p. 37; emphasis added)

To a chiasticist relationships should ideally be reciprocal. There should be a symmetry of feeling; both partners should have the same feeling towards one another; the same feeling should flow in both directions. In this passage, once it has been stated that parents loathe their daughters, it follows that daughters must loathe their parents.

It is significant that the feeling of hate in this, and a majority of other similar cases, is initiated on the parent-side. Chiastic reciprocity is a mirror-reflection. If you send out hate, then hate is what will be reflected back on you. This gives a special responsibility to the initiator of any feeling.

Yet on the other hand it also, paradoxically, means that if anyone is the victim of hate he himself is somehow to blame for it. If hate comes to him from other people, this must mean – must it not? – that it is returned; and in that case, if it is returned, he must have sent it out in the first place – such is the logic of chiasticism. A conspicuous feature of Butler's emotional life was a strong feeling of guilt, and the mechanism just described is the prime creator of that guilt. For any injustice, real or imagined, to which a chiasticist falls victim, he must in the end blame himself.

In life, when a relationship goes sour, it is often difficult to tell who was the initiator of the bad feeling. But in fiction some sort of order can be given, and since Butler's sympathy was generally (though not always and not entirely) with the offspring, he usually (though not always and not entirely) made parents the initiators of feelings of hate. By chiasticist definition that feeling must then be reciprocated by the offspring, but theirs is the pure mirror response – the parents have 'asked for it'.

In the passage quoted, note how the idea of mutuality extends even to physical development; 'and [your wife] has not fallen into such ill-health as lowers your own health in sympathy'. Even to the extent of bodily ailment there must be mutuality between two partners. (Butler easily noticed psycho-somatic and somato-psychic connections, but these connections need not be between the body and soul of one person; they can also be between the souls and bodies of two individuals.) Note also in the above quotation what it is implied that partners exist for; they exist to lower your health (through themselves becoming ill, so that you have to become ill too, in sympathy).

This passage involves 'loath[ing]'. In a passage of complement-ary chiastic inversion two paragraphs later, the underlying idea is deception:

Nevertheless it had got to be done, and poor Mrs Allaby never looked at a young man without an eye to his being a future son-in-law. Papas and mammas sometimes ask young men whether their intentions are honourable towards their daughters. I think young men might occasionally ask papas and mammas whether their intentions are honourable before they accept invitations to houses where there are still unmarried daughters.   (p. 38)

In a chiastic passage at the end of chapter 10 the superficial sense is quite positive:

With dinner his shyness wore off. He was by no means plain, his academic prestige was very fair. There was nothing about him to lay hold of as unconventional or ridiculous; the impression he created upon the young ladies was quite as favourable as that which they had created upon himself; for they knew not much more about men than he about women.   (pp. 42–3)

But this is attributed to mutual ignorance. Loathing, deception, ignorance – the list of negative words and concepts keeps accumulating. In fact, going through the passages of chiastic reciprocity in *The Way of All Flesh* is like a tour of the chapters on negative words in a thesaurus.

The setting of this last passage is also relevant. The very end of the chapter (the next paragraph), and the beginning of the next chapter, show the Miss Allabys at cards, with Theobald for the stake.

At the beginning of chapter 14 there is a similar occurrence of a chiastic construction ('She was so devoted too to her husband and her husband to her'), which also, on the surface of it, seems positive. But here too, the context is ironic:

By these the Pontifexes were welcomed as great acquisitions to the neighbourhood. Mr Pontifex, they said, was so clever; he had been senior classic and senior wrangler; a perfect genius in fact, and yet with so much sound practical common sense as well. As son of such a distinguished man as the great Mr Pontifex the publisher he would come into a large property by-and-by. Was there not an elder brother? Yes, but there would be so much that Theobald would probably get something very considerable. Of course they would give dinner parties. And Mrs Pontifex, what a charming woman she was; she was certainly not exactly pretty perhaps, but then she had such a sweet smile and her manner was so bright and winning. She was so devoted too to her husband and her husband to her; they really did come up to one's ideas of what lovers used to be in days of old; it was rare to meet with such a pair in these degenerate times; it was quite beautiful, etc., etc. Such were the comments of the neighbours on the new arrivals.   (p. 61)

The best way to describe this paragraph is perhaps to say that in it Butler had anticipated Martha Garnett's criticism. The Pontifex household, like that of Canon Butler, might well seem idyllic and ideal to outsiders, but to those who knew it it was a whited sepulchre.[42]

This is even clearer in the next example, from chapter 16, in which the theme is the same, but now presented with open irony and biting sarcasm: 'Happy indeed was Christina in her choice, for that she had had a choice was a fiction which soon took root among them – and happy Theobald in his Christina' (p. 68). Butler goes on to say that 'Christina was always a little shy of cards when her sisters were staying with her' (ibid.).

In chapter 20 the theme of parent–offspring hatred is resumed, and significantly again in that order, with Theobald as the initiator of the hatred: 'Theobald had never liked children. He had always got away from them as soon as he could, and so had they from him.... ' (p. 87). Once it is a given that Theobald hates children, it automatically follows that children hate him; yet the guilt is primarily his, since he initiates the feeling.

There is one qualification to be made however. We must distinguish between points of view. In his role as impartial narrator Butler takes the parent-as-initiator attitude. But, when he enters the point of view of Theobald, the case is different. Then he makes Theobald resort to all those mental defence mechanisms which a chiasticist can use in order to let himself come out on top.

If there is a mutual feeling of hate, you must make out that your opponent rather than yourself has initiated the feeling, since the guilt lies with the initiator. This is the first rule of chiastic sophistry. Therefore, in chapter 29, when we get ruminations *from Theobald's point of view* on the reciprocal feeling of hate between father and children, the children are made out to be the initiators. Theobald's interior monologue puts this in a 'conditional' formula of reciprocity: 'If he was fond of me I should be fond of him, but I cannot like a son who, I am sure, dislikes me.' In the elaboration of this idea, with many vacillations hither and thither, Theobald's solipsistic logic reaches the desired conclusion:

He is not fond of me, I'm sure he is not. He ought to be, after all the trouble I have taken with him, but he is ungrateful and selfish. It is an unnatural thing for a boy not to be fond of his own father. If he was fond of me I should be fond of him, but I cannot like a son who, I am sure, dislikes me. He shrinks out of my way whenever he sees me coming near him. He will not stay five minutes in the same room with me if he can help it. He is deceitful. He would not want to hide himself away so much if he were not deceitful. That is a bad sign and one which makes me fear he will grow up extravagant. I am sure he will grow up extravagant. I should have given him more pocket-money if I had not known this – but what is the good of giving him pocket-money?   (p. 122)

Even though he may not know what attitude to take to it, a chiasticist feels attracted to the injunction of 'doing unto others as you would be done by', which is said to be central in the teachings of many religions.

In chapter 23 a feeling closely kin to the 'do-unto-others' formula is put into words by the narrator Overton when he reflects,

Then my thoughts ran back to the bees and I reflected that after all it was perhaps as well at any rate for Theobald that our prayers were seldom marked by any very encouraging degree of response, for if I had thought there was the slightest chance of my being heard I should have prayed that some one might ere long treat him as he had treated Ernest.   (p. 99)

(Ernest has just been beaten savagely for saying 'tum' instead of 'come'.) The ideal structuring would have been Ernest treating Theobald as Theobald has treated Ernest. This being impractical, because of the disparity in power between the adult Theobald and the child Ernest, the complementary other half of 'Theobald mistreating Ernest' (i.e. 'Ernest mistreating Theobald') must be farmed out to a vicarious unnamed agent. Whenever practical considerations could be ignored, however, Butler indulged in mutuality in its perfect form, without substitute agents. In *Erewhon,* at the end of chapter 20, we are told of the scheme whereby old and young are to take turns at flogging each other:

A party of extreme radicals have professed themselves unable to decide upon the superiority of age or youth. At present all goes on the supposition that it is desirable to make the young old as soon as possible. Some would have it that this is wrong, and that the object of education should be to keep the old young as long as possible. They say that each age should take it turn and turn about, week by week, one week the old to be topsawyers, and the other the young, drawing the line at thirty-five years of age; but they insist that the young should be allowed to inflict corporal chastisement on the old, without which the old would be quite incorrigible.   (pp. 155–6)

Erewhon is a dream-world – Butler's dream-world. In other dream-worlds too – the dream-worlds of his characters, particularly in *The Way of All Flesh* – the theoretical ideal of mutuality is within reach. Day-dreams of infanticide (on the parts of parents) are perfectly matched by symmetrical day-dreams of patri- or matricide (on the part of the children), or *vice-versa*. One of the most common forms that the day-dreams of patricide take is the inversion of the story of Abraham and Isaac, with Isaac offering Abraham as a sacrifice, instead of the other way round. In *The Way of All Flesh* the ideal state of orphanhood occurs repeatedly – for instance, in the biography of Towneley, who is the darling of fortune in every way, particularly since 'his father and mother had been drowned by the overturning of a boat when he was only two years old and had left him as their only child and heir to one of the finest estates in the South of England' (ch. 48, p. 215). Important in the lore of happy orphans, and a decided favourite of Butler's, is also Melchizedek. At the end of chapter 67, Ernest, in prison, 'brood[s] over the bliss of Melchizedek who had been born an orphan, without father, without mother, and without descent' (p. 295).[43]

The murder-fantasies of the children are reciprocated in corresponding fantasies of infanticide on the part of parents. In *The Way of All Flesh* we are treated – humorously, but still – to such speculations in Theobald's interior musings in chapter 20:

Then there were the Romans – whose greatness was probably due to the wholesome authority exercised by the head of a family over all its members. Some Romans had even killed their children; this was going too far, but then the Romans were not Christians, and knew no better.   (p. 88)

A favourite event of history for a parent in infanticidal mood is also the tenth plague of Egypt:

Then his [Theobald's] thoughts turned to Egypt and the tenth plague. It seemed to him that if the little Egyptians had been anything like Ernest, the plague must have been something very like a blessing in disguise. If the Israelites were to come to England now he should be greatly tempted not to let them go. (Ibid., ch. 29, p. 123)

A chiasticist will be infuriated by any implied or explicit denial of reciprocity. Overton's (and Butler's) fury over Christina's 'death-bed' letter to her sons in chapters 25 and 26 owes much to the lack of reciprocal balance in the parent–offspring relations depicted in the letter. Children have many duties towards their parents, but the parents seem to have no duties towards their children.

He [Theobald] was to 'find his sons obedient, affectionate, attentive to his wishes, self-denying and diligent', a goodly string forsooth of all the virtues most convenient to parents; he was never to have to blush for the follies of those 'who owed him such a debt of gratitude', and 'whose first duty it was to study his happiness'. How like maternal solicitude is this! Solicitude for the most part lest the offspring should come to have wishes and feelings of its own, which may occasion many difficulties, fancied or real.   (p. 107)

At the end of chapter 29 there is a long pathetic section on Ernest's unhappiness at Roughborough, and the focal point of the section is again a complaint about a lack of reciprocity: 'His duty towards his neighbour was another bugbear. It seemed to him that he had duties towards everybody, lying in wait for him upon every side, but that nobody had any duties towards him' (p. 125).

Early in chapter 27 comes the next passage with a chiastic construction in which the feeling is one of enmity. Since the allusion is to Ishmael, it can be taken as a continuation of the theme of isolation and loneliness:

Some boys, of course, were incapable of appreciating the beauty and loftiness of Dr Skinner's nature. Some such boys, alas! there will be in every school; upon them Dr Skinner's hand was very properly a heavy one. His hand was against them, and theirs against him during the whole time of the connection between them.   (p. 111)

It is true that this time the opponent of the offspring is not a parent, but a headmaster. But Dr Skinner is a parent-figure. In chapter 30 we learn that Ernest 'was far from happy. Dr Skinner was much too like his father' (p. 127).

A remarkable feature of Butler's use of reciprocal chiastic constructions is the fact that, though he was perfectly capable of seeing through chiastic sophistry in his characters, and could expose it without mercy, yet he used precisely the same kind of chiastic sophistry himself in his personal life. In chapter 29 he is, as usual, holding up Ernest's mother to ridicule. Mrs Pontifex is deep into one of her customary reveries, in the course of which she puts herself on an equal footing with Dr Skinner in terms not only of piety but also of genius:

> I think we have done *most wisely* in sending Ernest to Dr Skinner's. Dr Skinner's piety is no less remarkable than his genius. One can tell these things at a glance, and *he must have felt it about me no less strongly than I about him.* I think he seemed much struck with Theobald and myself – indeed, Theobald's intellectual power must impress any one, and I was showing, I do believe, to my best advantage. When I smiled at him and said I left my boy in his hands with the most entire confidence that he would be as well cared for as if he were at my own house, I am sure he was greatly pleased. I should not think many of the mothers who bring him boys can impress him so favourably, or say such nice things to him as I did. (pp. 123–4; in third sentence, emphasis added)

Chiasmus presupposes balance, and one variety of balance is *equality*. In the case of manifestly unequal individuals a reciprocal chiastic construction is therefore presumptuous and absurd. Butler was perfectly capable of satirizing Christina in this passage; yet he was fairly often guilty of similar presumption himself.[44]

In fact all the techniques of chiastic sophistry that Butler satirizes in his works were used by himself at one time or another in his private life. To describe his personal relationships he would pragmatically use whatever variant of chiastic construction fitted the case. Reporting on his relationship with his father, Butler would generally follow the technique of making his father the initiator of the feeling of mutual hatred between them. The following note *'My Father and Myself'*, is typical:

> *He never liked me, nor I him;* from my earliest recollections I can call to mind no time when I did not fear him and dislike him; over and

over again I have relented towards him and said to myself that he was a good fellow after all; but I had hardly done so when he would go for me in some way or other which soured me again. I have no doubt I have made myself very disagreeable; certainly I have done many very silly and very wrong things; I am not at all sure that the fault is more his than mine. But no matter whose it is, the fact remains that for years and years I have never passed a day without thinking of him many times over as the man who was sure to be against me, and who would see the bad side rather than the good of everything I said and did. He used to say to his nurse, so my aunt, Mrs Bather, said: 'I'll keep you: you shan't leave: I'll keep you on purpose to torment you.'

And I have felt that he has always looked upon me as something which he could badger with impunity, or very like it, as he badgered his nurse.   (Jones, ι 20–1; emphasis added)

Even in this note, however, as we can see, the picture is far from clear. Having first saddled his father with the guilt, by putting him first in the chiasmus, Butler immediately half relents and says he does not know whose fault it was.[45]

By chiasticist definition, we know, it is the fault of neither or of both. By chiasticist definition either partner in a chiastic relationship can always play either role. Chiasmus abolishes the distinction between the halves of any pair of opposites: left and right, active and passive, beginning and end. Thus it also abolishes the distinction between subject and object. Therefore, in a relationship of hate between two, either person plays either role. Hater is hated and hated is hater.

Butler was fond of coining complementary words for the object-role of any verb. If there exists a *bore* there must also exist a '*boree*', since in chiasticist logic the existence of one presupposes the existence of the other. And in the activity of boring, the bore and the 'boree' are equally implicated, and equally guilty – though the way that Butler usually puts this is that the 'boree' is *more* guilty; compare Miss Savage's letter of 18 December 1875: 'Have you not taught me that there is nothing so contemptible as a boree? and a boree I shall be when you are worshipped by your spins' (Jones, ι 226).

When Butler, in writing his text, has mentioned either the subject- or the object-function, his addition of the other (remaining) one is often quite automatic, as in 'he [Professor Hanky] was log-rolled and log-rolling, but still, in a robust wolfish fashion, human' (*Erewhon Revisited,* ch. 4, p. 31). Once Butler has put down 'log-rolled', he (fairly automatically) adds 'and log-rolling'. Had he put down 'log-rolling' first, he would have been likely to add 'and log-rolled' automatically, in the same way.

In Butler, painer is pained and pained painer. Butler sent the manuscript of *Erewhon Revisited* to Streatfeild asking him to point out anything bordering on bad taste (Jones, II 338). Butler worried about the possible reaction to the more daring passages, realizing that there was much that 'would pain those whom to pain is a severe pain to myself' (Ibid., p. 337).

Obviously initiality cannot in the end mean too much, because attributing too much significance to it goes against ambilateralism. Admitting status to initiatorship would be the same as admitting that the subject-function exists, which would be a grave chiasticist heresy. Thus, clearly, ambilateralism and initiality are at war, and the whole question was exceedingly problematical for Butler.

Making someone an initiator, i.e. putting him leftmost in the reciprocal chiastic construction, *must* carry *some* meaning, the chiasticist muses, but what? Significance is marked through sequential order, and the second half of a chiasmus exists precisely to neutralize the significance of order in the first. Yet, though the second half of the chiasmus negates the first half, it does not do so completely. It remains a stubborn fact that, in writing, the English language proceeds from left to right. With *ab–ba* the chiasticist has, it is true, negated the order between the *a* and the *b* in his original *ab*. But now, instead of an order in the relation between the elements *a* and *b,* he has an order in pairs of elements, i.e. the first half of the chiasmus and the second half – the first coming first and the second second. The chiasticist can further weaken the distinction between left and right by repeating the chiasmus as a whole, with an inversion of the elements of the first half of the chiasmus; thus: '*ab* and *ba*, and *ba* and *ab*'. But even then, though further weakened, some residue of significance still remains in the left-versus-right distinction. You may add inversions of inversions *ad infinitum;* yet you will never completely get rid of the lopsidedness created through initiality, since there will always be a beginning, by definition.

Then, for a further pebble in the chiasticist's shoe, there remains the question of which role is preferable anyway, if there does indeed exist *some* – no matter how minute – difference in role between subject and object. Making his father the initiator of the relationship of mutual hatred between them, Butler at the same time makes himself a victim. The question is, whether it is all that desirable to be a victim. Butler was not sure. His wavering on this point resulted in his cruel attitude to various kinds of victims throughout his writings. He is not quite sure whether he is on the side of the judge or on that of the consumptive in chapter 11 of *Erewhon*. Often it seems preferable to him to be the perpetrator of a wrong rather than the victim. He sometimes put forward such views ironically, as in the following passage from the end of chapter 26 of *The Way of All Flesh:*

> This was how it came to pass that their children were white and puny; they were suffering from *homesickness*. They were starving, through being over-crammed with the wrong things. Nature came down upon them, but she did not come down on Theobald and Christina. Why should she? They were not leading a starved existence. There are two classes of people in this world, those who sin, and those who are sinned against; if a man must belong to either, he had better belong to the first than to the second.   (p. 109)

But, though this is ironic, elsewhere Butler very often comes down squarely on the side of the victimizers rather than the victims – without even a trace of irony – and in fact it is debatable whether most of the irony of such passages as the one just quoted is not being read into the text by benevolent critics.

If hostile relations between two parties are obligatory, then it may seem sensible to be the victimizer rather than the victim. In chapter 27 of *Erewhon,* when the argument for the rights of vegetables has been taken to its absurd extreme, the verses of the oracle state that there are no alternatives except eating or being eaten, killing or being killed, and the implication is clearly that it is better to choose the former:

> He who sins aught
> Sins more than he ought;
> But he who sins nought
> Has much to be taught.
> Beat or be beaten,
> Eat or be eaten,
> Be killed or kill;
> Choose which you will.   (p. 221)

If the relationship between parents and offspring is of necessity reciprocal, and if, also, the only imaginable relation is one of struggle, then there is a certain logic in a parent acting on the advice, 'Break your child's will early, or he will break yours later on' (cf. Jones, 1 20). Thus even Butler's most infernal portraits of parents are not entirely devoid of ambivalence.

There is no shortage of passages in which Butler makes a doctrine of behaviour out of the feeling that it is better to be a victimizer than a victim:

> I was to have my travelling expenses paid and was going to charge 2nd class fare when Mr Jacques, the head-master, hearing of my intention, said to me rather sternly:
>   'Young man, there are two classes of people in this world: there are those who prey and those who are preyed upon: never you belong to the latter.'
>   So I charged first class fare and travelled 2nd.   (Jones, 1 63)

A chiasticist, for all his habitual siding with the underdog, is perhaps in a sense also a cowardly person, who would rather be hurting than hurt. Cole argues that Butler was a timid man:

> Butler had too little personal bravery for his ideas to shelter behind in comfort. Satirists, I think, often have. They yelp at the world, because they find it uncomfortable; but they do not like it when the world hits back. And they are apt to fancy that the world is hitting back at them when it is not thinking about them at all. Indeed, that it should not be thinking about them is the unkindest cut; for surely it ought to be thinking how right, after all, they are.[46]

Undoubtedly there is much in this. But the patterns are quite varied. Whoever 'hits' first, the world or the chiasticist, it of course follows, first of all, that the other must then hit back. But, in the manipulations of chiastic sophistry, *which* is preferable: to be the party that hits first, or the party that hits back?

The answer is not unambiguous; often Butler manipulates history so that in the end he stands as initiator, when quite clearly he had in reality started out as the victim. When Butler sent the manuscript of *Erewhon* to Chapman and Hall, their reader, George Meredith, recommended them to reject it. This situation clearly starts out with Meredith as the victimizer and Butler as the victim. But now a duality has been created – Butler, Meredith – and in Butler's hands the relationship begins to undergo some strange metamorphoses. In his

Preface to *Erewhon,* Butler tries to see the whole thing from Meredith's point of view:

> As regards its rejection by Messrs Chapman and Hall, I believe their reader advised them quite wisely . They told me he reported that it was a philosophical work, little likely to be popular with a large circle of readers. I hope that if I had been their reader, and the book had been submitted to myself, I should have advised them to the same effect.   (p. xvi)

The last sentence means that, if Butler had been Meredith and Meredith Butler, he would have done the same thing. In a further comment in 1899, however, there is an interesting shift of grounds: 'This is not strange, for I should probably have condemned his *Diana of the Crossways,* or indeed any other of his books, had it been submitted to myself. No wonder if his work repels me that mine should repel him' (Jones, I 148). Now, suddenly, it is no longer a question of what Butler would have done if Butler had been Meredith reviewing Butler's book; now it is a question of what Butler would have done if Butler had been Butler and Meredith Meredith, and Butler had been reviewing *Meredith's* book! Such a situation never was; it is only a dream. But in the dream Butler stands as the initiator of a wrong against Meredith, rather than Meredith of one against Butler (as it was in reality). In the last sentence the variant of the chiastic formula used, i.e. 'His works repel me, my works repel him', implies that Meredith's act is a reaction to Butler's.

The tendency of a chiasticist to use chiastic sophistry to make his opponents the initiator of any negative relationship between them clashes with another tendency of his: namely, his wish to see the universe revolve around himself – even if it means that he will be presented in a bad light. 'Meredith hurting Butler and Butler reacting' suggests that Meredith is important, when in the view of a chiasticist the important person should be himself. Accordingly Butler turns the tables, and makes the episode a case of 'Butler disliking Meredith and Meredith responding'.

Let us now return to the survey of reciprocal chiastic constructions in *The Way of All Flesh.* At the beginning of chapter 33 occurs a reciprocal chiastic construction which is very uncharacteristic of the novel.

> All these excellent reasons for letting her nephew alone occurred to her, and many more, but against them there pleaded a woman's love

for children, and her desire to find someone among the younger branches of her own family *to whom she could become warmly attached, and whom she could attach warmly to herself.* (p. 137; emphasis added)

That any mutual feeling could be one of warm attachment seems highly incongruous in this novel. But then aunt Alethea is a very foreign element in *The Way of All Flesh*. Butler was very successful in evoking the general atmosphere of hate and misery in *The Way of All Flesh,* but not equally skilful in creating any alternative or contrast. Unconvincing cases of reciprocal chiastic constructions are the tell-tale sign of his failure. Further instances of such constructions occur in the section depicting the relationship between Ernest's children and their fosterparents, and between Ernest and Overton's friends; and all these sections of the book are unconvincing. All other characters and episodes give the impression of being real, but Alethea and some of the developments at the end of the novel come over as fantasy.

By stretching our tolerance we can perhaps still believe in Alethea and the bliss of the reciprocal relationship of 'warm attachment' – the first of its kind in the novel so far. We can perhaps also accept a mutual positive chiastic construction depicting the similarity of Overton's and Ernest's feelings at the beginning of chapter 70:

He told me how his father and mother had lain in wait for him, as he was about to leave prison. I was furious, and applauded him heartily for what he had done. He was very grateful to me for this. Other people, he said, would tell him he ought to think of his father and mother rather than of himself, and it was such a comfort to find someone who saw things as he saw them himself. Even if I had differed from him I should not have said so, but *I was of his opinion, and was almost as much obliged to him for seeing things as I saw them, as he to me for doing the same kind office by himself.* Cordially as I disliked Theobald and Christina, I was in such a hopeless minority in the opinion I had formed concerning them that it was pleasant to find someone who agreed with me. (pp. 306–7; emphasis added)

After all, the reason for this cordiality, and mutuality of feeling, is only that Ernest and Overton can join in a feeling of hate for Ernest's parents; which almost makes the passage a normal instance of reciprocal chiasmus in this novel.

Maybe, with some further stretching of our tolerance, we can even swallow the instantaneous mutual attachment between Ernest and 'three or four' of Overton's friends, at the beginning of chapter 81: 'So he fell away from all old friends except myself and three or four old intimates of my own, *who were as sure to take to him as he to them,* and who like myself enjoyed getting hold of a young fresh mind' (p. 361; emphasis added). This, however, is the last we see of these 'old intimates' and the reader is left with a feeling that they have been a mirage.

But with the best will in the world it is difficult to accept the instantaneous love between Ernest's children and Overton's laundress, and later between the children and their fosterparents:

> Before the day was two hours older we had got the children, about whom Ellen had always appeared to be indifferent, and had confided them to the care of my laundress, a good motherly sort of woman, *who took to them and to whom they took at once.*   (Ch. 77, p. 342; emphasis added)

What is so special about laundresses and barge-operators that they should be allowed to love rather than hate? It is true that Butler has presented working-class people in a positive light earlier in the novel, in chapter 23, where we are shown how a villager, Mrs Heaton, does not beat her son Jack even though he has broken an egg and caused her an economic loss. But Emma Heaton seems to function as a contrast to Ernest's parents more as an individual *ad hoc* invention than as a representative of her class. After all, Ellen is working-class too, and in the novel she represents one of the things that Ernest has to be weaned from. It is highly significant that even their union begins with an agreement to remain separate: 'Ellen and he got on capitally, all the better, perhaps, because the disparity between them was so great, that neither did Ellen want to be elevated, nor did Ernest want to elevate her' (ch. 73, p. 326). It is a strange sort of union that begins with an insistence on separateness. 'Union' means 'coming together', but in chapter 77 Ellen again insists that change or movement, on the part of either of them – towards the other – is impossible. The only way to get two partners who would be closer to each other would be *to start out* with an Ernest who would be more like Ellen and an Ellen who would be more like Ernest:

> As regards his breaking with her, she said it was a good job both for him and for her.

'This life', she continued, 'don't suit me. Ernest is too good for me; he wants a woman as shall be a bit better than me, and I want a man that shall be a bit worse than him.'   (p. 343)

We also recall that at the one stage in the novel when Ernest suffered from the illusion that working-class people were nice, this threepenny-bit of bad money was dramatically returned to him by Towneley, who taught him that they are not.

The people on the river (the fosterparents of Ernest's children) are pure fantasy in the context of the rest of the novel, and they come over as such. They, like Overton's friends, and to a large extent Alethea, foreshadow *Erewhon Revisited,* which is almost entirely populated by this race of dream-people, who are not human at all in that they feel love instead of hatred.

Returning now to further exemplification of reciprocal chiastic constructions in *The Way of All Flesh,* we immediately strike the keynote of normality again in chapter 38, with some further information on what parents and offspring exist for – to 'disturb' each other: 'Ernest used to get up early during the holidays so that he might play the piano before breakfast *without disturbing his papa and mamma – or rather, perhaps, without being disturbed by them*' (p. 162; emphasis added). One by one these passages may mean little, but the cumulative effect of them all, when taken together, is crushing. When love between parents and offspring is mentioned at all in a chiastic construction, it is ironic, or set in an incongruous context, as in chapter 40, when Ernest is the victim of the parental inquisition, this time with his mother as the torturer. And even here the gist of the remark is a complaint about *lack* of reciprocal love:

'Papa does not feel', she continued, 'that you love him with that fulness and unreserve which would prompt you to have no concealment from him, and to tell him everything freely and fearlessly as your most loving earthly friend next only to your Heavenly Father. Perfect love, as we know, casteth out fear: your father loves you perfectly, my darling, but he does not feel as though you loved him perfectly in return. If you fear him it is because you do not love him as he deserves, and I know it sometimes cuts him to the very heart to think that he has earned from you a deeper and more willing sympathy than you display towards him.   (p. 172)

One of the strange consequences of chiasticist obligatory reciprocity is that, if you want to extol your own virtues in a relationship, then, by chiasticist definition, you either have to admit that the virtue of your opponent is equal to your own, or, if this is impossible, refrain from praising yourself in the first place. In chapter 41 of *The Way of All Flesh* the muscular coachman John, who has just been dismissed by Theobald, threatens to come back and break every bone in Theobald's skin if Master Ernest is harmed. During his speech John wants to add some moral stature to his physical, and he does this by saying that he has been a good servant to Theobald. Having said this, however, he is now forced to admit that Theobald has been a good master to him.

> 'No, Master Ernest, you shan't', said John, planting himself against the door. 'Now, master,' he continued, 'you may do as you please about me. *I've been a good servant to you, and I don't mean to say as you've been a bad master to me,* but I do say that if you bear hardly on Master Ernest here I have those in the village as 'll hear on't and let me know; and if I do hear on't I'll come back and break every bone in your skin, so there!'   (pp. 179–80; emphasis added)

A very bad problem for the chiasticist is that obligatory mutuality gives hostile people the power of depriving the chiasticist not only of their own love towards him *but also of his love towards them.* For the chiasticist whose starting-point is his own love, there are only two strategies that preserve reciprocity. Either he has to admit that other people love him too, as he loves them; or else – if he cannot by hook or by crook convince himself that this is the case – he must deny his own love towards them too, since it should not exist unless reciprocated.

Both directly and through the history of Ernest Pontifex, Butler repeatedly claims that he tried to love his family relations (this, by chiasticist definition, at the same time means trying to make *them* love *him*) but they *would not let him.* Once this stage has been reached the rest is automatic. If they do not *love* him, then they must *hate* him (the rule of obligatory antithetical extremism). Further, if now *they* hate *him,* then – if he cannot reciprocate one way he must another – *he* must hate *them,* and this he proceeds to do, with a heavy heart.

It is important to put the stress on the point that others *will not let* the chiasticist love them. What grieves the chiasticist most is perhaps not that other people do not love him, but that this also prevents *him* from loving *them.* Again and again, Butler comes back to this point in reporting the relationship between himself and his family relations. At

the end of chapter 20 in *The Way of All Flesh,* there is a moving and
pathetic passage characterizing Ernest as a young child: 'As for the child
himself, he was naturally of an even temper; he doted upon his nurse, on
kittens and puppies, and on all things that would do him the kindness of
allowing him to be fond of them' (p. 88). The stress is not so much on
other things being fond of Ernest as on his being fond of them. The
former is a necessary prerequisite for the latter, it is true, but the latter is
more important. The paragraph ends with the oft-quoted 'But she
persevered'; but here too we must note that the damage is perceived
primarily not in terms of Christina's feelings for her son but in terms of
her son's feeling for her.

There exists one variety of chiastic construction which, some critics
have claimed, could have solved this problem for Ernest and Butler. As
the chiastic saying goes, if the mountain cannot come to Muhammed,
then Muhammed must go to the mountain. If there was a lack of
initiative in the matter of love on the part of his parents, then Butler (and
Ernest) should have taken the initiative himself, these critics say.

With Butler's views on reciprocity and symmetry in mind, we realize
at once that this is an irrelevant suggestion. A chiasticist cannot accept
such an asymmetric solution. (Nor, in fact, is it at all obvious why
anyone – chiasticist or non-chiasticist – should. It is generally thought
that a person has the right to expect *some* give-and-take, *some*
reciprocity in a relationship.)

The 'mountain-prophet' statement is symmetric in form, but
asymmetric in content (i.e. it does not endorse ambilateralism). In *The
Way of All Flesh* this variety of chiasmus is consistently used ironically.
In Ernest's career as a clergyman, in chapter 54, he is first convinced that
in the relationship between him and his parishioners it is the duty of *them*
to come to *him:*

> When Ernest came to London he intended doing a good deal of
> house-to-house visiting, but Pryer had talked him out of this even
> before he settled down in his new and strangely-chosen apartments.
> The line he now took was that if people wanted Christ, they must
> prove their want by taking some little trouble, and the trouble
> required of them was that they should come and seek him, Ernest,
> out; there he was in the midst of them ready to teach; if people did not
> choose to come to him it was no fault of his.   (p. 243)

In the next chapter, however, he begins to change his mind: if they do
not come to him maybe he ought to go to them: 'What he should do was

to go into the highways and byways, and compel people to come in. Was he doing this? Or were not they rather compelling him to keep out – outside their doors at any rate?' (p. 248). In chapters 58–60 Ernest acts on this suspicion and the initiative ends in disaster.

An even sharper thrust at the 'prophet-mountain' philosophy is given in chapter 69, in which Theobald and Christina decide that they must catch Ernest when he is released from prison. In the preceding chapter they have forbidden him to contact them, but when he shows signs of intending to take them at their word they turn. The idea was not that he should take them at their word. The idea was that he *should* return to them, but that the return should be made difficult and painful.

> 'He has been his own worst enemy', said Theobald. 'He has never loved us as we deserved, and now he will be withheld by false shame from wishing to see us. He will avoid us if he can.'
>
> 'Then we must go to him ourselves,' said Christina; 'whether he likes it or not we must be at his side to support him as he enters again upon the world.'
>
> 'If we do not want him to give us the slip we must catch him as he leaves prison.'   (p. 301)

The 'prophet–mountain' philosophy of a unilateral relationship is not really ever presented as a viable solution for any of Butler's characters. Neither was it a real option for Butler himself in his private life, in his relationship with his parents.

In some sense Martha Garnett seems to realize this; yet her criticism against Butler, and her defence of his family relations, in the end seems to come to little more than this: that since *they* did nothing to meet *him, he* ought to have met *them* – an unacceptable proposition to an ambilateralist.

Martha Garnett argues two theses in her book, and the first damages the second. The first thesis is that Butler was 'lacking in moral robustness': 'The fact is that Butler was a man of extreme sensibility, and not a little lacking in moral robustness' (*Samuel Butler: And his Family Relations,* p. 130; see also pp. 152, 185, and *passim*). This is convincing, and most critics agree. Throughout her book Garnett stresses Butler's 'sensitivity': 'He really had too much sensibility. A diffident, affectionate, generous nature I read in him, warped for life by the repressions and severities of his childhood' (pp. 226–7). She also implicitly recognizes that for Butler loving was impossible unless it simultaneously meant being loved. Butler 'could not be fond of those that repulsed him':

> I will not say courage, for if in his whole age there was anyone who stood up more resolutely against vested interests and powers and potentates and the whole weight of the world's opinion, I do not know his name. Yet the very method of his attack proves my assertion, that he was lacking in moral robustness. He could not face overt unpleasantness. Look at his portrait of himself as a child: a little submissive, affectionate, trembling creature, unhappy, cowed and acquiescent. 'He was naturally of an even temper, he doted upon his nurse, on kittens and puppies, and on all things that would do him the kindness of allowing him to be fond of them.' But he could not be fond of those who repulsed him: he could not retain his affection through trial. (pp. 130–1)

Garnett shows again and again how closely Butler's sensitivity (his 'lack of moral robustness') was connected with the idea of reciprocity. For Butler, to look at suffering meant suffering for the onlooker too – by sympathy: 'Still, however one criticises the scientist, the tender heart that could not bear to look on irremediable suffering, the vivid sympathy, remains as the most permanent impression' (p. 184). For Butler to hear of his mother's suffering meant acute suffering for himself as well: 'I find nothing so depressing to myself as the sight of suffering in others; but how much more so when the sufferer is the one whom one would naturally most desire to save from suffering' (p. 208; a letter from Butler to his sister). To stab others means stabbing oneself at the same time:

> He had then no trace of the moral robustness that does not care a jot what is thought, which welcomes opposition, and is unmoved by vituperation. So far from standing unmoved, strong in his own opinion, he felt vividly and even to excess the effect he was producing upon his opponents. He stabbed himself with every thrust at his enemies. (p. 132)

Martha Garnett's second point is her defence of Butler's family relations. But occasionally her defence of them, as commentators –often gleefully – have pointed out, serves to damn them even further, particularly the oft-quoted passage on Harriet's behaviour during Butler's final illness:

It really is pitiable; for to the devout and tender-hearted sister, the estrangement was anguish, especially when the last scene arrived. Misunderstandings persisted to the end. When Butler was taken ill abroad, and his devoted man, Alfred, was sent to Naples to nurse him and bring him home, the yacht of one of Harriet's nephews by marriage was lying off the coast, and offered a pleasant and easy means of conveyance. But Harriet dared not expose a young man to the contaminating influence of the infidel.   (p. 140)

Quite apart from the picture of Butler's relatives that emerges, the very logic of the 'mountain–prophet' formula of defence invites an entire merry-go-round of chiastic counter-questions. Why should the argument cut only one way? Why should one argue that, since Butler's relatives did nothing to meet *him, he* ought to have met *them?* Why not the other way round? First Martha Garnett shows, convincingly, that love for Butler was possible only via 'subject–object' fusion; yet she gives as a solution the 'mountain–prophet' formula which negates that fusion – being unidirectionalist in content, though symmetric in form.

Chiasticist arguments such as these never lead anywhere, because each new phase in the argument generates the beginning of its own refutation as well as itself. If you wish to apply the 'mountain–prophet' formula, the question arises, 'Who should be given the role of mountain and who that of prophet?' and you are back to subjectivist assumptions. To settle for Butler's family as mountain is seen to be arbitrary.[47]

Martha Garnett's recommendation of an asymmetric 'mountain–prophet' solution (of Butler unilaterally going out to meet his opponents) is symmetrically matched by C. E. M. Joad, who applies the enantiomorph of Garnett's argument. Joad writes that Butler made fun of the world because *it* made fun of *him:*

The mischievous destructiveness for which Butler is so famous to-day was, in fact, a comparatively late and entirely incidental development of his genius, and it was developed as the crab develops its shell, for purposes of defence rather than of offence. It was a kind of protective colouring, designed to shelter a sensitive organism from the ill-usage of the world. To put the point in another way, Butler refused to take the Victorian pundits seriously because they refused to take him seriously; he only made fun of his world because it made fun of him.[48]

He further argues that Butler refused to take the world seriously because the world refused to take *him* seriously:

> We may put the point briefly, by saying that Butler very frequently refused to take the world seriously because the scientists refused to take him seriously; he would not accept the experts at their pretended value, because the pretence of the experts was that his own value was negligible.[49]

Naturally this has to be true, since these arguments are indisputable corollaries of the axiom of obligatory reciprocity.

But we easily realize that these two applications of 'mountain–prophet' arguments to Butler's biography are too simplistic. Martha Garnett misuses the 'mountain–prophet' asymmetry one way and Joad another. These critics have hit on the truth, but haphazardly. They extract from Butler's chiasticist system of thought one specific variety – the 'mountain–prophet' formula – and use it themselves rather than comment on it. They try, as it were, to see chiasticism with the aid of chiasticism (i.e. one part of it). But it is not good methodology to make chiasticism both the vehicle and the object of one's study. If you want to pare Butler down to essentials, and study the morphology of his thought and behaviour, you have to stand back and look at chiasticism dispassionately from the outside. Joad errs on one side as much as Martha Garnett on the other, because he, like her, has entered the fray himself and taken sides.[50] Against the background of the complexity of chiastic thought, such approaches as these are seen to be oversimplification. The truth is less easy to get at.

The world was not blameless – neither Butler's relatives, nor the scientists, nor the classicists, nor the Shakespeare scholars, nor any of Butler's opponents. On the other hand, it may be rather difficult to be the partner of a chiasticist, no matter what the relation.

For the chiasticist, reciprocity is always a problem. Sometimes there is too little of it because one's partner does not match one's own performance. In the relationship with Pauli, Butler complains that Pauli had not dealt as unreservedly with him as he had with Pauli:

> I always hoped that, as time went on, and he saw how absolutely devoted to him I was, and what unbounded confidence I had in him, and how I forgave him over and over again for treatment that I should not have stood for a moment from any one else – *I always hoped that he would soften and deal as frankly and unreservedly with*

me as I with him; but, though for some fifteen years I hoped this, in the end I gave it up, and settled down into a resolve from which I never departed – to do all I could for him, to avoid friction of any kind, and to make the best of things for him and for myself that circumstances would allow.   (Jones, i 113; emphasis added)

Sometimes, again, Butler feels that he has been deficient himself. Such comments usually concern either Miss Savage or Moorhouse, the two people Butler felt he had mistreated most. Jones very shrewdly goes right to the centre of the problem in the relationship between Butler and Moorhouse: 'When he suspected people of attempting to browbeat him he hit back fiercely. But Moorhouse did not hit back and this was like coals of fire on his head' (ibid., p. 170).

The necessity of achieving reciprocity made Butler almost pathologically kind if he had become the object of kindness in the first instance: 'if any one was kind to him he could never do enough in return, and if he thought he had neglected an opportunity it made him miserable' (ibid., pp. 170–1).

Sometimes Butler would seek a solution to the problem through *imbalance:* by making sure that he treated people better than they treated him. The most grotesque example of this is in his relationship with Pauli, in which he went to extraordinary lengths in tolerating this parasite, who battened on him for years, even at times when Butler could hardly feed himself, let alone anyone else.

Jones, again, has some perceptive remarks on this. He suggests first of all that the relationship was an example of Butler's attempts to achieve emotional peace by making sure that he treated other people better than they treated him:

On Pauli's death, in 1897, he had the memory of the failure of a quixotic episode, but nothing to reproach himself with.

There was, however, a third person causing anxiety which began to assume serious proportions about this time. He believed that Miss Savage wanted to marry him, and he did not want to marry Miss Savage. When this situation arises between a man and a woman intercourse cannot be continued for long unless one or the other yields. Miss Savage yielded, and thereby covered Butler with shame and disgrace in his own eyes. His father and Pauli died leaving him no wound in his conscience; he knew that he had treated them better than they had treated him. Miss Savage's death, in 1885, brought him no relief; he knew that she had treated him better than he had treated her, and far better than he deserved.   (Ibid., p. 224)

He also gives a highly interesting hint of what may have been the motivating force, psychologically, behind Butler's behaviour in the Pauli affair. In the Butler–Pauli relationship, Butler 'considered himself to be in loco parentis, and was not going to behave like Theobald' (ibid., p. 223)

In the end, however, it is not really imbalance but balance that a chiasticist aims for (although he naturally will try out imbalance – usually in a grossly excessive way – in his attempts to achieve that balance). It is the perfect balance of mutually matching feelings in a relationship that a chiasticist strives for; this we must keep in mind when we read Butler's numerous detailed accounts of how he and someone else 'cut each other by mutual consent'.

> I did not see him [the Revd Edwin A. Abbott] again for some years, and then we met in Oxford Street. We looked at each other to see if we should greet or no; but there was a common, mutual instinct which made us equally settle the question in the negative, so we passed; the blame, if any, being, I should say, as nearly equal as possible. After we had passed we each turned round and caught the other doing so, but again we immediately went on in opposite directions. Now we always cut each other.
>
> [The second note ends thus:] We cut each other now by mutual consent, but it is years since I even met him in the street. I do not know who began the cutting, but I should say it was six of one and half-a-dozen of the other.   (Ibid., p. 182)

This narrative is certainly complete, even to the extent of the mutual turning and re-turning, and the preoccupation with who was first – who 'began'. In his final comment Butler is able, in retrospect, to achieve perfect balance, when the decision is said to have been shared exactly half-and-half by himself and Mr Abbott.

The constant hunt for balance in relationships is what makes a chiasticist so sensitive in his dealings with others. It is as if he were trying to tune a fine instrument, taking the most imperceptible disharmony into account. The intellectual 'tools' he uses for this 'tuning', such as the 'wedges' philosophy, could hardly be less suited to the task. The smallest thing that disturbs equilibrium gives rise to consequences out of all proportion. The minutest shortcoming on the part of the partner of a chiasticist in the relation between them brings out a disproportionately violent response of hate, repulsion and contempt. Correspondingly the smallest shortcoming on the part of the chiasticist himself causes him pathologically strong feelings of regrets, remorse, self-recrimination and self-hatred:

> *Ghosts:* It is a mercy that the dead cannot come back and haunt us while we are alive – not but what a good many dead people, as William Sefton Moorhouse and Miss Savage, not to mention others, haunt me every day of my life. I do not suppose a day ever passes but it comes up to me with a stab that these people were kinder and better friends to me than I to them – however, let that be. [1895.]   (Ibid., p. 443)

Butler's strangely disproportionate reactions to minute details in his relationship with others should be seen in connection with extremism. He tended to have only extreme friends and extreme enemies – there were no other categories of fellow humans. In his appreciation of music, painting and literature Butler normally made use of only two categories: fools and geniuses. People might occasionally cross over from one camp to the other, but they had to be in either. Things were usually black or white – there were seldom any nuances or shades.

The remaining examples of passages dealing with reciprocal relationships that I want to draw attention to in *The Way of All Flesh* all conform to the type which is by now familiar. In chapter 67 Ernest has decided that he must drop his parents if he is to have any chance of survival. When he occasionally wavers he is able to strengthen his resolution with this chiastic reflection: 'He still felt deeply the pain his disgrace had inflicted upon his father and mother, but he was getting stronger, and reflected that as he had run his chance with them for parents, so they must run theirs with him for a son' (p. 293). Ernest's parents have now become victims, but the victim of a wrong is as guilty as the perpetrator, and if Ernest's parents have been wronged, they only have themselves to blame.

In chapter 70 Ernest, having come out of prison, contemplates a career as a tailor. But no employer is willing to hire him, because 'he would not get on with the men, nor the men with him' (p. 309).

In chapter 73 Ernest does not 'get on' any better with his old, pre-prison-time, friends, than the tailor-shop owners have estimated that he would get on with their previous employees: 'At first it had been very painful to him to meet any of his old friends, as he sometimes accidentally did, but this soon passed; either they cut him, or he cut them ...' (p. 327). Butler goes on to explain that being cut is really a rather pleasant experience once you get used to it:

> it was not nice being cut for the first time or two, but after that, it
> became rather pleasant than not, and when he began to see that he
> was going ahead, he cared very little what people might say about his
> antecedents. The ordeal is a painful one, but if a man's moral and
> intellectual constitution are naturally sound, there is nothing which
> will give him so much strength of character as having been well
> cut.   (Ibid.)

We may end this survey of reciprocal hateful chiastic constructions in *The Way of All Flesh* with a passage from the last chapter (86), from one of the last few paragraphs of the whole novel. In the last chapter we learn that Ernest has now become an author. But he is completely isolated; he does not know any colleagues, nor does he want to. Everybody tacitly recognizes that it is not likely that he would get on any better with his fellow authors than he has been able to get on with anyone else: 'I replied, "Mr Pontifex is the exact likeness of Othello, but with a difference – he hates not wisely but too well. He would dislike the literary and scientific swells if he were to come to know them and they him ..." ' (p. 409).

From first to last, reciprocal relations in *The Way of All Flesh* tend to be reciprocal relations of hate, and this is particularly true of the relations between parents and offspring.

(c) Chiastic reciprocity in *Erewhon Revisited:* the reciprocity of love

As soon as we open *Erewhon Revisited* we realize that we have entered a different world. In the first example of chiastic reciprocity worth noting, in chapter 1, the reciprocal feeling is one of strong sentimental love: 'Let the reader spare me, and let me spare the reader any description of what we both of us felt' (p. 11). This is a cliché of Victorian sentimental fiction, meant to hint at yet deeper depths of emotions than the author has been able to convey. But even as a cliché the passage is symptomatic. Butler did not normally use such clichés; only in *Erewhon Revisited*.

The mutuality of 'sparing' in the passage ostensibly concerns the relationship between the narrator and the reader. But that is only the superficial sense. The context makes it clear that in reality the mutuality concerns the relations between Higgs's son (the narrator) and his father. There is a deep sympathy between the two; heightened on the narrator's part by a feeling of compassion for his father who gradually succumbs to illness and death.

Although this first example sets the tone for reciprocal relations in the rest of the novel, there is a jarring note in the next example, which concerns George's duties as a ranger:

'Whereas it is expedient to prevent any of his Majesty's subjects from trying to cross over into unknown lands beyond the mountains, and in like manner to protect his Majesty's kingdom from intrusion on the part of foreign devils, it is hereby...'   (Ch. 3, p. 25)

Even in *Erewhon Revisited*, with its climate of paradisiacal reciprocal love, such elements as these are necessary. The paradise has to be protected, to begin with. But we later learn that there exist, even in *Erewhon Revisited*, characters who are survivals from Butler's earlier works, and feel a reciprocity of hate instead of one of love. Such characters are above all the two professors Hanky and Panky.

In chapter 4, in our next example of a reciprocal chiastic construction, the difference between these people and the new breed of people (i.e. those who feel love instead of hate) is brilliantly focused in their different reaction to an occurrence of the reciprocal construction itself.

When all was now concluded, my father laughingly said, 'If you have dealt unfairly by me, I forgive you. My motto is, "Forgive us our trespasses, as we forgive them that trespass against us." '

'Repeat those last words', said Panky eagerly. My father was alarmed at his manner, but thought it safer to repeat them.

'You hear that, Hanky? I am convinced; I have not another word to say. The man is a true Erewhonian; he has our corrupt reading of the Sunchild's prayer.'

'Please explain.'

'Why, can you not see?' said Panky, who was by way of being great at conjectural emendations. 'Can you not see how impossible it is for the Sunchild, or any of the people to whom he declared (as we now know provisionally) that he belonged, could have made the forgiveness of his own sins depend on the readiness with which he forgave other people? No man in his senses would dream of such a thing. It would be asking a supposed all-powerful being not to forgive his sins at all, or at best to forgive them imperfectly. No;

Yram got it wrong. She mistook "but do not" for "as we". The sound of the words is very much alike; the correct reading should obviously be, "Forgive us our trespasses, but do not forgive them that trespass against us." This makes sense, and turns an impossible prayer into one that goes straight to the heart of every one of us.' Then, turning to my father, he said, 'You can see this, my man, can you not, as soon as it is pointed out to you?'

My father said that he saw it now, but had always heard the words as he had himself spoken them.   (pp. 40–1)

If the mutuality is to be one of forgivenesss, the old breed of people (i.e. the professors) cannot accept it, and Panky insists on an emendation that would uphold asymmetry. But Higgs accepts reciprocal symmetry of forgiveness.

Butler has indeed come a long way from his old self when he endorses such Christian maxims as this one! In his earlier books he would have used such a maxim ironically, inverted its sense, or attacked it. Butler's exaggerated suspicion of reciprocal love during his earlier life is only matched by his exaggerated acceptance of it once he lets himself go, in *Erewhon Revisited*. When his defences finally crumbled, they crumbled completely.

In our next example, from the end of chapter 6, George is fooling the professors into suspecting each other of theft:

'If I take nothing but the nuggets,' he argued, 'each of the Professors will suspect the other of having conjured them into his own pocket while the bundle was being made up. As for the handkerchief, they must think what they like; but it will puzzle Hanky to know why Panky should have been so anxious for a receipt, if he meant stealing the nuggets. Let them muddle it out their own way.'

Reflecting further, he concluded, perhaps rightly, that they had left the nuggets where he had found them, because neither could trust the other not to filch a few, if he had them in his own possession, and they could not make a nice division without a pair of scales.   (p. 60)

Such balance of mutual hatred is tolerated in *Erewhon Revisited* when the only participants involved are the professors. But, as soon as any such balance of hate threatens to include any of the love-people it is immediately condemned, and great pains are taken to have it destroyed. Thus in chapter 20, for instance, George says, ' "Meanwhile the Professors will be living in fear of intrigue on my part, and I, however unreasonably, shall fear the like on theirs" ' (p. 191). He then immediately goes on, ' "This should not be. I mean, therefore, on the day following my return from escorting the prisoner, to set out for the capital, see the King, and make a clean breast of the whole matter" ' (pp. 191–2).

Yram, George and the other members of the 'love-people' tribe even engage in what might be called 'merciful deception'. They talk in terms of balance of hate, but act in terms of mutuality of love. Thus Yram in chapter 21:

> She then told him briefly of what had passed after luncheon at her house, and what it had been settled to do, leaving George to tell the details while escorting him towards the statues on the following evening. She said that every one would be so completely in every one else's power that there was no fear of any one's turning traitor. But she said nothing about George's intention of setting out for the capital on Wednesday morning to tell the whole story to the King.   (p. 197)

On the surface is a mutuality of hate – a sort of 'double-blackmail' situation. But underneath the deceptive hate-surface the truth is that Yram and George have already decided to tell the King – the balance of hate must not be allowed to be real. In this example we can see that *Erewhon Revisited* represents a total reversal in Butler's views on reciprocity. Earlier in his life he would have suspected any reciprocity of love in a relationship of being a sham, and would have been secretly convinced that beneath such a surface must be a *real* relationship of mutual hate. Now, in *Erewhon Revisited*, it is the relationships of mutual hate that are suspect. Even though someone, as, for instance, Higgs in the above example, *can see* only a reciprocity of hate, there is the pleasant possibility that he is the victim of a 'merciful deception', and that beneath the illusion of a mutuality of hate there is a reality of a mutuality of love.[51]

Just as the most typical reciprocal relations of hate in *The Way of All Flesh* are relations within the family, so the most typical reciprocal relations of love in *Erewhon Revisited* are also within the family. But in *The Way of All Flesh* the hate is allowed to spill over into other relationships. Similarly in *Erewhon Revisited* the love is allowed to spill over into relationships outside the family. In chapter 8 we learn that there is mutual love between George and his men: ' "My son," she said innocently, "is always considerate to his men, and that is why they are so devoted to him. I wonder which of them it was? In what part of the preserves did you fall in with him?" ' (p. 74).

There is a lot of kissing and hugging, as well as other outward manifestations of mutual affection in *Erewhon Revisited*.

'I shall give Mrs Humdrum a double dose of kissing,' said George thoughtfully, 'next time I see her.'

'Oh, do, do; she will so like it. And now, my darling boy, tell your poor mother whether or no you can forgive her.'

He clasped her in his arms, and kissed her again and again, but for a time he could find no utterance. Presently he smiled, and said, 'Of course I do, but it is you who should forgive me, for was it not all my fault?'

When Yram, too, had become more calm, she said, 'It is late, and we have no time to lose.'   (Ch. 9, p. 89)

An important mechanism of reciprocity of love in this passage is what we may call *inverted haggling*.

Many social rituals of love (or similar emotions) depend on reciprocity of actions. In the ritual of 'making-up', for instance, when one of the antagonists in a quarrel has taken the initiative (for instance, by saying, 'It was all my fault') it is very important that the other should reciprocate immediately (for instance, by saying, 'No, really, it was mine as much as anybody else's'). A failure to reciprocate at such a point may set the quarrel going again.

Haggling involves two people who start out from two widely different positions on the question of price and gradually get nearer a compromise which they can both accept. It is perfectly possible and normal, in many cultures and situations, for the roles of the hagglers to be inverted, so that the seller tries to beat down the price and the buyer raise it. Such inverted haggling may be caused by conventions of politeness, modesty or generosity, or by feelings of friendship, admiration, and so on. The processes of haggling and inverted haggling are basically the same; the roles are only reversed.

In the passage just quoted, Yram asks George's forgiveness, and he immediately reciprocates by saying that it is really he who should ask forgiveness. This reciprocity works in all directions among the individuals in the love-people tribe in *Erewhon Revisited*. A few paragraphs earlier there is a similar passage:

'And you are going to ask me to forgive you for robbing me of such a father.'

'He has forgiven me, my dear, for robbing him of such a son. He never reproached me. From that day to this he has never given me a harsh word or even syllable.'   (p. 88)

In chapter 11, entitled 'President Gurgoyle's Pamphlet "On the Physics of Vicarious Existence" ', the argument is largely based on various aspects of the question of reciprocity. The philosophical starting-point of the discussion is the oxymoronic phrase, 'the livingness of the de[a]d' (p. 103). An author, the argument goes, lives a vicarious life through his books, although he and his audience know nothing of each other:

A man, we will say, has written a book which delights or displeases thousands of whom he knows nothing, and who know nothing of him. The book, we will suppose, has considerable, or at any rate some influence on the action of these people. Let us suppose the writer fast asleep while others are enjoying his work, and acting in consequence of it, perhaps at long distances from him. Which is his truest life – the one he is leading in them, or that equally unconscious life residing in his own sleeping body? Can there be a doubt that the vicarious life is the more efficient?   (p. 104)

Dr Gurgoyle has here become entangled in a 'which-one' ambiguity: i.e. which life is more important, the 'real' life or the vicarious life? Such questions have only one ultimate answer in Butler: i.e. both are equally important. Dr Gurgoyle, therefore, runs into problems with the subject–object equation when he continues his argument. Subject ought to be object and object subject, influencer should be influenced and influenced influencer. But he has to admit that perfect reciprocity of influence is no longer possible:

'It may be urged that on a man's death one of the great factors of his life is so annihilated that no kind of true life can be any further conceded to him. For to live is to be influenced, as well as to influence; and when a man is dead how can he be influenced? He can haunt, but he cannot any more be haunted. He can come to us, but we cannot go to him. On ceasing, therefore, to be impressionable, so great a part of that wherein his life consisted is removed, that no true life can be conceded to him.'   (p. 105)

Having had to admit this defeat of reciprocity, Dr Gurgoyle falls back on the Butlerian yin-and-yang philosophy – i.e. there is at least *some* life in the dead:

> 'I do not pretend that a man is as fully alive after his so-called death as before it. He is not. All I contend for is, that a considerable amount of efficient life still remains to some of us, and that a little life remains to all of us, after what we commonly regard as the complete cessation of life.'   (Ibid.)

But like any decent ambilateralist Dr Gurgoyle then immediately turns the tables on his imaginary opponents by shifting the target of the objection to its enantiomorph:

> 'In answer, then, to those who have just urged that the destruction of one of the two great factors of life destroys life altogether, I reply that the same must hold good as regards death.
>
> 'If to live is to be influenced and to influence, and if a man cannot be held as living when he can no longer be influenced, surely to die is to be no longer able either to influence or be influenced, and a man cannot be held dead until both these two factors of death are present. If failure of the power to be influenced vitiates life, presence of the power to influence vitiates death. And no one will deny that a man can influence for many a long year after he is vulgarly reputed as dead.'   (pp. 105–6)

He then returns to reciprocity through the typical alloy-metaphor, which regularly finds its way into such passages:

> 'It seems, then, that there is no such thing as either absolute life without any alloy of death, nor absolute death without any alloy of life, until, that is to say, all posthumous power to influence has faded away. And this, perhaps, is what the Sunchild meant by saying that in the midst of life we are in death, and so also in the midst of death we are in life.'   (p. 106)

But, having already summed up his argument, he is struck by a further thought and sees his way to a paradox which will neutralize the admission of a lack of reciprocity (i.e. in the power of dead people not only to influence but to be influenced):

> 'And there is this, too. No man can influence fully until he can no

more be influenced – that is to say, till after his so-called death. Till then, his 'he' is still unsettled. We know not what other influences may not be brought to bear upon him that may change the character of the influence he will exert on ourselves. Therefore, he is not fully living till he is no longer living. He is an incomplete work, which cannot have full effect till finished.'   (Ibid.)

The rest of the chapter continues in the same vein, with the same kind of vocabulary: 'And the converse of this is true ...' (p. 107); 'What an ineffable contradiction in terms have we not here. What a reversal, is it not ...' (p. 109); 'Our sense of moral guilt varies inversely ...' (p. 110); and so forth.

Whatever Dr Gurgoyle (Butler) can think of, he can immediately afterwards think of 'another side' to it: 'I can do nothing with those who either cry for the moon, or deny that it has two sides, on the ground that we can see but one' (p. 108). Everything has two sides: everything *must have.* A few paragraphs later Dr Gurgoyle restores symmetry to the Erewhonian philosophy of the unborn, arguing that, as there is a life before birth, so there must be one after death: 'He argued that as we had a right to pester people till we got ourselves born, so also we have a right to pester them for extension of life beyond the grave' (p. 109).

The narrator ends the chapter by assuring the reader that there are more inversions where those came from, but that these must suffice:

I shall adhere to my determination not to reproduce his arguments; suffice it that though less flippant than those of the young student whom I have already referred to, they were more plausible; and though I could easily demolish them, the reader will probably prefer that I should not set them up for the mere pleasure of knocking them down. Here, then, I take my leave of good Dr Gurgoyle and his pamphlet; neither can I interrupt my story further by saying anything about the other two pamphlets purchased by my father.   (p. 110)

Chapter 11 shows that the old inversionist Adam was still as strong as ever within Butler – in fact *Erewhon Revisited* is if anything *richer* in inversion than many previous works. But it does seem as if the aim and objectives of all the philosophizing on problems of reciprocity had changed. Even in Dr Gurgoyle's ruminations, the basic aim is to reduce the importance of death. All his previous life Butler had trained his perception to see the skull beneath the flesh. Changing now, at the end of his life, he changed in the only way a chiasticist knows how: i.e. inverted his habit and tried to cover the skull up with something that might pass for flesh.

The whole of chapter 11 is, however, a kind of throwback to *Erewhon*. There is much more narrative in *Erewhon Revisited* than in *Erewhon*, and the narration of events is not held up by philosophical chiasticist discourse in the same way as in *Erewhon*. In chapter 15, however, further chiasticist mumbo-jumbo is recited during the dedication ceremony, when extracts are read from the Sunchild's Sayings. Some of these sayings, such as no. 12, express chiastic reciprocity: ' "12. Therefore, as man cannot live without God in the world, so neither can God live in this world without mankind" ' (p. 151).

The list of sayings starts with three that express typically chiasticist contradiction:

'1. God is the baseless basis of all thoughts, things, and deeds.

'2. So that those who say that there is a God, lie, unless they also mean that there is no God; and those who say that there is no God, lie, unless they also mean that there is a God.

'3. It is very true to say that man is made after the likeness of God; and yet it is very untrue to say this.'   (p. 150)

Probably the reciprocity of mutual dependence expressed in no. 12 should not be read as a case of Butler supplying a complementary inversion (complementing the conventional truth – of man depending on God – by adding the missing other half: i.e. of God depending on man) but as a genuine defence of reciprocity, fully endorsed by Butler.

In any case, let us leave these cases of philosophical chiastic reciprocity and return to the realistic ones expressing mutuality of feeling between people. In chapter 16 there is an interesting occurrence of an alleged reciprocal affection: ' "I loved him dearly, and it will ever be the proudest recollection of my life that he deigned to return me no small measure of affection" ' (pp. 155–6). Without context this sounds fairly normal. But the person saying this is Hanky, and it concerns his relation with the Sunchild! The effect of such blasphemy is quite dramatic. Hanky's lie infuriates Higgs; we may imagine that it infuriated Butler while he was writing; and it is meant to infuriate the reader. The worst crime that a villain can commit in *Erewhon Revisited* is to abuse the sanctity of reciprocal affection.

Nothing could make Hanky more dislikable than his pernicious assertion of a mutual affection where there had in fact been none.

'Merciful deception', which is so important in *Erewhon Revisited*, need not be one-sided, as in the examples already quoted. Ideally it should be mutual, as when Higgs and George change boots: 'When the change was made, each found – or said he found – the other's boots quite comfortable' (ch. 17, p. 170). Apart from the mutual merciful fraud we should also note the *exchange* of possessions. On the plot-level this is a necessary stratagem at this point. But exchanging possessions is also a very important element in rituals of reciprocal friendship, or love. (Even heads of state give each other presents when they meet.) For the rest of the novel George's boots become a fetish for Higgs, and he dies with the boots in front of him. The exchange of boots, although on one level merely an element of plot, is on another level a symbolic act affirming reciprocity of love.

There is something magic in exchange itself. In chapter 21 the following episode occurs in the narrative:

> Up to this time they had been standing, but now Yram, seeing my father calmer, said: 'Enough, let us sit down.'
>
> So saying she seated herself at one end of the small table that was in the cell, and motioned my father to sit opposite to her. 'The light hurts you?' she said, for the sun was coming into the room. 'Change places with me, I am a sun worshipper. No, we can move the table, and we can then see each other better.'
>
> This done, she said, still very softly: 'And now tell me what it is all about. Why have you come here?'   (p. 195)

Offering to exchange places if one's own is better than that of one's partner may seem a trifling detail. The semiotic significance of such an episode in the narrative of a non-chiasticist would be to signal, through this minor act of kindness, the politeness of the character offering the exchange. But in the narrative of a chiasticist the semiotic significance of an exchange like this is greater. Changing places is a ritual signifying some kind of mystical union.

By now everyone in *Erewhon Revisited* loves everyone else (excepting, of course, the professors). Two paragraphs after the exchange of places in chapter 21, we learn through a reciprocally chiastic construction that Yram and her husband (the Mayor) love one another: ' "I love my husband with my whole heart and soul, and he loves me with his" ' (ibid.).

Strangely perverse mutations of family-structures exist in this love-world. It is explained in chapter 23 that, whereas in some families the father has two sons, in George's family the son has two fathers:

> 'Very well; then I will say something myself. I have a small joke, the only one I ever made, which I inflict periodically upon my wife. You, and I suppose George, are the only two other people in the world to whom it can ever be told; let me see, then, if I cannot break the ice with it. It is this. Some men have twin sons; George in this topsy-turvy world of ours has twin fathers – you by luck, and me by cunning. I see you smile; give me your hand.'
>
> My father took the Mayor's hand between both his own. 'Had I been in your place,' he said, 'I should be glad to hope that I might have done as you did.'
>
> 'And I', said the Mayor, more readily than might have been expected of him, 'fear that if I had been in yours – I should have made it the proper thing for you to do. There! The ice is well broken, and now for business.'   (p. 212)

Note, incidentally, the palladian handshake! This is the prevalent form of handshake in *Erewhon Revisited*.[52] Note also, in this example, another variant of speculations about 'changing places'. One conventional form of 'ritual-of-reciprocity' is to affirm a unity of purpose and outlook through assurances that each one of a pair would have done the same as the other had they been in each other's places and roles.

A few paragraphs later comes a passage which exemplifies inverted haggling quite literally. Higgs has decided to settle a sum on George, who has no money, so that he will be able to marry. Higgs discusses the matter with the Mayor. 'In the end it was settled that George was to have £2000 in gold, which the Mayor declared to be too much, and my father too little' (p. 213).

Just as abuse of reciprocity in this new world of love is felt to be a terrible crime, so failure to achieve reciprocity is felt to be a terrible shortcoming. In chapter 23 Higgs admires Yram's boys and regrets that he cannot reciprocate in the activity of blushing:

> The two elder boys – or rather young men, for they seemed fully grown, though, like George, not yet bearded – treated him as already an old acquaintance, while the youngest, a lad of fourteen, walked straight up to him, put out his hand, and said: 'How do you do, sir?' with a pretty blush that went straight to my father's heart.

'These boys,' he said to Yram aside, 'who have nothing to blush for – see how the blood mantles into their young cheeks, while I, who should blush at being spoken to by them, cannot do so.'

'Do not talk nonsense', said Yram, with mock severity.

But it was no nonsense to my poor father. He was awed at the goodness and beauty with which he found himself surrounded. His thoughts were too full of what had been, what was, and what was yet to be, to let him devote himself to these young people as he would dearly have liked to do. He could only look at them, wonder at them, fall in love with them, and thank heaven that George had been brought up in such a household.   (pp. 214–15)

A little later his conscience smites him because he had failed to preserve reciprocity in the relationship between Yram and himself. They had given each other a lock of hair; she had kept his, but he had thrown hers away.

'If you notice a little box on the dressing-table of your room, you will open it or no as you like. About half-past five there will be a visitor, whose name you can guess, but I shall not let her stay long with you. Here comes the servant to take you to your room.' On this she smiled, and turned somewhat hurriedly away.

My father on reaching his room went to the dressing-table, where he saw a small unpretending box, which he immediately opened. On the top was a paper with the words, 'Look – say nothing – forget.' Beneath this was some cotton wool, and then – the two buttons and the lock of his own hair that he had given Yram when he said good-bye to her.

The ghost of the lock that Yram had then given him rose from the dead, and smote him as with a whip across the face. On what dust-heap had it not been thrown how many long years ago? Then she had never forgotten him? To have been remembered all these years by such a woman as that, and never to have heeded it – never to have found out what she was though he had seen her day after day for months. Ah! but she was then still budding. that was no excuse. If a loveable woman – aye, or any woman – has loved a man, even though he cannot marry her, or wish to do so, at any rate let him not forget her – and he had forgotten Yram as completely, until the last few days, as though he had never seen her. He took her little missive, and under 'Look', he wrote, 'I have'; under 'say nothing', 'I will'; under 'forget', 'never'. 'And I never shall', he said to himself, as he replaced the box upon the table. He then lay down to rest upon the bed, but he could get no sleep.   (pp. 215–16)

At the end of chapter 24 Higgs takes leave of Yram and the Mayor and, as could be expected, there is an orgy of reciprocal constructions:

'I am glad you came – I am glad you have seen George, and George you, and that you took to one another. I am glad my husband has seen you; he has spoken to me about you very warmly, for he has taken to you much as George did. I am very, very glad to have seen you myself, and to have learned what became of you – and of your wife. I know you wish well to all of us; be sure that we all of us wish most heartily well to you and yours. I sent for you and George, because I could not say all this unless we were alone; it is all I can do', she said, with a smile, 'to say it now.'
    Indeed it was, for the tears were in her eyes all the time, as they were also in my father's.   (p. 222)

Apart from all the reciprocal constructions there are also innumerable handshakes, culminating in a palladian one at the very end of the chapter ('My father grasped his hand in both his own' – p. 224).
    The next chapter opens with George escorting Higgs out of Erewhon, and they begin the journey with some inverted haggling, mock-quarrelling over who should carry what:

'I have a rug for myself as well as for you.'
    'I saw you had two', answered my father; 'you must let me carry them both; the provisions are much the heavier load.'
    George fought as hard as a dog would do, till my father said that they must not quarrel during the very short time they had to be together. On this George gave up one rug meekly enough, and my father yielded about the basket and the other rug.   (p. 225)

The mock-quarrel and the inverted haggling, of course, only occur so as to give them the chance of another ritual of reciprocity.
    So truly universal is reciprocal affection in *Erewhon Revisited* that it takes in not only human actors but canine ones as well. At the beginning of chapter 28, not only the narrator, but the dog too, fawns on George:

I have said on an earlier page that George gained an immediate ascendancy over me, but ascendancy is not the word – he took me by storm; how, or why, I neither know nor want to know, but before I had been with him more than a few minutes I felt as though I had known and loved him all my life. And the dog fawned upon him as though he felt just as I did.   (p. 253)

The dog has his show of affection reciprocated a little later when it is confirmed that not only does the dog like George, but George likes the dog: 'Then he thanked me a thousand times over, shouldered the knapsack, embraced me as he had my father, *and caressed the dog,* embraced me again, and made no attempt to hide the tears that ran down his cheeks' (p. 261; emphasis added).

A little later the narrator again laments a case of unachieved reciprocity. Since this is the last passage I shall quote from *Erewhon Revisited* in this chapter, let me include a little more context than necessary in order to give us a final taste of the extraordinary tone of sentimentality that characterizes the novel:

For I had never seen, and felt as though I never could see, George's equal. His absolute unconsciousness of self, the unhesitating way in which he took me to his heart, his fearless frankness, the happy genial expression that played on his face, and the extreme sweetness of his smile – these were the things that made me say to myself that the 'blazon of beauty's best' could tell me nothing better than what I had found and lost within the last three hours. How small, too, I felt by comparison! If for no other cause, yet for this, that I, who had wept so bitterly over my own disappointment the day before, could meet this dear fellow's tears with no tear of my own.   (pp. 261–2)

On the basis of this survey of reciprocal, chiastic constructions in *Erewhon Revisited* we may conclude that the novel is an antithetical complement not only to *Erewhon* but above all to *The Way of All Flesh*. *The Way of All Flesh* depicts reciprocal relations between people as Butler pessimistically thought they really are. *Erewhon Revisited* depicts them as he would have liked them.

3 Chiasticism in Some of Butler's Works

I JUVENILIA, *A FIRST YEAR IN CANTERBURY SETTLEMENT* AND EARLY ESSAYS

(a) Cambridge writings

In his Introduction to volume I of the Shrewsbury Edition (to which all page references to Butler's early works in section I of this chapter relate, and from which the relevant quotations are taken, unless otherwise stated), Henry Festing Jones says that Butler repeatedly claimed he had been a slow grower and had developed late in life. 'But', says Jones, 'since his death, and since reading his early writings and comparing them with his later works, I have begun to doubt' (p. xvi). Jones points out that, just as Butler discovered and adopted his straightforward style of writing early in his career, so he also seems to have 'discovered and adopted, quite early, those principles of philosophy on which he based the views which he continued to hold until his death' (pp. xvi–xvii). Jones concludes, 'I suppose now that his note should be read as meaning that he only gradually came to understand fully the significance of what had already commended itself to him, rather than that, as he grew older, he developed any startlingly new opinions' (ibid.).

Precisely the same picture emerges from a study of the relationship between Butler and chiasmus. Butler acquired his chiastic habits very early. In embryonic form most of the components of chiastic thinking can be found even in his earliest writings, and occasionally there are passages in the juvenilia in which chiasticism is already in full bloom.

In the very first paragraphs of the first essay that Butler ever published, 'On English Composition and Other Matters' (1858), he already states his preference for a prose style which is not only graphic, vigorous and concise but also 'straightforward' (p. 3). 'Straight', of

149

course, is a complementary term to such words as 'turn'. In the second paragraph of the essay, when he exemplifies, Butler chooses Jeremy Taylor's saying, 'Tell them it is as much intemperance to weep too much as to laugh too much' (ibid.), showing that already dualist divisions and balance fascinated him.

In the third paragraph he deals with the interrelationship between rules and writers, and characteristically begins to wonder whether men should follow rules, or rules men: 'rules, for the most part, are but useful to the weaker among us. Our greatest masters in language ... have been those who preceded the rule and whose excellence gave rise thereto ...' (pp. 3–4). Already Butler was preoccupied with questions of sequential order. Later on, in this very short essay, he criticizes the tendency 'unconsciously to follow in the wake of public opinion, while professing to lead it' (pp. 5–6).

There are other dualistic divisions apart from the 'weep–laugh' dichotomy already mentioned: 'too many – too few' (p. 4) and 'blunts–sharpens' (p. 6).[1] The former concerns the heaping-up of unnecessary illustrations: 'it is as great a fault to supply the reader with too many as with too few', says Butler, and, significantly, continues 'having given him at most two, it is better to ...' (p. 4). Apart from revealing how early the number two got a hold on Butler's psyche, these dualistic passages also show him grappling with the idea of a middle between two extremes.

Longing for the *via media* is an integral part of chiasticism, and is likely to follow if the other components of chiasticism are already in existence, but there may have been an external reason as well as an internal. Ruth Gounelas has shown convincingly how deeply the atmosphere at Cambridge in Butler's days was imbued with the spirit of 'impartiality', a concept which often seems to have been visualized as a middle position between two extremes.[2]

Whether for internal or external reasons, Butler's intellectual growth was stunted at Cambridge; he was never in later life able to transcend dualism, the longing for a mean, and all those other mental habits that were, if not born, then at least well fed and nursed at Cambridge.

One more idea in Butler's essay is worthy of attention. At the end of his text Butler deals with the question of subjects. He is groping for an idea, and he does not say it in so many words, but behind the verbiage of this part of the essay is the first occurrence of Butler's hobby-horse idea that the writer should not hunt for a subject but rather let the subject hunt for him.

Scattered chiastic passages in Butler's other Cambridge juvenilia show that the chiastic flavour of 'On English Composition' was not an isolated instance. In the essay 'Our Tour' (1859), which relates a journey Butler made with a friend during a vacation, he professes not to care what came first, a river or a valley: 'from this point we begin definitely, though slowly, to enter the hills and ascend by the side of the Romanche through the valley, which that river either made or found – who knows or cares?' (p. 13). In reality, of course, Butler always 'cared' when it came to questions of sequential order – his denial is merely another manifestation of his interest.

Further, possibly Cambridge-induced, dualism is found in Butler's humorous piece 'Prospectus of the Great Split Society' (1856?). *Division* ('split') is essential to dualism. If Butler already had a tendency towards dualism when he came to St John's, the Cambridge atmosphere of 'impartiality' can hardly have done anything else than confuse him, since it professed abhorrence of extremes, yet defined an alternative (impartiality) in terms which nevertheless presuppose the extremes. 'The Great Split Society' satirizes division; therefore Butler is ostensibly insincere when he writes, 'He is to call the present members to witness, and all are to take one side or the other, so that none be neutral ...' (p. 32). But, even if Butler invertedly echoes Cambridge applause of neutrality, the concept of 'neutral' furthers his indoctrination into dualism. You may refuse to join one side or the other, but that there are two sides you are not allowed to doubt. Even though you might be uncomfortable about the number two, you are not to replace it with other numbers, such as one, three or four.

The 'horror-of-the-middle-ground' idea is presented satirically here, since, in a sense, Cambridge undergraduates – as Ruth Gounelas shows – were rather taught to seek out a middle ground than to avoid it. There are further examples of satiric 'horror-of-the-middle-ground' passages in Butler's Cambridge writings. In the satiric piece 'Powers' his persona advises those that would be 'powers' to make a choice, either to pray much, or talk much during chapel service:

When thou goest to chapel talk much during the service, or pray much; do not the thing by halves; thou must either be the very religious power, which kind though the less remarked yet on the whole hath the greater advantage, or the thoughtless power, but above all see thou combine not the two, at least not in the same company, but let thy religion be the same to the same men.

(p. 37)

The insistence here, if we disregard the irony and read the passage straight, is on the necessity of a choice between two, and the necessity of extremism. Already Butler secretly rebelled at Cambridge condemnation of these two. 'Same with same' at the end of the quote is directed against the idea of 'any with any', and the very act of attacking the latter idea at the same time inevitably brings it into one's consciousness.

But in fact Cambridge 'impartiality' itself did not demand that one should *stay* in a middle position. What was essential was to *start out from* a middle position, there weighing the evidence (of 'one side and the other') carefully before taking sides. Throughout his career Butler was fond of using as material for metaphors those British institutions which are structured on a dualistic principle, such as the law-courts (with their dualist division of forces into defence and prosecution, and the impartial judge and jury).

From another point of view 'impartiality' is the same as ambivalence, and to an insecure character such as Butler the adoption of Cambridge attitudes was fatal. He acquired a mental habit of vacillation that he could never after shake off. He developed into an inveterate ambilateralist.

Caution and scepticism, which seem to have been positive Cambridge values at this time, also invade the chiastic passages expressing reciprocity in these early writings. At the end of 'Powers' Butler's persona says, 'And of distrust, distrust all men, most of all thine own friends; *they will know thee best, and thou them...*' (p. 40; emphasis added).

That friendship and distrust should be coupled is certainly an early indication of Butler's problems with reciprocity of relationships, despite the fact that the passage, like the rest of the text, is offered as satire. There is in Butler's text a strong flavour of a conviction that, though not the way they should be, this is the way things are.

Even in incidental cases of chiasmus to express reciprocity there seems to be a tendency to select negative feelings – if not distrust (as above), then perhaps indifference. Jones quotes the following passage from a notebook which Butler kept in New Zealand, but later destroyed: 'While we were at breakfast a robin perched on the table and sat there a good while pecking at the sugar. We went on breakfasting with little heed to the robin, and the robin went on ecking with little heed to us' (Shrewsbury, I xxxvii).

Apart from several passages concerned with reciprocity (see also p. 33) these early writings also contain, for instance, a full-fledged example of the 'toppling-over' variety of the idea of inversion: 'Nevertheless I would have thee keep within certain bounds, lest men turn upon thee if thy rule is too oppressive to be borne' ('Powers', p. 36).

In his Cambridge writings Butler also made 'decorative' use of chiasmus. A good example is the poem 'The Battle of Alma Mater', which Butler wrote on the subject of the 'Cambridge Tobacco Riot' of 1854. Butler makes use of ornamental chiasmus several times in the poem, beginning with the first stanza:

> The Temperance Commissioners
>   In awful conclave sat,
> Their noses into this to poke
> To poke them into that....   (p. 50)

This is probably as close as Butler ever comes to a use of chiasmus which concerns form only and not content. But even here I am not quite sure that Butler's chiasmus is only a matter of form, and that it does not affect content.

The above example could be regarded as an instance of 'chiasmus as repetitious redundancy' (a usage which I should have liked to call βαττολογία, after Ovid, *Metamorphoses*, II. 703–5; but unfortunately the consensus among commentators on this passage and on the term βαττολογία seems to be that it specifically refers not to chiastic repetitious redundancy, but to 'nonsense' in a more general sense[3]). A term should, however, be found for chiastic repetitious redundancy.

Reptitious redundancy is stupid or funny in itself, and making fun (i.e. of the anti-smokers) is Butler's object here. Butler quickly became too fond of chiasmus to take much notice, in his later career, of its repetitious-redundancy aspect, but at this point he may well have used superfluousness (i.e. repetition) in form to suggest superfluousness in content (i.e. anti-tobacco people and ideas are superfluous). In the lines 'Their noses into this to poke/ To poke them into that', the second half says the same thing as the first half, which is an image of the tedious sameness, and single-minded fanaticism, of the anti-tobacconists.

This impression is further strengthened when we proceed to consider one of the most important pieces of evidence of Butler's chiasticism during his Cambridge days. This is an English adaptation of a Tuscan proverb. The original goes:

> Con arte e con inganno si vive mezzo l'anno
> Con inganno e con arte si vive l'altra parte.   (p. 54)

Butler's English version:

> In knavish art and gathering gear
> They spend the one half of the year;
> In gathering gear and knavish art
> They somehow spend the other part.

The idea behind this anticlerical saying is that the priests are always the same. The second half of the proverb says precisely the same thing as the first, though it may appear at first to be different. There is a seeming difference, but in reality an actual sameness. The priests never change; one half of the year with them is like the other half, any appearances to the contrary notwithstanding.

Chiasmus, thanks particularly to its existential variety, is well suited to express pseudo-difference, since the '*a* is *b*, and *b* is *a*' formula suggests that, though *a* and *b* ought to be different (being separate entities each with its own name), they are nevertheless the same (which is expressed – optionally – through the verb 'to be' and through the switch of roles and positions).

There is, then, a specific philosophical thrust in the content of this proverb, and it is expressed through form. But the significance of the example as testimony of Butler's developing chiasticism goes far beyond this. Of all the proverbs he could have translated he picked a chiastic one. This reveals his fascination with chiasmus in general, not just with the specific variety in hand. Already the process had started whereby Butler filtered his experience so that he took in only what chiasticism let through.

In the general picture of Butler's Cambridge writings a significant feature is his choice of genres. He wrote satires and parodies. He mocked, attacked, imitated and distorted. The nature of parody or satire as a genre involves an antithetical relationship between two works, the parody and its target. Already Butler's way of putting himself in relation with the world was to put himself in hateful relation with it. Already he needed the number two, and already, through chiasmus, he showed that, despite the hate, he longed for reciprocity, union and fusion.

(b) *A First Year*

Butler's first book was *A First Year in Canterbury Settlement* (1863). Butler himself, however, always professed to dislike this work and insisted on regarding *Erewhon* (1872) as the start of his literary career.[4]

Some of the reasons for his attitude are obvious enough. Butler's father had made changes in the manuscript, and Butler could not stand such interference, least of all from his father. But the major reasons for Butler's attitudes should probably be sought within chiasticism.

First of all we must question Butler's sincerity. He often riled against those genres that were his own favourites, as the following comment shows: 'He became "one of Mr Darwin's many enthusiastic admirers, and wrote a philosophic dialogue (the most offensive form, except poetry and books of travel into supposed unknown countries, that even literature can assume) upon the *Origin of Species*."'[5] Of course Butler could not genuinely dislike philosophic dialogues, since a dialogue presupposes the number two, and the number two in a philosophic dialogue is achieved through a split of the self – both of these very desirable things to a chiasticist. Butler would have liked someone to attack his favourite genres; failing that he was, however, always willing to do it himself. Chiasticists are like those plants in nature that rely on self-fertilization as a last resort if everything else fails. It does not follow that Butler means what he is saying; or rather it follows that he means both what he is saying and the opposite.

The only really perfect partner for a chiasticist is his own self; and a chiasticist is perfectly willing to be self-sufficient in creating a self-contained dialectic that needs no outside help. (Butler's fascination with the idea of 'self' and self-sufficiency comes over, for instance, in his frequent etymological comments on the word 'idiot', which – as Butler points out – means no more than one who thinks for himself[6]). When, therefore, Butler says disparaging things about *A First Year*, that is only another way of praising *Erewhon*, or whichever book is being contrasted with *A First Year*. There is even a hint of a rule that, the more he blackens the one, the more will the other shine (because of the increase in contrast). This is the chiasticistic fallacy of see-saw thinking, which rules that if one goes down the other comes up, and, further, that if you want one to come up you must make the other go down.

The self-sufficiency of chiastic thinking influences the behaviour of a chiasticist in odd ways. It is easy for the chiasticist to be victorious if he can set up only such difficulties as he solves, and himself be sole judge of success or failure.

If the self-sufficiency of the chiasticist extends to the distribution of praise and blame, the chiasticist's activities as his own judge will create some views of the relationships between various works in his *oeuvre* that should not necessarily be accepted by other critics. At the end of chapter 11 of *Erewhon Revisited*, the narrator writes,

> I shall adhere to my determination not to reproduce his arguments; suffice it that though less flippant than those of the young student whom I have already referred to, they were more plausible; and though I could easily demolish them, the reader will probably prefer that I should not set them up for the mere pleasure of knocking them down.   (p. 110)

This, however, is often what every stage in a development that a chiasticist creates *exists for* – if not exactly to be knocked down by the subsequent stage, then at least in one way or another to form a basis or a stepping-stone for it.

A First Year was a stepping-stone to *Erewhon*, and being a stepping-stone involves being trodden on. Henry Festing Jones very perceptively comments on this,

> The proofs [of *A First Year*], however, were fished up [after a shipwreck], though so nearly washed out as to be almost undecipherable. Butler would have been just as well pleased if they had remained at the bottom of the Indian Ocean, for he never liked the book and always spoke of it as being full of youthful priggishness; but I think he was a little hard upon it. Years afterwards, in one of his later books, after quoting two passages from Mr Grant Allen and pointing out why he considered the second to be a recantation of the first, he wrote: 'When Mr Allen does make stepping-stones of his dead selves he jumps them to some tune.' And he was perhaps a little inclined to treat his own dead self too much in the same spirit.[7]

That the interrelationship between Butler's works often forms a zig-zagging dialectic is easily apparent. In the case of *A First Year* versus

Erewhon, the relation involves purely hostile antithesis. More often, of course, the relation is complementary, as between *Erewhon* and *Erewhon Revisited*, or, most obviously of all, between the two operas *Narcissus* and *Ulysses*. Jones's report of the birth of the latter is highly interesting:

> The delay was caused ... and partly by something that arose out of *Narcissus,* which we published in June 1888.
>
> Butler was not satisfied with having written only half of this work; he wanted it to have a successor, so that by adding his two halves together, he could say he had written a whole Handelian oratorio.   (Shrewsbury, I lviii)

Jones then goes on to relate how they decided on the *Odyssey* as a subject and how that in turn eventually led Butler to his theory of the female authorship of the poem. Jones's account of Butler's dissatisfaction with his uncomplemented half of a work is a very good description of a chiasticist's predictable reactions and emotions.

In general Jones's synopses of the history of the birth of Butler's works are all very suggestive and revealing. Take, for instance, the following example from Jones's 'Sketch' of S. B., published repeatedly at the beginning of the century and printed in Volume I of the Shrewsbury Edition:

> Following his letter in *The Press,* wherein he had seen machines as in process of becoming animate, he went on to regard them as living organs and limbs which we had made outside ourselves. What would follow if we reversed this and regarded our limbs and organs as machines which we had manufactured as parts of our bodies? In the first place, how did we come to make them without knowing anything about it? But then, how comes anybody to do anything unconsciously? The answer usually would be: By habit. But can a man be said to do a thing by habit when he has never done it before? His ancestors have done it, but not he. Can the habit have been acquired by them for his benefit? Not unless he and his ancestors are the same person. Perhaps, then, they are the same person.   (p. xlvii)

Here is a typical chain of chiasticist logic. First inversion has allowed the thinker to see machines as animate. This abolishes the distinction between limbs and machines, metaphor aiding in the process. Then inversion is again used – chiasticists always believe in the heuristic value of inversion; inversion – they think – is always bound to lead to some discovery. At the end of the chain of chiasticist logic the distinction-abolishing power of existential chiasmus is used to make a man the same as his ancestors, i.e. 'He is they, and they are he.'

In addition to the reasons already mentioned, Butler's dislike of *A First Year* was probably dictated by another important chiastic mechanism. In his view the relation between an author and his work should be reciprocal. The work should come to the writer no less than the writer to the work. Probably the main reason why Butler disliked *A First Year* was that, unlike all his other works, *A First Year* had not forced itself upon him.

We may again quote Jones: '[Butler] looked upon himself as a painter and upon *Erewhon* as an interruption. It had come, like one of those creatures from the Land of the Unborn, pestering him and refusing to leave him at peace until he consented to give it bodily shape' (Shrewsbury, I xlv). In the same way ever after, Butler yielded to the importunities of each of his unborn books as they came to him clamouring to be allowed to be born.

Finally, from the point of view of this study, it may be relevant that the text of *A First Year* makes less use of chiasmus and chiastic thinking than any of Butler's other books (with the obvious exception of such works as the life and letters of his grandfather, the text of which is for the most part not by Butler himself).

Despite the relative scarcity of chiasmus and chiasticistic thought in *A First Year*, a brief survey will add to the total picture of Butler's psychomorphology and his development as a chiasticist. Let us therefore look at some of the most important examples of chiasmus in the text.

In *A First Year*, as in Butler's other works, chiasmus is sometimes found in rather unexpected contexts, and from the point of view of a study of chiasticism some of these unusual occurrences can be quite instructive. Part of chapter 4 of *A First Year* is on the mineral nature of Canterbury settlement – one of the objectives of Butler and his companion during their expedition being to prospect for gold – and Butler puts some of his observations into chiastic language:

We saw no masses of quartz; what we found was intermixed with sandstone, and was always in small pieces. The sandstone, in like manner, was almost always intermingled with quartz. Besides this sandstone there was a good deal of pink and blue slate, the pink chiefly at the top of the range, showing a beautiful colour from the river-bed. In addition to this, there were abundance of rocks, of every gradation between sandstone and slate – some sandstone almost slate, some slate almost sandstone.   (p. 104)

Butler's choice of textual strategy for such passages reveals that chiasmus was more to him than one method of expressing a certain content. He *could* have been content with a noun, such as 'proportion', to express the intermixture of varieties of stone ('slate and sandstone being mixed, in varying proportions'). He *could* also have used a reciprocal pronoun – 'each other', or 'one another' – ('sandstone and quartz being mixed with one another'). But one gets the impression that Butler uses reciprocal pronouns comparatively seldom, considering how often reciprocity is his subject. Likewise he does not seem to use nouns to express reciprocity as often as he might, or as often as other authors. He usually prefers to express reciprocity through word-order, i.e. through chiasmus. That this is the case comes over particularly clearly in examples, such as the present, in which there is no discernible reason why he should favour chiasmus over nouns or pronouns as a means of expressing reciprocity. Chiasmus has a value of its own, apart from its usefulness as a means of expressing reciprocity.

The last part of the quotation – 'some sandstone almost slate, some slate almost sandstone' – expresses the insecurity of the chiasticist about definitions and identities. What is sandstone? What is slate? Where is the border between them? When does sandstone become slate; when does slate become sandstone? This insecurity about categories, which is created through the influence of existential chiasmus, plagues chiasticists severely. When Butler refers to the works of his namesake, Samuel Butler the author of *Hudibras,* it is usually to one out of a small number of favourite passages, and in particular he is fond of quoting the following couplet: 'He knows what's what, and that's as high, / As metaphysic wit can fly.'[8] The reason why this couplet fascinated Butler is obvious. Knowing 'what's what' is precisely what a chiasticist finds problematical.

Some other chiastic passages on similar themes in *A First Year* are fairly conventional and usually occur to express a lack of reciprocity, or an inversion of imbalance (i.e. what could have been expected to be less important is in fact more so, and *vice-versa*). Lack of perfect reciprocity is expressed in Butler's report on the marital relations of the New Zealand paradise duck:

Her mate is much fonder of her than she is of him, for if *she* is wounded he will come to see what is the matter, whereas if *he* is hurt his base partner flies instantly off and seeks new wedlock, affording a fresh example of the superior fidelity of the male to the female sex.   (p. 158)

Observations on inverted imbalance in a relationship are also to be found in Butler's comments on the relative positions of masters and men, and sheep and humans. In New Zealand the balance has shifted so that servants' work has become an employee's market.

> You and your men will have to be on rather a different footing from that on which you stood in England. There, if your servant were in any respect what you did not wish, you were certain of getting plenty of others to take his place. Here, if a man does not find you quite what he wishes, he is certain of getting plenty of others to employ him.   (p. 166)

One might similarly have thought that man is ruler of the beasts, but in New Zealand the needs of sheep come first, those of humans after:

> You must remember they [the sheep] are your masters, and not you theirs; you exist for them, not they for you. If you bear this well in mind, you will be able to turn the tables on them effectually at shearing-time. But if you once begin to make the sheep suit their feeding-hours to your convenience, you may as well give up sheep-farming at once.   (p. 170)

This quotation also contains the interesting expression and concept of 'turning the tables'. In the preceding chapter of *A First Year* there is another case of a turning-of-the-tables inversion, this time used mainly for humorous purposes. Pursuer becomes pursued, and pursued pursuer, as an eel turns the tables on a cat which had tried to eat him.

> I am told that the other night a great noise was heard in the kitchen of a gentleman with whom I have the honour to be acquainted, and that the servants, getting up, found an eel chasing a cat round the room. I believe this story. The eel was in a bucket of water, and doomed to die upon the morrow. Doubtless the cat had attempted to take liberties with him; on which a sudden thought struck the eel that he might as well eat the cat as the cat eat him; and he was preparing to suit the action to the word when he was discovered.   (p. 163)

Such episodes as this are presumably funny to everyone, but to a chiasticist they are irresistibly funny, and always worthy of being noted down and handed on.

The cat and the eel exchange roles, and any form of exchange rings a bell in the consciousness of a chiasticist. In describing the voyage to New Zealand in the early chapters of *A First Year,* Butler reflects that he feels as if he had always been at sea; as if he had exchanged lives with someone else: 'it seems as though I had always been on board the ship, and was always going to be, and as if all my past life had not been mine, but had belonged to somebody else, or as though someone had taken mine and left me his by mistake' (ch. 2, p. 78).

When Butler tells his readers how a team of bullocks get frightened and confused, and mess up the harness, he is particularly struck by the fact that the confusion develops according to a chiastic pattern of exchange, the off bullock turning upon the near side and the near bullock upon the off:

> In the small River Ashburton, or rather in one of its most trivial branches, we had a little misunderstanding with the bullocks; the leaders, for some reason best known to themselves, slewed sharply round, and tied themselves into an inextricable knot with the polars, while the body bullocks, by a manoeuvre not unfrequent, shifted, or, as it is technically termed, slipped, the yoke under their necks, and the bows over; the off bullock turning upon the near side and the near bullock upon the off. By what means they do this I cannot explain, but believe it would make a conjuror's fortune in England. (p. 138)

It would certainly make a conjuror's fortune if his audience was always made up of chiasticists, because for them chiastic exchange has a limitless appeal.

It would actually be quite interesting to study in some depth 'the aesthetics of confusion', and the role of symmetry in the creation and appreciation of various kinds of confusion.

Given dualism and repetition, and given the possibility of inversion, chiastic combinations are bound to result sooner or later from a random process of distribution or reorganization, the table of possibilities being

$$a\,a - b\,b$$
$$b\,b - a\,a$$
$$a\,b - b\,a$$
$$b\,a - a\,b$$

The probability that Butler's bullocks should sooner or later achieve a chiastic exchange during confusion is a result of the dualist division of the team into off bullocks and near bullocks and the reported zeal of Butler's team in testing out all combinational possibilities. Once Butler's bullocks had achieved chiasmus, Butler was sure to remember it.

Mental preference for symmetry over asymmetry is an important factor in both the production and the perception of chiastic confusion. Let us consider the latter first.

The chiastic exchange, as compared with other combinational variants, is sometimes only in the eye of the beholder. Let us consider an example. In speaking English some orientals do not properly distinguish between 'l' and 'r'. The phonetic facts of this confusion are fairly complicated and cannot be dealt with here. The native speaker of English will possibly think it typical of the Chinese to pronounce 'r' as 'l', and of the Japanese to pronounce 'l' as 'r', but above all a disinterested listener will note the confusion of 'l' and 'r'.

But if speakers of English want to create a caricature of an Oriental, for purposes of comedy, it is likely that the caricature character will be one that regularly pronounces 'r' as 'l' and 'l' as 'r'. This chiastic stylization is created by the listeners through the structuring of the way they perceive reality. They discard other possibilities and keep and exaggerate the chiastic one, because of the intrinsic appeal of chiasmus and symmetry. Fun should be maximized; inversion is funny; obligatory chiastic (i.e. double-sided) inversion is therefore most funny. The audience will gladly, through their method of perception, do some violence to the facts for symmetry's sake. Even if other possibilities do exist (i.e. 'l' and 'r' pronounced correctly; both 'r' and 'l' always pronounced as 'r'; and both 'r' and 'l' always pronounced as 'l') what they *prefer to hear,* and accordingly most likely *will hear,* is the chiastic version of 'l' pronounced as 'r' and 'r' as 'l'. If, in actual fact, the pronunciation tends to be halfway between 'l' and 'r', this makes it even easier for the listener to impose chiasticism than if the pronunciation is lopsided either way, or random. Then, to the listener, every time the intermediate form is pronounced it will sound wrong: 'l' as 'r' and 'r' as 'l'.

In life Cockneys may be somewhat unsure about their 'haitches' when they try to speak Standard English. But in certain forms of comedy they are not unsure at all: they leave 'h' out where it should be, and put it in where it should not be, with perfect regularity.[9] Such chiastic order need not be intrinsic to reality; it may be imposed on reality by minds using a chiastic model in their perception.

It is thus, to sum up, possible that much of the chiasticity in mispronunciation – as in so much else – is in the eye of the beholder. Many combinational variants may occur, but only chiastic ones will be remembered. Of the theoretical possibilities – i.e. (1) correct pronunciation, (2) random pronunciation, (3) 'h'-dropping (leaving 'h' out incorrectly), (4) hypercorrectness (putting 'h' in where it should not be), and (5) 'h'-dropping and hypercorrectness combined (leaving 'h' out where it should be, and putting it in where it should *not* be) – it is (5), 'h'-dropping and hypercorrectness combined that will be remembered, because of the appeal of symmetry.

Whatever the Cockney pattern of aspirating and not aspirating the 'h' may have been in Butler's days, it was predictable that he would notice and report chiastic inversion. Thus in a note dating from 1881 he writes, 'The first shop I saw was Byle's eating house; the young man in the seat opposite me began reading *John Inglesant* and, outside, the Salvation Army began singing about "'eav'nly, 'eav'nly music floating through the hair" ' (Jones, II 69).

The question of to what extent switch-mechanisms are involved in the *production,* as opposed to the perception, of chiastic mispronunciation is difficult. Since spoonerisms must be produced by some kind of mental 'switch-mechanism' it is likely that the same mechanism could produce double mispronunciation of related sounds or mispronunciations which would give such results as *"eavenly hair' for 'heavenly air'*.

Dualism may conceivably influence the behaviour of the potential mispronouncer. If the difficulty is in reproducing two related sounds (let us here represent them by the arbitrary symbols *a* and *b*) and a word contains one case of *a* and one of *b,* in a certain order, then a preponderance of chiastic double mispronunciation rather than cases of getting one right and the other wrong might ensue. The speaker presumably braces himself for the task of pronouncing a word with two difficult, related, sounds; having pronounced one (the first) he knows that he should then use the other (which is different from the first). If he has then got the first one wrong, he will get the other one wrong too, if his consciousness of the fact that they were to be different is stronger than his ambition to try to produce either (in this case the latter) correctly as a separate undertaking.

In chapter 3 of *A First Year* Butler jokingly mentions homoeopathy. He writes that he has 'purchased a horse, by name Doctor. I hope he is a homoeopathist' (p. 86). Butler's interest in homoeopathic medicine becomes fully understandable only against the background of chiasticism. A career as a homeopathic doctor was one of the options for a professional future that Butler contemplated after he had left Cambridge and decided not to take orders. In his correspondence with his father at this time a number of projects are discussed and rejected, either by Butler himself or by his parents. Some critics want to explain Butler's interest in homoeopathy against this background. Butler's parents were prudish and disliked the thought of all the unsuitable things that their son might come into contact with if he chose a medical career. At least homoeopathy would in this respect be better than other varieties of medicine.[10]

There may be something in this argument. Nevertheless I think that the chief explanation for Butler's fascination with homoeopathy should, as usual, be sought in his chiasticism. As the first part of the term '*homoeo*pathy' suggests, this medical philosophy is concerned with the questions of sameness and otherness, similarity and difference – precisely those questions that dominate the lives of a chiasticist. Should one go in for homoeopathy or allopathy? Should one fight like with like, or different with different – in other words '*a* with *a* and *b* with *b*', or '*a* with *b* and *b* with *a*'? Which answer a chiasticist will choose is not predictable. But that he will be interested in the question is entirely predictable.

There are other features in the homoeopathic philosophy that appeal to a chiasticist. Homoeopathists often prescribe extremely small doses of the substances they think efficacious. This naturally is a very familiar type of thought to a chiasticist (cf. the 'wedge' metaphors). If something goes a little way it will go all the way. If something helps a little it will help completely.[11]

Some of Butler's typical chiasticist thought-patterns can be found exemplified in *A First Year*. Thus his 'palladian' thinking structures the way he reports the development of the settlers' attitudes to rivers in New Zealand. First they fear rivers extremely, and take great care in crossing them (stage *a*); then, by and by, they get indifferent and careless (stage *b*); until they are almost drowned, and return to their first attitude (stage *a* or *a*₁):

> On their first few experiences of one of these New Zealand rivers, people dislike them extremely; they then become very callous to them, and are as unreasonably foolhardy as they were before timorous; then they generally get an escape from drowning or two, or else they get drowned in earnest. After one or two escapes their original respect for the rivers returns, and for ever after they learn not to play any unnecessary tricks with them. (p. 109)

In addition to 'palladianism' there are also some good examples of Butler's relativism. In chapter 1 Butler reports that the passengers aboard the emigrant ship began to wonder about the climate of their new hemisphere when they met with some very cold weather during the voyage. He then makes a characteristic comment to assert his typical chiasticistic belief that 'cold' does not exist except in relation to its opposite, 'warm': 'No doubt we felt it [the cold] more than we should otherwise on account of our having so lately crossed the line' (p. 72). A little later he writes that

> Sailors generally estimate a gale of wind by the amount of damage it does, if they don't lose a mast or get their bulwarks washed away, or at any rate carry away a few sails, they don't call it a gale, but a stiff breeze; if, however, they are caught even by comparatively a very inferior squall, and lose something, they call it a gale.   (p. 74)

Some of Butler's comments on the landscape of Canterbury settlement in *A First Year* find their way into the text because the outer landscape of Canterbury fits an inner landscape of Butler's mind. It is, for instance, inevitable that a chiasticist should be fascinated by anything similar in shape to the letter χ, which has given chiasmus its name. One such thing is the hour-glass, which Butler predictably introduces to describe a natural formation in the Canterbury landscape:

> Therefore, though, when first looking at the plains and river-bed flats which are so abundant in the back country, one might be inclined to think that no other agent than the rivers themselves had been at work, and though, when one sees the delta below, and the empty gully above, like a minute-glass after the egg has been boiled – the top glass empty of the sand, and the bottom glass full of it – one is tempted to rest satisfied; yet when we look closer, we shall find that more is wanted in order to account for the phenomena exhibited, and the geologists of the island supply that more, by means of upheaval.   (p. 133)

An additional source of fascination for a chiasticist is of course that an hour-glass is periodically inverted – by necessity every time you want to use it, in fact.

Another congruity between Butler's mental landscape of chiasticism and the actual landscape of Canterbury province was found in oscillation – the oscillation of the chiasticist between left and right (one and the other, beginning and end, first and after, subject and object, active and passive), corresponding to the oscillation of New Zealand rivers from one side of their bed to the other: 'I said the rivers lie on the highest part of the delta; not always the highest, but seldom the lowest. There is reason to believe that in the course of centuries they oscillate from side to side' (p. 131)

Above all there is a double significance in the endless crossings and recrossings of rivers in *A First Year*. On the one hand, of course, this *was* a prominent fact of colonial life in Canterbury settlement; on the other, however, the zigzagging of crossings and recrossings traced, in reality, a pattern that already existed in Butler's mind. The congruity reinforced the impression made by this fact of a settler's life, so that Butler lays great stress upon it both in *A First Year* and in other early articles or essays, such as 'Crossing the Rangitata'.[12]

It is obvious from this brief survey of chiastic passages in *A First Year* that, although among all of Butler's books it is one of those least dominated by chiasticism, still there is enough of it to show that there was really no dramatic change or development in Butler's career as a chiasticist. Even in Butler's early work chiasmus is already highly important.

(c) Early articles and essays

The main significance of Butler's early articles and essays – published partly in New Zealand and partly after his return to London in 1864 – is their function as finger-exercises for *Erewhon, The Fair Haven* and Butler's works on evolution. The early 1860s was a formative period during which Butler acquired not only chiastic attitudes, but also those basic chiastic ideas which later on develop into doctrines.

The exchange in *The Press* on Darwinism (see Shrewsbury, I 184–207), contains the germ of Butler's later works on the teleological theory of evolution. It is not in his own text, but in that of his anonymous opponent. The structure of *Erewhon* is made up of a number of existential formulae. One of these concerns the relation between the animate and the mechanical, and the difficulty of drawing a border-line between the two. The formula 'The mechanical is animate and the animate mechanical' forms the chiastic basis for chapters 23, 24 and 25 of *Erewhon*, as well as for some scattered passages on the same theme throughout the book. The first half of this formula, 'Machines are animate' was prefigured in the article 'Darwin among the Machines', an essay published in *The Press* in 1863. The second half of the formula was foreshadowed in 'Lucubratio Ebria' (*The Press*, 1865). The argument of the latter essay is not a pure

cceptance of the sentence 'Men are machines', but indirectly this
entence underlies the views put forward. The essay deals with the
lifficulty of determining the border between the animate and the
nechanical. Is not a spade, for instance, merely an extracorporeal
imb?

The starting-point of the chiastic formula was the half 'machines are
nimate' – the second half then followed automatically as the
obligatory complement of the first. The origin of the first half of the
ormula again was Butler's urge to contradict by inversion contempor-
iry public (largely Darwinian) opinion, which said, in effect, 'Man is a
nachine.'

There is no need to deal further with the general significance of
hese articles here; most of them were incorporated into later works –
he pamphlet *The Evidence for the Resurrection of Jesus Christ as
contained in the Four Evangelists critically examined* (1865), for
nstance, was finally worked into the text of *The Fair Haven*. Instead
et/us look at some details that further illustrate Butler's chiastic
hinking at this time.

Passages expressing reciprocity are fairly frequent in these works.
Writing about men and machines, Butler envisages various forms of
interdependence. In 'Darwin among the Machines' he argues that
machines cannot exist without men, nor men without machines: 'The
fact is that our interests are inseparable from theirs, and theirs from
ours' (p. 212). In the dualistic world-picture of a chiasticist
everything exists only in relation to its opposite. If, then, that opposite
is destroyed, it means a destruction also of that of which it is an
opposite. An image that naturally comes easily to the chiasticist mind
to express this absolute interdependence is therefore that of Siamese
twins – an image that Butler uses at the beginning of 'Lucubratio
Ebria': 'We know that what we see is but a sort of intellectual Siamese
twins, of which one is substance and the other shadow, but we cannot
set either free without killing both' (p. 214).

In 'The Mechanical Creation' Butler again writes about machines
that 'Their desires will probably never clash with ours, nor ours with
theirs ...' (p. 237). The insecurity that Butler feels, even while
asserting reciprocity, comes out in the word 'probably'. The context is
negative. Butler is speculating on the future of men as slaves under the
machines.

It is interesting to note the *quality* of Butler's view of interdependence. In his use of the image of Siamese twins, the relation he
immediately envisages is one of hostility, and the speculation concerns

the feasibility of *killing* either without also killing the other. It is important, in assessing the significance of all such passages as these, to forget the superficial sense of what is being said, and instead listen to what sort of words are being used ('kill', 'clash', and so forth); what subjects are being dealt with (slavery, killing, hostility, and the like) and so on. The semiotic significance of these passages goes beyond the straightforward meaning of what is being specifically said in each case, and there may be more meaning in the general than in the specific.

In a passage expressing reciprocity in 'Crossing the Rangitata' Butler congratulates himself on receiving more confidence than could have been expected: 'I walked my mare quickly into it [a ford], having perfect confidence in her [the mare], and, I believe, she having more confidence in me than some who have known me in England might suppose' (p. 181). Again, let us disregard facts about Butler's skills in horsemanship. What matters is the general pattern of insecure belief in reciprocity, coupled with a strong longing for it. Butler expected – or imagines his English friends as expecting – that the mare would have little confidence in him, yet he 'believes' that there is more than he expected.

The longing for reciprocity makes chiasticists clutch even at the straw offered by established religious doctrine, in the reciprocity implied in certain commandments or injunctions. In 'Precaution in Free Thought' (1865) Butler repeats the commandment of 'doing to others as [you] would be done by' (p. 240). This is a rare instance. Usually Butler attacked this injunction.

In Butler's world there are always two sides, and shifting from one side to the other does not really change anything, because, if you make an improvement in the side you go to, this will be offset by a corresponding deterioration in the side you leave. Thus, if you convert a number of Indians to Christianity, it is true that you have made a number of Christians, but you have also spoiled the same number of Hindus. At the beginning of 'Precaution in Free Thought' Butler quotes Sydney Smith, who 'said well, that when a missionary wrote home from India of his having made so many converts to Christianity, the chances were he had only spoiled that number of Hindoos' (p. 238). This must not be taken to mean only that the Indians had left off being good Hindus without therefore becoming good Christians; that is of course one variant of meaning, but Butler always had in mind (and always worked out) all variants of meaning, and what really matters is the deep conviction of the chiasticist that nothing ever changes: therefore there are two aspects to any event – increasing the number of

Christians may be progress, but that, inevitably, at the same time means decreasing the number of Hindus, which is a retrogression that neutralizes the effect.

The initial state and the resulting state are in the end the same, which is symbolized in Butler's essay by his argument coming full circle, so that he ends his text with the same thought with which he began it: 'instead of becoming a good Freethinker, he is after all nothing but a spoiled Christian' (p. 241).[13]

That there are two sides to everything is insisted upon as strongly in these early essays as elsewhere in Butler's writings. The phrase 'both sides', which implies that there are two sides to things – rather than one, three, four, five, or any other number of sides – is becoming habitual. At the beginning of 'The Mechanical Creation' Butler structures reality according to his two half formulae, asking whether the mechanical kingdom is really animate or whether perhaps the animate kingdom is developing an extension of itself into the mechanical. 'Much has to be said on both sides...' (p. 231).

In Butler's art-criticism of the period his chiasticism is no less apparent than in the other essays. Commenting on a painting by Dedomenici da Rossa, in an article of the same name, he begins to wonder about the date of the painting. Now a date could be anything – Butler could for instance have made a guess at a particular year or decade. Instead Butler as usual structures possibilities dualistically by suggesting two alternatives, 'old' versus 'modern', and then begins to worry about the interrelationship between these two, and brings them into chiastic contact: 'if an old picture, it was an anachronism as too modern, if a modern one, it was infinitely more so, as being instinct with a feeling that had been supposed to have been long dead' (p. 244).[14]

In Butler's essay 'Instead of an Article on the Dudley Exhibition' (1871), his worry over the number two leads him into a philosophical digression on the use of the first person plural by critics. 'We', he argues, 'carries with it a certain weight to which, in critical articles, it is not entitled. It suggests two, and two are better than one; if this were not so it would soon be discarded ...' (p. 246). Note how Butler's compulsive need to structure reality dualistically is revealed in his unwarranted assumption that the pronoun 'we' 'suggests two'. This is not true. 'We' suggests a number larger than one, and, though the pronoun can be used to refer to two individuals, it can equally well be used to refer to any larger number, and Butler's singling out of the number two is as usual arbitrary – the guided arbitrariness of the committed dualist who always happens to end up with the number two.

In the same article, however, Butler also writes that 'there are three positions which [a critic] can take with regard to any picture. He may like it, dislike it, or be unable to tell whether he does the one or the other' (p. 247). The reader is startled to find Butler mentioning the number three, but soon realizes that the third possibility is not a genuine third option at all, only a way of combining the first two.

Butler's comments on inability to choose are interesting. In a kind of logical regression he argues that, though not being able to choose is admissible, at least one ought to be able to make up one's mind whether one is unable to choose or not. A chiasticist loves this kind of 'reduplicative' construction, which takes you back from one 'which-one' duality to another (and, if need be, from that one back to yet another and so on *ad infinitum*). 'Life is not a donkey-race in which everyone is to ride his neighbour's donkey, and the last is to win. It *is* a hard matter to know whether one likes a picture or no, but it ought not to be a hard matter to know that one doesn't know whether or not one likes it' (ibid.). These regressive constructions presumably appeal to a chiasticist because of their self-sufficiency. In this passage Butler couples the idea of logical 'reduplicative' regression with one of his favourite concepts – the donkey-race (see also, for instance, *The Way of All Flesh,* p. 137). Appealing features in a donkey-race are inversion (the last wins), and exchange (everyone rides his neighbour's donkey). Typical is also Butler's use of the word 'whether' – a word that implies two possibilities and is therefore a favourite with a chiasticist. In the use of 'whether', the addition of '... or not' (or '... or no') is optional. Characteristically Butler nearly always uses it. A chiasticist can never be *too* sure about dualism; the more he makes sure the better. (Butler's normal variant of the phrase is 'whether or no').

Other typically chiastic phenomena can be found in these texts. Our old narcissistic friend 'echo' is found at the beginning of 'Dedomenici da Rossa', the opening paragraph of which is chiastically structured (p. 242). 'Turning' imagery is found in Butler's mock-heroic poem 'The English Cricketers', on the occasion of an England–Canterbury match: 'Fortune turned her wheel, / And Grace, disgracéd for the nonce, was bowled / First ball ...' (p. 226). 'Grace, disgracéd' is a type of construction that a chiasticist loves, and such constructions are numerous in Butler's prose. These self-sufficient constructions should probably be seen as akin to oxymoron, but the appeal of reduplicative regression perhaps also enters the picture, or maybe that variety of 'toppling-over' inversion in which you upset an extreme by taking it still further. Let us call these phrases *sartor resartus* constructions.

Literalism and personification were two difficult subjects for Butler. His thoughts went with equal ease from the abstract to the concrete and from the concrete to the abstract. He therefore did not know what to think of personifications and literalism, and in his writings gropes around, without success, for a comfortable opinion. Usually his comments themselves become chiastic when he deals with the subject.

> I say personal Deity – I should have said Deity alone – for I see not how to believe in an impersonal Deity. It is as easy to believe the trinity in unity and unity in trinity, as it is for me to conceive the notion of Deity without personifying it. If I do not personify the idea, the idea itself eludes my grasp ...   (p. 240)

Butler's chiasticism expresses itself in these early writings in the way he structures his perception of the subject material. In 1872, for instance, he published a review titled 'Handel's "Deborah" and Bach's "Passion" '. The review is divided into two parts. Characteristically the parts are not separate – i.e. one on Handel and one on Bach. Instead the two composers are juxtaposed, contrasted and compared (naturally to Handel's advantage). To write about first one thing, and then about another, without bringing the two into (antithetical) relation with one another, was not a thing that Butler's temperament would easily allow him to do.

II   *EREWHON*

A survey of chiasticism in *Erewhon* may begin with the title itself, which is an anagram of 'nowhere'.[15] Anagrams, usually of personal names, occur throughout the work: 'Yram' (Mary; pp. 53 ff.);[16] 'Senoj Nosnibor' (Robinson Jones; p. 59 and *passim*);[17] 'Ydgrun' (Grundy; p. 116 and *passim*);[18] 'Thims' (Smith; p. 161 and *passim*).[19]

The principle of inversion is thus already exemplified in the title through anagram. The full title, *Erewhon: Or, Over the Range,* exemplifies not only inversion but also dualism and 'palladian' geography. 'Over' is not there in the title only to suggest the narrator *going over* the range; 'over' primarily means *on the other side of,* i.e. there are two sides, divided by the range in the middle.[20]

For a motto Butler chooses a line from Aristotle's *Politics,* 'τοῦ γὰρ εἶναι δοκοῦντος ἀγαθοῦ κάριν πάντα πράττουσι πάντες', which Butler paraphrases as follows: 'There is no action save upon a balance of considerations'. Balance, as we know, is one of the central concepts of chiasticism and the motto reveals the chiasticist's perpetual worry over his inability to choose.

Precisely that inability is dramatically further demonstrated in the form of the motto itself when Butler sent his manuscript to the printer. In his Introduction to the Shrewsbury Edition, Jones includes a facsimile of the manuscript title-page (facing p. xii) and comments, 'Nor do I know why, in the quotation from Aristotle, εἶναι in the MS. is the fourth word and in the published book the third word. πάντες and πάντα are also reversed' (p. xiii). Well, Jones may not know, but the reader who has become alerted to Butler's chiasticism will know.

Just as Jones wonders in his Preface to *Erewhon,* so Streatfeild too wonders in similar fashion in his Preface to *Life and Habit:*

> One more point deserves notice. Butler often refers in *Life and Habit* to Darwin's *Variations of Animals and Plants under Domestication.* When he does so it is always under the name *Plants and Animals.* More often still he refers to Darwin's *Origin of Species by means of Natural Selection,* terming it at one time *Origin of Species* and at another *Natural Selection,* sometimes, as on p. 278, using both names within a few lines of each other. Butler was as a rule scrupulously careful about quotations, and I can offer no explanation of this curious confusion of titles.   (Shrewsbury, IV xv)

The reader who has become alerted to chiasticism need not wonder. Butler's 'curious confusion' was to be expected. In referring to Darwin's *Origin of Species by means of Natural Selection* Butler dutifully vacillates between one end of the title and the other. In referring to *Animals and Plants,* which is too short to allow that kind of vacillation, he is consistent, but consistently wrong, so that there has at least been *one* inversion.

Erewhon is rich in inversion. This is evident even from the vocabulary. At the end of chapter 1 the narrator – whom we may call Higgs, though he is given that name only in *Erewhon Revisited* – resolves to 'cross' the range to find out what is 'on the other side of it' (p. 6). If few overtly chiasticistic ideas occur in the early chapter of *Erewhon,* at least a chiasticistic vocabulary immediately appears, 'cross' and 'other side' being typical chiasticist words.

More chiasticist vocabulary is introduced at the end of chapter 3: the narrator discovers that Chowbok has 'turned' (p. 17) back and left him. At the beginning of chapter 4 the narrator reports that he 'crossed and recrossed' (p. 19; see also pp. 30, 64) a stream several times.[21] In fact all over the pages of *Erewhon* there is a liberal sprinkling of chiasticist vocabulary, and particularly words connected with Latin *vertere* or English 'turn': for instance, 'turn' (p. 99), 'turned' (pp. 33, 52, 63), 'turning' (p. 114), 'conversion' (pp. 41, 45, 132, 224, 236), 'converter' (p. 132), 'convert' (pp. 42, 132, 239), 'converting' (pp. 59, 130), 'perversions' (p. 56), 'perversion' (pp. 83, 151, 156), 'perversity' (pp. 60, 104), 'subversionary' (p. 81), 'subverters' (p. 92), 'reverse' (p. 121), 'reversion' (p. 192), 'aversion' (p. 123).

In chapter 3, the narrator reports a special technique of catching birds. The presence of this passage in the text is dictated by chiasticism.

We had caught half a dozen young ducks in the course of the day – an easy matter, for the old birds made such a fuss in attempting to decoy us away from them – pretending to be badly hurt as they say the plover does – that we could always find them by going about in the opposite direction to the old bird till we heard the young ones crying: then we ran them down, for they could not fly though they were nearly full grown.   (p. 13)

By inverting what the grown-up birds are doing it is possible for the humans to unmask the real purpose of their action. A chiasticist always believes that inversion will automatically bring about some sort of valuable discovery; some sort of brilliant success.[22] Acting on this in real life, he will afterwards tend to remember, and pass on, those cases in life and reality in which inversion *did* lead to a successful result, but forget and ignore those cases in which it did not.[23]

Once Butler has got into the mood, in chapter 3, by reporting on the inversionary bird-catching technique, he goes on in the next paragraph to invert a Virgilian saying from the *Georgics,* in the process complementing the word *fortunatos* with its negative twin *infortunatos.* He ends the paragraph with a reference to what is perhaps the most important object of all in the world of a chiasticist – a mirror: 'Let us be grateful to the mirror for revealing to us our appearance only' (p. 14).

Three paragraphs later the narrator, even while he is making good progress on his journey, already thinks about the difficulty of returning: 'I cannot conceive how our horses managed to keep their footing, especially the one with the pack, and I dreaded the having to

return almost as much as going forward' (p. 15). Naturally *all*
mountain-climbers dread having to return, since descent in reality is
often more difficult than ascent. But a chiasticist has a double reason
for thinking of return even while going forward. For a chiasticist there
is no going-forward without also a going-backward. Movement is
never unidirectional – it must never be. Of course there is a perfectly
natural explanation in terms of the narrative: Higgs would not want to
have his retreat cut off. But the fear of being unable to return, which
(according to the logic of the narrative and the type of reality it
imitates) it is natural that Higgs should feel, is matched in Butler's
psyche by his strong aversion to the idea of anything existing on its
own, without an inversionary complement.

In the final chapter the narrator envisages a shuttlecock traffic of
slave-ships going 'backwards and forwards as long as there was a
demand for labour in Queensland, or indeed in any other Christian
colony, for the supply of Erewhonians would be unlimited, and they
could be packed closely and fed at a very reasonable cost' (p. 238).

In chapter 7 Higgs gets into trouble over his watch, which gives him
an opportunity to invert Paley's argument from design:

> I remember that when they first found it I had thought of Paley, and
> how he tells us that a savage on seeing a watch would at once
> conclude that it was designed. True, these people were not savages,
> but I none the less felt sure that this was the conclusion they would
> arrive at; and I was thinking what a wonderfully wise man
> Archdeacon Paley must have been, when I was aroused by a look of
> horror and dismay upon the face of the magistrate, a look which
> conveyed to me the impression that he regarded my watch not as
> having been designed, but rather as the designer of himself and of
> the universe; or as at any rate one of the great first causes of all
> things.   (p. 48)

The underlying existential formula, 'Designer is designed and
designed is designer', abolishes the distinction between subject and
object.

In these middle and late chapters of the book the inverted
institutions of the Erewhonians are presented. These institutions are
complementary inversions of normal institutions or concepts; thus
'reason' is complemented with 'unreason' and there are Colleges of
Unreason (pp. 157ff.). Yet it is important to remember that to a
chiasticist it all in the end comes to the same thing, and we are

reminded of this periodically, for instance through the recurrence of opposites oxymoronically brought together: 'So convincing was his reasoning, or unreasoning ...' (p. 65).

Reason and unreason come to the same thing partly because they cannot exist without one another: 'With unreason the case is different. She is the natural complement of reason, without whose existence reason itself were non-existent' (p. 164). If either half of an antithetical duality seems to be unduly neglected, the chiasticist feels he must help it. The Erewhonians help unreason because they think reason is able to fend for herself, while unreason is the underdog:

> Reason might very possibly abolish the double currency; it might even attack the personality of Hope and Justice. Besides, people have such a strong natural bias towards it that they will seek it for themselves and act upon it quite as much as or more than is good for them: there is no need of encouraging reason.   (Ibid.)

Inversion serves to bring into existence necessary antithetical complements. Once these have been brought into existence, inversion is further used to remind us that either half of the created duality has an equal claim. There are always two points of view. If there is a duality 'humans–plants', and humans have opinions on plants, then plants will also, of course, have opinions on humans, as in chapter 23: 'If it seems to us that the plant kills and eats a fly mechanically, may it not seem to the plant that a man must kill and eat a sheep mechanically? (p. 177; cf. also the lilies on Solomon – ch. 27, p. 220).

When Butler created an alternative through inversion he often went to extraordinary lengths of vivid literalization. The vegetarianism of the Erewhonians in chapter 26 makes it normal for them to eat rotten eggs, and this inverted state of affairs is presented in great detail, complete with the 'inspector, who, on being satisfied that they were addled, would label them "Laid not less than three months" from the date, whatever it might happen to be' (p. 209).

Such detailed working-out of inverted practices demonstrates Butler's capacity to imagine antithetical complements to existing things. Nevertheless he supplemented his own power of imagining inversionary variants with a thorough knowledge of existing cases of inversion, and a keen observation of inversionary phenomena in nature and reality. In *Erewhon* Butler as usual reminds the reader of the Orpheus-myth:

the memory of this existence which you are leaving endeavours vainly to return; we say in such a moment, when you clutch at the dream but it eludes your grasp, and you watch it, as Orpheus watched Eurydice, gliding back again into the twilight kingdom ...

(p. 147)

One of Butler's variants of obligatory turning was the type of turning which is done in desperation, as by a rat cornered. In *Erewhon* this type occurs quite literally: 'I felt like a rat caught in a trap, as though I would have turned and bitten at whatever thing was nearest me'

(p. 33).

Inversion as a principle is subservient to dualism, and exists to complete a chiasmus, of which one half is a given. The perfect variety of inversion is multiple inversion, since its inherent alternation highlights dualism. When Butler writes on existing things he may present only one inversion, since his aim is then to complement an existing sequential order with its opposite. But when he writes on imaginary things he frequently prefers a series of inversions, as in 'The series of revolutions on which I shall now briefly touch shows this ...' (ch. 26, p. 206). One name for a series of inversions is 'vacillation', and vacillation, we remember, is in *Erewhon* honoured with almost an entire chapter of its own: chapter 14, 'Mahaina'. The Nosnibor ladies vacillate back and forth between hypocritically accepting the alleged dipsomania of their friend Mahaina, and suggesting indirectly that she does not drink at all but suffers from indigestion.

In Butler's 'palladian' thinking the two extremes, on either side of a different middle, are in the end same or similar. This compulsive mental vision is brought out in many forms, one of them being the idea of 'extremes meeting'. When you go from one to something else, if you only persevere and go far enough you will always – because a chiasticistic universe is circular – sooner or later return to the same or the similar.[24] This is the case in biology, for instance: 'Thus the butterfly lays an egg, which egg can become a caterpillar, which caterpillar can become a chrysalis, which chrysalis can become a butterfly ...' (p. 189).

In chapter 2, when Higgs tries to make the native Chowbok tell him about the range and what is beyond it, the idea of extremes meeting is introduced in the form of the conventional saying that the sublime and the ridiculous are near: 'I am afraid my description will have conveyed only the ridiculous side of his appearance; but the ridiculous and the sublime are near, and grotesque fiendishness of Chowbok's face approached this last, if it did not reach it' (p. 9). Butler pointed out hundreds of cases of extremes meeting which were his own inventions or his own observations, but naturally he was not averse to repeating well-known clichés on the subject either, if they fitted his pattern of thought.

A chiasticist is likely to perceive the three tempora of the past, the present and the future as a case of 'palladianism' (see *Erewhon*, ch. 25) which is his psychological reason for adopting the attitude that nothing ever changes. The reason he will still spend much time muddling out similarities and differences between one time and another is merely technical: like need not follow like *immediately;* different may follow like, like and different may alternate – and in the end everything is both similar and different anyway. A chiasticist finds an absorbing interest in the question of similarity and difference. In chapter 25 of *Erewhon*, an Erewhonian philosopher speculates on similarity: 'The assurance that the future is no arbitrary and changeable thing, but that like futures will invariably follow like presents, is the groundwork on which we lay all our plans – the faith on which we do every conscious action of our lives' (p. 195).

But should like be combined with like, and different with different? Or should like be combined with different and different with like? A chiasticist is never sure, since in the short run like and different are neighbours, even though each case of difference is flanked by two cases of like, and each case of like flanked with two cases of different. Whenever an *aa–bb* formula occurs in Butler's text, it is usually followed fairly quickly by an *ab–ba* formula or a *ba–ab* formula. Chapter 6 opens with Higgs's descent into Erewhon. He begins one of his descriptions of the view with a list that initially combines like with like: 'Nearer beneath me lay ridge behind ridge, outline behind outline ...' (p. 35). This is at a point when he will soon have to put himself in reciprocal relation with the Erewhonians; similar will soon no longer associate with similar alone, but must be brought into contact with different, and different with similar. The description immediately turns chiastic as it continues: 'Nearer beneath me lay ridge behind ridge, outline behind outline, sunlight behind shadow, and shadow behind sunlight ...' (ibid.). In the next paragraph the Erewhonians look at Higgs and he at them: 'They did not run away, but stood stock still, and looked at me from every side, as I at them' (p. 36).

If, as 'palladianism' has it, there is no difference between the extremes on either side of a middle, then it does not matter which you aim for if you want to achieve one; you will achieve it anyway, since both are the same. In *Erewhon,* chapter 24, on the tyranny of the machines, it is said about them that 'they serve that they may rule' (p. 184). 'Serving' and 'ruling' must be the same since they are opposites. Subject and object are also the same: 'So that even now the machines will only serve on condition of being served ...' (p. 185). Negation of the difference between subject and object is further exemplified in chapter 13 in the phrase, 'some coterie that was trying to exalt itself in exalting some one else' (p. 99).

The most important 'which-one' ambiguity in *Erewhon* is the 'unequivocal' (p. 221; note word) saying of the Erewhonian oracle at the end of chapter 27:

> He who sins aught
> Sins more than he ought;
> But he who sins nought
> Has much to be taught.
> Beat or be beaten,
> Eat or be eaten,
> Be killed or kill;
> Choose which you will.   (p. 221)

This passage should be explicated at great length, since it contains a number of important chiasticist ideas, but most of these will be obvious by now. Stronger than most other chiasticist ideas in the passage, however, is perhaps the notion that, since a choice is anyway obligatory (even though it is between 'pest and cholera'), and since killer and killed are really the same, you may as well be the killer. The passage is one of Butler's periodic endorsements of cruelty, and it results from his 'wedge' thinking – the thinking that combines lability and extremism. If it is a little cruel to kill and eat something, then it must be *all* cruel, and one must stop killing and eating altogether; not only animals but plants too, since 'vegetables are only animals under another name' (p. 220). On the other hand, if scruples have been shown to be *a little* absurd then they must be *all* absurd, and if a little cruelty does not matter then no amount of cruelty matters, and cruelty should be wholeheartedly accepted.

Butler mentions inconsistency in his Preface to the second edition (p. xxi), blaming it on the Erewhonians; and also in chapter 13, where in passing he uses the phrase, 'wrong to be out of health that good may come' (p. 103). The firm belief of the chiasticist that it is possible to do evil that good may come (and good that evil may come) is a corollary of the formula that 'Good is evil and evil is good.' If they are the same it means that, no matter which one you aim for, if you achieve it you will also achieve the other.

In 'palladian' thinking the choice between the two extremes is often a choice between pest and cholera. But, if the extremes seem at times fairly impossible, yet to get to the middle, or to stay in it, is more impossible still, as is evident from the imagery of some of the palladian passages in *Erewhon*.

One such variant of palladian thinking occurs in chapter 4, when the narrator reflects that he must either go back or forth: 'To stay where I was would be impossible; I must either go backwards or forwards' (pp. 20–21). Another comes at the very end of the chapter, when Higgs philosophizes that 'Exploring is delightful to look forward to and back upon, but it is not comfortable at the time, unless it be of such an easy nature as not to deserve the name' (p. 25). What is noteworthy in both these instances, as revealing the true anatomy of palladian thinking, is the feeling that, when there is one unit in the middle, and two symmetrical units, one on each side, although it may be difficult to go for either of the extremes, and, in that case, to decide which one, on the other hand staying in the middle is also uncomfortable, impossible, and so on – in fact always in the end in some sense forbidden.

In another palladian image, a boy is pictured as being torn between conscience, on the one hand, and Common Sense and Nature, on the other:

> All the time his health kept on improving, and though he felt sure that he owed this to the beefsteaks, the better he became in body, the more his conscience gave him no rest; two voices were for ever ringing in his ears – the one saying, 'I am Common Sense and Nature; heed me, and I will reward you as I rewarded your fathers before you.' But the other voice said: 'Let not that plausible spirit lure you to your ruin. I am Duty; heed me, and I will reward you as I rewarded your fathers before you.' (Ch. 26, p. 213)

The mind of this boy can be seen as an amphisbaena whose two ends have both decided to go their opposite ways at one and the same time. When your 'staying in the middle' is only the result of the fact that you are dragged in opposite directions by contrary impulses, then staying in the middle must be extremely uncomfortable. If you cannot stay in the middle, and if both extremes are equally bad, then things are hopeless indeed, and the chapter ends with the boy hanging himself.[25]

Butler chose as the motto of *Erewhon* a saying about balance. But his attitude to balance is ambivalent. In the chapter on Mahaina he exemplifies the ridiculous side of balance when inability to choose causes a paralysis of vacillation. The frightening side is exemplified in chapter 15, 'The Musical Banks', in which the action of choosing is likened to 'a leap in the dark': 'Few indeed were those who had the courage to insist on seeing both sides of the question before they committed themselves to what was practically a leap in the dark' (p. 118). To structure reality dualistically into two balanced alternatives is easy enough for the chiasticist, but to go on from there, and make a choice, seems frightening, ridiculous or in some other way negative.

At the end of chapter 10 comes one of Butler's numerous 'alloy' passages making use of the word 'balance' (note that 'balance' in this case means *imbalance* – Butler was fond of some words which are intrinsically ambiguous) and the chiasticist idea of the *via media*.

> For the Erewhonians hold that unalloyed virtue is not a thing to be immoderately indulged in. I was shown more than one case in which the real or supposed virtues of parents were visited upon the children to the third and fourth generation. The straighteners say that the most that can be truly said for virtue is that there is a considerable balance in its favour, and that it is on the whole a good deal better to be on its side than against it; but they urge that there is much pseudo-virtue going about, which is apt to let people in very badly before they find it out. Those men, they say, are best who are not remarkable either for vice or virtue. I told them about Hogarth's idle and industrious apprentices, but they did not seem to think that the industrious apprentice was a very nice person.   (p. 80)

It is strange, by the way, that Butler in his comments on Hogarth's idle and industrious apprentices – a subject which he commented on several times – apparently does not suspect any irony in Hogarth's series. Yet Hogarth can hardly have arranged, for example, the pattern of positions without any intention of irony. At the beginning of the series the two apprentices are well to either side of the picture, but if one superimposes the prints the two antithetical characters move progressively closer to the centre, so that at the end they are both in the middle. There must be some implied comment on the possible actual sameness of seeming antitheses here, one would think. It is strange that Butler, who was a master at creating this type of ambivalence himself, sometimes failed to detect it in others. Equally strange is the parallel fact that Butler, who was himself a master of metaphor, sometimes failed to recognize metaphor in other authors' texts, and often read literally passages which are obviously meant to be read metaphorically.

Metaphor is. the result of an ability to play around with the two principles of similarity and difference. To Butler the interplay of these two principles was enormously important, and his preoccupation with them explains his skill as a metaphorizer. But the fact that he sometimes read metaphoric expressions literally suggests that to Butler similarity and difference meant far more than to those authors who are good metaphorizers and retain control over the device. The interplay of similarity and difference led to many consequences in Butler; metaphor was one result, but the influence did not stop at that.[26]

Occasionally the dark and hopeless 'pest-and-cholera' variety of palladianism is seemingly denied in Butler. In chapter 20 of *Erewhon* it is claimed that there is a bright side as well as a dark: 'The mythology is obviously an unfair and exaggerated representation of life and things; and had its authors been so minded they could have easily drawn a picture which would err as much on the bright side as this does on the dark' (p. 149). Such passages merely prove the rule, i.e. that there always are two sides. If you disregard individual examples and look statistically at the distribution of negative and positive, the crushing majority of palladian passages with a negative content speaks for itself.

The same holds for passages expressing reciprocity, to which we now turn our attention.

Chapter 11, in the later version,[27] opens with a trial in the Personal Bereavement Court. A man is 'accused of having just lost a wife to whom he had been tenderly attached, and who had left him with three little children, of whom the eldest was only three years old' (p. 81). The spouses had loved each other. This reciprocity is, for a change, not expressed through chiasmus, but through a reciprocal pronoun – 'one another' ('the couple had been devoted to one another' – ibid.). Nevertheless I wish to include the example, because the scene is so pregnantly symbolic of values in Butler's world. In his world (except in *Erewhon Revisited*) mutual attachment, particularly within the family, is a crime. Chapter 11 of *Erewhon* is only the literalization of this idea. The chiasticist longs for emotional attachments, particularly reciprocal ones, but feels that if he is caught out in any he will be punished for it.

The chapter deals with trials in an Erewhonian court of law, and, as I have already pointed out, the dualist structure of English law-courts appealed to Butler. The idea of judicial impartiality implies equal willingness to consider either of two possible alternatives. The narrator commends the Erewhonian court for being perfectly 'impartial': 'The evidence for the prosecution was very strong; but I must do the court the justice to observe that the trial was absolutely impartial' (p. 83). Someone reading *Erewhon* for the first time, without having read any other of Butler's books, may be inclined to read comments of this kind as irony, and doubtless there is an ironic dimension to them. But when one becomes more familiar with Butler's psychomorphology one realizes that he could never be wholeheartedly ironic about anything as dear to him as dualism. Thus, for instance, it is clear that not only the Erewhonian courts (with their dual structure of defence and prosecution) but also the Erewhonian Musical Banks (with their dual currency) could not for long remain a target of ironic attack – sooner or later the dualism would seduce Butler into siding with, rather than against, these institutions. Accordingly he tends to be less ironic and more friendly in his late additions than in the original text.

As a dualist Butler could not condemn the 'two distinct commercial systems' and the 'two distinct currencies' (p. 108) which are described in chapter 15 ('The Musical Banks') and his reluctance is particularly apparent in the paragraphs he added in the 1901 edition:

Yet we do something not so very different from this even in England, and as regards the dual commercial system, all countries have, and have had, a law of the land, and also another law, which, though professedly more sacred, has far less effect on their daily life and actions. It seems as though the need for some law over and above, and sometimes even conflicting with, the law of the land, must spring from something that lies deep down in man's nature; indeed, it is hard to think that man could ever have become man at all, but for the gradual evolution of a perception that though this world looms so large when we are in it, it may seem a little thing when we have got away from it.

When man had grown to the perception that in the everlasting Is-and-Is-Not of nature, the world and all that it contains, including man, is at the same time both seen and unseen, he felt the need of two rules of life, one for the seen, and the other for the unseen side of things. For the laws affecting the seen world he claimed the sanction of seen powers; for the unseen (of which he knows nothing save that it exists and is powerful) he appealed to the unseen power (of which, again, he knows nothing save that it exists and is powerful) to which he gives the name of God.   (pp. 118–19)

In the additions the sense is also reinforced that in any situation of choice you cannot really win; that two alternatives may be equally possible but both are equally bad. The man accused of pulmonary consumption cannot really win; he is a victim and a victim is guilty – as guilty as the victimizer. In the words of the judge

'Lastly, I should point out that even though the jury had acquitted you – a supposition that I cannot seriously entertain – I should have felt it my duty to inflict a sentence hardly less severe than that which I must pass at present; for the more you had been found guiltless of the crime imputed to you, the more you would have been found guilty of one hardly less heinous – I mean the crime of having been maligned unjustly.'   (Ch. 11, p. 87)

That to be a victim or a victimizer is really the same is spelt out in the chiastic sentence immediately preceding this paragraph: 'You may say that it is your misfortune to be criminal; I answer that it is your crime to be unfortunate' (ibid.).

On the subject of the attitudes of victims and victimizers in Butler's world, it is worth noting that victims accept their fate:

So was it also with the jury and bystanders; and – most wonderful of all – so was it even with the prisoner. Throughout he seemed fully impressed with the notion that he was being dealt with justly: he saw nothing wanton in his being told by the judge that he was to be punished, not so much as a necessary protection to society (although this was not entirely lost sight of), as because he had not been better born and bred than he was. But this led me to hope that he suffered less than he would have done if he had seen the matter in the same light that I did. And, after all, justice is relative.   (Ch. 12, p. 92)[28]

Chapter 13, which is an addition, is based on the existential formula 'Birth is death and death birth', as are also chapters 18, 19 and 20. Like all other antithetical concepts, birth and death are to a chiasticist really the same thing, and the Erewhonians 'insist that the greater number of those who are commonly said to die, have never yet been born' (p. 97).

These chapters – 18 ('Birth Formulae'), 19 ('The World of the Unborn') and 20 ('What They Mean by It') – should be read very carefully by anyone who wishes to understand Butler's psyche. Chapter 11 was his literalization of the feeling that mutual attachment *is a crime* and liable to be punished as such. The chapters now under consideration are literalizations of the feeling that *it is a crime to have been born.*

But *how* could it be a crime – surely one has no choice in the matter? To be able to shift the blame and create a choice Butler envisages a world of the 'unborn', which the inhabitants voluntarily choose to leave and be born. Butler is able to imagine a world of the 'unborn' because, if the concept 'born' exists, then it must have a negative complement 'unborn'. Once *that* is a given it will be easy to shift the blame from parent to child. (The phrase 'shift the blame' is actually used in the opening paragraph of chapter 18, p. 136.)

There is no mistaking the reality of Butler's feeling that to have been born is an offence. This can be seen even in the vocabulary in which suitable punishments are discussed: 'kill'[29] (p. 138), 'suicide' (p. 142), 'infanticide' (p. 153).

The feeling between parents and children is one of mutual hate. The role of the children is to 'pester' the parents, and life is an endless chain of pestering and being pestered: 'Delude not yourself with thinking that you will be wiser than your parents. You may be an age in advance of those whom you have pestered, but unless you are one of the great ones you will still be an age behind those who will in their turn pester you' (p. 145).

The three chapters are full of examples of inversion, of which I shall not repeat any here, since I have quoted some of them in Chapter 2. But these inversions do not signify that guilt is now all on the side of the parents. The inversions are there in the text only to strengthen the alternative which Butler sees as the weaker, and it is repeatedly spelled out, chiastically, that guilt and the like are equally shared between parents and children: 'It is hard upon the duckling to have been hatched by a hen, but is it not also hard upon the hen to have hatched the duckling?' (ibid.). There is no distinction between active and passive, hatching and being hatched. 'To injure' is the predicate (the palladian middle), but the subject and object (the wings) are the same: 'a painful struggle in which it will be hard to say whether you have suffered most injury, or inflicted it' (ibid.).

Immediately after this comes yet another negative image expressing the idea of the motto of the book, this time calling it 'free will' and likening it to 'fetters':

> 'Remember also, that if you go into the world you will have free will; that you will be obliged to have it; that there is no escaping it; that you will be fettered to it during your whole life, and must on every occasion do that which on the whole seems best to you at any given time, no matter whether you are right or wrong in choosing it. Your mind will be a balance for considerations, and your action will go with the heavier scale. How it shall fall will depend upon the kind of scales which you may have drawn at birth, the bias which they will have obtained by use, and the weight of the immediate considerations. If the scales were good to start with, and if they have not been outrageously tampered with in childhood, and if the combinations into which you enter are average ones, you may come off well; but there are too many "ifs" in this, and with the failure of any of them your misery is assured. Reflect on this, and remember that should the ill come upon you, you will have yourself to thank, for it is your own choice to be born, and there is no compulsion in the matter.'   (pp. 145–6)

At the beginning of chapter 20 the reciprocal 'do-as-you-would-be-done-by' rule is briefly considered as a solutuion to the problem of parent–child relations, only to be immediately rejected:

> yet I firmly believe that the same thing would happen in nine families out of ten if the parents were merely to remember how they felt when they were young, and actually to behave towards their children as they would have had their own parents behave towards themselves. But this, which would appear to be so simple and obvious, seems also to be a thing which not one in a hundred thousand is able to put into practice.   (p. 150)

Four paragraphs later we are back to a normal view of parent–child relations:

> There is no talisman in the word 'parent' which can generate miracles of affection, and I can well believe that my own child might find it less of a calamity to lose both Arowhena and myself when he is six years old, than to find us again when he is sixty – a sentence

which I would not pen did I not feel that by doing so I was giving him something like a hostage, or at any rate putting a weapon into his hands against me, should my selfishness exceed reasonable limits.   (p. 152)

To have parents is a 'calamity'; children need 'weapon[s]' against their parents; and so on. About two pages later Butler recommends that children should learn a trade early, the main boon being that 'they will not press on the parents, nor the parents on them' (p. 154). Parents and children are a burden to one another. Another two pages later, at the end of the chapter, parents and children take turns at flogging each other.[30]

The relations between spouses are hardly any happier than those between parents and children in Butler's world. This may seem to be belied by the development of chapter 21 of *Erewhon,* in which Higgs and Arowhena fall in love, and where their love is even described in a chiasmus expressing reciprocity: 'she said that she believed I loved her as much as she loved me' (p. 159).[31] But even in *Erewhon* Arowhena's love for Higgs is immediately complemented, in the same family, by the hatred of her elder sister Zulora. But, more importantly, in *Erewhon Revisited* we learn that Arowhena has been wasting away in exile, very unhappy. The cause of her ultimate death is ostensibly given as her exile, but is in reality her marriage.

> Early in 1890, I being then home from Oxford (where I had been entered in the preceding year), my mother died; not so much from active illness, as from what was in reality a kind of *maladie du pays.* All along she had felt herself an exile, and though she had borne up wonderfully during my father's long struggle with adversity, she began to break as soon as prosperity had removed the necessity for exertion on her own part.
>
> My father could never divest himself of the feeling that he had wrecked her life by inducing her to share her lot with his own; to say that he was stricken with remorse on losing her is not enough; he had been so stricken almost from the first year of his marriage; on her death he was haunted by the wrong he accused himself – as it seems to me very unjustly – of having done her, for it was neither his fault nor hers – it was Ate.   (p. 7)

Clearly she died from marriage, and Higgs blames himself although only indirectly: the marriage entailed exile for her and he did not kill her directly by marriage but indirectly through a marriage that presupposed exile. If not directly fatal, marriages in the works of a chiasticist *will* usually presuppose something that *is* fatal.

But either party to a crime such as marriage is of course equally guilty – thus Arowhena is guilty too. There is no subject and no object; either partner is both. This is asserted in chapter 1 of *Erewhon Revisited,* in a passage which quotes an Italian proverb:

The Italians say:

> Chi lontano va ammogliare
> Sarà ingannato, o vorrà ingannare.

'If a man goes far afield for a wife, he will be deceived – or means deceiving.' The proverb is as true for women as for men, and my mother was never quite happy in her new surroundings. Wilfully deceived she assuredly was not, but she could not accustom herself to English modes of thought... (pp. 4–5)

There is no compelling reason to introduce this proverb at this point – neither the narrative nor the logic of the exposition demands it. The real reason it is introduced is because it makes out that marriage is about deception, and that deception is mutual, and both parties equally guilty – deceiver and deceived.

Of the chiastic passages expressing reciprocity in *Erewhon* there are hardly any positive ones at all. On the other hand, there is a wealth of negative ones. In chapter 27 the reciprocity is one of reciprocal stupidity: ' "And when we call plants stupid for not understanding our business, how capable do we show ourselves of understanding theirs?" ' (pp. 216–17). At the end of chapter 26 two parties mutually model themselves on each other, only to be mutually fooled: 'And they used him for a model much as he did them' (p. 213). In the anecdote the protagonist does not eat meat because he thinks that *they* (the others) do not, and *they* do not because they think *he* does not. The chapter, we recall, ends with the boy committing suicide.

A chiastic construction at the end of chapter 27 reveals what the poles of an antithesis exist for – reciprocally to 'correct' one another: 'Indeed, I can see no hope for the Erewhonians till they have got to understand that reason uncorrected by instinct is as bad as instinct uncorrected by reason' (p. 222). These negative cases of reciprocal chiastic constructions imply that there is little to be gained from reciprocal relations with others; and in fact the alternative strategy of self-reliance is pointed out in the same paragraph, through the use of the word 'self': 'thinking for themselves'.

In the machine chapters the reciprocal relationship between machines and men is seen in terms of mutual dependence, with all the predictable overtones of slavery and imprisonment and the hateful dependence of one Siamese twin on the other: 'their existence is quite as much a *sine qua non* for his, as his for theirs' (p. 184). In another reciprocal passage, the text proceeds from the chiasmus to present a choice for humans between 'suffering' and slavery:

> it is the machines which act upon man and make him man, as much as man who has acted upon and made the machines; but we must choose between the alternative of undergoing much present suffering, or seeing ourselves gradually superseded by our own creatures, till we rank no higher in comparison with them, than the beasts of the field with ourselves.   (Ch. 25, p. 199)

In chapter 16 ('Arowhena') we may take note of a humorously ridiculous chiastic word-sequence expressing reciprocity: 'whether the stone knew that the man's head was there, or the head the stone' (p. 125). The context is humorously ironic and absurd; the neighbouring sentences make use of such words as 'punishment' and 'death'; and the subject is a *clash* (between a stone and a man's head). The evidence of the chiasticist's doubt about the possibility of reciprocity keeps on accumulating in one way or another, if not in the main point of what is being said then in minor details in passing.

> Thus they have a law that two pieces of matter may not occupy the same space at the same moment, which law is presided over and administered by the gods of time and space jointly, so that if a flying stone and a man's head attempt to outrage these gods, by 'arrogating a right which they do not possess' (for so it is written in one of their books), and to occupy the same space simultaneously, a severe punishment, sometimes even death itself, is sure to follow, without any regard to whether the stone knew that the man's head was there, or the head the stone .... (Ibid.)

Thus the picture gradually becomes fairly clear. In fact, if Butler speaks positively of reciprocity at all in *Erewhon,* he is ironic, as in the Conclusion, when he argues that turning the Erewhonians into slaves would 'be mutually advantageous both to us and them' (p. 238). Butler is probably sincere in his antislavery attitude in this passage and the irony is pure and transparent. What we should note is Butler's choice of tool in his condemnation of slavery. He wanted to sneer at those who defend slavery, and he chose to do it through a vehicle – reciprocity – which he chose all the more readily because subconsciously he regarded it as something contemptible in itself.[32] Nothing is more worthless, empty and hollow than reciprocity in Butler's world at this point in his life; therefore he puts it into the mouth of the advocate of slavery in chapter 29 of *Erewhon*.[33]

Most important of all passages on reciprocity in *Erewhon* is of course the 'lamb-ewe' passage quoted in Chapter 1. As I said there, the symbolic value of that vignette can hardly be overestimated. It goes straight to the heart of the matter of what is problematical in the life of Butler: loneliness, the desire for reciprocity; the frustrated longing for a union of separates, and, above all, unhappy parent–child relationships.

One of Butler's attempts to bring about the fusion of separates is expressed in the word 'cross' – one of his favourites. In *Erewhon*, as elsewhere, the word is used in Butler's idiosyncratic quasi-genetic sense: 'I got very melancholy as these reflections crossed me ...' (p. 30). Here, since it is the negative emotion of melancholy which is his partner in the fusion, the union is allowed to take place. Otherwise Butler normally frustrates quasi-genetic crossing, usually by claiming that the cross is too wide: i.e. that the partners are too different.

Most chapters in *Erewhon* are based on a chiastic existential formula of one kind or another. The machine chapters are based on the formula, 'Machines are men and men machines'; the 'rights-of-animals-and-vegetables' chapters are based on the formula, 'Animals are plants and plants animals'; the 'crime-and-illness' chapters are based on the formula, 'Illness is crime and crime illness.'

To justify such formulae Butler brought in some auxiliary tools of chiastic thinking, of which the most important is his 'wedge' imagery. In chapter 12 we may note a typical occurrence of the wedge-metaphor itself:

> It may be said that the classification was not sufficiently careful, and that the remedies were ill chosen; but it is a hard thing to initiate any reform, and it was necessary to familiarize the public mind with the principle, by inserting the thin end of the wedge first; it is not, therefore, to be wondered at that among so practical a people there

should still be some room for improvement.   (p. 93)

The wedge-metaphor rules that if something has gone a little way it will go all the way, because 'Little is much and much is little.' Where can anyone draw any line? The wedge-rule becomes very important in Butler's scientific works. It underlies his implicit belief that, if something can be shown to be a little true it will be all true (this is usually applied to his own arguments), and that if something can be shown to be a little false it will be all false (usually applied to the arguments of his opponents).

In *Erewhon* it is mostly not the narrator but the various Erewhonian prophets who argue that it is impossible to draw lines. The author of the 'book of machines' argues in chapter 24 that 'the servant glides by imperceptible approaches into the master' (p. 183). 'Servant' and 'master' are extremes on a *continuum,* and Butler's habit of using continua to visualize reality alternates with his habit of committing the crime he condemns: i.e. drawing arbitrary lines and making divisions and classifications. The favourite Butlerian idea of continuity is important because it is related to his use of continua to visualize reality.

'Some one may say,' he continued, "What do you mean by talking about an infinite number of past occasions? When did a rose-seed make itself into a rose-bush on any past occasion?"

'I answer the question with another. "Did the rose-seed ever form part of the identity of the rose-bush on which it grew?" Who can say that it did not? Again I ask: "Was this rose-bush ever linked by all those links that we commonly consider as constituting personal identity, with the seed from which it in its turn grew?" Who can say that it was not?

'Then, if rose-seed number two is a continuation of the personality of its parent rose-bush, and if that rose-bush is a continuation of the personality of the rose-seed from which it sprang, rose-seed number two must also be a continuation of the personality of the earlier rose-seed. And this rose-seed must be a continuation of the personality of the preceding rose-seed – and so back and back *ad infinitum.* Hence it is impossible to deny continued personality between any existing rose-seed and the earliest seed that can be called a rose-seed at all.'   (pp. 218–19)

'Palladian' thinking allows Butler to disregard every second link in the chain of alternation between rose-seed and rose-bush.

The taboo on division and classification leads to doubt about identity. Identity again is dependent on the interplay of the two principles of similarity and difference. Accordingly many of these passages arguing the impossibility of making distinctions deal prominently with similarity and difference. In chapter 26 the Erewhonian prophet points out that there is more similarity than difference between animals and humans:

'Now it cannot be denied that sheep, cattle, deer, birds, and fishes are our fellow-creatures. They differ from us in some respects, but those in which they differ are few and secondary, while those that they have in common with us are many and essential. My friends, if it was wrong of you to kill and eat your fellow-men, it is wrong also to kill and eat fish, flesh, and fowl.'   (pp. 207–8)

In chapter 27 another philosopher argues that plants and animals are similar:

He contended, therefore, that animals and plants were cousins, and would have been seen to be so, all along, if people had not made an arbitrary and unreasonable division between what they chose to call the animal and vegetable kingdoms.   (p. 215)

Further:

Granting that vegetable intelligence at first sight appears to differ materially from animal, yet, he urged, it is like it in the one essential fact that though it has evidently busied itself about matters that are vital to the well-being of the organism that possesses it, it has never shown the slightest tendency to occupy itself with anything else.   (p. 216)

Immediately before this a chiasmus has as usual brought two complementary oppositions into conjunction: 'He therefore connected all, both animal and vegetable development, with intelligence, either spent and now unconscious, or still unspent and conscious ...' (ibid.).

The impossibility of drawing lines, and the creation of conceptual chaos through existential formulae, leads to a state of 'not knowing what is what', and as usual at such points Butler, in *Erewhon* too, quotes his namesake's couplet about knowing what's what:

Apropos of its [a potato's] intelligence, had the writer known Butler he would probably have said –

> He knows what's what, and that's as high,
> As metaphysic wit can fly. (p. 177)

In chapter 5 Butler (through Higgs) makes use of a type of ambiguity which – unfortunately – is rather rare in his prose, i.e. referential ambiguity:

> Moreover, I had set my heart upon making him a real convert to the Christian religion, which he had already embraced outwardly, though I cannot think that it had taken deep root in his impenetrably stupid nature. I used to catechize him by our camp fire, and explain to him the mysteries of the Trinity and of original sin, with which I was myself familiar, having been the grandson of an archdeacon by my mother's side, to say nothing of the fact that my father was a clergyman of the English Church.   (p. 28)

Butler manipulates two grammatical rules in the text so that the 'with which' could refer either to 'original sin' or to 'mysteries'. Ambiguity was in Butler's blood, but, in contrast to Henry James, he seldom put this particular variety to witty uses of this kind, and in fact hardly ever used it at all.

What, in conclusion, could be said to be the most important effect of chiasticism in *Erewhon?*

The most important overall effect of *Erewhon* is to indoctrinate the reader with relativism. To pay much attention to the book's irony and satire *as such* would be a shallow reading, and to deduce any very definite or coherent 'message' or 'programme' would be, I fear, a misreading.[34]

Much of the behaviour of a chiasticist is accounted for by his special philosophy of the word 'no' – the philosophy of negation. The use of 'no' involves the assumption of a duality of 'is' and 'is-not'. To most of us the 'is-not' represents an absence of existence; to a chiasticist, however, it represents a complementary form of existence. A chiasticist feels he has to work out the 'not-actual', the 'not-present', the 'not-real', and so on, even if only to bring 'the actual', the 'present' and the 'real' into proper existence.

Utopian literature would seem to be a highly legitimate genre in which to do this, since usually in this genre it is precisely a matter of working out the 'not-real' and 'not-actual' without therefore quite letting go of the real (in contrast to such a genre as that which we call 'fantasy'). 'U-topia' (no-where) is the negative complement of 'some-where' in a form which is not a void, an absence of existence, but a concept with body and reality, albeit an inverted, complementary, form of reality. In many utopias what is interesting for the reader is not so much what is being said about the utopian society directly, but rather what is indirectly being said about the author's own society. But is this the case in Butler's utopia?

Butler is above all a relativist. The reformer and the relativist do not approach dualism in the same way. The reformer, if he perceives a dualist division, looks for a side with which to align himself; an asymmetry whose champion he can become. If he is an ardent reformer and a committed dualist he will possibly already have a few dualist divisions in residence when he welcomes a new one, and his instinct will be to assimilate all new dualities to the existing ones so that they form a set with the good–bad duality at bottom. To him two plus two makes two.

The relativist, on the other hand, tries to work out all possible combinations of anything. If one possibility seems to be lacking, he will work on it and try to bring it into existence. The reformer cares about that particular variety of the theoretical combinational possibilities which he has chosen, while the relativist is ultimately indifferent to everything except the working out of the relativism itself.

If we accept momentarily, for heuristic purposes, this generalization and the concepts of 'relativist' and 'reformer', it is easy to see that the description of the 'relativist' fits Butler. But how much of the 'reformer' is there in Butler?

The answer, surely, must be, 'Very little.' When we first encounter a work such as *Erewhon,* we may perhaps try to read into the narrative qualities of social or political satire, moralism, reformism, and other manifestations of a programmatic attitude to life that we later recognize are just simply not there – at least not to any noticeable extent, or with any degree of sincerity or consistency. The more we read, the more we realize that what ultimately matters to Butler is only the relativism itself.

Many of Butler's other works, particularly his four books on evolution, are far more deeply imbued with chiasticist relativism than *Erewhon.* But the work in which Butler, for good or bad, most successfully infects the reader with his own mental ambilateralism is without doubt *Erewhon.*

III   *THE WAY OF ALL FLESH*

Let us begin our survey of chiasticism in *The Way of All Flesh* with a closer look at one particular justification of Butler's ambidirectionalism – namely, the philosophy that Ernest calls 'kissing the soil'. In chapter 67 Ernest, making his plans for a career after prison, rejects the idea of clinging to some sort of gentility, and instead decides to fall still lower, hoping for an ultimate rebound:

> He knew his father and mother would object to being cut; they would wish to appear kind and forgiving; they would also dislike having no further power to plague him; but he knew also very well that so long as he and they ran in harness together they would always be pulling one way and he another. He wanted to drop the gentleman and go down into the ranks, beginning on the lowest rung of the ladder, where no one would know of his disgrace or mind it if he did know; his father and mother on the other hand would wish him to clutch on to the fag-end of gentility at a starvation salary and with no prospect of advancement. Ernest had seen enough in Ashpit Place to know that a tailor, if he did not drink and attended to his business, could earn more money than a clerk or a curate, while much less expense by way of show was required of him. The tailor also had more liberty, and a better chance of rising. Ernest resolved at once, as he had fallen so far, to fall still lower – promptly, gracefully and with the idea of rising again, rather than cling to the skirts of respectability which would permit him to exist on sufferance only, and make him pay an utterly extortionate price for an article which he could do better without.
>
> He arrived at this result more quickly than he might otherwise have done through remembering something he had once heard his aunt say about 'kissing the soil'. This had impressed him and stuck by him perhaps by reason of its brevity; when later on he came to know the story of Hercules and Antaeus, he found it one of the very few ancient fables which had a hold over him – his chiefest debt to classical literature. His aunt had wanted him to learn carpentering, as a means of kissing the soil should his Hercules ever throw him. It was too late for this now – or he thought it was – but the mode of carrying out his aunt's idea was a detail; there were a hundred ways of kissing the soil besides becoming a carpenter.   (p. 291)

Just like the amphisbaena, Butler's mind too is equally willing to crawl in either of two opposite directions, and, in the search for some philosophical justification for this perverse ambidirectionalist attitude, the idea of 'kissing the soil' comes in handy.

Through habit, education and intrinsic necessity human beings acquire all kinds of set asymmetric preferences and leanings. Wherever we are on a scale of good-to-bad, for instance, we will naturally try to move towards the good. Wilfully to go towards the bad is perverse. Even if we have only small hopes of changing our positions and circumstances, still every change for the better, no matter how minute, is welcome, and every change for the worse unwelcome, we think.

The chiasticist, however, wishing to be able to go in either of two opposite directions, will seize on any philosophical excuse to see both directions as similar or equally good. Images of a 'rebound' were dear to Butler. Going in one direction presents itself to his imagination in terms of an elastic band being stretched. Built into the idea of 'going in one direction' is the concomitant idea of an obligatory return, and there is an additional rule to the effect that, the further and faster you go, the swifter and more certain will be your return. Therefore, if you are on your way towards the bad, as Ernest is in chapter 67, it is not a clever idea to cling to the rudiments of good you have left; rather you should look in the other direction and go for the bad as fast as you can. It is obligatory that you should go to the extreme; therefore, the sooner you go, and get it over with, the better. Also, if you go there with some speed, you can use the extreme as a springboard and rebound back into the good – to a position further up the scale than you would have been in had you tried to cling to the place where you were.

Butler's favourite verb 'to pitchfork' expresses perhaps better than anything else his conviction that there is no such thing as unidirectionalism; no going without a return.

In the quotation above, the narrator says that the story of Hercules and Antaeus had made a deep impression on Ernest ('he found it one of the very few ancient fables which had a hold over him – his chiefest debt to classical literature'). The myth gave Ernest a rationale for his ambidirectionalism. Antaeus's strength was magically restored to him every time he touched his mother, Earth. Myths such as this provide an external reason to believe that going to an extreme, even the wrong one, will bring a reward.

The real reason for the wild rushes of the chiasticist from extreme to extreme is probably mirror-image symmetry itself. The symmetric alternative of an extreme on a scale is the opposite extreme, not the middle, or anywhere in between. If you have to leave one extreme, the only acceptable alternative is the symmetric position at the other end. Thus mirror-image symmetry defines the concept of 'alternative' position in very strict terms. In chapter 3 of *The Way of All Flesh*, the narrator describes how the children 'passed, therefore, in a short time from extreme depression to a no less extreme exultation' (p. 43). There is no halting in any middle position, whether an absolute middle or an imperfect middle. It is a question of either *one* extreme position, or its mirror-image alternative.

There are further traces of the doctrine of 'kissing the soil' in *The Way of All Flesh*, apart from its appearance in chapter 67. In chapter 35 Aunt Alethea, making her will, feels confident that Ernest will have to reach bottom before he can start climbing. Therefore she instructs Overton to hold the money in trust until Ernest is twenty-eight.

> 'Let him make his mistakes', she said, 'upon the money his grandfather left him. I am no prophet, but even I can see that it will take that boy many years to see things as his neighbours see them. He will get no help from his father and mother, who would never forgive him for his good luck if I left him the money outright; I daresay I am wrong, but I think he will have to lose the greater part or all of what he has, before he will know how to keep what he will get from me.'
>
> (p. 149)

Butler's mental extremism and his horror of the middle ground mean that in his world things have to be done in order. It does not matter whether they are done beginning-to-end or end-to-beginning, but they must be done extreme-to-extreme. You must not turn before you have reached the extreme. Butler's scientific books are full of observations on the impossibility of starting anywhere else than at the extremes. If a sparrow is disturbed halfway through building its nest, it has to start all over again from the beginning. If a musician is interrupted in the middle of a performance, he often has to start from the beginning in order to remember, and so on. The penalties for not doing things extreme-to-extreme are often very severe in Butler's world.

There is a passage with such a scientific variety of the 'kissing-the-soil' philosophy in chapter 81 of *The Way of All Flesh*, where Ernest is likened to a caterpillar that has to do his work strictly in the order beginning-to-end.

> 'It seems to me', he said once, 'that I am like one of those caterpillars which, if they have been interrupted in making their hammock, must

begin again from the beginning. So long as I went back a long way down in the social scale I got on all right, and should have made money but for Ellen; when I try to take up the work at a higher stage I fail completely.' I do not know whether the analogy holds good or not, but I am sure Ernest's instinct was right in telling him that after a heavy fall he had better begin life again at a very low stage, and as I have just said, I would have let him go back to his shop if I had not known what I did. (pp. 364–5)

From the chiasticist's habit of 'touching the ground' let us now move on to his habit of 'setting himself the other way'.

The emotional enantiomorphism of the chiasticist is reflected in many ways in the behaviour of Ernest in *The Way of All Flesh*. At the end of chapter 30 we learn that Ernest, in forming friendships with the other boys at school, 'sets himself the other way', even though it makes him unhappy: 'He did not like the boys whom he thought like himself. His heroes were strong and vigorous, and the less they inclined towards him the more he worshipped them' (p. 129). This habit of 'setting oneself the other way' in choosing one's friends is one of Ernest's many attempts to create symmetry in the relationship between himself and the world. What he is looking for in his heroes is his own enantiomorph. He is a Tweedledum without a Tweedledee, a Hanky without a Panky, or a Siamese twin separated from his other half.[35]

Tenniel drew the Tweedle twins as enantiomorphs. Twin pairs such as they are popular in literature and art because of symmetry – in such pairs we have come as close as we can to the idea of seeing two human beings as each other's mirror-images.

It seems, by the way, that physically Siamese twins are each other's enantiomorphs. One will be right-handed; the other, it seems, left-handed. The whorl of hair goes one way on the head of one and the other way on the head of the other, and so on. Finger-prints are similar, but inverted. The asymmetric inner organs are arranged in bilateral symmetry, one of the twins having the organs on the other side (this phenomenon is known as *situs inversus*). Thus one of the twins will have his heart on the right and his liver on the left, contrary to what is normal and contrary to what is the case in the other twin.[36]

Intrigued by this kind of symmetry, authors and artists have tried to extend the symmetry from the sphere of the physical to other areas, such as emotion and language. It is interesting to see what conventions authors have created to express the idea of the symmetry of twin pairs in language. One fairly common convention is to have the pair share sentences: i.e. one twin begins a sentence and the other completes it. This device is meant to show the similarity of the twins: i.e. that they are identical to the extent of being able to finish each other's sentences.[37] But some authors and artists, realizing that not only similarity but inversion too is needed for symmetry, have made their twin characters not only complete or repeat each other's utterances but invert them too. Such inversions are usually spoonerisms, metatheses or chiastic puns. A typical example are the two blundering detectives in the Tintin comics by Hergé. One of the detectives usually repeats what the other has just said, but with some inversion so that the result is a spoonerism or a chiastic pun. The author has instinctively felt – quite correctly – that spoonerisms, metatheses and chiastic puns create linguistic forms of symmetry.

It is symptomatic that Butler invented such a twin pair as Hanky and Panky in *Erewhon Revisited*. It is also instructive to note what he saw as constituting enantiomorphism in the pair. Apart from obvious superficial details such as the fact that one of the professors wears his European costume reversed and the other the normal way, there are also attempts to create what Butler apparently thought of as emotional enantiomorphism.

Hanky and Panky are each other's 'emotional' enantiomorphs in several ways. The two professors are different, yet stick together. They are often set against one another in purpose and action, and perverse rules of cause and effect govern their intercourse – thus Panky only encourages Hanky's outspokenness by trying to check it, for instance.

The complexities of the relationship between Hanky and Panky reveal that enantiomorphism between two individuals was a multifaceted phenomenon for Butler, and we may be sure that it influences Butler's behaviour and his ideas in all kinds of subtle ways and on all kinds of unlikely occasions. Someone who has read no other work by Butler than *The Authoress of the Odyssey* would probably find it a fantastic and improbable suggestion that Butler's theory of the female authorship of the *Odyssey* is caused by his wish to bring the *Iliad* and the *Odyssey* into a symmetrical relationship. But after reading all of Butler's works, and some reflection on such phenomena as the Hanky–Panky pair, the suggestion is far from fantastic.

Ernest Pontifex in *The Way of All Flesh* is looking for someone who could function as his Siamese twin brother in an 'emotional' sense. Butler and Ernest are not quite certain what such emotional enantiomorphism would entail, but obviously the missing half would have to be different, and so they settle for people who are different from themselves; even hostile towards themselves. Such people can become human mirrors, allowing oneself to see oneself clearly.

The longing for an external other half of the self is expressed explicitly in chapter 64 when Ernest realizes that he hates being a clergyman and wonders why he had not discovered this earlier: 'I suppose people almost always want something external to themselves, to reveal to them their own likes and dislikes' (pp. 279–80). There are many ramifications of the split-person theme, and the longing for a reflector outside oneself, in *The Way of All Flesh*. A rather interesting case is the beginning of chapter 56, which links the longing for an outside influence with the 'Buridan's-ass' syndrome, suggesting that indecision stems from the lack of an outside influencing force:

> By and by a subtle, indefinable *malaise* began to take possession of him. I once saw a very young foal trying to eat some most objectionable refuse, and unable to make up its mind whether it was good or no. Clearly it wanted to be told. If its mother had seen what it was doing she would have set it right in a moment, and as soon as ever it had been told that what it was eating was filth, the foal would have recognized it and never have wanted to be told again; but the foal could not settle the matter for itself, or make up its mind whether it liked what it was trying to eat or no, without assistance from without. I suppose it would have come to do so by and by, but it was wasting time and trouble, which a single look from its mother would have saved, just as wort will in time ferment of itself, but will ferment much more quickly if a little yeast be added to it. In the matter of knowing what gives us pleasure we are all like wort, and if unaided from without can only ferment slowly and toilsomely.
>
> (p. 250)

In the next paragraph there is a definite change of tack:

> My unhappy hero about this time was very much like the foal, or rather he felt much what the foal would have felt if its mother and all the other grown-up horses in the field had vowed that what it was eating was the most excellent and nutritious food to be found anywhere. He was so anxious to do what was right, and so ready to believe that every one knew better than himself, that he never ventured to admit to himself that he might be all the while on a

hopelessly wrong tack. It did not occur to him that there might be a blunder anywhere, much less did it occur to him to try and find out where the blunder was. Nevertheless he became daily more full of *malaise*, and daily, only he knew it not, more ripe for an explosion should a spark fall upon him.   (Ibid.)

The passage, significantly, is once again about a parent–offspring relationship, and Butler is reminded that parents *do* exist; *they* can be used as a reflector; *they* can reveal one to oneself. But how? Butler's answer in this paragraph, as so often elsewhere, is to grope around for the possibility of a rule of permanent inversion (cf. Ch. 2). Maybe, by inverting everything the grown-ups do and say, a rule for one's own behaviour can be found, he muses.

Though the idea of permanent inversion is really self-created, Butler and Ernest, through a typical case of the kind of chiastic sophistry with which we have become familiar, shift the initiative to the parent-generation, so that the permanency of the clash between generations is seen to be all the doing of one side. In chapter 86 the constant enmity between Theobald and Ernest is reported as if initiated solely by Theobald:

He [Ernest] felt that there were only three people in the world who joined insincerely in the tribute of applause [of his father's memory], and these were the very three who could least show their want of sympathy. I mean Joey, Charlotte, and himself. He felt bitter against himself for being of a mind with either Joey or Charlotte upon any subject, and thankful that he must conceal his being so as far as possible, not because of anything his father had done to him – these grievances were too old to be remembered now – but because he would never allow him to feel towards him as he was always trying to feel. As long as communication was confined to the merest commonplace all went well, but if these were departed from ever such a little he invariably felt that his father's instincts showed themselves in immediate opposition to his own. When he was attacked his father laid whatever stress was possible on everything which his opponents said. If he met with any check his father was clearly pleased. What the old doctor had said about Theobald's speaking ill of no man was perfectly true as regards others than himself, but he knew very well that no one had injured his reputatiuon in a quiet way, so far as he dared to do, more than his own father. This is a very common case and a very natural one. It often happens that if the son is right, the father is wrong, and the father is not going to have this if he can help it.   (pp. 403–4)

Despite the fact that Theobald is made out to be the initiator, it is obvious even in this quote that what is more important than the question of initiatorship is simply the fact of antitheticality itself. Note, in this quotation, how Ernest regrets being of the same mind with Joey and Charlotte. Joey and Charlotte being against his father, if *he* wants to be against his father it means he must be *with* them. He regrets this because it destroys his chance of achieving a perfect antithetical relationship with everyone.[38]

I have already pointed out in Chapter 1 that the distinction between contraries and contradictories in traditional logic helps one understand how the mind of a chiasticist works. Of two contrary propositions, both cannot be true but both can be false. Thus from the truth of one the falsity of the other can be inferred, but from the falsity of one the truth of the other can not be inferred. Of two contradictory propositions both cannot be true and both cannot be false; therefore from the truth of one the falsity of the other can be inferred and from the falsity of one the truth of the other can be inferred.

As we readily recognize, this distinction depends on the difference between asymmetry and symmetry. The former category (contraries) concerns asymmetric, unidirectional relations. The latter category (contradictories) concerns symmetric, ambidirectional relations. Since the world of the chiasticist is governed by symmetry, it follows that contraries are normally lacking in his thinking. To a chiasticist all relations tend to be contradictories.

The domain of the fallacy of seeing contraries as contradictories should be enlarged to cover all the varieties of chiastic fallacies of logic that arise from the misuse of symmetry. It should cover the thinking behind such a sentence as 'If the son is right, the father is wrong' (cf. quotation), and explain why it is regarded as a given that, if the son is right, the father must be wrong – in other words, why, if two pairs (father and son; right and wrong) are mentioned, they must always be arranged crosswise in chiastic symmetry.

There are many passages in *The Way of All Flesh* which remind us directly that an important function of antithesis and inversion is to create bilateral symmetry between the chiasticist (in this case Ernest) and his environment, by making the two each other's mirror images. It is not only in his relationship with his father that Ernest feels compelled to 'set himself the other way'. The same is true of his attitude to prevalent doctrines and fashions – for instance, in religion. In chapter 50 Ernest has become infatuated with ultra-Evangelicalism, at a time when fashion is moving towards Catholicism:

> Theobald hated the Church of Rome, but he hated dissenters too, for he found them as a general rule troublesome people to deal with; he always found people who did not agree with him troublesome to deal with: besides, they set up for knowing as much as he did; nevertheless if he had been let alone he would have leaned towards them rather than towards the High Church party. The neighbouring clergy, however, would not let him alone. One by one they had come under the influence, directly or indirectly, of the Oxford movement which had begun twenty years earlier. It was surprising how many practices he now tolerated which in his youth he would have considered Popish; he knew very well therefore which way things were going in Church matters, and saw that *as usual Ernest was setting himself the other way*. The opportunity for telling his son that he was a fool was too favourable not to be embraced, and Theobald was not slow to embrace it.   (p. 228; emphasis added)

This quotation is again characteristic in that it shows once again that Ernest's 'perversity', even when it concerns matters such as his religious attitudes, is somehow mixed up with his relationship with his father. If we surmise that Ernest's (and Butler's) 'perversity', i.e. his 'setting himself the other way', in matters of religion, science, politics, and so on, was a carry-over from his habit of 'setting himself the other way' in relation to his father, this passage could be regarded as a place where the seam shows.

It is a psychological necessity to Ernest to 'set himself the other way'. In fact, Theobald's attitude in the passage just quoted is not presented as being utterly unreasonable. There are other people apart from Theobald who comment on Ernest's perversity. At the beginning of chapter 54 his friends pass similar judgement on him: 'This move on Ernest's part was variously commented upon by his friends, the general opinion being that it was just like Pontifex, who was sure to do something unusual wherever he went ...' (p. 241). A little later we learn that Ernest's rector does not like Ernest's wish to turn everything 'topsy-turvy':

> The present London Rectors are hopeless people to deal with. My own is one of the best of them, but the moment Pryer and I show

signs of wanting to attack an evil in a way not recognized by routine, or of remedying anything about which no outcry has been made, we are met with, 'I cannot think what you mean by all this disturbance; nobody else among the clergy sees these things, and I have no wish to be the first to begin turning everything topsy-turvy.' And then people call him a sensible man. I have no patience with them.

(pp. 242–3)

Ernest's habit of 'setting himself the other way' is meant to ease into existence emotional enantiomorphism – a symmetric relationship between Ernest and some other character or phenomenon. This is emotional enantiomorphism when you yourself take the initiative in trying to bring it into existence. But naturally the initiative can be taken by the outside world too. Then it is Ernest's duty to respond. As the concept of emotional enantiomorphism explains Ernest's habit of 'setting himself the other way', so it also explains much of his zigzagging. 'Setting oneself the other way' results from active attempts to bring symmetry of personal relationship into existence; zigzagging results from Ernest's willingness to respond, and do his share of the work, if the outside world approaches him in a way which he interprets as a proposal for the establishment of a symmetrical relationship. His ideas of precisely what kind of response is demanded of oneself on such occasions are hazy and vague, but he is always willing to respond.

In his snipe-like zigzagging Ernest is always willing to be influenced even if it means a complete reversal. Before an occurrence of the snipe-image in chapter 45 we are told that Ernest was 'a good deal on the look-out for cants that he could catch and apply in season, and might have done himself some mischief thus if he had not been ready to throw over any cant as soon as he had come across another more nearly to his fancy' (p. 199; the snipe-image reappears in chs. 51 and 59).

Willingness to turn is clearly a positive thing in *The Way of All Flesh*, and it is therefore fitting that a eulogy on the subject, in chapter 35, is given to Alethea who preaches quite a sermon against permanency and stability, and in favour of zigzagging and turning:

When all this had been done she became more easy in her mind. She talked principally about her nephew. 'Don't scold him,' she said, 'if he is volatile, and continually takes things up only to throw them down again. How can he find out his strength or weakness otherwise? A man's profession', she said, and here she gave one of her wicked little laughs, 'is not like his wife, which he must take once for all, for better for worse, without proof beforehand. Let him go here and there, and learn his truest liking by finding out what, after all, he catches himself turning to most habitually – then let him stick to this; but I daresay Ernest will be forty or five and forty before he settles down. Then all his previous infidelities will work together to him for good if he is the boy I hope he is.' (pp. 150–1)

We can now see the connection between emotional enantiomorph- ism and zigzagging. There is an extraordinary amount of zigzagging in *The Way of All Flesh*. It is found in the twists and turns of the plot. It is found in the plots of the micro-narratives. The inversions and inversions of inversions in the story (ch. 55) of Ernest's and Pryer's speculations on the stock-market present a miniature variant of the zigzagging on the macro-level. Zigzagging is further found in the important snipe-image. That zigzagging is intimately connected with emotional enantiomorphism becomes obvious if we consider chapter 64, in which, it is interesting to note, the sentence, already quoted, about people always wanting something external to reveal their own likes and dislikes, comes immediately before a summary of Ernest's zigzaggings so far.

It puzzled him, however, that he should not have known how much he had hated being a clergyman till now. He knew that he did not particularly like it, but if anyone had asked him whether he actually hated it, he would have answered no. I suppose people almost always want something external to themselves, to reveal to them their own likes and dislikes. Our most assured likings have for the most part been arrived at neither by introspection nor by any process of conscious reasoning, but by the bounding forth of the heart to welcome the gospel proclaimed to it by another. We hear some say that such and such a thing is thus or thus, and in a moment the train that has been laid within us, but whose presence we knew not, flashes into consciousness and perception.
Only a year ago he had bounded forth to welcome Mr Hawke's sermon; since then he had bounded after a College of Spiritual Pathology; now he was in full cry after rationalism pure and simple; how could he be sure that his present state of mind would be more lasting than his previous ones? He could not be certain, but he felt as though he were now on firmer ground than he had ever been on before, and no matter how fleeting his present opinions might prove to be, he could not but act according to them till he saw reason to

change them. How impossible, he reflected, it would have been for him to do this, if he had remained surrounded by people like his father and mother, or Pryer and Pryer's friends, and his rector. (pp. 279–80)

The language of the first paragraph of this quotation is highly revealing. In the mind of a chiasticist quiet rumination and consistency of purpose alternate with violent flashes of insight and sudden turns which are produced by something outside the self. These responses to outside stimuli become so violent, sudden and total because the chiasticist's longing for emotional enantiomorphism has prepared the ground for them and undermined all consistency. The chiasticist may try very hard to stick to a course, but he has a traitor at the back door of his mind, i.e. the longing to achieve emotional enantiomorphism by responding to outside stimuli, and the more he tries to ward off new, contrary impulses, the more total, sudden and violent is his defeat when he gives in.[39]

It is possible to see a connection not only between emotional enantiomorphism and zigzagging but also between emotional enantiomorphism and Butler's yin-and-yang philosophy. The chiasticistic belief that in anything there always exists a little quantity of its own opposite can be seen as the chiasticist giving his pledge that, although he may now be seen to go almost totally for one out of two alternatives, the little bit of yin that he leaves in yang (or *vice-versa*) is the hostage which guarantees that he will be true to a chiasticist's promise of being always willing to turn. Through the yin-and-yang philosophy the chiasticist signals his never-ending willingness to respond, if the outside world should happen to issue an invitation for him to do so. It is symbolic that *The Way of All Flesh* ends with a passage preaching the yin-and-yang philosophy. In the last paragraph of the text we are told that Ernest now makes a habit of periodically inverting his beliefs, for purposes of relief, and as an antidote to the danger of consistency and permanency:

Such is my friend's latest development. He would not, it is true, run much chance at present of trying to found a College of Spiritual Pathology, but I must leave the reader to determine whether there is not a strong family likeness between the Ernest of the College of Spiritual Pathology and the Ernest who will insist on addressing the next generation rather than his own. He says he trusts that there is not, and takes the sacrament duly once a year as a sop to Nemesis lest he should again feel strongly upon any subject. It rather fatigues him, but 'no man's opinions', he sometimes says, 'can be worth holding unless he knows how to deny them easily and gracefully upon occasion in the cause of charity'.   (p. 410)

A few words on narcissism may be called for at this point. It is important to realize that the chiasticist's willingness to respond (so as to create emotional enantiomorphism) is not in conflict with narcissism. When a chiasticist longs for something outside the self, this does not really mean that he wants to get away from the self, since the outside influence he longs for is primarily a reflector – a mirror. The longing for something outside the self in this form is in itself narcissistic.

Studying narcissism in *The Way of All Flesh,* we should not restrict our examples to those obvious cases that we find on the surface such as Christina's reveries. Narcissistic ideas influence the narrator's (and Butler's) thinking in subtle ways.

The Christina episodes do show, however, in a drastic way, how superior the reflected self is to any other partner. In chapter 29 Christina and Theobald, travelling home in a coach after visiting Ernest at Rockborough, do not speak to each other, but both nevertheless carry on lengthy conversations – with themselves: 'Though they spoke not to one another, there was one nearer to each of them with whom they could converse freely. "I hope," said Theobald to himself, "I hope he'll work – or else that Skinner will make him. I don't like Skinner, I never did ..." ' (p. 122; see rest of chapter). In chapter 34, after one of Christina's usual reveries, the narrator comments, 'The advantage of doing one's praising for oneself is that one can lay it on so thick and exactly in the right places' (p. 145).

At the end of *The Way of All Flesh* Ernest is in 'a very solitary position', but it is the role that he claims suits him. Being very solitary is not perhaps only a curse to a chiasticist. If he needs other people mainly as reflectors in order to see himself clearly, perhaps having only enemies does not matter all that much.

I could see the publisher, who ought to know, had lost all faith in Ernest's literary position, and looked upon him as a man whose failure was all the more hopeless for the fact of his having once made a *coup.* 'He is in a very solitary position, Mr Overton', continued the publisher. 'He has formed no alliances, and has made enemies not only of the religious world but of the literary and scientific brotherhood as well. This will not do nowadays. If a man wishes to get on he must belong to a set, and Mr Pontifex belongs to no set – not even to a club.'

I replied, 'Mr Pontifex is the exact likeness of Othello, but with a difference – he hates not wisely but too well. He would dislike the literary and scientific swells if he were to come to know them and they him...' (p. 409)

As readers we are not sure whether Ernest has been the victim of adverse circumstances, or whether he has in fact worked himself into precisely the position he wanted, or both of these.

Before going on to a review of some passages expressing reciprocity in *The Way of All Flesh,* let us briefly note that Ernest's propensity for 'turning' is shared by other actors in the novel. There are many examples of obligatory 'toppling-over' reversals in the novel. If the weak are pressed hard enough, or long enough, they will in the end turn, like a rat cornered. In the early and middle part of *The Way of All Flesh* Ernest is pictured as utterly weak and defenceless, but even Ernest feels an instinct to turn when pressed beyond endurance.

'You may imagine how shocked I was when I discovered that the watch had been brought for sale by that miserable woman Ellen' – here Ernest's heart hardened a little, and he felt as near an approach to an instinct to turn as one so defenceless could be expected to feel; his father quickly perceived this and continued, 'who was turned out of this house in circumstances which I will not pollute your ears by more particularly describing.' (Ch. 41, p. 178)

In chapter 43 Dr Skinner turns on Ernest's father:

This infamy was more than he could own to, and he kept his counsel concerning it. Fortunately he was safe in doing so, for Dr Skinner, pedant and more than pedant though he was, had still just sense enough to turn on Theobald in the matter of the school list.

(p. 188)

Immediately after this we are told about another turn of opinion, concerning the attitude of the other boys towards Ernest:

Ernest got off with the head boys easier than he expected. It was admitted that the offence, heinous though it was, had been committed under extenuating circumstances; the frankness with which the culprit had confessed all, his evidently unfeigned remorse, and the fury with which Dr Skinner was pursuing him tended to bring about a reaction in his favour, as though he had been more sinned against than sinning.   (Ibid.)

A paragraph later Ernest feels 'that he had arrived at one of the great turning points of his life'.

In chapter 83 there is a sketch of the progressive changes within the Church, from Evangelicalism towards High Church practices. Theobald used to preach in his master's gown, but exchanges it for a surplice. Charlotte and Christina prevail on Theobald to allow the canticles to be sung. Then the 'Glory be to the Father' is to be chanted instead of spoken. Then Charlotte observes that 'Glory be to the Father' should really be 'Gloria'. When Theobald goes away for a long holiday a High-Church clergyman takes his place, and on returning Theobald finds that whole psalms are being chanted as well as the Glorias. During Theobald's absence Mrs Goodhew and old Miss Wright have taken to 'turning towards the east' while repeating the Belief. Charlotte convinces Theobald that the 'Belief' should not be called that but the 'Creed'.

Thus the thing is taken further and further. But finally the 'toppling-over' moment occurs:

So Mrs Goodhew and old Miss Wright continued to turn to the east during the time the Creed was said, and by and by others followed their example, and ere long the few who had stood out yielded and turned eastward too; and then Theobald made as though he had thought it all very right and proper from the first, but like it he did not. By and by Charlotte tried to make him say 'Alleluia' instead of 'Hallelujah', but this was going too far, and Theobald turned, and she got frightened and ran away.   (p. 383)

A little later the narrator speculates in the possibility of 'the toppling over of the whole system' (p. 384).

Things will ultimately topple over even without outside help, but when an individual's latent willingness to turn is combined with an outside influence the reasons are doubled.

We shall now proceed to examine a few passages in *The Way of All Flesh* expressing reciprocity, but not dealt with in Chapter 2. In reading these we may still keep the concept of emotional enantiomorphism in mind. With such examples as Hanky and Panky, and Ernest's habit of 'setting himself the other way', emotional enantiomorphism is obvious. But, if we try to extend its use and apply it to increasingly complex phenomena of reciprocity, the concept becomes gradually more diluted and its usefulness decreases. But, although the applicability of the concept diminishes, still the various features of chiasticism are all interconnected and probably there is an overlap between Ernest's and Butler's emotional enantiomorphism and the chiasticist's attitude to reciprocity.

The chiasticist's wish to use others to reflect his own self, and his corresponding willingness to be a reflector, should naturally result in reciprocity. Ernest's willingness to be reflected is repeatedly brought up in *The Way of All Flesh* – for instance, in chapter 32:

> The boy had plenty of prattle in him when he was not snubbed, and Alethea encouraged him to chatter about whatever came uppermost. *He was always ready to trust anyone who was kind to him;* it took many years to make him reasonably wary in this respect – if indeed, as I sometimes doubt, he ever will be as wary as he ought to be – and in a short time he had quite dissociated his aunt from his papa and mamma and the rest, with whom his instinct told him he should be on his guard   (p. 135; emphasis added)

in chapter 51: 'Pryer, in fact, approved of him sufficiently to treat him civilly, and Ernest was immediately won by anyone who did this' (p. 231); and in chapter 63: 'the readiness the boy had shown to love anything that would be good enough to let him' (p. 274). The last example is made all the more pathetic by the context (see the whole paragraph, which begins with the narrator in a 'Buridan's-ass' position: 'Never do I remember to have halted more between two opinions than on my journey to Battersby upon this unhappy errand').

Ernest is not only willing to be a reflector; he is sometimes said to be compulsively anxious to be one. If he thinks he has been guilty of a failure to reflect he is conscience-stricken to an absurd degree (or at least Butler says he is). Compare chapter 77, and Ernest's separation from Ellen:

> Then came the odious task of getting rid of their unhappy mother. Ernest's heart smote him at the notion of the shock the break-up would be to her. He was always thinking that people had a claim upon him for some inestimable service they had rendered him, or for

some irreparable mischief done to them by himself; the case however was so clear, that Ernest's scruples did not offer seious resistance.   (p. 342)

At the same time as there are innumerable chiastic passages expressing reciprocity in Butler's works, there are also the familiar references to Ishmaels and other outcasts. How is this contradiction to be explained? On the one hand, Butler and his characters long for relationships with others; yet it is obvious that much of Butler's isolation, and the isolation of his characters, is self-sought. Doubtless some of Butler's bragging about his solitary position is sour-grapes-type rationalization or whistling in the dark. When, at the beginning of chapter 84, Ernest talks about his solitary Ishmael-like position, the stress is on the vulnerability of anyone who enters into relationships, and how isolation removes the danger of being wounded:

On our way to town Ernest broached his plans for spending the next year or two. I wanted him to try and get more into society again, but he brushed this aside at once as the very last thing he had a fancy for. For society indeed of all sorts, except of course that of a few intimate friends, he had an unconquerable aversion. 'I always did hate those people,' he said, 'and they always have hated and always will hate me. I am an Ishmael by instinct as much as by accident of circumstances, but if I keep out of society I shall be less vulnerable than Ishmaels generally are. The moment a man goes into society, he becomes vulnerable all round.'   (pp. 386–7)

In the end everything seems to come back to Butler's sensitivity. Relationships with other people can lead to situations in which one is hurt; therefore it is safest to stick to mirror reflections – they are predictable.

It will be remembered that, in Chapter 2, most of the quoted passages from *The Way of All Flesh* expressing reciprocity were negative. The fact that they are there in Butler's text should be interpreted as proof of the chiasticist's longing for relationships with others; the fact that they are negative should be interpreted as evidence of the chiasticist's doubts that such reciprocal relationships could really come into existence, and be happy ones. The only reciprocity that Ernest is shown as coming near to achieving is reciprocity of misfortune. At the beginning of chapter 61 a form of symmetry is almost achieved in the complementary ruining of characters:

> Miss Snow's charms had ruined – or would have done so but for an accident – his moral character. As for Miss Maitland, he had done his best to ruin hers, and had damaged himself gravely and irretrievably in consequence. The only lodger who had done him no harm was the bellows-mender, whom he had not visited. (pp. 266–7)

As others try to ruin his moral character, so Ernest tries to ruin the moral character of others.

The following example conveniently sums up the discussion so far by mixing most of the ingredients one expects:

> Sometimes, like all whose minds are active, Ernest overworks himself, and then occasionally he has fierce and reproachful encounters with Dr Skinner or Theobald in his sleep – but beyond this neither of these two worthies can now molest him further.
>
> To myself he has been a son and more than a son; at times I am half afraid – as for example when I talk to him about his books – that I may have been to him more like a father than I ought; if I have, I trust he has forgiven me.   (p. 408)

In this passage we note that Ernest has nightmares quite literally about personal relationships. Of the two partners mentioned, one is his father and the other a father-figure. As the passage continues there is the joke which inverts the usual sense of 'being like a father to someone'. In this passage reciprocity is connected with sensitivity; fear of all personal relationships grows out of fear of the father–son relationship; and Butler's aggressive humour (particularly his use of inversion) is connected with all of these.

The 'willingness to respond' and 'willingness to be influenced', even if it means giving up entirely the direction one has just been going in, and going in precisely the opposite direction, is important in connection with reciprocity of personal relationships, but reciprocity becomes important to a chiasticist only because some of its principles happen to get entangled to some extent with those of ambilateralism. The main significance of Ernest's impressionability is that it provides yet another reason for lability. In *The Way of All Flesh,* at the beginning of chapter 53, Ernest's ideological to-ing and fro-ing on the question of religion is explained in terms of his willingness to be influenced.

> The foregoing conversation and others like it made a deep impression upon my hero. If next day he had taken a walk with Mr Hawke, and heard what he had to say on the other side, he would have been just as much struck, and as ready to fling off what Pryer had told him, as he now was to throw aside all he had ever heard from anyone except Pryer; but there was no Mr Hawke at hand, so Pryer had everything his own way.   (p. 237)

Ernest's ambilateralism is here portrayed as something latent or dormant; the urge to 'go the other way' needs an outside influence to be triggered into action. In the next paragraph the narrator presents some typical Butlerian philosophy of a kind that we are by now thoroughly familiar with. What is interesting, for what it reveals about ambilateralism, is the way the paragraph first holds out a hope of an end to zigzagging ('before they adopt their final shape'), but then later on undermines the belief by saying that at least the zigzagger himself will never know whether his latest turn is his last or not.

> Embryo minds, like embryo bodies, pass through a number of strange metamorphoses before they adopt their final shape. It is no more to be wondered at that one who is going to turn out a Roman Catholic, should have passed through the stages of being first a Methodist, and then a free thinker, than that a man should at some former time have been a mere cell, and later on an invertebrate animal. Ernest, however, could not be expected to know this; embryos never do. Embryos think with each stage of their development that they have now reached the only condition which really suits them. This, they say, must certainly be their last, inasmuch as its close will be so great a shock that nothing can survive it. Every change is a shock; every shock is a *pro tanto* death. What we call death is only a shock great enough to destroy our power to recognize a past and a present as resembling one another. It is the making us consider the points of difference between our present and our past greater than the points of resemblance, so that we can no longer call the former of these two in any proper sense a continuation of the second, but find it less trouble to think of it as something that we choose to call

new.   (Ibid.)

In this example the reason for turning is external. But the reason for every 'turn' in zigzagging processes is not always made out to be external in Butler's works. Often it is admitted to be internal, and often no reason at all is given.

An uncompromising dualism is a prerequisite for chiasticism, and in *The Way of All Flesh* there are many passages that show both Butler's tendency to pick out or create dualistic pairs and his vacillation between the halves of the pair once the pair has been established. If there exists a pair 'men and goddess' out of which one influences the other, ambilateralism makes Butler willing to consider either one of the pair a candidate for the subject-role, and thus his habitual vacillation on the 'chicken-and-egg' question can begin. Who made whom? Did men make Fortuna a goddess? Or did she make them, so that they could make her? Or did they make her, so that she could make them make her? – and so on in infinite regression.[40]

Was George Pontifex one of Fortune's favoured nurslings or not? On the whole I should say that he was not, for he did not consider himself so; he was too religious to consider Fortune a deity at all; he took whatever she gave and never thanked her, being firmly convinced that whatever he got to his own advantage was of his own getting. And so it was, after Fortune had made him able to get it.

'Nos te, nos facimus, Fortuna, deam', exclaimed the poet. 'It is we who make thee, Fortune, a goddess'; and so it is, after Fortune has made us able to make her. The poet says nothing as to the making of the 'nos'. Perhaps some men are independent of antecedents and surroundings and have an initial force within themselves which is in no way due to causation; but this is supposed to be a difficult question and it may be as well to avoid it. Let it suffice that George Pontifex did not consider himself fortunate, and he who does not consider himself fortunate is unfortunate.   (Ch. 5, pp. 17–18)

The narrator says it may be as well to avoid such questions, but that is after he has dwelt on it at some length, and, rather than being avoided, such ambivalent vacillation is sought out in *The Way of All Flesh*.

Another kind of ambivalence in Butler is the vacillation between humour and seriousness. In chapter 86 of *The Way of All Flesh*, Ernest is accused by being always in jest: 'With the public generally he is not a favourite. He is admitted to have talent, but it is considered generally to be of a queer unpractical kind, and no matter how serious he is, he is always accused of being in jest' (p. 408).

To create ambilateralist vacillation Butler presses any device, no matter how humble, into service, and he does not despise ordinary, simple uncertainty as a means of achieving dualist vacillation: 'whereon I believe we did something like fighting and I rather think John Pontifex got the worst of it, *but it may have been the other way*' (ch. 3, p. 12; emphasis added).

The familiar ideal of 'impartiality' is another favourite way of justifying an ambilateralist attitude. In chapter 64 Ernest studies the New Testament impartially:

> now he was well enough to read he made the New Testament his chief study, going through it in the spirit which Mr Shaw had desired of him, that is to say as one who wished neither to believe nor disbelieve, but cared only about finding out whether he ought to believe or no. (p. 279)

In chapter 73 Ernest again does not care which way a conclusion goes: 'All he wanted, he said, was to know which way it was to be ...' (p. 329).

In chapter 5 Butler picks out the antithetical pair of God and Mammon: 'Yet when a man is very fond of his money it is not easy for him at all times to be very fond of his children also. The two are like God and Mammon' (p. 20). Where another Victorian author might only have made fleeting reference to the pair, Butler on the contrary makes the duality a matrix for elaborate parallels and analogies. Mr Pontifex cannot like both his money and his children, and, faced with the choice, naturally chooses the money.

In chapter 49 it is mentioned that the unpleasant Simeonite Badcock has a nickname, deriving from the deformity of the lower parts of his back. The name is not revealed, and critics have not put their guesses into print.

> Badcock was one of the most notorious of all the Simeonites. Not only was he ugly, dirty, ill-dressed, bumptious, and in every way objectionable, but he was deformed and waddled when he walked so that he had won the nickname which I can only reproduce by calling it 'Here's my back, and there's my back', because the lower parts of his back emphasized themselves demonstratively as though about to fly off in different directions like the two extreme notes in

the chord of the augmented sixth, with every step he took.   (p. 217)

Forgetting the humour for a moment, we should note that a situation in which different parts of one and the same living organism want to go off in different directions is a problem that unconsciously troubled Butler to no small extent. To return to the amphisbaena, a spontaneous reaction that the snake often calls forth in people is the realization of a possible problem. The amphisbaena is supposed to function in such a way that, while one half sleeps, the other wakes; when one head wants to go in its direction, the other head submits; and so on; and the two heads must take turns at domination and submission. But what, we ask, would happen if both heads simultaneously wanted to go forth, each in its own direction? There would then be an insoluble conflict; the two halves of the self would be pitted against one another in a frustrating, self-destructive war.

This possibility makes us aware that some forms of symmetry – such as that of an amphisbaena – are biologically impractical. A snake should have only one head, and that head at the front. In the head are the eyes and other sensory organs, and the snake wants to know where it is going, not where it has been. The only useful head at the tail-end is a fake head – this has survival value, as it makes snake-eating birds uncertain of which end to swoop down on. *That* kind of ambilateralist uncertainty is useful (for the snake if not for the birds), but the kind of symmetry which would divide an amphisbaena, as seen from the side, into two symmetric halves is too self-destructive to be viable.

Monstrous births of snakes and turtles with two heads (at the same end) occur in zoos. Such double-headed creatures are severely disabled because of their conflicting wills, and obviously do not survive for long in nature. Siamese twins can manage by devising rules – of absolute rigidity – of turn-taking, and alternating domination and submission. The original Siamese twins took turns, changing every twenty-four hours, at making decisions and submitting. Even so, their scheme ran into tragic difficulties in the end when one of them took to drink, late nights and so on.

To most people the idea of an amphisbaena is vaguely frightening or abhorrent. People sense that such symmetry is self-destructive and could not work. Many kinds of potential symmetry are impractical in a biological sense, and have no place in nature.

Not only biologically, but in many other ways too, some forms of symmetry seem impossible. Despite his longing for symmetry Butler seems to have sensed the difficulties, and misgivings about the result of achieved symmetry find their way into his thinking and writing. The typical indecision of Butler's characters is often pictured as a mortal internal conflict, with two halves of the self wishing to go in opposite directions. ' "Instinct tore me one way and reason another" ', says Higgs in *Erewhon Revisited*.

'And my easy method with spiritual dilemmas proved to be but a case of *ignotum per ignotius*.

'If Satan himself is at times transformed into an angel of light, are not angels of light sometimes transformed into the likeness of Satan? If the devil is not so black as he is painted, is God always so white? And is there not another place in which it is said, "The fear of the Lord is the beginning of wisdom", as though it were not the last word upon the subject? If a man should not do evil that good may come, so neither should he do good that evil may come; and though it were good for me to speak out, should I not do better by refraining?

'Such were the lawless and uncertain thoughts that tortured me very cruelly, so that I did what I had not done for many a long year – I prayed for guidance. "Show me Thy will, O Lord," I cried in great distress, "and strengthen me to do it when Thou hast shown it me." But there was no answer. Instinct tore me one way and reason another. Whereon I settled that I would obey the reason with which God has endowed me, unless the instinct He had also given me should thrash it out of me. I could get no further than this, that the Lord hath mercy on whom He will have mercy, and whom He willeth He hardeneth; and again I prayed that I might be among those on whom He would show His mercy.

'This was the strongest internal conflict that I ever remember to have felt, and it was at the end of it that I perceived the first, but as yet very faint, symptoms of that sickness from which I shall not recover. Whether this be a token of mercy or no, my Father which is in heaven knows, but I know not.'   (Ch. 7, pp. 65–6)

Higgs dies of an illness which is symbolically tied up with the difficulty of choosing 'which one' out of two. John Pickard Owen in *The Fair Haven* dies of a brain-fever, exhausted by his vacillation. There are several other such deaths – for instance, the youth who hangs himself in *Erewhon*. The disease that these characters die from, and which many of Butler's characters suffer, should be unhesitatingly diagnosed as symmetry itself. Butler kills these people off because at some level of consciousness he is convinced that perfect symmetry is incompatible with life. We know today that life is asymmetric in a molecular sense; Butler was subconsciously convinced that life has to be asymmetric in a behavioural sense, even though he consciously strove to prove the opposite all the time.

Let us recall a few more cases of (mostly trivial) dualism in *The Way of All Flesh*. At the end of chapter 69 Ernest feels that his life has been cut in two.

> Each step he took, each face or object that he knew, helped at once to link him on to the life he had led before his imprisonment, and at the same time to make him feel how completely that imprisonment had cut his life into two parts, the one of which could bear no resemblance to the other.   (p. 305)

Characters in *The Way of All Flesh* make divisions and classifications, but they are not going to be bothered with too many categories. Two will do quite nicely. It is a pity Ernest and Ellen do not get on, because chapter 71 shows that they are well matched at least in one respect – Ellen too makes dualist divisions: 'For her [Ellen] there were two classes of people, those who had been in prison and those who had not' (p. 312).

Another humorous case of dualism is found in chapter 83. Theobald's musical repertoire consists of two tunes only .

> After their early dinner, when Joey and Ernest and their father were left alone, Theobald rose and stood in the middle of the hearthrug under the Elijah picture, and began to whistle in his old absent way. He had two tunes only, one was 'In my Cottage near a Wood', and the other was the Easter Hymn; he had been trying to whistle them all his life, but had never succeeded; he whistled them as a clever bullfinch might whistle them – he had got them, but he had not got them right; he would be a semitone out in every third note as though reverting to some remote musical progenitor, who had known none but the Lydian or the Phrygian mode, or whatever would enable him to go most wrong while still keeping the tune near enough to be recognized. Theobald stood before the middle of the fire and whistled his two tunes softly in his own old way till Ernest left the room; the unchangedness of the external and changedness of the internal he felt were likely to throw him completely off his balance.   (p. 376)

The detail, Jones tells us, was drawn from life. Canon Butler too knew only two tunes; and, moreover, people were not always sure which one he was whistling. Thus, to the dualism of Butler's version (two tunes) Jones adds ambilateralism (the 'which-one' uncertainty). (Cf. Jones I 27 and II 153.)

All through *The Way of All Flesh* there is a dualistic structuring into two opposing 'sides' on various occasions. There is always the possibility of 'another side', but only one 'other side', not several 'other sides'. At the end of chapter 7 these 'sides' are the usual ones of parents and children, and the narrator complains about imbalance:

> I think the Church Catechism has a good deal to do with the unhappy relations which commonly even now exist between parents and children. That work was written too exclusively from the parental point of view; the person who composed it did not get a few children to come in and help him; he was clearly not young himself, nor should I say it was the work of one who liked children – in spite of the words 'my good child' which, if I remember rightly, are once put into the mouth of the catechist and, after all, carry a harsh sound with them.   (p. 31)

In chapter 26 the narrator points out that a clergyman is not impartial – he is a paid advocate for 'one side':

> A clergyman, again, can hardly ever allow himself to look facts fairly in the face. It is his profession to support one side; it is impossible, therefore, for him to make an unbiassed examination of the other.
>
> We forget that every clergyman with a living or curacy, is as much a paid advocate as the barrister who is trying to persuade a jury to acquit a prisoner. We should listen to him with the same suspense of judgement, the same full consideration of the arguments of the opposing counsel, as a judge does when he is trying a case. Unless we know these, and can state them in a way that our opponents would admit to be a fair representation of their views, we have no right to claim that we have formed an opinion at all. The misfortune is that by the law of the land one side only can be heard.   (pp. 108–9)

The moral of the second paragraph is that, if clergymen are asymmetrically all on one side, we at least should stay ambilaterally impartial. The idea of stating one's opponents' view in a form which they would admit to be a fair representation (i.e. in practice in an extreme form) is another easily recognizable regular Butlerism.

The theme of the clergy as paid advocates is taken up again in chapter 59, when the freethinker Mr Shaw is allowed to score a few good points by appealing to impartiality. The connection between the ambilateralism of 'impartiality' and chiasmus shows very clearly in this episode, because Mr Shaw structures his description of the ambilateralist possibility as a chiasmus:

'If you really want to know,' said Mr Shaw, with a sly twinkle, 'I think that he who was so willing and able to prove that what was was not, would be equally able and willing to make a case for thinking that what was not was, if it suited his purpose.' (p. 260)

Ernest is much impressed by this: 'Ernest was very much taken aback. How was it that all the clever people of Cambridge had never put him up to this simple rejoinder?' (ibid.). However, Mr Shaw does not think any worse of the clergy for their asymmetric approach. The blame always falls squarely on yourself for failing to stick to symmetry. The world may be brimful of asymmetry, and rightly so, but we, as observers, must stick to symmetry:

'You see,' continued Mr Shaw, 'these writers all get their living by writing in a certain way, and the more they write in that way, the more they are likely to get on. You should not call them dishonest for this any more than a judge should call a barrister dishonest for earning his living by defending one in whose innocence he does not seriously believe; but you should hear the barrister on the other side before you decide upon the case.'

This was another facer. Ernest could only stammer that he had endeavoured to examine these questions as carefully as he could. (Ibid.)

The structuring into 'sides' is finally reinforced a few paragraphs later when Mr Shaw concludes, ' "You know nothing of our side of the question, and I have just shown you that you do not know much more of your own" ' (p. 261).

One attempt to come to terms with the problem of symmetry and asymmetry is to seek a solution in 'palladianism', by equating the two 'sides', but seeing the self as somehow in the middle. In chapter 53 Pryer and Ernest make plans for their 'College of Spiritual Pathology', which is to outbid the two 'sides' of Rome and scepticism: 'we should set on foot a spiritual movement somewhat analogous to the Young England movement of twenty years ago, the aim of which shall be at once to outbid Rome on the one hand, and scepticism on the other' (p. 238). Also 'Such a college, as you will probably admit, will approach both Rome on the one hand, and science on the other ...' (pp. 238–9). But such attempts seldom work. To stay in the middle is uncomfortable. The plans for a College of Spiritual Pathology come to nothing, and Pryer is revealed to be a swindler.

In chapter 5 there is an interesting example of a palladian structure, in a passage of which the moral is that the middle is bad. Out of the alternation of generations the narrator lifts a palladian structure 'father–son–grandson', explaining that the son (the palladian middle) will be bad, but the father and grandson (the palladian wings) good:

> the more brilliant the success in any one generation, the greater as a general rule the subsequent exhaustion until time has been allowed for recovery. Hence it often happens that the grandson of a successful man will be more successful than the son – the spirit that actuated the grandfather having lain fallow in the son and being refreshed by repose so as to be ready for fresh exertion in the grandson.   (p. 19)

On closer inspection Butler's views on compromise (*via media,* the average, the mean, and so on) turn out to be far less straightforward than one may have thought at first. To begin with, Butler is usually not, strictly speaking, in favour of the middle. Most often he speaks against the extremes. It is true, of course, that in Butler's logic this should come to the same thing.

Most of the passages in *The Way of All Flesh* that deal with the question of the middle do so indirectly through symmetric implication, i.e. by condemning the extremes rather than praising the middle directly. In chapter 15 the farmers of Battersby are said to be 'tolerators, if not lovers, of all that was familiar, haters of all that was unfamiliar; they would have been equally horrified at hearing the Christian religion doubted, and at seeing it practised' (p. 65). These farmers are thus clearly middle-of-the-road-people primarily by virtue of symmetric inference; if they dislike the extremes they must like the middle.

Aunt Alethea, we are told in chapter 32, 'went to church, but disliked equally those who aired either religion or irreligion' (p. 134). At the end of chapter 47 this commendable attitude is even briefly attributed to Ernest, before he begins his wild zigzagging: 'like the

farmers in his father's village, though he would not stand seeing the
Christian religion made light of, he was not going to see it taken
seriously' (pp. 208–9). This professed hatred of extremes is, however,
already rather shaky, and the narrator admits as much in the rest of the
paragraph:

> Ernest's friends thought his dislike for Simeonites was due to his
> being the son of a clergyman who, it was known, bullied him; it is
> more likely, however, that it rose from an unconscious sympathy
> with them, which, as in St Paul's case, in the end drew him into the
> ranks of those whom he had most despised and hated.   (p. 209)

In chapter 85 the mature Ernest, in one of his essays, preaches to
others the very virtues that he has so far so conspicuously failed to
attain in his own life:

> Christianity was true in so far as it had fostered beauty, and it had
> fostered much beauty. It was false in so far as it fostered ugliness,
> and it had fostered much ugliness. It was therefore not a little true
> and not a little false; on the whole one might go farther and fare
> worse; the wisest course would be to live with it, and make the best
> and not the worst of it. The writer urged that we become persecutors
> as a matter of course as soon as we begin to feel very strongly upon
> any subject; we ought not therefore to do this; we ought not to feel
> very strongly even upon that institution which was dearer to the
> writer than any other – the Church of England. We should be
> churchmen, but somewhat lukewarm churchmen, inasmuch as
> those who care very much about either religion or irreligion are
> seldom observed to be very well bred or agreeable people. The
> Church herself should approach as nearly to that of Laodicea as was
> compatible with her continuing to be a Church at all, and each
> individual member should only be hot in striving to be as lukewarm
> as possible.   (p. 394)

The internal conflict within Butler's attitude is well symbolized in the
paradox at the end of the quotation, which has to bring in the 'hot'
even while advocating the 'lukewarm'.

Extremes are half-heartedly condemned in various ways in *The Way
of All Flesh*. One variant is the idea of extremes as 'signposts' – i.e. the
extremes are there so as to show us what we should avoid. The most
famous instance of this is Butler's metaphor in chapter 26 of the

clergyman as 'a kind of human Sunday' (p. 108). Sometimes extremism is mildly condemned in humorous terms, in passages which are quite often genuinely funny, and among the most memorable in *The Way of All Flesh*:

> He called Ernest 'an audacious reptile' and said he wondered the earth did not open and swallow him up because he pronounced Thalia with a short i. 'And this to me,' he thundered, 'who never made a false quantity in my life.' Surely he would have been a much nicer person if he had made false quantities in his youth like other people.   (Ch. 30, p. 127)

Even when the middle is praised directly, and not indirectly through dispraise of its antithesis, the very names that the middle position are given reveal Butler's uncertainty and ambivalence. In chapter 86 Ernest's name for the middle position is 'mediocrity' – not a very positive-sounding term:

> 'I do not know nor greatly care whether they [the books] are good or not. What opinion can any sane man form about his own work? Some people must write stupid books just as there must be junior ops and third class poll men. Why should I complain of being among the mediocrities? If a man is not absolutely below mediocrity let him be thankful ...'   (p. 409)

The best name that Butler can find for the mean is 'common sense', and this concept is sometimes invested with a downright mystical significance. But it is usually brought in only as a magical word, and, if the proof of this pudding is in the eating, although there is talk about common sense in *The Way of All Flesh* there is no show of common sense in operation. In chapter 75, for instance, 'common sense' is mentioned very reverently, but everything that has gone before, and much of what is to follow, undercuts this reverence:

> It seemed to him that in his attempt to be moral he had been following a devil which had disguised itself as an angel of light. But if so, what ground was there on which a man might rest the sole of his foot and tread in reasonable safety?
> He was still too young to reach the answer, 'On common sense' –an answer which he would have felt to be unworthy of anyone who had an ideal standard.   (p. 335)

One of Butler's attempts at reconciliation of his conflicting feelings on the subject of the choice between extremism and middle-of-the-roadism was to explain that it is necessary to go to the extremes and burn one's fingers so that one knows to stay in the middle thenceforth – in other words, that one cannot know what the middle is until one has learnt what its opposite, the extremes, is. Butler usually exemplifies this theory with anecdotes about speculation on the stock-market, as in chapter 78 of *The Way of All Flesh:*

> It is only on having actually lost money that one realizes what an awful thing the loss of it is, and finds out how easily it is lost by those who venture out of the middle of the most beaten path. Ernest had had his facer, as he had had his attack of poverty, young, and sufficiently badly for a sensible man to be little likely to forget it. I can fancy few pieces of good fortune greater than this as happening to any man, provided, of course, that he is not damaged irretrievably. (p. 347)

In chapter 49 advocacy of extremism and the obligatoriness of dual antithetical structuring is put into the mouth of a dislikable character – Mr Hawke (see in particular pp. 221–2). Mr Hawke is suspect; therefore his love of disjunctive structuring should be so. But Ernest, who is a portrait of Butler, is shown as acting immediately on this antithetical mania in chapter 51 (cf. pp. 229–30).

In many of Butler's works, particularly as he gets older, the problematical relationship between extremism and middle-ism occurs in clearly recognizable patches of text in which Butler's thoughts settle into a number of well-worn grooves and then rumble on inevitably, one well-known chiastic idea suggesting another, until Butler has made his ritual tour of them all, and can return to more normal writing. There is such a patch of prose in chapter 19 of *The Way of All Flesh*, in which Butler makes his typical round of chiasticist landmarks, calling at such well-known features as asymmetry; the 'mean'; the difficulty of 'drawing lines'; things existing by virtue of their opposites; dualism (including two cases of chiasmus on the sentence-level); complementariness; making the most of both worlds; the impossibility of accepting both of two opposites; extremists as warning-posts (burnt fingers); and, finally, the 'mean' again. At the end of the chapter comes yet another mention of 'average': 'Judge him according to a fair average standard ...' (pp. 85–6).

I shall quote the whole of this tirade as an example of the kind of chiastic reveries that Butler, particularly in his later works, was frequently liable to fall into:

I submit it as the result of my own poor observation, that a good deal of unkindness and selfishness on the part of parents towards children is not generally followed by ill consequences to the parents themselves [*asymmetry: lack of reciprocity*]. They may cast a gloom over their children's lives for many years without having to suffer anything that will hurt them. I should say, then, that it shows no great moral obliquity on the part of parents if within certain limits they make their children's lives a burden to them [*ambilateralist siding with perpetrator rather than victim*].

Granted that Mr Pontifex's was not a very exalted character, ordinary men are not required to have very exalted characters. It is enough if we are of the same moral and mental stature as the 'main' or 'mean' part of men – that is to say as the average [*middle-ism*].

It is involved in the very essence of things that rich men who die old shall have been mean. The greatest and wisest of mankind will be almost always found to be the meanest – the ones who have kept the 'mean' best between excess either of virtue or vice. They hardly ever have been prosperous if they have not done this, and, considering how many miscarry altogether, it is no small feather in a man's cap if he has been no worse than his neighbours. Homer tells us about some one who made it his business αἰέν ἀριστεύειν καὶ ὑπείροχον ἔμμεναι ἄλλων – always to excel and to stand higher than other people. What an uncompanionable disagreeable person he must have been! Homer's heroes generally came to a bad end, and I doubt not that this gentleman, whoever he was, did so sooner or later.

A very high standard, again, involves the possession of rare virtues, and rare virtues are like rare plants or animals, things that have not been able to hold their own in the world. A virtue to be serviceable must, like gold, be alloyed with some commoner but more durable metal [*alloys*].

People divide off vice and virtue as though they were two things, neither of which had with it anything of the other [*difficulty of drawing lines*]. This is not so. There is no useful virtue which has not some alloy of vice, and hardly any vice, if any, which carries not with it a little dash of virtue; virtue and vice are like life and death, or mind and matter – things which cannot exist without being qualified by their opposite [*things coming into existence by virtue of their opposites*]. The most absolute life contains death, and the corpse is still in many respects living; so also it has been said, 'if thou, Lord, wilt be extreme to mark what is done amiss', which shows that even the highest ideal we can conceive will yet admit so much compromise with vice as shall countenance the poor abuses of the time, if they are not too outrageous. That vice pays homage to virtue is notorious; we call this hypocrisy; there should be a word found for the homage which virtue not unfrequently pays, or at any rate would be wise in paying, to vice [*complementariness*].

I grant that some men will find happiness in having what we all feel to be a higher moral standard than others. If they go in for this, however, they must be content with virtue as her own reward, and not grumble if they find lofty Quixotism an expensive luxury, whose rewards belong to a kingdom that is not of this world. They must not wonder if they cut a poor figure in trying to make the most of both worlds [*making the best of both worlds*]. Disbelieve as we may the details of the accounts which record the growth of the Christian religion, yet a great part of Christian teaching will remain as true as though we accepted the details. We cannot serve God and Mammon [*obligatory choice*]; strait is the way and narrow is the gate which leads to what those who live by faith hold to be best worth having, and there is no way of saying this better than the Bible has done. It is well there should be some who think thus, as it is well there should be speculators in commerce [*extremes as signposts*], who will often burn their fingers – but it is not well that the majority should leave the "mean" and beaten path [*the mean*].   (pp. 83–4)

One of the most idiosyncratic forms that Butler's enantiomorphistic desires take is his eccentric theory of 'crossing'. In applying his quasi-genetic concept of 'crossing', Butler spends most of his time on cases of unachieved union, or semi-achieved union. An example of the latter is the sterility of hybrids (hybrids exemplifying a case in which union between two different species has been just barely possible and it is impossible to perpetuate the strain).

In *The Way of All Flesh*, however, the impossibility of crossing is kept in the background. At the end of chapter 23 crossing is mentioned in the metaphoric sense, and given as a reason why one should not feel sympathy with the unfortunate:

As it was, I was glad to get away from him, for I could do nothing for him, or chose to say that I could not, and the sight of so much suffering was painful to me. A man should not only have his own way as far as possible, but he should only consort with things that are getting their own way so far that they are at any rate comfortable. Unless for short times under exceptional circumstances, he should not even see things that have been stunted or starved, much less should he eat meat that has been vexed by having been over-driven, or under-fed, or afflicted with any disease; nor should he touch vegetables that have not been well grown. For all these things cross a man; whatever a man comes in contact with in any way forms a cross with him which will leave him better or worse, and the better things he is crossed with the more likely he is to live long and happily. All things must be crossed a little or they would cease to live – but holy things, such for example as Giovanni Bellini's saints, have been crossed with nothing but what is good of its kind.   (pp. 100–1)

All these tiny little bits of Butlerian wisdom serve the same purpose in the end: they all exist to justify ambilateralism. Butler knows that conventional morality expects one to feel sympathy with the unfortunate. He therefore begins to hunt for something to be said 'on the other side'. His usual line of reasoning on such occasions is that, no matter what morality says we *should* do, what we *do* do is side with the fortunate rather than the unfortunate. Butler then usually turns this around and says that what we *do* do is also what we *should* do.[41]

In chapter 79 we return to the concept of crossing, this time with Ernest's doctor as the theorist:

'Cross him', said the doctor, 'at once. Crossing is the great medical discovery of the age. Shake him out of himself by shaking something else into him.'

I had not told him that money was no object to us and I think he had reckoned me up as not over rich. He continued:

'Seeing is a mode of touching, touching is a mode of feeding, feeding is a mode of assimilation, assimilation is a mode of re-creation and reproduction, and this is crossing – shaking yourself into something else and something else into you.'

(p. 352)

The passage begins and ends with a chiasmus, showing clearly the connection between chiastic thinking and the idea of 'crossing'.

Overton doubts the doctor's seriousness, but the doctor is in earnest: 'He spoke laughingly, but it was plain he was serious' (ibid.). Also:

> Had the doctor been less eminent in his profession I should have doubted whether he was in earnest, but I knew him to be a man of business who would neither waste his own time nor that of his patients. As soon as we were out of the house we took a cab to Regent's Park, and spent a couple of hours in sauntering round the different houses. Perhaps it was on account of what the doctor had told me, but I certainly became aware of a feeling I had never experienced before. I mean that I was receiving an influx of new life, or deriving new ways of looking at life – which is the same thing – by the process.   (p. 353)

Overton is brought round to believing the doctor by the persuasive appeal of ambidirectionalism. He was 'receiving an influx of new life, or deriving new ways of looking at life – which is the same thing'; in other words life passed in two directions: from him to something else, and from something else to him; and how could you doubt anything which does that? Such doubts would be sacrilegious in a chiasticist's world. For an ambilateralist the highest appeal is always to the authority of symmetry.

In the doctor's speeches in chapter 79 there are nice distinctions as to what would be too wide a cross for Ernest, and what would be too little. When Ernest goes to the zoo, the hippopotamus, the rhinoceros and the elephants are just about right, but 'The monkeys are not a wide enough cross; they do not stimulate sufficiently' (ibid.); and going abroad, again, would be too wide a cross.

For a final example of a passage illustrating Butler's typical difficulties in vacillating between extremism and middle-ism, let us turn to chapter 69:

> All our lives long, every day and every hour, we are engaged in the process of accommodating our changed and unchanged selves to changed and unchanged surroundings; living, in fact, in nothing else than this process of accommodation; when we fail in it a little we are stupid, when we fail flagrantly we are mad, when we suspend it temporarily we sleep, when we give up the attempt altogether we die. In quiet, uneventful lives the changes internal and external are so small that there is little or no strain in the process of fusion and accommodation; in other lives there is great strain, but there is also

great fusing and accommodating power. A life will be successful or not according as the power of accommodation is equal to or unequal to the strain of fusing and adjusting internal and external changes.

The trouble is that in the end we shall be driven to admit the unity of the universe so completely as to be compelled to deny that there is either an external or an internal, but must see everything both as external and internal at one and the same time, subject and object – external and internal – being unified as much as everything else. This will knock our whole system over, but then every system has got to be knocked over by something.

Much of the best way out of this difficulty is to go in for separation between internal and external – subject and object – when we find this convenient, and unity between the same when we find unity convenient. This is illogical, but extremes are alone logical, and they are always absurd, the mean is alone practicable and it is always illogical. It is faith and not logic which is the supreme arbiter. They say all roads lead to Rome, and all philosophies that I have ever seen lead ultimately either to some gross absurdity, or else to the conclusion already more than once insisted on in these pages, that the just shall live by faith, that is to say that sensible people will get through life by rule of thumb as they may interpret it most conveniently without asking too many questions for conscience' sake. Take any fact, and reason upon it to the bitter end, and it will ere long lead to this as the only refuge from some palpable folly.   (pp. 304–5)

Comment is hardly necessary. This is again one of those occasions when Butler has fallen into one of his usual trances and recites his chiastic refrains quite mechanically, ticking off, as it were, on his chiasticist rosary one obligatory formula after another. The first of these chiastic reveries that the reader happens to come across in Butler may sound interesting and deeply philosophical. But, after one has read thirty or forty of them, all their various ingredients have become so predictable that one reads them not for what they may be saying about their subject but for what they say about Butler.

In Butler chiasmus is always in the end symmetry-oriented, whether it expresses a symmetric or an asymmetric content. In form any chiasmus is always an example of symmetry, but a chiasmus may assert asymmetry in content even while being symmetric in form. The sentence, 'As *a* is *b*, so also is *b a*', is symmetric both in form and content. A sentence, 'It was not *a* that *b* but *b* that *a*', is symmetric in form but expresses an asymmetric content. This latter variety is probably, it seems to me, the kind of chiasmus that people most need and most use in ordinary language. Such statements are meant to sort out which of two asymmetric possibilities is the correct one. It is a choice between asymmetry and asymmetry, not between asymmetry and symmetry. Such a chiastic sentence affirms one asymmetry and negates its enantiomorph, thereby making doubly sure. Such asymmetry-oriented chiasmus loses most of its normal function in Butler because he uses it mainly, and sometimes almost exclusively, to help the underdog, whereby it somehow becomes a servant of symmetry after all.

The chiasmus that Butler really longs for is one symmetric both in form and content: 'As *a* is *b;* so also is *b a.*' But, if an asymmetric tradition exists, Butler thinks that he does symmetry a greater service by helping it indirectly through the creation of the enantiomorph to the asymmetry of conventional tradition. A man's family is normally thought to be more important to him than his money, so Butler inverts this by insisting on the inverted asymmetry, and pointing out, in chapter 66, that Job could enjoy his money without his family but not his family without his money: 'Job probably felt the loss of his flocks and herds more than that of his wife and family, for he could enjoy his flocks and herds without his family, but not his family – not for long – if he had lost all his money' (p. 288). But such (superficially) asymmetry-oriented cases of chiasmus are not as frequent as one would expect, whereas the symmetry-oriented types of chiasmus are relatively plentiful (cf. Ch. 2, section iii) – i.e. plentiful in relation to what one would expect.

With Butler's asymmetry-oriented chiastic passages in *The Way of All Flesh* it is often expressly stated that they are brought in only to challenge a conventional asymmetry: 'They say it takes nine tailors to make a man, but Ernest felt that it would take at least nine Ernests to make a Mr Holt' (ch. 58, p. 256). Such passages are often temporary, and exist only thanks to the 'helping-the-underdog' philosophy. Indeed, this can clearly be seen in the many instances in which symmetric and pseudo-asymmetric cases of chiasmus are put together into the same passage. Take, for instance, the following from chapter 85:

Ere long, however, he found out all about it, and settled quietly down to write a series of books, in which he insisted on saying things which no one else would say even if they could, or could even if they would.

He has got himself a bad literary character. I said to him laughingly one day that he was like the man in the last century of whom it was said that nothing but such a character could keep down such parts.

He laughed and said he would rather be like that than like a modern writer or two whom he could name, whose parts were so poor that they could be kept up by nothing but by such a character. (pp. 396–7)

At the end of the quotation Ernest inverts Overton's statement, and that inversion may be taken as a mild backing of asymmetry. But even in this quotation the mildly asymmetry-oriented inversion comes immediately after a case of perfect symmetry: 'which no one else would say even if they could, or could even if they would'.

Usually symmetry is allowed to reign unchallenged. Many statements in *The Way of All Flesh* are mechanically complemented with their enantiomorphs: 'he had allowed himself for so many years to say things he ought not to have said, and not to say the things he ought to have said' (ch. 44, p. 192).

Symmetry is such a powerful positive value in Butler's world that it cancels out everything else. In chapter 35 Aunt Alethea forgives Ernest his numerous sins because of symmetry: 'She saw also that his conceit was not very profound, and that his fits of self-abasement were as extreme as his exaltation had been' (p. 148).

Ambilateralism is the idea behind those passages in Butler in which two different individuals work together to achieve the same result, with a reciprocity of enantiomorphically matching reasons. In chapter 10 Mrs Allaby has to scheme and plot in order to find husbands for her daughters. For her scheming she desperately needs the help of a celebrated matchmaker, Mrs Cowey. But she need not worry. Not only is Mrs Cowey willing to help, but she is almost as eager to do her part of the work as Mrs Allaby is to do hers.

Professor Cowey had published works through Theobald's father, and Theobald had on this account been taken in tow by Mrs Cowey from the beginning of his University career. She had had her eye upon him for some time past, and almost as much felt it her duty to get him off her list of young men for whom wives had to be provided, as poor Mrs Allaby did to try and get a husband for one of her daughters. (p. 40)

Whether two separates in Butler join each other eagerly or find their longings frustrated, separates, and in particular antithetical opposites, always keep an eye on one another. There are innumerable types of bonds between separates. Things exist only thanks to their opposites. There would be no St Anthony (in the role in which we know him) without the devils:

'Oh, no,' he replied, still laughing, 'no more than St Anthony felt towards the devils who had tempted him, when he met some of them casually a hundred or a couple of hundred years afterwards. Of course he knew they were devils, but that was all right enough; there must be devils. St Anthony probably liked these devils better than most others, and for old acquaintance sake showed them as much indulgence as was compatible with decorum.
    'Besides, you know,' he added, 'St Anthony tempted the devils quite as much as they tempted him....' (Ch. 44, pp. 191–2)

Another bond between separates is the 'logic of contradictories' which automatically takes your thought to the opposing party (since for every thing that happens to either of the pair there is a symmetric inverted repetition with the other). Compare, for instance, the end of chapter 81:

A little later I remember his saying with a laugh that had something of a family likeness to his aunt's: 'It is not the pleasure it causes me which I enjoy so, it is the pain it will cause to all my friends except yourself and Towneley.'
    I said: 'You cannot tell your father and mother – it would drive them mad.'
    'No, no, no,' said he, 'it would be too cruel; it would be like Isaac offering up Abraham and no thicket with a ram in it near at hand. Besides, why should I? We have cut each other these four years.' (p. 365)

If you have two dualities, i.e. Ernest and his friends (except Overton and Towneley), and pleasure and pain, and, if something causes pleasure to one party, it must cause pain to the other, and *vice-versa*.
    The need to have opposites present extends even to the most common idioms of the language. The frequency of such phrases as 'He

may or may not do so' (p. 53), which are habitual with all the characters, shows the need to complement the 'may' with 'may not', even though 'may' in itself signals uncertainty. One is reminded of the story of the Welshman who emigrated to Mars, and on arrival built two chapels. Asked why he built two he answers, 'This chapel here is the chapel I go to. And that chapel over there is the chapel I do not go to.'

There is always this kind of connection between things in Butler. He always felt he had to build two chapels too, one for going to and one for not going to. And always both chapels are equally important, and always both are kept in mind.

If they are both absent, that is worth noting. The epitaph at the end of chapter 18 does not say anything either positive or negative: 'There is not a syllable of either praise or dispraise' (p. 110).

If they are sufficiently different they can be taken as a case of extremes meeting, as at the beginning of chapter 43, where extreme heroism and extreme cowardice are alleged to be the same:

> A boy of barely sixteen cannot stand against the moral pressure of a father and mother who have always oppressed him any more than he can cope physically with a powerful full-grown man. True, he may allow himself to be killed rather than yield, but this is being so morbidly heroic as to come close round again to cowardice; for it is little else than suicide, which is universally condemned as cowardly.   (p. 187)

If extreme opposites are really the same then it may be convenient to put them close together in oxymora and paradoxes, as at the beginning of chapter 65: 'There was no hope left if this were so; if this were so, let him die, the sooner the better. "Lord," he exclaimed inwardly, "I don't believe one word of it. Strengthen Thou and confirm my disbelief" ' (p. 282).

If you put them close together then it becomes much easier to bring them into contact with each other and see what may come out of that, as at the end of chapter 68:

> What was his position? He had lost all. Could he not turn his having lost all into an opportunity? Might he not, if he too sought the strength of the Lord, find, like St Paul, that it was perfected in weakness?
>
> He had nothing more to lose; money, friends, character, all were gone for a very long time if not for ever; but there was something else also that had taken its flight along with these. I mean the fear of that

which man could do unto him. *Cantabit vacuus.* Who could hurt him more than he had been hurt already? Let him but be able to earn his bread, and he knew of nothing which he dared not venture if it would make the world a happier place for those who were young and lovable. Herein he found so much comfort that he almost wished he had lost his reputation even more completely – for he saw that it was like a man's life which may be found of them that lose it and lost of them that would find it. He should not have had the courage to give up all for Christ's sake, but now Christ had mercifully taken all, and lo! it seemed as though all were found.

As the days went slowly by he came to see that Christianity and the denial of Christianity after all met as much as any other extremes do; it was a fight about names – not about things; practically the Church of Rome, the Church of England, and the freethinker have the same ideal standard and meet in the gentleman; for he is the most perfect saint who is the most perfect gentleman. Then he saw also that it matters little what profession, whether of religion or irreligion, a man may make, provided only he follows it out with charitable inconsistency, and without insisting on it to the bitter end. It is in the uncompromisingness with which dogma is held and not in the dogma or want of dogma that the danger lies. (p. 299)

Once you have established your pair, one of the topics that you can spend endless time on is the question of who should come (or go) to whom. Should *a* go to *b?* Should *b* go to *a?* Or should everybody always be willing to go in any (i.e. either) direction? Probably Butler's single most important specific belief in ambidirectionalism is his lifelong insistence that an author should not go hunting for a subject, but let the subject come to him. This philosophy is expressed in *The Way of All Flesh* too, in chapter 46, in a paragraph which, again, sends Butler (or Overton) into a brief chiasticist trance:

He did not understand that if he waited and listened and observed, another idea of some kind would probably occur to him some day, and that the development of this would in its turn suggest still further ones. He did not yet know that the very worst way of getting hold of ideas is to go hunting expressly after them. The way to get them is to study something of which one is fond, and to note down whatever crosses one's mind in reference to it, either during study or relaxation, in a little note-book kept always in the waistcoat pocket. Ernest has come to know all about this now, but it took him a long time to find out, for this is not the kind of thing that is taught at schools and universities.

Nor yet did he know that ideas, no less than the living beings in whose minds they arise, must be begotten by parents not very unlike themselves, the most original still differing but slightly from the parents that have given rise to them. Life is like a fugue, everything must grow out of the subject and there must be nothing new. Nor, again, did he see how hard it is to say where one idea ends and another begins, nor yet how closely this is paralleled in the difficulty of saying where a life begins or ends, or an action or indeed anything, there being an unity in spite of infinite multitude, and an infinite multitude in spite of unity. He thought that ideas came into clever people's heads by a kind of spontaneous germination, without parentage in the thoughts of others or the course of observation; for as yet he believed in genius.... (pp. 203–4)

In this devout pilgrimage Butler pauses at such chiasticist shrines as *crossing* ('cross one's mind'), *learning by doing* ('this is not the kind of thing that is taught at schools and universities'), *similarity and difference* ('must be begotten by parents not very unlike themselves, the most original still differing but slightly from the parents'), *drawing lines* ('Nor, again, did he see how hard it is to say where one idea ends and another begins'), a chiasmus proper ('there being an unity in spite of infinite multitude, and an infinite multitude in spite of unity'), *initiality* ('spontaneous germination, without parentage in the thoughts of others or the course of observation'),[42] and *changing one's mind* ('as yet he believed').

Contact between the two partners in a pair should always be possible both ways (and, if one direction is usually thought less likely, particularly that direction). The thinker and his thought are a pair. Should the thinker think his thought? Or should the thought come to the thinker? English usage today seems to suggest that we master our thoughts. Of the word 'think' itself the first of its variants has now become extinct, except for the archaic 'methinks'. Butler, like an ancient prophet, inclines more to the view that a thought should come to the thinker, or at least there should be a two-way street. He was so afraid of inadvertently refusing some thought access to his brain, when that thought should gracefully see fit to make a visit, that he took to carrying a small notebook and pencil around with him wherever he went, and would stop and record it on the spot whenever he had a visit from a thought.

If an antithetical pair is established there are further things to be done with it. You can comment on the behaviour of an individual faced with the choice between the two. You can commend him for his ambilateralism as Ernest is praised in *The Way of All Flesh* for his willingness to turn, and in the way Butler in his *Notebooks* and correspondence pats himself on the head for his willingness to turn. Alternatively, villains can be mildly criticized for their willingness to turn. In chapter 24 Joey and Charlotte vacillate between 'the hare' (Ernest) and 'the hounds' (his parents). They may like running with the hare, even going all the way, but they are nevertheless willing to turn at any point, in true ambilateralist fashion.

> The worst of it was that I could never trust Joey and Charlotte; they would go a good way with me and then turn back, or even the whole way and then their consciences would compel them to tell papa and mamma. They liked running with the hare up to a certain point, but their instinct was towards the hounds.   (p. 102)

If your two opposites have shown signs of coming together to the extent of merging then you can start worrying about 'drawing lines' and the question of where one ends and the other begins, though the impossibility of drawing lines can also be used as an argument to bring opposites together. Ernest finds it difficult to 'draw the line' in chapter 60:

> What should he do? Fly, fly, fly – it was the only safety. But would Christ have fled? Even though Christ had not died and risen from the dead there could be no question that He was the model whose example we were bound to follow. Christ would not have fled from Miss Snow; he was sure of that, for He went about more especially with prostitutes and disreputable people. Now, as then, it was the business of the true Christian to call not the righteous but sinners to repentance. It would be inconvenient to him to change his lodgings, and he could not ask Mrs Jupp to turn Miss Snow and Miss Maitland out of the house. Where was he to draw the line? Who would be just good enough to live in the same house with him, and who just not good enough?   (pp. 264–5)

If you decide that it is not impossible to draw a line, the question still remains of where it should be drawn. Very interesting examples in this context are the two passages describing the death of Ernest's mother and father, in chapters 83 and 86, respectively. By blurring the line of division between life and death Butler obeys his ambilateralist impulse to try and make out that life and death are the same.

> A week passed slowly away. Two or three times the family took the sacrament together round Christina's death-bed. Theobald's impatience became more and more transparent daily, but fortunately Christina (who even if she had been well would have been ready to shut her eyes to it) became weaker and less coherent in mind also, so that she hardly, if at all, perceived it. After Ernest had been in the house about a week his mother fell into a comatose state which lasted a couple of days, and in the end went away so peacefully that it was like the blending of sea and sky in mid-ocean upon a soft hazy day when none can say where the earth ends and the heavens begin. Indeed she died to the realities of life with less pain than she had waked from many of its illusions.   (Ch. 83, p. 385)

Sea and sky are the same; life and death are the same, because there is a blending. Non-ambilateralist readers might object that there is too little blending to warrant the equation of sea and sky, life and death. Butler, however, has a precise idea of how much blending there is. In the other death passage he states the proportions: they are half-and-half. Theobald's death is only half dying, but neither had his life been more than half living.

> There was no doubt that Theobald passed peacefully away during his sleep. Can a man who died thus be said to have died at all? He has presented the phenomena of death to other people, but in respect of himself he has not only not died, but has not even thought that he was going to die. This is not more than half dying, but then neither was his life more than half living. He presented so many of the phenomena of living that I suppose on the whole it would be less trouble to think of him as having been alive than as never having been born at all, but this is only possible because association does not stick to the strict letter of its bond.   (Ch. 86, p. 402)

By transferring half the amount of life to death, and half the amount of death to life, Butler has again created his ideal version of symmetry – the symmetry that satisfies his desire for ambilateralism. As long as people claimed that life and death were separate and different things, it would have been difficult to insist that they were the same. But, once it has been shown that no dividing line exists, and that in each of the two there is half of the other, it becomes possible to settle for either, no matter which, and to flit back and forth without let or hindrance or asymmetric restriction of direction of any sort.

If you have a pair, again, one of the principles that will afford most scope of all for endless musings is the principle of relativism. Belief in relativism chains two differents to one another, without any possibility of separation. If one is a function of the other, and the other a function of the one, then no separation is possible, and whichever you go for, it means that you also ambilateralistically go for the other at the same time. Butler did not start saying that opposites were 'a function of each other' until he had read Hering, but once he had seen the phrase he eagerly made it his own.[43]

Butler's relativism must be studied primarily in his scientific works. In *The Way of All Flesh* there are few really good illustrations of it. Relativism is evident in the following paragraph from chapter 1:

> 'My boy,' returned my father, 'you must not judge by the work, but by the work in connection with the surroundings. Could Giotto or Filippo Lippi, think you, have got a picture into the Exhibition? Would a single one of those frescoes we went to see when we were at Padua have the remotest chance of being hung, if it were sent in for exhibition now? Why, the Academy people would be so outraged that they would not even write to poor Giotto to tell him to come and take his fresco away. Phew!' continued he, waxing warm, 'if old Pontifex had had Cromwell's chances he would have done all that Cromwell did, and have done it better; if he had had Giotto's chances he would have done all that Giotto did, and done it no worse; as it was, he was a village carpenter, and I will undertake to say he never scamped a job in the whole course of his life.' (p. 4)

This, however, is a primitive example compared to those available in Butler's scientific works. In *Erewhon Revisited* Butler spends most of chapter 10 (q.v.) preaching relativism.[44]

A side effect of the rule of obligatory connection between one thing and another is that Butler develops a talent for the kind of joke in which you arbitrarily assume a relation (usually made out to be causative) between two things that happen to be brought together. In chapter 14 Butler uses this trick to argue that restoration of temples causes national disaster (pp. 61–2). The idea of obligatory connection between any two things made it particularly easy for Butler to invent such humorous quasi-connections.

The proportion of chiastic passages in *The Way of All Flesh* is lower than in some of Butler's other works. Neither is their importance always as great as in most of the other works. Therefore a survey of chiastic passages in *The Way of All Flesh* can be an aid to interpretation and understanding only to a limited extent. But if we have become thoroughly familiar in general with Butler's ambilateralist habits of thought, then we will understand *The Way of All Flesh,* Butler's greatest literary achievement, in an entirely new way. Superficially puzzling features such as the zigzagging of the plot will fall neatly into place, as bits of an overall pattern of Butler's psychomorphology. Most important, such a knowledge will help us understand one particular effect of the novel which readers have reported again and again – i.e. the unsettling effect of the particular quality of savagery of the text. It is the ambilateralism which has this effect on readers. Our lives as human beings, in the 'social' sense, function on the tacit assumption of innumerable asymmetries taken for granted. In thousands of separate little instances, Butler's ambilateralism destroys our confident assumption that things are one way and not another. He shatters our asymmetric assurances and tempts us with symmetry. And symmetry again is a complex thing. It appeals to us; it creates beauty. But it is also associated with negative results and ultimately death. Even the title emphasizes everyone's ultimate fate.[45] The way of all flesh is 'to the kitchen'. The novel is intriguing, elegant, unsettling, appealing and repulsive – all of this because of chiasticism.

4   Chiasmus and Butler's Life

Henry Festing Jones's *Memoir* gives sufficient evidence that Butler's private rhetoric was much the same as his public. All through Jones's two massive volumes we find Butler doing in his private life what he was doing in his public as regards chiasmus. Often the chiastic passages quoted in Jones's *Memoir* are even more revealing than corresponding ones in Butler's own published works, because we are allowed to see more of the feelings they gave rise to – feelings such as satisfaction, triumph and anxiety.

Familiar uses and forms of chiasmus abound. Complementary inversion occurs, as in the following example in a letter to Miss Savage: 'I am still alive, but I have fallen among thieves. Well, I believe I may also truly say that the thieves have fallen among *me*...' (I 216). Chiastic inversion is often used in connection with humour, as in another letter to Miss Savage.

> By the way, I did not mean the hero to be sentimental towards the old flirt; but I meant the old flirt, in the end, to be sentimental about the hero, and to wind up a long theological argument, during which her attention has evidently been wandering, by flinging her arms about his neck and saying she would do anything for him if he would only love his Saviour.   (I 160–1)

In his letters and his notes Butler uses chiasmus for exposition of his ideas in the same way as he does in his books and articles. The following sentence is from a letter to Professor Mivart on the subject of pantheism: 'I see him [God] as animating the universe – he in us, and we in him ...' (I 407). Another example of this kind is a passage from a summary of *Life and Habit* that Butler wrote: 'Then comes Descent with Modification. Similarity tempered with dissimilarity and dissimilarity tempered with similarity – a contradiction in terms like almost everything else that is true or useful or indeed intelligible at all' (II 445). Butler liked to express his doctrines in chiastic aphorisms if

239

possible. Therefore it is natural to find his ideas about 'learning and doing' reported by Jones in a form that implies chiasmus through equation of 'learning' and 'doing': 'Do not learn to do, but learn in doing' (II 105).

Since a chiasticist believes that of any two there is always some amount of one in the other, he will often fall to speculating which one out of two contains more of the other. Butler constantly turned such things over in his mind. In a letter to Jones from Monte Erice he describes a procession: 'The whole thing was pagan with the slightest varnish of Christianity; all other such things I have seen were Christian with a touch of paganism' (II 193). If there is a conventional proportion of the two ingredients in a mixture, the well-known type of joke that results from an inversion comes very easily to a chiasticist – as witness Butler reporting from Shrewsbury, where he was visiting his sisters: '*2nd Aug. 1895* – I am all right, but have said that there was chicory in the coffee (I *should* have said, to be nearer the truth, that there was perhaps some coffee in the chicory)...' (II 231).

Butler never tired of chiasmus; he always found it impressive. Many episodes in Jones's *Memoir.* show that he also thought others did the same, and accordingly would find *him* impressive if he made use of chiasmus. Compare the following note about Butler, Jones and two Frenchmen:

> The Frenchmen could not make it out, and I thought it incumbent upon me to explain briefly what it was all about. They mollified at once at the name of the British Museum and entered into conversation. What did I think of Freeman's *Sicily?* I said, doubtless in bad French, but that did not matter, that I did not like the book, and fired off a remark which I concocted once about Cuvier:
> 'Monsieur Freeman est grand dans les petites choses et petit avec les grandes.' I suppose they thought this was impromptu, but I could see that it impressed them.   (II 269)

Butler's keen sense of satisfaction in remembering such episodes was never blunted. Such notes as this give us a measure of his emotional addiction to chiasmus.

Satisfaction, however, is not the only emotion connected with chiasmus in Butler. Despair is another, as when Butler, writing to Mrs Bovill, reflects on variants of a 'Catch-22' problem:

> Then I was a year and a half in Canada, mainly Montreal. I think you

know the little 'Psalm' which was the outcome of that sojourn. It is at the end of my Selection book. When they have nicer things to eat they will be nicer people, and when they are nicer people they will have nicer things to eat; but so long as their food is what it is the Lord will harden their hearts and they will not bring forth the fruits of good living. What a vicious circle it all is! For good living is both the fruit that is to be borne and the thing that is to bear the fruit, is it not? (ɪɪ 124)

Butler's desire to find chiasmus can be seen in a letter to his father in which he asks for help in finding a chiastic line that he half remembers. First Butler wrote to his sister:

29 Dec. 1885 – Please ask my father if he remembers a line in Horace, 'Nec mihi res, sed me rebus componere...' Does he remember the last word? It sounds as if it ought to be 'conor', but I have a half fancy that the 'o' in 'conor' may be short; if he remembers, ask him to supply the missing word; if he doesn't, I will look through the Epistles and Satires of Horace. I want the passage as summing up the Lamarckian system, according to which modification is effected by animals and plants adapting themselves to their surroundings as well as they can and, as the surroundings gradually change, changing too. (ɪɪ 29)

Two days later he wrote to his father:

31 Dec. 1885 – I thank you for your kindness in trying to find my line. I thought the 'o' in 'conor' was long, but have generally found that when I feel pretty sure a vowel is long it turns out short, and I could not remember a passage with the word in it. On receipt of yours I took out my small Horace, intending to look through the Epistles and find the line, which had been kind enough to place itself within the first 25 lines of the First Epistle of the First Book. I had it all wrong – the passage runs:

> Nunc in Aristippi furtim praecepta relabor,
> Et mihi res, non me rebus subiungere conor.

So he does the exact opposite of what I want him to do. However, he evidently disapproves of what he is doing, and acknowledges the normal and proper thing to be the trying to adapt self to circumstances, rather than circumstances to self, and this is what I want. Of course in real life we do both as much as we can and bear with what we cannot change; still I think there is a decided balance in favour of adaptation of self to things rather than of things to self; this, if Lamarck's view is right, pervades the whole animal kingdom and underlies all modification. (Ibid.)

Forgetting for the moment the evolutionary debate, we see most clearly in letters such as these Butler's strong desire to find a chiastic way of putting this ideas, and his worry over 'which-one' questions. Which is primary: self or environment, environment or self?

The most typical expression of Butler's anxiety over a 'which-one' problem is a letter to Edward James Jones (1884) in which Butler rumbles on and on in his chiasticist grooves, which became ever deeper as time went on:

In *Unconscious Memory* I said that we should start with life, not death, as we could never smuggle life in if we started without it. This was badly put, for we can no more smuggle death in than life, if we start without it. We must start with matter eternally both alive and dead at the same time. This will be very nice, will it not? We must see life and death as we see heat and cold, never either of them absolute, but in the highest life still some death, and in the lowest death still some life. The greatest heat and cold we know of can always be imagined as becoming a little hotter and colder, which means that there is a little cold even in the highest heat we can deal with. There is no such thing as either perfect life or perfect death. And the personal identity between the dying man and the corpse is quite as close as that between the embryo at a day old and the same embryo at three months. True, there is a great change, but every change is pro tanto a death, and death is only a very big change after which we change our ways of looking at things so completely that the new life has no more in common with the old than our present has with our embryonic. The change is, indeed, more sudden than most other changes; but it is neither so sudden nor so complete as to admit of no subdivision whatever, and, if so, there is gradation, and the continuation of identity between life and death (I mean between the dying man and the corpse) goes on all fours with all other changes; so that you must either deny personal identity, as we are accustomed to think of it, or else in the end deny, not death in a modified sense, but certainly death as the end of the individual. Strictly speaking, the individual is born and dies from moment to moment; that is to say, he is never an individual at all except during the present moment – which present moment has no logical existence, but lives on the sufferance of times past and present. Any change is a kind of death, and this is why it is so rude of our friends to notice changes in us.

That life is closely connected with memory may be seen in the fact that death is so closely connected with forgetfulness. Hence the ancients called their river of death Lethe, The River of Forgetfulness.

Also we know the closeness of the analogy between growth, the repair of wasted tissues, and reproduction; they are only phases of the same thing. It is curious that his analogy extends to the mental condition which precedes both eating and the act of generation; in each case there is an appetite – a strong desire to unify some foreign body with ourselves as closely as possible. Love involves an effort after identifying something with ourselves, which ends either in assimilation, by eating, or in connection and reproduction and, consequently, in assimilation after all. Even the desire to pat a horse or dog is a pro tanto effort after physical unification. When we love we desire to draw what we love as closely to us as we can; when we hate we push what we hate away as far as we can. All affinity is a mode of loving, all dissolution a mode of hating. It is curious that we use the same words for the appetite of eating and for that of reproduction. We say we love roast beef and we should like to have roast beef. The residuous parts are also analoguous in eating and reproduction – in the one case, faeces; in the other, afterbirth.

Also unity and separateness are a puzzle. When is 'a thing' a thing at all? If you go down to your atoms and get them quite separate, without a particle of unity with anything else, you can never afterwards get them to join with any other atom; again, if you once get them perfectly united you can never disjoin them. In the most complete isolation there must be still a little union and linking on to something else. In the most complete union there must lurk a germ of disunion – as with heat and cold and life and death. It is only by looking at it thus that we can see the universe either as one thing or as a number of things, and this is how we have got to see it.   (I 430–2)

A little later Butler writes, 'I have no doubt I have written a great deal of rot in this letter, but I can't read it over again' (ibid.). The 'rot' he wrote came straight from his heart. It concerned the two things he found most problematical in life: the question of initiality and the question of identity.

A subcategory of the second of these is the impossibility of fusion, and, though Butler in his notes and letters often uses chiasmus to express mutuality, it is often a mutual lack of something, so that any coming-together can be frustrated, as in the following case of the two categories of music-lovers and poetry-lovers:

> I find that those who are devoted to music and the arts of painting and sculpture are unwilling to turn to the art of literary poetry. On the other hand those who are devoted to the art of literary poetry are less interested in music and in the fine arts.   (II 84)

One of the most distasteful occasions on which Butler used chiasmus is his letter to Miss Savage of 10 February 1885, telling her that his brother had died:

> I have lost my brother, so you see some of us do die sometimes. ... My father remains much in statu quo, but he has never recovered the ground he lost last November; still he gets driven to church in a fly, and is not acutely ill. How is your mamma?
>
> I don't write on black edged paper because you would think that I had become an orphan; but next time I write you will know, so I shall use black edged paper.
>
> I am overworked and low, my neck is full and troublesome, and this always means that I am doing too much, but then I have got too much to do. I cannot help it.
>
> I lost my friend Mr Tylor at the end of December. Curious! as soon as I got a really useful friend, able and willing to back me, *he*, poor man, as soon as he came 'to know me well' 'was sure to die'. Those people have died who ought not to have died, and those people who ought to have died have not died, and there is no sense of propriety in them.   (I 439)

By a masterstroke of dramatic irony, fate gave a final twist to the chiasmus, 'Those people have died who ought not to have died, and those people who ought to have died have not died', when Butler received a letter, not from Miss Savage herself but from a doctor, saying that she had undergone an operation for cancer and was in hospital. She died soon after.

When Butler adds its enantiomorph to a statement, to make it a chiasmus, he may sometimes seem to have a rational reason. In the following example one might think that he is genuinely and carefully considering who can lay greater claim to their common theory, Professor Hering or himself, or who brought it out first: 'Instinct and not only instinct but bodily growth, which, after all, is only a phase of instinct, are certainly according to me and Professor Hering – or rather, according to Professor Hering and myself ...' (I 346). But ultimately, when one has become familiar with Butler's idiosyncrasies of style, one realizes that these additions of enantiomorphs are automatic and unthinking, and need not always, or even usually, mean very much, as witness: 'something has disagreed with me or I have disagreed with something' (II 158). The addition of the second part of such chiastic constructions was often purely automatic in Butler.

Jones's *Memoir* gives a good picture of how Butler soaked up chiasticism from his environment as well as imparted it to whatever he came into contact with. Chiastic events in his own life would impress themselves on his memory, stay there for years, and ultimately find their way into his writing. The muddle of putting two letters into the wrong envelopes occurred in Butler's own childhood (cf. Jones, II 5):

When [Charlotte] wrote to Crampsford to desire the prayers of the congregation (she was sure her mother would wish it, and that the Crampsford people would be pleased at her remembrance of them), she was sending another letter on some quite different subject at the same time, and put the two letters into the wrong envelopes. Ernest was asked to take these letters to the village post-office, and imprudently did so; when the error came to be discovered Christina happened to have rallied a little. Charlotte flew at Ernest immediately, and laid all the blame of the blunder upon his shoulders. (*The Way of All Flesh*, ch. 83, p. 375)

Butler stored the event up in his memory for years because it was chiastic.

Whether as a result of their acquaintance with Butler, or whether they became acquaintances because of it, the fact is that Butler's friends often had pronounced chiasticist habits. This is particularly true of Miss Savage and perhaps Jones; but actually even such people as Alfred, Butler's manservant, can be suspected of having caught the habit: 'I was very glad to see [the Governor] after such a long absence, and so was he to see me again' (Jones, II 164).

Alfred's use of such constructions may be the result of chance. But with Miss Savage and Jones the case is different. Miss Savage was quite clearly in many respects a chiasticist, as is evident from her letters and her reported sayings. Compare, for instance, 'it is rather droll to think that when we are playing upon the piano, the piano is playing upon us in exactly the same way' (I 235); or,

> I was provoked last night by the nonsense some people were talking about [Mr Carlyle], and, as they went on to excuse his bad temper on account of his bad digestion, I said that probably his bad digestion should be excused on account of his bad temper, as probably he had been born with a bad temper, but that bad digestions were generally made.   (I 429)

Miss Savage then goes on to acknowledge her indebtedness to *Erewhon* ('I remember *Erewhon* you see' – ibid.), but actually it is difficult to say precisely who influenced whom. (For Jones's comments on the question, see II 348–9.)

It is even possible to make out slight differences between Butler and Miss Savage in the profiles as chiasticists. One chiasticist idea which is comparatively neglected in Butler is the chiastic 'see-saw' rule of thinking: i.e. 'If one goes up the other must come down, and *vice-versa.*' This pattern is very strongly present in the thinking of Henry James, who wrote entire books on the theme, such as *The Sacred Fount.* It appears that it also came easily to Miss Savage:

> A Mr and Miss Lloyd whom I know slightly came to the gallery to-day. They looked so extraordinarily well and flourishing that I am sure there must be a corresponding depression in the health of the other Lloyds, or that there very soon will be.   (I 305)

Above all other chiastic traits, however, Miss Savage shared Butler's love of inversions, as is evident from Alethea in *The Way of All Flesh* – Alethea being modelled on Miss Savage. It was Miss Savage who originally wrote about her enemy that 'she combined the harmlessness of the serpent with the wisdom of the dove' (I 247). Particularly interesting is Miss Savage's inversion of the first and second names of Grant Allen: 'That flippant creature Allen Grant was soon ready with his notice...' (I 304). Jones explains this as humour: 'Her quiet assumptions of an inability to remember correctly the name of so insignificant a person as Grant Allen amused Butler more than the reviews annoyed him' (ibid.). With Butler inversion of names was not a device which was always under artistic control, and it would be interesting to know the full truth of this matter. Was there perhaps a private tradition of inversion of names in the circle of Butler and his friends?

It is sometimes difficult to make out what should be attributed to Jones and what to the people whose speech he reports in the *Memoir*. When Jones reports chiastically Rockstro's instructions (Jones and Butler went to Rockstro regularly for music-lessons) 'about ornamenting your construction and not constructing your ornament' (II 229), should we take this as evidence of Rockstro's or Jones's love of chiasmus?

Certainly Jones became more and more like Butler as time went by, and the *Memoir* reflects Jones's as well as Butler's love of chiasmus. Indeed, the very birth of the *Memoir* was Butlerian. Jones says it 'came to him', as Butler's books used to come to *him:* 'The book came to me, as he used to say his own books came to him, and insisted on being written' (I viii). Sometimes in the *Memoir* it is difficult to know whether Jones or Butler is speaking:

> Young John Pickard Owen and young Ernest Pontifex did not understand that nothing can exist at all unless it contains some of its opposite. Later, they came to realise that the enemy sows tares in every wheat-field, and we must have patience. ... But nothing came of this desire for reconciliation – perhaps because there is no possibility of any agreement as to which is wheat and which tares; or the difficulty may lie in the hearts of the disputants and not in the nature of the crops.   (I 183)

Throughout the *Memoir* Jones shows an excellent understanding of the motivating forces in Butler's psyche, and makes many interesting comments. He compares Butler's reactions at different times, noting similarities: 'Butler's whole nature revolted against the idea that the universe was without intelligence, just as it had revolted against the idea that Rossura porch had not been designed' (I 300). He explains apparent contradictions:

> This was part of the tidiness of Butler's nature which Ernest inherited from the author.
> Again, any statement involving a contradiction, not realised as such by the person making it, outraged his sense of tidiness. No one

felt more acutely than he did that life depends upon the equilibrium resulting from the clash of opposites, and this involves the
existence of contradictions. But these are not untidy contradictions
springing from muddle-headedness and carelessness; there is no
untidiness in intentional contradictions which are pigeon-holed as
such from the first.   (II 10)

He suggests motives: 'He felt that the position was all wrong; but he
considered himself to be in loco parentis [in relation to Pauli], and
was not going to behave like Theobald' (I 223).

Jones also comments on the one-sidedness of Butler's friendship
with Pauli, apparently not worried that his own friendship with
Butler might qualify for the same category – with himself in the role
of the dog: 'It seems to have been one of those one-sided friendships
sometimes met with in real life, as well as in books, when the
diffident, poetical, shy man becomes devoted to the confident,
showy, worldly man, as a dog to his master' (I 108). There were
several cases of one-sided relationships in Butler's life – one-sided
one way or the other – and not only of friendship but also of enmity
and guilt. Jones very perceptively comments on the fact that Butler
did not really need a rational reason for his feelings in this respect:

> Butler gave no reason; he thought he had done a high-handed and
> shabby action in calling in his money without consulting Moor-
> house, whose good opinion he thought he must have forfeited by
> behaving in such an overbearing manner. When he suspected
> people of attempting to browbeat him he hit back fiercely. But
> Moorhouse did not hit back and this was like coals of fire on his
> head. He may have had some reason which he would not tell me,
> but I think not; for, as I saw over and over again, if any one was
> kind to him he could never do enough in return, and if he thought
> he had neglected an opportunity it made him miserable.   (I 170–1)

If we now turn to the manifestations of the various subcategories
and constituent elements of chiastic thinking in the *Memoir,* and
begin with reciprocity, there is ample proof that Butler's use of
reciprocal constructions was as frequent in his private rhetoric as in
his public.

Butler's relationship with his father is summed up in the first
sentence of a note which he wrote in 1883: '*My Father and Myself*: He
never liked me, nor I him...' (I 20). Butler then immediately goes on

to worry about the question of balance, saying he does not know whose fault it was (cf. Ch. 2, *supra*).

The pattern of Butler's problems with reciprocity is intricate and varied, but all the features are predictable. At the basis of it all is Butler's passionate longing for reciprocity. From this follows his sharp sense of betrayal if other people did not match the feelings he had towards them. Thus he is upset that Pauli did not treat him as he treated Pauli:

> I always hoped that, as time went on, and he saw how absolutely devoted to him I was, and what unbounded confidence I had in him, and how I forgave him over and over again for treatment that I should not have stood for a moment from any one else – I always hoped that he would soften and deal as frankly and unreservedly with me as I with him... . (I 113)

After the burial of Pauli, when Butler eats the funeral luncheon, he reflects with macabre satisfaction that here at last is a grain of something to restore reciprocity:

> After the coffin had been duly lowered and the service ended, we were asked to a luncheon which had been brought down with us from London. Everything was done regardless of expense and I was wondering who in the world was paying for it – or rather I should have wondered if I had not heard about ... [the well-to-do friends] – when I reflected, with a certain satisfaction, that for once in my life I was making a hearty meal at what was very nearly Pauli's expense. It was the nearest thing to a dinner from him that I had ever had. (II 285)

The complementary mirror-image of Butler's indignation, if people had treated him worse than he them, was deep remorse if he thought he had treated them worse than they him. Such people were above all Miss Savage and Moorhouse (cf. Ch. 2, *supra*). Editing his literary remains in 1901, Butler writes in a note on Miss Savage,

> I have got on with Miss Savage's and my correspondence – being now just half way through. I am shocked to see how badly I treated her, always thinking and writing about myself and never about her. If I have been as selfish and egoistic to you as I was to her, it will explain a good deal. I must endeavour, late as it is, to mend my ways. (II 349)

Editing the correspondence between himself and Miss Savage in 1877, Butler comments in a note,

> I never had such a good chance of seeing my past self, not vaguely, but with the documentary evidence of my own handwriting; and I am shocked at the selfishness which pervades all my letters, and the marvellous unselfishness which pervades all Miss Savage's. How patient under suffering she was I never knew till after her death; but what pains me most as I edit this correspondence – the only thing that I can do to express the remorse I feel as strongly now as I did when she died nearly twenty years ago – what pains me most is to see the way in which, all through, I was thinking of myself and my own doings, while taking no heed, letter after letter, of things she had told me about her own... .   (I 251–2)

On the imbalance in the relationship between Butler and Moorhouse, note the following passage from Butler's letter to the editor of *The Press* in 1902:

> I am glad also to possess photographs of my old friend, Mr William Sefton Moorhouse, who dwells ever in my memory as one of the very finest men whose path I ever crossed, but who also haunts me bitterly as one of the very few men – at least I trust it may be so – who treated me with far greater kindness than I did him. His memory is daily with me, notwithstanding all these years, and ever will be, as long as I can remember anything. But, alas! it is as that of one who showed nothing but extreme kindness and goodwill to me and who did not receive from me the measure which he had meted out. Not that I ever failed in admiration and genuine affection but (it is true, under great stress) I did not consider things which a larger knowledge of the world has shown me I ought assuredly to have considered.   (II 362)

From Butler's feelings of remorse over those cases in which he thought there had been an imbalance because of his treating other people worse than they him follow naturally those strategies that he devised to counteract such faults. The simplest way to make sure that a relationship (involving kindness) would not be unbalanced one way (i.e. with him treating people less kindly than they him) was of course to make it ridiculously unbalanced the other way (i.e. with him treating people unconscionably better than they him). No amount of overkill along these lines would ever strike Butler as unreasonable. If it was best to make sure, why not then very sure; why not even ridiculously oversure?[1] Why not tolerate even such a parasite as Pauli? Jones, again, has a good comment on this:

> When Edward Overton doubts whether Ernest ever will be as wary as he ought to be about trusting any one who is kind to him – this is a dig at himself. He was always thinking, as he says of Ernest (chap. lxxvii), that people had a claim upon him for some inestimable service they had rendered him or some irreparable mischief done to them by himself, so much so that I used to say of him that he must always pay double and other people might only pay him half. (ii 9)

Even in Butler's personal habits, in matters such as gestures, we find traces of this strategy. He would not – even literally – 'turn away' from anyone, and scrupulously left rooms, in which he had been with friends, walking backwards, facing the company. Compare the Revd Cuthbert Creighton's reminiscences of Butler: 'When my father took him away to his study later on, he said good-night to us all and left the room, walking backwards, smiling and bowing to the company in the quaint old-fashioned way which I understood was his habit on such occasions' (ii 179).

When reciprocity is an ideal the presence of perfect reciprocity is a cause for rejoicing and praise, and the absence of it a cause for reproach and bitterness. As examples of the first, let us take some passages dealing with the intimate relationship between Hans Faesh and Butler/Jones; Faesch and Butler; or Faesch and Jones. In a letter to Faesch dated 16 February 1895 Butler writes, 'nothing but goodness and kindness ever came out of you, and such as our best was we gave it to you as you gave yours to us' (ii 202). In another letter a little later he writes, 'then, my dear Hans, let me beseech you in the name of all the affection a dear father can bear to a very dear son, by the absurd, idiotic tears that you have wrung from me, by those we wrung from yourself, by the love which Jones bears you and you bear towards him...' (ii 203–4).

If a friendship demanded reciprocity of action (of gift-making, for instance) Butler could certainly rise to the occasion, even if his friendliness had started as a joke or a charade. Very instructive is

Butler's relationship with a Turk named Ismail (see II 220ff.). Butler reciprocates with a gift, having first received one.

> Ismail was much affected. The good fellow immediately took off his watch-chain (happily of brass and of no intrinsic value) and gave it me assuring me that it was given him by a very dear friend, that he had worn it for many years and valued it greatly – would I keep it as a memorial of himself? Fortunately, I had with me a little silver match-box which Alfred had given me and which had my name engraved upon it. I gave it to him, but had some difficulty in making him accept it.   (II 223)

But in the end Butler could not keep it up, and Ismail becomes yet another of those ghosts that rise up and smite him, in waking nightmares.

> I sent him his photograph which I had taken, and I sent the soldiers their groups also – one for each man – and in due course I received the following letter of thanks. Alas! I have never written an answer. I knew not how to do it. I knew, however, that I could not keep up a correspondence, even though I wrote once. But few unanswered letters more often rise up and smite me. How the Post Office people ever read 'Bueter, Ciforzin St.' into 'Butler, Clifford's Inn', I cannot tell. What splendid emendators of a corrupt text they ought to make! But I could almost wish that they had failed, for it has pained me not a little that I have not replied.   (Ibid.)

As an example of Butler's annoyance with someone guilty of destroying the symmetry of reciprocity, we may take his indignation at Grant Allen, who went ahead and reviewed Butler's book, though Butler had declined to review *his* book:

> *Butler to Mrs Bridges: 16 Dec. 1886* – To-morrow (the Editor of *The Academy* tells me) there is to be a very hostile review of *Luck or Cunning?* in *The Academy*. The Editor apologised a good deal and hum'd and ha'd, but I told him I had survived a good many hostile articles in *The Academy* already, and he need not distress himself. The review is to be by Grant Allen who, doubtless, asked for the job. Grant Allen is the man whose book I declined to review in *The Athenaeum* on grounds which ought to have deterred him from reviewing myself, and that they have not done so confirms the

opinion which I have long formed concerning him.   (II 44)

Butler being a bad lover but a good hater, his problems with reciprocity of hostility are nothing like his problems with reciprocity of affection.[2] If the mutual feeling is to be one of hate, Butler enthusiastically rushes in to supply the enantiomorph that is lacking to complete a chiasmus expressing reciprocity. There are numerous passages on Butler and his partner cutting each other by mutual consent. For instance: 'and Lewis Morris, the poet, and I (who know each other perfectly well and used to meet continually at the Century) cut each other by mutual consent' (I 417). Also, on the same page:

> My impression is that I dislike them quite as much as they me, and though I do not for a moment believe men of science to be in a conspiracy against myself, I am quite ready to admit that I am in a conspiracy of one against men of science in general, with an extra slouch of the hat for Mr Grant Allen in particular. It was because Clodd told me of Grant Allen's having said this, that I told him I did not like Grant Allen or his work when I met Clodd at Webster's. [July 1885].

The following concerns Dr Kennedy:

> I spoke to Kennedy before dinner, and found him surly, and, as it appeared to me, anxious to avoid me – which I no sooner perceived than I avoided him. ... Why should I, knowing that I do not particularly like these people nor they me, why should I, who never liked my school nor got much good from it, go and pay a guinea for a bad dinner, and eat and drink what it takes me a whole day to recover from?   (II 39)

In the next example Butler starts out with a case of deception, the guilt of which is as usual equally shared between deceiver and deceived:

> Fortunately for them [the scientific establishment] the public has developed such hereditary aptitude for being cheated, and they have themselves developed such not less hereditary aptitude for gulling the public that, thanks to the universities and academies, they will probably find enough supporters to last their time, after which the deluge will not much matter.   (II 116)

He then immediately goes on to a specific reciprocal negative relation

– between himself and Francis Darwin: 'As for Frank Darwin – he is a Cambridge professor and knows better than to go about breathing fire and smoke against me. No more, I trust, do I against him' (ibid.). Reciprocity of hostility as a general principle would often put Butler in mind of a specific case in this way. Conversely he would deduce a general rule from a specific, as in the following example (a letter to Fernand Henry):

> I am sorry your French critics have treated you in a superficial manner, but I have always observed that it is only the shallow books that are received with a chorus of applause. The critics can understand these at once; but as for being at any pains to study what requires sustained attention – is it to be expected of them? Besides – do you write reviews yourself? If you do, by all means let the fact be known in literary circles. The reviewers themselves sometimes write books and, if they know that you may be able to belaud them, they will belaud you; otherwise if you write on a subject of which they know nothing, if they deign to notice you at all, they will make it quite plain that they have not thought it worth while to read what you have said.   (II 316)

Not only with reciprocity but also with inversion – to which we now turn – it was true that Butler's private language was as full of it as his public. Again, the question of what *was* private and what public in Butler's life is debatable. As critics have suggested, maybe what Butler liked more than anything else was to invert in private, with his friends such as Jones or Miss Savage, but think about it as if it had been done in public. (This may be taken as a sign of that moral cowardice which critics have so often and unanimously detected in Butler.) Typical of this kind of inversion would then be Butler's suggestion to Jones that his (Butler's) biography should begin with the sentence, 'The subject of this Memoir was born of rich but dishonest parents' (I viii).

The idea that a possible source of Butler's chiasticism was his unhappy relationship with his father is supported by the fact that Butler inverted some of his father's sayings.

Thomas Butler went to school at Shrewsbury under his father, Dr Butler. Having to write a theme upon 'Silence' he began:

'Silence is a virtue which renders us agreeable to our fellow creatures.'

He wrote another on 'Inconsistency' which began:

'Inconsistency is a vice which degrades human nature and levels man with the brute.'

He was not intending to be satirical, but his son was when he afterwards used both these aphorisms in *Erewhon;* he edited the second, however, by changing 'Inconsistency' into 'Consistency'.

(I 12)

Butler wished his father would die. Then he could have his way, he thought. He was disappointed when Canon Butler did not die of an attack of bronchitis, and invoked the familiar Orpheus-myth inverted:

Butler to Miss L. I. Jones: 16 Jan. 1902 – I am editing the very painful years in my correspondence, 1883–1886. I am at the point when I was sent for post-haste to Shrewsbury to a supposed perfectly hopeless illness of my father who recovered and lived three years longer. I see I wrote to Miss Savage that it was Orpheus and Eurydice only the other way about.　(II 364)

Butler's habit of inverting proverbs and sayings was so inveterate in private life too that other people remembered it as being 'singularly characteristic' of him:

My friend Mr Phipson Beale told me that he went out to America on the same steamer with Mr Butler, and that on a lovely moonlight evening they were gazing over the Atlantic – a long time silent – when Mr Butler turned to him and said: 'Yes, Beale – yes, an honest God's the noblest work of man.' Singularly characteristic.　(I 212)

Butler's love of inversion extended to double-inversion, i.e. inversion of an inversion, so as to re-create the original, uninverted state: 'I gathered moreover that she shared the common, but absurd, opinion according to which "the child is father of the man" (just as if everyone did not know that it is the other way on)' (II 36).

The familiar variety of inversion which is meant to achieve something by aiming for the opposite is found in this example: 'She [the Church] attacks reasonable conclusions under the guise of defending them, with a view to impose on those who have not wit enough to find her out' (I 182).

Inversion influenced Butler's creative processes in subtle ways – it may be at work even when it is quite invisible. Jones suggests that 'Old

Mr Owen, the father of the brothers in the Memoir, is Butler's own father by contraries; that is, he is just what Canon Butler was not' (i 177). This is an important observation, not so much for the specific point it makes, as for the general. The inversionary tactic was one of Butler's strategies of invention. We may imagine that he sometimes relied on the technique of inversion as a kind of scaffolding so that inversion aided in the creative process even though it may be invisible in the finished product.

Butler was fascinated by states of vacillation (cf. Ch. 2). In the *Memoir* Jones relates the following anecdote involving himself, Butler's sister and Butler:

> On the Sunday morning after breakfast, Mrs Bridges began:
> 'You know, Sam, we don't wish you to think that we expect you to go to church. We know you and Mr. Jones always go into the country on Sunday for a walk, and we want you to try and think you can do just as you would wish. We shall go to church; and if you think you would like to come with us, you would find it a bright little service; that I can promise you. And the music is good. Or, there is St So-and-so's where you would have a sermon from the vicar. But of course you can go into the country if you think you would prefer it, and we shall not be in the least offended. All we wish is that you should try and understand that we want you to think you are free to try and do exactly as you think you would like'...
>
> This rambled on like a first movement by Beethoven; the two skilfully contrasted themes of Church and Country-walk were worked out and developed, and led to a coda which threatened to assume considerable dimensions. In imitation of the master, Mrs Bridges introduced 'points of independent interest, variety of modulation and new treatment of the themes of the movement being alike resorted to, to keep up the interest until the last'. Presently she paused; not that she had exhausted her themes or herself, but she paused; and I interpolated:
> 'Suppose we toss up?'
> It had the effect of silencing Mrs Bridges.
> 'Come away!' said Butler sternly.   (ii 404–5)

Jones's *Memoir* provides overabundant evidence of Butler's inability to choose between two alternatives. Butler time and again got caught in an inability to decide which one of two alternatives was the likelier. In a note he relates a clash between his schoolmaster Dr

Kennedy and himself over a Greek word and ends his note with the following reflection: 'We were both of us very silly and very lazy; but which of us was the sillier and lazier our Father which is in heaven knoweth, but I know not. By "us" I mean Kennedy and myself' (1 35).

One would have thought that, with the violence of his quarrel with his father, Butler would come down all on his own side, but, on the contrary, it is perhaps especially in the case of a dual choice with such (seemingly) wildly unbalanced alternatives that he most strongly confirms his belief in ambilateralism. Thus, while editing his literary remains he often adds postscripts such as the following to portions of his and his father's correspondence: 'I do not know which is the more comic in its own melancholy way – my letter or my father's note. – S. B. 1901' (1 65).

Butler's ambilateralism was a source of pride and satisfaction to him. He thought that his capability of seeing two sides of any question ought to earn him praise and approval from others. Thus he can cite his changes of opinion in his favour: 'I feel strongly and write as I feel; but I am open to conviction, and that I can take in more sides of a question than one is proved by the many changes my opinions have undergone' (1 98). That Butler *did* have an extraordinary ability to change his mind is suggested by the following report by Jones:

And then when Butler came to my rooms in the evening he would generally say something of this kind:

'You know that Rembrandt at the Old Masters – that thing they call a Rembrandt, I mean – in the third room?'

And I would reply, 'Yes.'

'Well, Ballard has been this afternoon; says he is convinced they are right. I don't believe a word of it. Why it hasn't any of the – '

Here would follow all the reasons for the attribution being absurd; and it would seem to me that there must have been something like a row between Butler and Ballard. Next evening Butler would say:

'I've been to the Old Masters again to see that Rembrandt, and, do you know, I believe Ballard is quite right. What I took for – '

Here would follow all the reasons for changing his opinion and agreeing with Ballard after all. He nearly always came round to agreeing with Ballard in the end; he always told him so, and they never really quarrelled.   (1 139)

Butler's reasons for changing his mind were varied, and probably the rules of his chiasticism about turning, not turning, and so forth, may have meant as much or more than any actual state of facts.[3]

'Which-one' ambiguities occupied Butler's mind for years on end. No matter how trivial the question might be intrinsically, if only it was posed in the form of 'whether-or-not?' it was sure of keeping Butler's attention. Compare the following note:

> Moorhouse once said to Butler, 'Very handsome, well-dressed men are seldom very good men.' On this Butler wrote:
>
>> I liked Moorhouse very much, and, being young, listened deferentially to all he said. I did not like to hear him say this, for I knew I liked men to be handsome and well-dressed. I have thought about it a great deal during the more than twenty years that have passed since Moorhouse's words were spoken, and even now I do not know what to say. Sometimes they are and sometime they are not. [1882] (i 106)

The following anecdote is of a type well recognized in humorous literature. The basic structure is inversion, i.e. the real wisdom of the fool (which implies symmetrically the foolishness of the wise), rather than the foolishness of the fool (and the wisdom of the wise). The inversion naturally made Butler remember any such anecdote. But what really dots the 'i' is the 'which-one' ambiguity:

> T. W. G. Butler was once taxed with having spoken disrespectfully of the three Persons of the Trinity. He had not even been present when the words were spoken, but he gravely considered the accusation and replied:
> 'No. That wasn't me. There must be some mistake. I cannot have said that because I don't know any of them.'
> 'Which of us,' Butler used to say, 'which of us, I wonder, ought to be in the workhouse asylum?'   (i 134–5)

There are other humorous uses of 'which-one' ambiguities. One variety concerns lack of difference, in cases, such as the following, where difference and distinctness are of the essence: 'His father, like Theobald, knew two tunes, "God save the Queen" and "In my cottage near a wood", and I have been given to understand that people were not always sure which he was whistling ...' (i 27).

Since the most natural subject of a debate for Butler was a

'which-one' ambiguity, he imagines that the topic of Christ's disputation with the Doctors must have been such a question.

> He also intended to fall asleep and have a dream in front of the chapel that contains the figures representing Christ disputing with the Doctors. We had often wondered what the dispute was all about; in his dream the Doctors were to propound this question:
>   'Which is best – prose or poetry?'
> And Christ, ticking off the alternatives on his fingers, as Italians do, was to be heard giving His decision:
>   'Poetry, because there is less of it on a page.'   (II 26)

In vacillating between the two possible answers to a 'which-one' ambiguity, the pleasure is prolonged in proportion as the number of turns or switches from one side to the other can be multiplied.[4] Butler therefore loved such ambiguities the more the more numerous were the switches. In deciding which episodes (of 'which-one' ambiguities of vacillation) from his life and experience were worthy of being remembered and put on record, an important criterion was probably the number of switches – the principle being, the more the better. Butler and Jones especially loved the following episode, because there is a final additional switch when they discover that they had been wrong:

> We had been told that two of the soldiers, in the chapel where Christ is taken in the garden, were made out of the old statues of Adam and Eve when the present Adam and Eve in the first chapel were made, and we had examined the chapel in the morning and made up our minds that the soldier with a moustache and real drapery was Adam and the other soldier with long hair and armour was Eve. Eve was bigger than Adam which was wrong, and she had no breasts to speak of, but that might have been because neither Cain nor Abel was yet born. Her breast had been painted to represent armour in silver scales, which stopped short of her girdle, her intervening belly being painted blue, like an ancient Briton. As we were going into chapels before dinner, we thought we might as well settle the Adam and Eve question for certain, so we went in and Dionigi investigated; I also pulled up their clothes and we found we had been quite wrong in the morning. It is Eve who has the moustache and the drapery hides her breasts; and it is Adam's stomach that is painted blue.   (II 57; cf. also *Ex Voto,* ch. 11, pp. 112–13)

Another, very similar, anecdote of this kind is the following, in which there is also a final twist, and no real certainty of a solution to the 'which-one' ambiguity:

This was not the only lesson he received that evening. The other was on a subject more difficult than the attractive displaying of type on a page. It was on the art of understanding women. Most of the other guests were ladies, and the conversation turned upon Stockton's story 'The Lady or the Tiger?' Butler had not read it, and they had to tell it to him shortly. The princess and a young man had fallen in love; he is to be punished by being brought into the arena where he is to open one of two doors; behind one door is a tiger, behind the other is a lady; if he opens the first, the tiger will come out and eat him; if he opens the second, the lady will come out and marry him; he does not know which is behind which, but the princess is in secret and is sitting among the audience; he looks to her for a sign and she directs him to open – here the story breaks off, hanging on the query, Which door did she indicate?

The ladies at Miss Zimmern's all agreed that it was a foolish query because, of course, no woman could bear to see her lover torn to pieces by a tiger; true, no woman could bear to see her lover marry a rival, still it would be the lesser of two evils, and women being by nature tender-hearted she would certainly spare his life. We listened with interest, and felt that we were learning something.

The conversation then turned, as it often does among English people in Florence, upon the Brownings – and what a remarkable pair they were! and what an ideal marriage! One of the ladies remembered that she had once before discussed 'The Lady or the Tiger?' in a company which included a lady who knew Mr Browning slightly. At the request of the others this lady had written to the poet stating the problem and asking what, in his opinion, the princess would have done. Mr Browning replied on a postcard that the princess would have let out the tiger, and so would any woman; he had no doubt about it. Whereupon the ladies at Miss Zimmern's all agreed that Mr Browning was right. And they attributed the correctness of his solution of the problem to his consummate knowledge of women, acquired no doubt from that wonderful woman his wife. And so the conversation was left hanging on a query no less perplexing to us than the query of the story, and we were not sure that, after all, we had learnt anything.   (II 240–1)

We realize that psychologically Butler did not want any solution to a 'which-one' problem. What he was after was not the solution, only the problem itself.. A solution would have created asymmetry; the question, on the contrary, represented symmetry preserved.

Butler's urge to find symmetry everywhere was with him from a very early age and concerned all his activities. In the following letter, from Butler to his mother, at the early date of 1851, Butler's interest in mathematics concerns precisely questions of symmetry and reversibility:

I have just been interrupted in this letter to prove to the whole private room except More that when $d = 0$, $r\,a\,d = 0$ none of them being for some time able to comprehend the simple fact that 4 times 0 is 0 and all insisting that 0 times 4 is a very different thing from 4 times 0!!!! and not above half believing that 5 times 6 = 6 times 5!!!! so much for the mathematical education at Shrewsbury: it really has been a most animated argument.   (I 41)

Even earlier than this Butler had acquired a chiasticist vocabulary. In the earliest preserved letter from Butler to his mother (August 1850) we already find the word 'reverse': 'Which is not bad but the reverse' (I 38). Throughout his life he went on adding to his chiasticist vocabulary. Although Butler strived for simplicity of style and would not use rare words unless he had to, his range of vocabulary was enormous, and in no respect is this so true as in the case of the words connected with chiasticism. Butler would coin neologisms if he had to; above all he would adopt any existing word connected with chiasticism, no matter how rare. Thus one finds, say, such a word as 'animadversational' in one of his letters (II 314).

Butler's 'palladianism' permeates his thinking and his life. Nature is full of palladian symmetry, but few individuals are as open to the fact as Butler. There is hardly a scene or an episode in his life in which palladian influence is not at work. Even when Butler is coxing on the river at Cambridge, the simple fact that a river has two banks impresses itself on his consciousness, not only as a concrete fact, but probably also as a philosophical fact.

As we go over the course day by day there are plenty of gigs and traps running by our sides, and men, too, timing us and noticing every stroke; one feels very big and very responsible with the knowledge that if you steer a foot too wide round a corner or don't keep the boat's head *quite* straight, but budge a little bit to the one hand or the other, your misdeed is looked upon with untellable satisfaction or the contrary by heaps of foes or friends of the boat.

(1 53)

Freedom for Butler is often bound up with the question of reversibility. Lack of reversibility gives Butler a sense of being trapped. There are two ways of avoiding this. One is obviously if there does exist the possibility of turning. The other is if palladianism makes sure that there are two similar ends, so that, if only you continue – even without turning – there will at some time be a change and you will be back to a state similar to the initial one. Butler's feelings on the subject can be studied in the psychological overtones of the following dissertation on rat-traps:

Dunkett's Rat-Trap: Mr Dunkett found all his traps fail one after another, and was in such despair at the way the corn got eaten that he resolved to invent a rat-trap. He began by putting himself as nearly as possible in the rat's place.

'Is there anything', he asked himself, 'in which, if I were a rat, I should have such complete confidence that I could not suspect it without suspecting everything in the world and being unable henceforth to move fearlessly in any direction?'

He pondered for a while and had no answer, till one night the room seemed to become full of light and he heard a voice from heaven saying:

'Drain-pipes.'

Then he saw his way. To suspect a common drain-pipe would be to cease to be a rat. Here Skertchley enlarged a little, explaining that a spring was to be concealed inside, but that the pipe was to be open at both ends; if the pipe were closed at one end, a rat would naturally not like going into it, for he would not feel sure of being able to get out again; on which I interrupted and said:

'Ah, it was just this which stopped me from going into the Church.'

When he told me this I knew what was in his mind, and that, if he had not been in such respectable company, he would have said: 'It was just this which stopped me from getting married.'   (1 436)

In the following palladian remark the middle (matrimony) is just about right, one extreme (bigamy) is wrong one way, and the other extreme wrong the other way: '*Boss:* Boss's son, Tom, is illegitimate; but he has himself committed bigamy, first with Topsy and now with Phoebe – or 'Phoeb', as Boss calls her without sounding the final 'e'. Boss was not married quite enough; Tom is married a little too much' (II 11).

There is one type of use of the word 'or' in which what is on either side must be different. Because of his habitual checking whether what is on either side of a middle is the same or different, Butler was quick to realize the restraints in the use of the word:

> Be the day weary or the day long
> At last it ringeth to Evensong.

In thanking Miss Butler for her present I was careful not to say that I had met with 'Be the day weary' etc. in Ernest's bed-room at Battersby (chap. lxxxiii.), or to let her suspect that I remembered his comment:

'There's not enough difference between "weary" and "long" to warrant an "or",' he said, 'but I suppose it's all right.'   (II 422; see also the relevant passage in *The Way of All Flesh*)

Also, for the same reason, Butler was quick to add to his arsenal of jokes those that exploit the idea of underlying sameness despite seeming difference (signalled by 'or'):

Talking of doing nothing, did I tell you that in one of Miss Savage's letters she wrote of a man who had an unexpected holiday on a summer's day and could not make up his mind whether he should go to the Green Park and lie out all day under a tree, or whether he should do nothing?   (II 383)

Jones also had a keen eye for the occurrence of the similar where the different should have been, as in the following standard scene of comedy:

He was being attended only by Dr Dudgeon, who was eighty-two and deaf, and Butler also was a little deaf. The question of a second opinion was started; whereupon Butler said to Dudgeon:

'I am perfectly satisfied with you; but if you would like a second opinion, say so, and get any one you like.'

Dudgeon replied: 'I am sure I know what is the matter with you, and I am perfectly satisfied with your progress; but if you would like a second opinion, say so, and I'll get one in a moment.'   (II 398)

Butler's inability or unwillingness to distinguish between subject and object means that any activity of the subject affects itself as much as the (ostensible) object; therefore, to hurt is to *be* hurt:

If Mr Darwin chooses to take this ground, and does not mind going on selling a book which contains a grave inaccuracy, advantageous to himself and prejudicial to another writer, without taking any steps to correct it, he is welcome to do so as far as I am concerned – he hurts himself more than he hurts me.   (II 463)

One ritual affirming the sameness of subject and object is Butler's habit of automatically condemning both if he condemns one, or praising both, if he praises one. Compare the following example, in which Butler vows that his attitudes are the same whether he is subject or object: 'You are letting great talents and excellent opportunities go to waste. I am quite sincere – not being given to flatter nor liking to be flattered...' (I 175).

On some subject–object questions such as reviewing and being reviewed Butler chooses the object-role: 'I never write reviews; it is much easier to write a book than to review one, so I have drifted into the ranks of the reviewed, not of the reviewers' (I 209). Also: 'Besides I do not review books. I belong to the reviewed classes, not to the reviewers' (II 28). As usual, the varying surface meanings of such statements count for little in comparison with the stability in Butler's way of structuring the choice.[5]

Butler's passion for balance can be seen even in his personal habits. He kept account books, in which he entered and balanced his personal expenditure every evening (I v). He did this even during those periods of his life when he was financially secure. The attraction, it seems, lay mainly in the 'balancing' – in keeping the record of experience tidy, which to Butler meant balanced. Book-keeping by double entry had a special value to Butler; there are numerous references to it not only in his notes but also in his fiction.

Complementary inversion is found in many passages in the *Memoir*. If there is a social ritual of 'introduction' there should also be a complementary one of 'separation':

There ought to be some form of social separation as simple and void of offence as introduction. If ever I go to Erewhon again (which I do not suppose I ever shall, for I could never fill another volume or even half a volume) I shall introduce such a form, as one of the things I forgot to mention. (i 247–8)

If success is cumulative, so also, unfortunately, is failure, as Butler was to discover:

I have no doubt whatever about its success. Success is cumulative. *Erewhon* would make this successful even if it were not successful on its own account – I mean, of course, commercially successful.

[So we all thought and hoped, and the fact that almost any one in my place would have thought and hoped the same must be my excuse for going on eating up the dregs of my capital, and continuing to write. It was plain that writing was my strongest card; and I had not yet realised either Mr Darwin's character, or his irresistible hold on the public. I have since found out that if success is cumulative, failure is cumulative also; and for the last twenty years each one of my books has failed – of course I only mean commercially, for I admit no failure in any other respect – more completely than its predecessor – S. B., Sep. 16, 1901] (i 256)

Complementary inversion passes imperceptibly into mere dualism. Sometimes Butler thinks of complementariness even though there is no direct inversion. A proverb needs a 'help-meet', preferably a direct inversion, but, failing that, some other form of close relative:

Two are better than one: I heard some one say this and replied: 'Yes, but the man who said that did not know my sisters.' This proverb is the help-meet for The Half is Greater than the Whole of Hesiod. [1893.] (ii 8)

Butler's keen eye for dualities in his analysis of the works of others, such as the *Odyssey,* was the same as his keen eye for dualities in his personal life. Often the two were intermixed, and mutually reinforced one another, as in the following typical case of Butler's fascination with the expression 'double wages' in the *Odyssey:*

(From 'The Odyssey Rendered into English Prose' by S. Butler): Telepylus the city of the Laestrygonians, where the shepherd who is driving in his sheep and goats [to be milked] salutes him who is

driving out his flock [to feed after having been milked] and this last answers the salute. In that country a man who could do without sleep might earn double wages, one as a herdsman of cattle and another as a shepherd, for they work much the same by night as they do by day.

This is the prehistoric joke about the Laestrygonian man who could earn double wages if he could do without sleep, referred to by Butler in his letter to me of 30th August 1892 (ante, p. 146). We were told that the goats were driven into Cefalù to be milked from 6 till 8 in the morning and again from 5 till 7 in the evening; and this was the only town known to our informant where they were so driven and milked, and where fresh milk could be obtained twice a day, and therefore the only town where a sleepless man could earn double wages. In most Sicilian towns there was, in 1896, no evening supply; you had to take your milk when the goats passed in the morning or wait till to-morrow. No doubt, as Butler says in *The Authoress*, fresh milk could have been obtained in the evening in Palermo, Messina, or Catania, but it would not have been the usual thing. Even in Rome our landlord told us that it would be an exceptional thing for the goats to come to be milked in the evening.   (ii 246)

Butler's habit of adding enantiomorphic complements extended to his own (earlier) statements and to his own works. Evidence of his attitude are his numerous projects for sequels to earlier books:

Butler was not satisfied with having only written half of *Narcissus*, and was glad to get it published and off his mind, so that he could turn his attention to *Ulysses* which, as he wrote to his sister 3rd June 1886 (ante, ii, p. 38), was to be its succesor. He was only to write half of *Ulysses*, but by adding these two halves together he would be able to say that he had written and composed the equivalent of a whole Handelian oratorio. (ii 65; for a projected sequel to *Alps and Sanctuaries*, see i xivj, and for a general picture of how idea followed idea in this way, i 233–4)

In the interaction between the individual and his environment poetic convention licenses a number of peculiarities, above all the 'pathetic fallacy', according to which nature shows sympathy with an individual by matching, for instance in weather or season, the individual's state of mind or emotion. People who begin to believe literally that their moods affect the weather, however, have stepped into the world of the mentally disturbed.

In noticing corresepondences between ourselves and the world, we see what we have a motive for seeing. Therefore, if we have a cold ourselves we will notice other people's colds. But, again, the mark of sanity is the realization that our cold did not cause the colds of other people; it only caused us to notice them.

Some disorders of imagination such as megalomania and paranoia result when something goes wrong in the individual's observation of correspondences between self and the environment. People suffering from megalomania believe that they cause everything that happens – they are the measure of everything. Paranoid people relate everything to the self in that they believe all persecution to be directed against themselves.

Dedicated artists are often very self-centred, and in Butler's case his withdrawal into a fairly small and rather private world was in addition motivated by his fear of being hurt. Certainly the self is the centre of Butler's world, and certainly he notices correspondences between the self and the environment: 'Curiously enough, like all unimaginative people, I have a fancy that everyone else has a cold as soon as I get one myself; whereas, until I had caught one, I thought that really no one was at all likely to have one' (ɪɪ 3).

Although I cannot see that there is any justification for using such terms as 'megalomania' and 'paranoia' in their literal sense in a discussion of Butler's habit, we might perhaps sometimes use them metaphorically. Butler was often deluded in his ridiculously exaggerated estimates of changes of current opinion, for instance. If he had changed his mind himself, and had said so in print, he tended to believe that others had done so as well, although there was in fact little foundation for this belief. Butler certainly also felt persecuted much of the time; but then, objectively speaking, he often *was* persecuted.

Butler's most questionable manipulation of the normal rules for regulating relations between the self and the environment is perhaps his habit of splitting the self up into two halves, which can then communicate.[6] This behaviour could easily turn into an exercise in solipsism: 'I have been putting down anything that it seems to me can be urged against it with as much force as if I were a hostile reviewer, and really cannot see that I have a leg to stand upon when I pose as an objector' (ɪ 243). No matter how much Butler may assure the reader of his complete lack of partiality when he poses as an objector, experience teaches us that it *is* easier to overcome difficulties when one is allowed to invent them oneself, than if they are invented by others (i.e. *real* others).[7] Inevitably, in raising one's own objections, one raises only such as can be demolished.

> He used, therefore, to talk about the *Odyssey* to me, coming to my rooms evening after evening, inventing the objections which his opponents ought to have raised, considering them, adopting them tentatively, and finally embracing them with such ardour that he crushed them to pieces. In this way the evolution of his theory proceeded, and he assured himself that, when his book should be published, his critics (if any) would be able to bring forward only such objections as he had already considered and demolished.   (II 207)

It is true that Butler's capacity for 'seeing the other side', or at least his willingness to consider that there *was* another side was sometimes phenomenal. Even in his account of his quarrel with Pauli he concedes that there is Pauli's side as well: 'If ever it is read, however, it should be remembered that it is an ex parte statement and that Pauli's version of the matter can never be known' (II 287). Consider also his published dialogues with himself in *The Press* (mentioned in Chapter 1), and the extraordinary correspondence in *The Examiner* in 1879 known as 'A Clergyman's Doubts', in which Butler carried on a debate with himself in print for several months under different pseudonyms. (See Jones, I 238–9 and 295–8.)

But Butler did not really become solipsistic in any such way as to justify a very 'clinical' approach. There are some logical fallacies such as that of the undistributed middle that one might expect a chiasticist to fall victim to. But this does not seem to happen in a very clear cut way in Butler.[8] And when it does happen it is usually in context such as the machine chapters in *Erewhon*, in which Butler's degree of seriousness and involvement is difficult to determine. I have already stated which logical fallacies Butler is usually guilty of: i.e. seeing contraries as contradictories and imposing unjustifiable dualism on nature and reality.) The logic of a solipsistic mind allows the positions of evidence and conclusions to alternate until the solipsist is spiralled off into the blue. What was a moment ago conjecture becomes fact, upon which another conjecture can be fastened, and so the process feeds itself, and the thinker is catapulted further and further away from reason.

Butler did nurse his theories, and they grew and grew, but it is not, I feel, fair to say that illegitimate switches between evidence and conclusion characterize this growth. In fact, the most daring self-sustained flights of any mind in Butler's fiction are Christina's reveries in *The Way of All Flesh,* and they are made fun of.[9]

The self-sufficiency which it is predictable that chiasticism should foster instead found expression in Butler in those technical features of style with which we are familiar. Thus, for instance, *sartor resartus* constructions (cf: Ch. 3) occur in his private rhetoric as in his public. In one letter to Miss Savage, Butler writes that he might have 'out-Oliphanted Mrs Oliphant' (I 175). Miss Savage, in a letter to Butler, criticizes his 'reflex reflection':

> And I don't like 'reflex reflection'. I think you have been caught by the jingle of the words; would not 'reflex thought' mean the same thing, and sound better? Or do you mean 'reflex reflection' for a 'sotiltée' (as the cookery book I have been studying calls complicated and curious dishes), which my brain is too dull to penetrate?   (I 204)

In Butler's home there was a servant named William Williams; Jones tells us that he was spoken of as 'William Williams, the Butlers' butler' (I 279) a quip that one may assume he learned from Butler. As with the words themselves in these *sartor resartus* constructions, so with their content. In a note on *Life and Habit* Butler writes, 'One object of *Life and Habit* was to place the distrust of science upon a scientific basis' (I 266).

In choosing whether to attack or ignore his enemies the chiasticist finds it difficult to do the latter. Sometimes Butler considers the strategy of indifference as an alternative to the strategy of direct attack, but such cases are rare:[10]

> *Butler to Hans Faesch: 31 July 1896* – Never mind about De Galembert's being a Roman Catholic if he is a good fellow otherwise. It is a great thing that you should have anyone at all whom you can make a friend of. I hate all that rubbish, whether Catholic or Protestant, more and more the older I grow and, so far from becoming indifferent to it, the sense of the harm it does in a thousand ways and of its utter unworthiness impresses me more and more continually. I loathe it. But, at the same time, I think we oppose it more effectually by treating it with silent contempt than by arguing about it.   (II 248)

Actually even here Butler immediately proceeds to the more familiar idea of wrecking a cause by joining it, and to the 'mule-driver' ruse:

> In fact I am not sure that the best way of dealing with those who are
> on the other side is not to pretend to agree with them a little more
> than one really does rather than to argue with them. The more they
> see us anxious to get them to think as we do the more they will stick
> to their own opinion. It piques them far more and makes them far
> more uneasy if we make them see that we do not care one straw what
> they think. This makes them suppose we must feel strongly enough
> not to want their support and the more they think this the
> more of their support will they give us. It is always a sign of
> weakness... (Ibid.)

To stay with the self is a means of ensuring sameness. But in Butler's 'palladian' world, where even antitheses are ultimately the same, that reason is not so important. Everything is both true and not true, as Butler says in a conversation with Jowett. 'It [*Erewhon*] was like everything else, Sir, true, and not true' (ii 152).

Antithesis was a strategy of discovery for Butler. Reading the *Odyssey* he made his discovery of the female authorship by means of antithesis: 'It was not till I got to Circe that it flashed upon me that I was reading the work not of an old man but of a young woman' (ii 106). As 'young' antithetically replaces 'old', so in parallel fashion 'woman' replaces 'man'.[11]

The rule of the actual similarity of seeming opposites in Butler sometimes needs the help of an argument that relies not on direct contact but on contact through intermediate stages, each connected to the following through end-linking. In the following example Butler thinks he may be able to call Mr Darwin the 'Pecksniff of Science' via calling him 'Bacon':

> I do not see how I can well call Mr Darwin the Pecksniff of Science,
> though this is exactly what he is; but I think I may call Lord Bacon
> the Pecksniff of his age and then, a little later, say that Mr Darwin is
> the Bacon of the Victorian era. This will be like passing one item
> through two different accounts, as though I had made Pecksniff
> debtor to Bacon and Bacon debtor to Darwin, instead of entering
> Pecksniff debtor to Darwin at once.   (ii 75)

That this indirect bond between extremes, *via* an intermediate stage, is related to chiastic thought is brought to our notice very clearly when

Jones continues, 'Apropos of this there is a further note reminding himself to call Tennyson the Darwin of Poetry, and Darwin the Tennyson of Science' (II 76).

Intermediate stages are unimportant because it is impossible to draw lines. Only the extremes count, and they are the same. To remind us of Butler's inability to draw any lines of division let us quote just two sentences from Jones: 'After I have done my present book, I go on to the "Organic and Inorganic". I have finally made up my mind that there is no hard and fast line to be drawn...' (I 333; Butler then, significantly, goes on to praise Walt Whitman, who was also obsessed with the idea of fusion and an all-encompassing sympathy and union of everything).[12]

If one can not draw any line, then any seeming differents are really the same, because strings of end-linking units can prove them to be so. Thus liberals are in reality bomb-throwing anarchists: 'I am afraid of liberalism – or at any rate of the people who call themselves liberal; they flirt with radicals who flirt with socialists who flirt with anarchists who do something a deal more than flirt with dynamite' (II 172). With the aid of similar chains of end-linking Butler was able to condemn the most varied people. Butler disliked Gladstone; Gladstone liked Dante; hence Butler disliked Dante; from which followed a long chain of dislike, until Butler ends up with a dislike which, again, like his dislike of Gladstone, is a postulate, or a first principle:

Butler says to Miss Savage: 23 Jan. 1883 – I see Gladstone says he owes all the fine qualities of his mind to the study of Dante. I believe I owe whatever I have to the fact that no earthly power has induced, or ever could induce me to read him. I have not yet begun even to feel the want of Dante.

Blake, Dante, Virgil, and Tennyson: Talking it over, we agreed that Blake was no good because he learnt Italian at over 60 in order to read Dante, and we knew Dante was no good because he was so fond of Virgil, and Virgil was no good because Tennyson ran him, and as for Tennyson – well, Tennyson goes without saying. (*The Note-Books of Samuel Butler,* 1912) (I 382)

These chains of end-linking elements can be seen as related to Butler's labile rushing to extremes – his 'wedge' thinking. In trying to come to grips with the 'wedge' problem, Butler adopted alternating postures of condemnation and acceptance. Under one of his aliases in the debate 'A Clergyman's Doubts', he condemns the rule: 'If Christianity does not contain *all* truth, must we conclude that it contains *no* truth?' (ɪ 297). But that is merely the working-out of the antithetical shadow of his main attitude, which is acceptance of the 'wedge' rule. In his scientific writings Butler makes very extensive use of this rule. Let us refresh our memory with just one example from Jones: '7. Given a single creature capable of reproducing itself and it must reproduce a creature capable of reproducing itself and so on *ad infinitum*' (ɪɪ 445). The validity of the 'wedge' rule is also implied in Butler's frequent use of various proverbs which reinforce it: for instance, the English saying, 'In for a penny, in for a pound': 'Feeling, therefore, that if I was in for a penny I might as well be in for a pound...' (ɪ 258–9); and 'I was in for a penny and might as well be in for a pound' (ɪ 342).

In his private life as in his public Butler spent much time contemplating which direction events are tending in. Is an event going forward or backward? 'The chapel that the old Jew sculptor was using as a studio at Crea was littered with limbs half-formed and coming into being, and Butler said it was a topsy-turvy Golgotha' (ɪɪ 58). Do the souls of animals go downwards and the souls of men upwards?

He [Butler] even suspected the fathers [at the Sanctuary at Sammichele] of having some idea that he might be induced to write on their side. One of them in a conversation in Ely Place had been trying to show that the distinction between men and animals was not arbitrary, but founded on something essential, immutable, etc.

'Thus the Bible says that the soul of a man goeth upward and the spirit of a beast goeth downward.'

'No,' said Butler, 'let us have the whole passage.'

So the father turned to the Vulgate (Ecclesiastes, iii.21) and found: 'Quis novit si spiritus filiorum Adam ascendat sursum, et si spiritus jumentorum descendat deorsum?' (Who can say that the soul of a man goeth upward and the spirit of a beast downward?)

Our English version is wrong: it has, 'Who knoweth the spirit of man that goeth upward, and the spirit of the beast that goeth downward to the earth?' The context shows that the Vulgate is right in rendering the question as one involving scepticism concerning our knowledge on these points. The father was much scandalised. He said he did not think he had ever read the passage before. And I do not think he had.   (I 374)

The passage I have quoted from Jones's *Memoir* show that, as regards chiasmus, there is little or no difference between Butler's private rhetoric and his public. A study of Butler's correspondence and his notes yields the same result. Butler's chiasticism is basically always the same, whether it appears in his fiction, his scientific writings, his letters, his notes or his personal life.

Furthermore, I think it could be shown that, although Butler borrowed ideas from others, he preferred to borrow chiastic ones. In her study Ruth Gounelas 'attempts to correct the view of Butler as a man intellectually isolated from the thought of his day, who read little, and reached his conclusions almost entirely independently'; her 'main aim is to prove how heavily he drew on contemporary ideas, rather than simply his imagination, in writing his books'.[13]

The material – largely unpublished – which Ruth Gounelas brings forth from the British Library, the Library of St John's College, Cambridge, and the Chapin Library, Williams College, Williamstown, Massachusetts, does show that Butler was far from isolated. Butler used to brag that he had the smallest library of any literary man in London (cf. Jones, II 320), but he spent most of his days in the British Museum and therefore had the resources of one of the largest libraries of the period at his command. He read extensively and borrowed frequently – with or without acknowledgement (usually *with*).

One gets the impression that Butler's borrowing was far from random. If he happened to come across chiastic ideas in the material he was reading, they were certain to be adopted. In the same way, any arguments implicitly denying chiasticism would be noticed and denounced. Thus Butler denounces von Hartmann for his attempts to separate mind and matter: 'There was never yet either matter without mind, however low, nor mind, however high, without a material body of some sort...'[14]

The relationship between Butler's love of symmetry and the world's love of symmetry, however, is not primarily a matter of Butler and the world borrowing symmetrical ideas from one another. Much more important is the pattern according to which the world provided one half, and Butler the other half, of a symmetric whole. Gounelas argues convincingly that, for all his anti-Victorianism, Butler always worked within terms of contemporary ideas: 'He may have been against his age, but except at the end of his life, he was never outside it. "Prevailing opinion" was the source from which he derived all his ideas and on which he was deeply dependent, even if this dependence was a negative one.'[15] In one way or another, directly or indirectly, Butler in his reading of others found what he was looking for, and what he looked for was symmetry.

The chiastic passages reported by Jones, and similar passages which can be found in Butler's notes, his correspondence, anecdotes and other people's personal recollections of him show that Butler's chiasticism was always the same, on the technical level of form and mannerisms. My general thesis in this study has been that there is, in Butler's literary works, a correspondence between phenomena on the technical micro-level of style, and the thematic macro-level. In the same way I believe that there is a connection between stylistic mannerisms when they are found in Butler's private life, and the larger emotional and developmental patterns of that life. In my opinion the picture of Butler's life presented so competently by several biographers, particularly Furbank, Stillman, Muggeridge, Henderson and Cole, takes on an entirely new and deeper meaning when complemented with the insight that one's familiarity with Butler's chiasticism provides.

Conclusion

The rhetorical figure of chiasmus is not a mere superficial ornament in the style of Samuel Butler, but rather something that reflects the author's entire personality. Butler's love of symmetry – which is signalled through his use of chiasmus – influences not only the way that he writes but also the way that he thinks, feels and perceives.

A thorough knowledge of Butler's chiasticism opens up interesting perspectives. Familiarity with his patterns of thought is an excellent *vade mecum* when we encounter more sophisticated phenomena in which chiasticist thought, love of symmetry and ambilateralism play a role. Butler's chiasticism is easy to understand because it is pathetically all on the surface. In Butler we are allowed to see chiasticism as it were under laboratory conditions, and this is an opportunity we should not despise. Familiarity with Butler's chiasticism will not only stimulate our curiosity but also make us better equipped to deal with the questions that arise when we proceed from the comparatively simple case of Butler to more challenging tasks.

What other 'chiasticists' are there? Is their chiasticism similar to Butler's? If it differs, *how* does it differ? Is excessive love of symmetry characteristic primarily of individuals, or are there periods of history, philosophies, literary genres, and so forth, whose degree of 'chiasticity' it might be worthwhile to look into?

Such questions can be answered more successfully if we have first made ourselves thoroughly familiar with one particular case of symmetry-obsession. Indeed, I think it is only after submitting oneself to such an experience that one becomes capable of seeing to what extent all kinds of love of symmetry (including some illegitimate ones) play a role in our thinking and in our linguistic and literary behaviour.

The function of symmetry in language and literature is a fascinating subject. If we want to find out about some of the ways in which symmetry influences our lives, we will wish to give some thought to the meaning of chiasmus.

Notes and References

1. It is not important *per se* that the inversion of *two* elements – rather than
three, four, five, etc. – should be singled out as a feature of the definition.
For a structure to qualify as an example of bilateral symmetry the strict
requirement is that, whatever the order is in one half, it should be inverted
in the other half. Thus *abc–cba*, *abcd–dcba*, and so forth, are examples of
bilateral symmetry no less than *ab–ba*. The *ab–ba* structure, however, is
the most important, and it is convenient to use the term 'chiasmus' to refer
primarily to that variety. In order for us to know that an inversion of
sequentially ordered elements is taking place, we need a minimum of two
elements. The *ab–ba* structure is therefore the minimal version of bilateral
symmetry. If more elements than two in each half of the two-part structure
are inverted (*abc–cba*, etc.) this may be thought of as an added boon. But
on no account should the definition of chiasmus demand that the inversion
be of more than two elements. If the order of two elements is inverted,
then we already know that there is a tendency towards symmetry, and this
is most certainly so if the two inverted elements are, in one sense or
another, the most important elements of the structure (which, again,
repetition automatically tends to make them).
    Whether the name chiasmus should be given also to structures such as
abc–cba and *abcd–dcba*, or reserved for *ab–ba* structures, is a quibble over
words. The essential question is whether a tendency towards symmetry is
at work or not. It naturally *is* at work in meticulously inverted
multi-element structures such as *abc–cba* (which may be considered a
kind of palindrome on the sentence level). But it is equally at work in the
minimal variant *ab–ba*, and this is the case whether *a* and *b* are the only
elements in the structure, or the main elements – and often even when
they are just two elements out of several.
2. I have given some examples of this type of thematic chiastic
structuring in *The Insecure World of Henry James's Fiction: Intensity
and Ambiguity* (London: Macmillan; New York: St Martin's Press,
1982), chapter five, pp. 137–92.
3. One of the functions of the English passive, in the dynamics of textual
progression, is to allow the writer to get round left–right restrictions.
4. Chiasmus is a figure of repetition. In sentences such as 'Jack loves Jill, and
Jill (loves) Jack', repetition of the verb in the second half is optional, and
the verb is often left as implied, without visible manifestation. But the two

elements 'Jill' and 'Jack' must be repeated, since it is precisely the two operations of repetition and inversion that bring the chiasmus into existence.

5. *The Shrewsbury Edition of the Works of Samuel Butler*, ed. Henry Festing Jones and A. T. Bartholomew, 20 vols (London: Jonathan Cape; and New York: E. P. Dutton, 1923–5) XII: *The Authoress of the Odyssey*, p. xxi. (This edition is hereafter referred to as 'Shrewsbury', with volume and page numbers as appropriate.)

Other people, in mediaeval or modern times have detected feminine influence both in the *Iliad* and the *Odyssey*. Not so Butler. What he longed for was complementariness, and that longing would not have been satisfied by a theory of female authorship of both poems. One may still come across, however, the misconception that 'Butler thought Homer was a woman'. That misconception not only reveals ignorance of the facts, but also unfamiliarity with Butler's temperament and his way of thinking.

That Butler would not at all have been satisfied with a theory of female authorship of both poems can be seen in, for instance, Shrewsbury, XII xx:

he [Eustathius] was trying to prove too much, because by attributing both the finished poems to the result of Homer's having consulted the works of Phantasia, he must have detected the influence of woman in the Iliad as much as in the Odyssey, which of course will not do at all.

Cf. also Ibid., p. 8.

6. I shall quote from the Shrewsbury Edition throughout, and give page references to that edition (the volume number is given only on the first reference to a particular work). But to make things easier for people who read Butler in other editions I shall also mention which chapter each example is taken from.

7. *Samuel Butler's Notebooks*, selections edited by Geoffrey Keynes and Brian Hill (London: Jonathan Cape, 1951) p. 58. I have decided to quote Butler's notes from this collection. It is widely available, and sufficiently extensive for my purposes. The original master copy of Butler's *Notebooks*, in 8 volumes, is in the Chapin Library, Williams College, Williamstown, Mass. Keynes's and Hill's selection will hereafter be referred to as *Notebooks*. To save space I shall incorporate the titles of notes into the text of the quotation. Titles of notes will be given in italics, and separated from the rest of the note by a colon.

8. Critics often call Butler a 'controversialist'. See, for instance, Streatfeild, in Shrewsbury, III xi; John F. Harris, *Samuel Butler Author of 'Erewhon': The Man and His Work* (London: Grant Richards, 1916) p. 59 ('And Butler's mind was above everything a controversial mind').

For an excellent study of the subject, see Ruth M. Gounelas, 'Some Influences on the Work of Samuel Butler (1835–1902)' (diss., Oxford, 1977) Part III, pp. 184–249 ('The 1890s: Butler as Controversialist').

9. See ibid., pp. 172–3, and *passim*. William James's chiastic comment on sadness and crying appeared in his article 'What is an Emotion?', *Mind*, 1884, pp. 189–90. Cf. Gounelas, 'Some Influences', pp. 88–9.

10. Similarities between the pragmatistic beliefs of Butler and William James

should probably be explained to a large extent as resulting from the chiasticistic habits of thought that the two had in common.

Several critics have, with varying degrees of insight, commented on Butler's and William James's pragmatism. Cf., for example, Clara G. Stillman, *Samuel Butler: A Mid-Victorian Modern* (New York: Viking, 1932) pp. 224–8; Adam John Bisanz, 'Samuel Butler: A Literary Venture into Atheism and Beyond', *Orbis Litterarum* (Copenhagen), xxix iv (1974) 316–37, and 'Samuel Butler's "Colleges of Unreason"', *Orbis Litterarum*, xxviii i (1973) 1–22; Lee E. Holt, *Samuel Butler* (New York: Twayne, 1964) pp. 51, 90, 94, 152, 159.

11. For a discussion of this see Michael C. Corballis and Ivan L. Beale, *The Psychology of Left and Right* (Hillsdale, NJ: Lawrence Erlbaum Associates, 1976) esp. 11, pp. 160–76.

12. Shrewsbury, vii 29.

13. See Henry Festing Jones, *Samuel Butler: Author of 'Erewhon' (1835–1902). A Memoir* (London: Macmillan, 1920) i 264–5. (This memoir is hereafter referred to as 'Jones'.)

14. Cf. also Jones, i 151 ('Giles, who has brains, read it through, from end to end, twice …'), and ii 125 ('Mrs, Beavington Atkinson did *Narcissus* the week before last, from end to end …'); Shrewsbury, xii 6 ('I read it [the *Odyssey*] through from end to end …'); letter to Robert Bridges, 3 Mar 1900 ('I shall read all your plays from end to end'), in Donald E. Stanford, 'Robert Bridges on His Poems and Plays: Unpublished Letters by Robert Bridges to Samuel Butler', *Philological Quarterly*, l ii (Apr 1971) 289.

The expression 'end to end' is quite a favourite in Butler, at the expense of 'beginning to end'.

15. I wish to point out that here, as everywhere in this study, my interpretations are not necessarily offered as an alternative to those of other critics. My only interest is to find out in what way chiasticism was responsible for the end-product.

For further interpretation of the equation illness–crime, see, for instance, Thomas L. Jeffers's brilliant study *Samuel Butler Revalued* (University Park, Penn., and London: Pennsylvania University Press, 1981) pp. 48ff.

16. Cf. Jones, i 233: 'Butler had first assumed that man is a mechanism, whence followed the inference about machines becoming animate.'

Note Jones's use of the word 'inference'. Chiasticists have a logic of their own; a logic which is governed by the underlying rule of obligatory symmetry. Given one statement, chiasticists think that the truth of its enantiomorph follows automatically, and to proceed to the enantiomorph they call 'drawing the inference' (specifically *the* inference, not *an* inference – there is only one to be drawn in chiasticist logic).

This is, of course, a logical fallacy. The enantiomorphic 'inference' can be drawn only if and when the reality under consideration is intrinsically symmetric.

17. The problem has been a preoccupation of philosophers through the ages. To some philosophers, such as Immanuel Kant, the question of the nature of enantiomorphs was a subject that the philosopher consciously

commented on, as it were, 'from the outside'. But it is also likely that to some philosophers an obsession with symmetry has been an unconscious underlying factor shaping their ideas and determining the direction of their thought.

18. Alternatively red.
19. Critics have realized this. Cf., for instance, Dieter Petzold, 'This Blessed Inconsistency: Bemerkungen zu den Paradoxien in Samuel Butler's "Erewhon"', *Germanisch-romanische Monatsschrift* (Heidelberg), xxvii ii (1977) 196: 'Es ist ein kennzeichnendes Paradoxon dieses an Paradoxien so reichen Buches, dass man beiden entgegengesetzten Ansichten eine gewisse Berechtigung zuerkennen muss'; Holt, *Samuel Butler*, p. 29: 'Indeed, a trap lies open for any reader of Butler who concludes from a single statement he may make that this is his considered opinion, even at the time he makes it'; Stillman, *Samuel Butler: A Mid-Victorian Modern*, pp. 179–80:

> But a contradiction more or less was not likely to disturb him, for he saw contradiction as essential to life. He was penetrated with the sense of ambivalence that is far more common in our day than it was in his. Nature abounded in fluctuating and opposing values, in relativities and contradictions, in an eternal is and is-not. Every truth was both truth and falsehood, every virtue pushed too far became a vice, every thought pursued to its conclusion ended in its opposite.

20. The role of destruction in the world of a chiasticist may be connected with the nature of chiasmus. A chiasmus is made up of two evenly balanced halves, which, apparently, the chiasticist often experiences as being at war with one another. The destruction resulting from such a war is total, the hostile halves mutually destroying one another and leaving nothing – rather than one half destroying the other, leaving at least itself.

    One is rather reminded of the Kilkenny cats, or the speculations in physics about the possible existence of anti-matter and what would result if anti-matter were to come into contact with matter.

21. The word 'no' plays an important role in the kind of dualism that characterizes Butler's thought. For Butler the simplest way of creating the longed-for dualism was negation. Everything is complemented with its own negation; everything comes in pairs of the 'something' and the 'not-something'. This 'not-something' was for Butler never *an absence*; it was an alternative form of presence. Butler was one of those people to whom negation represents not a void, but a concrete, almost tangible complementary form of presence. Cf. also Ch. 3, section ii, on *Erewhon*.

    For an orientation into some aspects of the philosophy of the word 'no', see Gaston Bachelard, *La philosophie due non: essai d'une philosophie du nouvel esprit scientifique* (Paris: Presses Universitaires de France, 1973).

22. Cf. Jones, ii 74: 'There will be no comfortable and safe development of our social arrangements – I mean we shall not get infanticide, and the permission of suicide, nor cheap and easy divorce – till Jesus Christ's

ghost has been laid; and the best way to lay it is to be a moderate churchman.'

P. N. Furbank, in *Samuel Butler (1835–1902)*, 2nd edn (Hamden, Conn.: Archon Books, 1971) p. 34, comments on this passage,

> The desire to shock that dictates the passage does not make it the less remarkable how completely destructive and negative the programme is. Butler's anarchism is so genuine as to be unobtrusive. His adoption of the title of Conservative in politics and his dislike of Liberals or Radicals is really the indifference of the pure anarchist. Infanticide, suicide and divorce are as self-contained a programme as liberty, equality and fraternity.

Furbank's study, although short, is by far the best book that has been published on Butler.

23. On the internal struggle within Butler's psyche, see ibid., pp. 10–11 and *passim*.

24. 'Over' here means 'beyond' or 'on the other side of' (cf. Butler's earliest ideas for a title). In the novel itself there are of course several ranges, but that is immaterial.

25. Cf. Shrewsbury, ı lxiii:

> I am much better to-day. I don't feel at all as though I were going to die. Of course, it will be all wrong if I do get well, for there is my literary position to be considered. First I write *Erewhon* – that is my opening subject; then, after modulating freely through all my other books and the music and so on, I return gracefully to my original key and write *Erewhon Revisited*. Obviously, now is the proper moment to come to a full close, make my bow and retire; but I believe I am getting well, after all. It's very inartistic, but I cannot help it.

See also Shrewsbury, xvı xiii; and Jones, ıı 396–7.

One of the very last things Butler wrote was a letter to Fuller Maitland in which he adds in a postscript, 'You will not forget the pretty roundness of my literary career! α *Erewhon*, ω *Erewhon Revisited*.' Cf. Jones, ıı 393; also facing p. 388.

26. The scene was drawn from Butler's own childhood experience: cf. Jones, ı 24.

27. Edmund Wilson, in 'The Satire of Samuel Butler', *The Triple Thinkers: Ten Essays on Literature* (London: Oxford University Press, 1938) pp. 210–19, advocates a Freudian interpretation of Butler's lifelong habit of rebelling against figures of authority:

> The Freudian would be able to show how, even after Butler had escaped from the domination of his father, he was still forced to keep putting in his father's place other persons of high authority, and, identifying himself with some lesser person, to insist on the latter's superior claims. Dante, Virgil, Bach, Beethoven and Darwin had all to

play the role of the old Butler, while Handel, Giovanni Bellini, Tabachetti and Gaudenzio Ferrari figured the snubbed young man. When he did admire accepted reputations, as in the case of Shakespeare and Homer, he had to invent original heretical theories as to who they had really been and what they had really meant. And though in 'Erewhon' and 'The Way of All Flesh' his revolt against his father had inspired him to his most brilliant work, his controversies with substitute fathers became less and less interesting as he grew older, and he himself turned into a kind of crank. (p. 211)

28. For an example of a passage in which Butler asserts his belief in reversibility, see *The Way of All Flesh*, ch. 19: 'So the psalmist says, "The righteous shall not lack anything that is good." Either this is mere poetical licence, or it follows that he who lacks anything that is good is not righteous ...' (p. 82). Cf. also *Notebooks*: 'knowledge and condition are as convertible as force and heat. They say that knowledge is power. Is, then, knowledge a mode of heat, since force and heat are convertible?' (p. 176).

29. Or the convention of alternation in some early Greek script, in which every second line went from right to left, and the others left to right.

30. Butler's resentment against his parents is a constant theme, directly or indirectly, in most of his works. In Bernard Shaw's phrase from 'Samuel Butler, the New Life', *Manchester Guardian*, 1 Nov 1919 (quoted in Stillman, *Samuel Butler: A Mid-Victorian Modern*, p. 196), Butler is 'the only man known to history who has immortalized and actually endeared himself by parricide and matricide long drawn out'.

31. Cf. for instance, R. F. Rattray, *Samuel Butler: A Chronicle and an Introduction* (New York: Haskell House, 1974) p. 18.

32. Martin Gardner, *The Ambidextrous Universe: Mirror Asymmetry and Time-Reversed Worlds*, 2nd updated ed, illus. John Mackey (New York: Charles Scribner's Sons, 1979).

33. Hermann Weyl, *Symmetry* (Princeton, NJ: Princeton University Press, 1952). See in particular the section on bilateral symmetry, pp. 3–38.

34. *The Reversible World: Symbolic Inversion in Art and Society*, ed. Barbara A. Babcock (Ithaca, NY, and London: Cornell University Press, 1978).

The reader interested in the symbolism of left and right, a subject tangential to symmetry, is referred to the standard work on this subject: *Right and Left: Essays on Dual Symbolic Classification*, ed. Rodney Needham (Chicago and London: University of Chicago Press, 1973).

Though undoubtedly excellent, this collection of essays also raises the question of to what extent dualism is inherent in reality. Can the amount and importance of dualism that an investigator finds in a culture be influenced by the fact that dualism is what he studies?

35. See George S. Tate, 'Chiasmus as Metaphor: The "Figura Crucis" Tradition and "The Dream of the Rood"', *Neuphilologische Mitteilungen*, LXXIX ii (1978) 114–25.

CHAPTER TWO.   THE PSYCHOMORPHOLOGY OF CHIASTICISM

1. Malcolm Muggeridge, *The Ernest Atheist: A Study of Samuel Butler*

(London: Eyre & Spottiswoode, 1936) p. 9. Cf. also p. 26: 'He was one of those who smell death in life and hate in love.'
2. Graham Greene, in *The Lost Childhood: and Other Essays* (London: Eyre & Spottiswoode, 1951) pp. 126–8, esp. p. 127, comments on the triviality of Butler's notes:

> Better far to stick down everything as it came to mind, even when the note was as trivial as:
>
>> *The Ridiculous and the Sublime:* As there is but one step from the sublime to the ridiculous, so also there is but one from the ridiculous to the sublime;
>
> as cheaply smart as:
>
>> *Christ:* Jesus! with all thy faults I love thee still;
>
> as meaningless as:
>
>> *Everything:* should be taken seriously, and nothing should be taken seriously.
>
> There is a great deal of this kind of thing in the second selection from the note-books: a great many exhibitions of rather cocky conceit in his own smartness – 'So and so said to me ... I said to him', the smartness which makes *Erewhon* so insignificant beside *Gulliver*, many superficial half-truths in the form of paradoxes which have become aggravatingly familiar in the plays of his disciple; and always, in whatever subject he treats, the soreness of the unhealing wound. The perpetual need to generalize from a peculiar personal experience maimed his imagination. Even Christianity he could not consider dispassionately because it was the history of Father and Son.

After reading thousands of sentences like those which Greene calls 'trivial', 'cheaply smart' and 'meaningless' one may be inclined to share his feelings. However, if one's task is analysis rather than evaluation, it is important to realize that it is precisely these 'trivial' notes that most clearly reveal Butler's psychomorphology. The first note may be trivial to us, but complementary inversion (which is what the note exemplifies) was never trivial to Butler. Likewise, though the third note may be meaningless to us, it was the very basis of Butler's 'rationality'. The 'cocky conceit', finally, is reciprocity exemplified, and, since Butler's struggle with reciprocity is perhaps the most pathetic of all his struggles, 'cocky conceit' is a definite misnomer.

Greene's comment on the 'unhealing wound' is undoubtedly very accurate.
3. Cf. also *Ex Voto*, ch. 17, pp. 189–90.
4. The immediate reason for Butler's fury in this case was that these myths 'suppose pain and happiness to be absolute, not relative' (*Notebooks*, p. 244). Chiasticism demands relativism.

5. Anything involving fathers and sons, or, more broadly, parents and children, was irresistible to Butler, because of his own unhappy relationship with his family, particularly his father. Stereotype narratives, situations, characters, and so forth, on this subject were certain to be noticed by him and subjected to the inversion treatment, as in the Isaac–Abraham inversion. In one *Notebooks* entry Butler picks out the tenth plague of Egypt for inversion:

> *The eleventh plague of Egypt:* The tenth plague was no good at all. The Egyptians would have been strangely unlike any papas and mammas that I have ever known if they had emancipated their slaves merely because one of their children died. What made them let the Jews go was an eleventh plague in consequence of which their papas and mammas were endowed with immortality. On this they let the Jews go immediately. (p. 189)

Note here how the emphasis shifts halfway through the quotation so that the hate of parents for children is replaced (i.e. complemented) by the hate of children for parents, thus completing the chiastic chart through establishing reciprocity of hatred between generations. Every generation has a dual role, being both a parent-generation (i.e. in relation to its children) and an offspring-generation (in relation to its parents). Every generation has an antithetical relationship both to the preceding and to the following generation. The shift of emphasis in the quote shows how inversion is abandoned once it has served its purpose. Its purpose is not to replace or cancel out, but merely to complement.

There are numerous inversions of stereotypes involving parent–offspring relations in Butler. For a case involving the parable of the prodigal son, see *Notebooks,* p. 116.
6. For further examples of Solomon and the lilies, see *Notebooks,* pp. 176, 202, etc.
7. For a typical example of Butler's love of an abrupt 'no', with himself as the speaker rather than the one spoken to, see *Notebooks,* p. 15.
8. Many of Butler's critics have commented on inversion. Cf. W. G. Bekker, *An Historical and Critical Review of Samuel Butler's Literary Works* (Rotterdam: Nijgh & Van Ditmar, 1925) p. 28: 'His fondness of looking at things from another point of view than the current one sometimes degenerates into silliness.'; G. D. H. Cole, *Samuel Butler and 'The Way of All Flesh'* (London: Home & Van Thal, 1947)

> He had most of the Victorian obsessions, though he had many of them upside down. That, indeed, was how he enjoyed having things: witness his life-long delight in inverting a proverb or a text. 'It is better to have loved and lost than never to have *lost* at all' gave him the keenest pleasure: his correspondence with Miss Savage, who shared his taste, is full of such *bons mots:* they stood happily on their heads at each other, whenever a chance offered. (p. 11; cf. also pp. 21–2, 24)

> The faculties which he applied in these later studies were much the same as he had used in his 'religious' period – a refusal to take anything at all on trust from the people who were supposed to know, and indeed a

preconception that they were probably all wrong, a love of inverting current beliefs (the same love as made him delight in turning familiar proverbs inside out), and a readiness to be totally captured by an idea, in such a way that it took full possession of him and went buzzing round and round in his head until he had relieved himself of it by the expulsive force of literary creation. (p. 61)

he took his usual course with every falsehood he met with. He turned it inside out, or upside down, and saw what it looked like reversed. Many of the scientists were saying that men were 'just like' machines. Very well: how about seeing what would follow if one affirmed instead that machines were 'just like' men? (p. 84; see also p. 103)

and J.-B. Fort, *Samuel Butler l'écrivain: étude d'un style* (Bordeaux: J. Bière, 1935) pp. 72–3 and 118–22. See also Fort's *Samuel Butler (1835–1902): étude d'un caractère et d'une intelligence* (Bordeaux: J. Bière, 1935) pp. 366–8. (Fort is one of the few critics who deals with Butler's rhetorical mannerisms directly, but he does so only briefly and in passing); Furbank, *Samuel Butler (1835–1902)*, p. 122 (on Butler and Wilde): 'the quotations from memory and reversed proverbs to which both Butler and Wilde were addicted'; Harris, *Samuel Butler Author of 'Erewhon'*, pp. 28–9; Holt, *Samuel Butler*, (on the Notes): 'Their dominant characteristic is the way in which, like his books, they challenge all accepted views, turn traditional patterns upside down...' (p. 144), and '*The Way of All Flesh* is in many respects the apotheosis in nineteenth-century English fiction of the attempt to view everything from an unaccustomed angle. All novelists indeed must attempt this to some extent to achieve liveliness, but Butler in *The Way of All Flesh* attempts it almost all the time...' (p. 101); Jeffers, *Samuel Butler Revalued*, p. 19, and pp. 129–30 (further references); Stillman, *Samuel Butler: A Mid-Victorian Modern*: 'a power of turning accepted ideas upside down and inside out in order to get a fresh view of them' (p. 12), and 'Turning an idea inside out was a favourite device of his for testing its truth and following out its implications. He used this simple trick with such skill and power that it became in his hands a richly creative process' (p. 115); and J. L. Wisenthal, 'Samuel Butler's Epistle to the Victorians: *The Way of All Flesh* and Unlovely Paul', *Mosaic*, xiii i (1979) 20.

9. According to Gounelas ('Some Influences', p. 244) Butler probably never read any Marx – at least he does not refer to him.

10. To some extent Butler influenced political thinkers, at least George Bernard Shaw and also, apparently, George Orwell.

Shaw's own famous acknowledgement of his indebtedness to Butler is in the Preface to *Major Barbara – The Works of Bernard Shaw*, xi (London: Constable, 1930) 221:

It drives one almost to despair of English literature when one sees so extraordinary a study of English life as Butler's posthumous Way of All Flesh making so little impression that when some years later, I produce plays in which Butler's extraordinarily fresh, free and future-piercing suggestions have an obvious share, I am met with nothing but vague cacklings about Ibsen and Nietzsche.... Really, the English do not deserve to have great men.

Many critics have commented on Butler and Shaw: for instance, Gilbert Cannan, *Samuel Butler: A Critical Study* (London: Martin Secker, 1915) p. 158; Cole, *Samuel Butler and 'The Way of All Flesh'*, p. 17; P. J. De Lange, *Samuel Butler: Critic and Philosopher* (Zutphen: W. J. Thieme, 1925) pp. 167–70; Furbank, *Samuel Butler (1835–1902)*, p. 94 (and on Butler, Shaw and Wilde, pp. 117–24); Harris, *Samuel Butler Author of 'Erewhon'*, pp. 69, 96, 114, 144, 218, 257, 294; Philip Henderson, *Samuel Butler: The Incarnate Bachelor* (London: Cohen & West, 1953) pp. viii, 102, 117, 122–3, 157, 221, 228–9; Holt, *Samuel Butler*, pp. 14, 130, 137, 149, 150, 151, 152, 157, 165; Jeffers, *Samuel Butler Revalued*, pp. 25–6, 31–2, 47–8, 65–7, 116–17, and *passim*; Hugh Kingsmill, *After Puritanism 1850–1900* (London: Duckworth, 1929) p. 59; Gerald Levin, 'Shaw, Butler, and Kant', *Philological Quarterly*, LII i (Jan 1973) 142–56; Muggeridge, *The Earnest Atheist*, e.g. pp. 47, 167, 169, 251; Rattray, *Samuel Butler: A Chronicle and an Introduction*, p. 21, and *passim*; Stillman, *Samuel Butler: A Mid-Victorian Modern*, pp. 6, 8, 183, 218, 246, 247, 269. This is only an incomplete sample. The literature on the subject is very rich.

What Orwell may have taken from Butler, if anything, is probably a general sense of the possible political applications of chiasticism rather than any specific view.

Chiasticism is highly relevant in Orwell's thought. He is troubled by chiastic scenarios of political change in the future. Both *1984* and *Animal Farm* express his fear of revolutions that become only a chiastic change of roles. One of Orwell's themes is the possible actual sameness of seeming antitheses, and the possible actual antitheticality of seeming similars. An example of the latter are the various mottoes and slogans in *1984*, such as 'War is peace.' Orwell felt strongly about such assertions, in which what is actually different is made out to be the same. An example of his corresponding, complementary anger, when what is actually the same has been made out to be different, comes in the final paragraph of *Animal Farm – A Fairy Story* (London: Longmans, Green, 1964) p. 88: 'The creatures outside looked from pig to man, and from man to pig, and from pig to man again; but already it was impossible to say which was which.'

If change means no more than an inversion, or a new distribution of roles, it is worthless to Orwell, and in his fiction change is persistently viewed as a tool of tyranny. In *Animal Farm* the commandments of 'animalism' are changed, one by one. In *1984* all changes are for the worse.

In *Coming up for Air* there is the haunting symbol of the fish-pond which the narrator remembers from his childhood and thinks should by now be filled with giant trout, but which on inspection turns out to have become a rubbish-dump. This, at its extremest, is how Orwell viewed change.

11. Even some of Butler's personal changes of opinion took the form of a 'toppling-over'. Recording the origins of his beliefs, Butler often pictures himself as unconsciously prepared for some sudden revelation which occurred with or without an outside stimulus.

Stillman finds 'toppling-over' patterns in Butler's biography: 'there was an inherent trustfulness and conservatism in Butler's nature, especially where his emotions were involved, which led him, like Charity, to "suffer long and be kind", but which, once the breaking point was reached, made his reaction all the more violent' (*Samuel Butler: A Mid-Victorian Modern*, p. 22).

12. See Aeschylus, *Agamemnon*, 1233; Nicander, *Theiriaca*, 372–83; Lucan, *Pharsalia (Bellum civile)*, ix.719; Pliny the Elder, *Naturalis Historia*, viii.85, see also xx.216, xxx.85 and xxx.128; Solinus, *Collectanea rerum memorabilium*, 27.29; Aelian, *De natura animalium* ix.23; Ammianus Marcellinus, *Res gestae*, xxii.27. See also relevant passages in the Aristophanes fragment, in Hesychius, and in Isidor, *Origines*, xii.4.20.

13. Translated as follows by A. F. Scholfield – Aelian, *On the Characteristics of Animals*, ii (Cambridge, Mass.: Harvard University Press, 1959) pp. 243–4:

> The Amphisbaena however is a snake with two heads, one at the top and one in the direction of the tail. When it advances, as need for a forward movement impels it, it leaves one end behind to serve as tail, while the other it uses as a head. Then again if it wants to move backwards, it uses the two heads in exactly the opposite manner from what it did before.

14. Tennyson takes a similar attitude in a metaphor: 'Two vipers of one breed – an amphisbaena, / Each end a sting' – *Queen Mary*, iii. iv.39, p. 107 in *'Queen Mary' and 'Harold'*, annot. Alfred Lord Tennyson, ed. Hallam Lord Tennyson (London: Macmillan, 1908)

15. I am grateful to Jon Haarberg for discussing with me the views of the ancients towards the amphisbaena.

16. In an abusive epigram, probably by Alexander Pope, the amphisbaena is used in a metaphor to satirize two collaborating hostile authors:

> Burnet *and* Duckit, *friends in spite,*
> *Came hissing forth in Verse;*
> *Both were so forward, each wou'd write,*
> *So dull, each hung an A* ——
> *Thus* Amphisbœna *(I have read)*
> *At either end assails;*
> *None knows which leads, or which is led,*
> *For both Heads are but Tails.*

See Alexander Pope, *The Dunciad*, ed. James Sutherland, in *The Twickenham Edition of the Poems of Alexander Pope*, v (London: Methuen, 1965) p. 169 (this edn. first publ. 1943).

17. Note also the reference to King Dagobert (p. 24). Butler unerringly picked out all such details – his mind and memory functioning as a filter which let other things through but retained inversions.

18. Butler also reports the desperate attempts of others to reach stability:

> Her gardener, Curtis, had consulted her as to how and where some cabbages were to be planted. Later on the gardener came again with a

suggestion which was obviously an improvement. 'Curtis,' said she, 'if I tell you to plant the cabbages with their leaves in the ground and their roots in the air you will be pleased to do so.' And yet, as she said to my aunt, she knew Curtis's way was much better, but she was not going to have settled questions re-opened, and she was going to be mistress in her own house. (*Notebooks*, p. 14)

19. Again there is an extraordinary similarity between Butler and Henry James. James loved the idea that portraits tell us more about the painter than the sitter. One of his most famous novellas, 'The Liar' (1888), is devoted to this theme.
20. Cf. also *Notebooks*, p. 289, '*Walking up and pacing down*'.
21. This is one reason why I think a morphological approach, such as the present, is useful.

The morphological approach demands a particular intellectual discipline to which one may initially find oneself reluctant to submit. It is necessary to raise the level of abstraction in such a way that, for instance, two mutually contradictory statements in Butler's works may count as examples of the same thing. Such methods of classification may seem unnatural; still, they are necessary in this case.

Let us imagine four levels of generalization and specificity. On the first and most general level we have a subject-matter, say *man;* on the next (less general and more specific) level, *man and his environment* – a typically Butlerian dualist division. Then, on the next level (the third), which is even less general and more specific, let us assume we have a question: '*Which is primary, man or environment?*' (this being a typical Butlerian 'which-one' question). On the fourth level, which is least general and most specific, there will be an answer, either '*Man is primary*', or '*Environment is primary.*'

For the morphological analysis, which is meant to give us an insight into Butler's psyche, the important level is the third. With another author we would most likely be interested only in what specific answer he gives to a question, but in Butler the fact of his asking the question, and the way in which he asks it, is more important than the specific answer – which, anyway, as we have seen, is likely to vary. In the case of such an author as Butler, who is so dominated by certain patterns of thought, it may be practical to ignore, temporarily, the surface-meaning of his texts, and instead aim at a level slightly below surface-meaning. Quite a lot can be learnt by classifying and comparing different kinds of passages and studying frequencies, on this level.

The morphological analysis, by the way, does not necessarily always increase one's enjoyment of Butler's works. On the contrary, when we look behind the scenes, and see the creaking intellectual machinery, some of the mystery vanishes. But this is the curse of all analysis, and perhaps after the dissection we may put the scalpel aside and revert to reading, rather than studying, Butler. He definitely deserves to be read too, and not only studied.

The morphological approach is not of very much use to a critic or reader interested in aesthetic evaluation of Butler's works, because Butler's chiasticism caused both the successes and the failures in his art. Butler *is* whatever he is largely because of his love of symmetry. But that still leaves us with the task of making up our minds about the value of his works. Personally I agree with the view of most other critics that Butler is at his best in a work such as *The Way of All Flesh* in which the scheme and character of the work was most in harmony with his mental habits. But there are many minor triumphs in Butler's art. To mention only one, there is the particular variety of 'tenderness', the capacity for enjoyment and delight that Furbank draws attention to in *Samuel Butler (1835–1902)*, ch. 2 ('The Scratching of a Mouse', pp. 43–55); cf. also Jeffers, *Samuel Butler Revalued*, ch. 3 ('The Hedonics', pp. 47–70). This quality is found in *Alps and Sanctuaries*, sometimes in the *Notebooks*, but even, in scattered instances, in *The Way of All Flesh*.

22. Cf. Holt, *Samuel Butler*, pp. 48–57: 'It is satire, but what a many-voiced satire it is!' (p. 56).

23. See Samuel Butler, *Essays on Life, Art and Science*, ed. R. A. Streatfeild (Port Washington, NY, and London: Kennikat Press, 1970) pp. 176–233 (first publ. 1908).

24. Geoffrey Chaucer, *The Parlement of Foulys*, ed. D. S. Brewer (London and Edinburgh: Thomas Nelson, 1960) p. 75.

25. An important theme in *The Parlement of Foulys* is that of choice; the birds have gathered on St Valentine's Day to choose a mate. The clash between the ideal and the practical reappears later on in the poem. The upper-class birds are influenced by a 'courtly-love' type of lover's hesitation, while the lower-class birds usually want to stop dilly-dallying and get on with the business in hand.

The image of a piece of iron suspended between two magnets of equal strength occurs at an important point in the narrative. The author has had a dream in which Scipio Africanus takes him on a journey, and they have come to the wall which encloses the garden of love. There (ll. 120ff.) the protagonist faces a difficult choice. The gates to the garden of love carry two inscriptions that totally contradict one another. One of the inscriptions (stanza 19) urges the protagonist to accept love and enter:

> 'Thorw me men gon in to that blysful place
> Of hertis hele & dedly woundis cure;
> Thorw me men gon onto the welle of grace,
> Theere grene & lusty May shal euere endure;
> This is the weye to al good auenture;
> Be glad, thow redere, & thyn sorwe ofcaste
> Al opyn am I; passe in & sped the faste.'

The other (stanza 20) says the opposite:

> 'Thorw me men gon', than spak that othir side,
> 'Onto the mortal strokis of the spere
> Of whiche Disdayn & Daunger is the gyde,
> Ther neuere tre shal freut ne leuys bere;
> This strem ʒow ledith to [the] sorweful were
> There as the fisch in prysoun is al drye;
> Th' eschewing is only the remedye.'

Faced with this contradictory advice the protagonist is paralysed:

> These wers of gold & blak iwretyn were,
> Of whiche I gan astonyd to beholde;
> For *with* that on encresede ay myn fere,
> And with that othir gan myn hertė bolde;
> That on me hette; that othir dede me colde;
> No wit hadde I, for errour, for to chese,
> To entre or flen, or me to saue or lese.

After these reflections the protagonist then goes on to the famous image already discussed.

26. See *Iohannis Buridani quaestiones super libris quattuor de caelo et mundo*, ed. Ernest Addison Moody, The Mediaeval Academy of America, Publication no. 40 (*Studies and Documents, no. 6*) (Cambridge, 1942) p. xi:

> The one thing for which [Buridan] was remembered during these three centuries – the famous problem of the ass who starved to death from inability to choose between two equal bundles of hay –, is now asserted to be purely legendary, and to appear nowhere in his writings.

Moody quotes B. Geyer, *Ueberwegs Geschichte der Philosophie*, 11th edn (Berlin, 1928) II 597.

27. The entry in the *Britannica* reads as follows:

> The dilemma of a particular kind of moral choice, between two evidently identical items, is illustrated by the celebrated allegory of 'Buridan's ass', though the animal mentioned in Buridan's commentary on Aristotle's *De caelo* ('On the Heavens') is actually a dog, not an ass. His discussion centres on the method by which the dog chooses between two equal amounts of food placed before him. Discerning both a symmetry of information and a symmetry of preference about the two items, he concludes that the dog must choose at random; this outcome leads to the investigation of theories of probability.

28. It is possible that people's attitudes to questions of symmetry and asymmetry are determined to a certain degree by their temperaments and habits, so that idealistic people are drawn more towards symmetry than practical people. It may even be possible that Aristotle's curious insistence on the intrinsic superiority of the right over the left may have resulted from the fact that he was much more of a practical man than, say, Plato. Plato advocated bisexualism, and he thought that man is by nature ambidextrous, and becomes handed (right-handed) because of the influence of foolish nurses and mothers. (Cf. in particular *Leges*, 794d–795d.) Plato was, in the main, an idealist. (Aristotle was more of an empiricist, and maybe for that reason he argued that handedness (right-handedness) is of nature. But, when Aristotle argues other cases of laterality, and particularly when he insists that the right is intrinsically

superior to the left, we may speculate whether his thinking may have been influenced by a conviction that practice functions on asymmetry. In other words, though Aristotle may be wrong sometimes, is it the case that he is wrong in a good cause, as it were – the cause of asymmetry? Cf. particularly *De caelo*, 284b; *De incessu animalium*, 706b; and *De partibus animalium*, 665a. For comments on these, and other relevant passages, see Geoffrey Lloyd, 'Right and Left in Greek Philosophy', in *Right and Left*, ed. Needham, pp. 167–86.

29. Ultimately, however, Butler feels that fusion is impossible, and he often makes fun of people who attempt to bring two differents together (though he did this all the time himself!). In *The Way of All Flesh*, Butler feels particularly free to satirize an attempt to harmonize the Old and the New Testament, since the person making the attempt is Theobald:

> After breakfast he retires to his study; he cuts little bits out of the Bible and gums them with exquisite neatness by the side of other little bits; this he calls making a Harmony of the Old and New Testaments. Alongside the extracts he copies in the very perfection of handwriting extracts from Mede (the only man, according to Theobald, who really understood the Book of Revelation), Patrick, and the other old divines. He works steadily at this for half an hour every morning during many years, and the result is doubtless valuable.   (Ch. 16, 67–8)

On Theobald's death, the 'Harmony' is sold for ninepence a barrow-load:

> Theobald's effects were sold by auction, and among them the Harmony of the Old and New Testaments which he had compiled during many years with such exquisite neatness, and a huge collection of MS. sermons – being all in fact that he had ever written. These and the Harmony fetched ninepence a barrow load.   (Ch. 86, p. 404)

30. A good illustration of Butler's ambivalent attitude to vacillation is the following passage from *The Way of All Flesh*:

> Theobald, whenever this was touched upon as possible, would shake his head and say: 'We can't wish it prolonged', and then Charlotte caught Ernest unawares and said: 'You know, dear Ernest, that these ups and downs of talk are terribly agitating to papa; he could stand whatever comes, but it is quite too wearing to him to think half-a-dozen different things backwards and forwards, up and down in the same twenty-four hours, and it would be kinder of you not to do it – I mean not to say anything to him even though Dr Martin does hold out hopes.'   (Ch. 83, p. 374)

Vacillation is said to be 'wearing', but then this is said by a character whose motives for saying it are questionable.

31. Again a comparison with Henry James is justified. There are substantial traces of chiasticism in James's thinking, and therefore we may expect to find hesitation, inability to act, paralysis and destruction in his fictional

world. Find them we also most certainly do! The sterility of James's world is extraordinary, and the hesitation of his characters a by-word in literary criticism. As Edmund Wilson remarks, 'the men are always deciding *not* to marry the women in Henry James' – 'The Ambiguity of Henry James', in *A Casebook on Henry James's 'The Turn of the Screw'*, ed. Gerald Willen, 2nd edn (New York: Thomas Y. Crowell, 1971) p. 123.

Vacillation between two contradictory alternatives that cancel one another out also became a paralysing mannerism for Herman Melville. This is particularly evident in *The Confidence-Man*.

32. Furbank points out how *Erewhon Revisited* is in this sense similar to the other two books – *Samuel Butler (1835–1902)*, ch. 5, pp. 82–94 (*'Erewhon Revisited, The Coming Race* and *News from Nowhere'*).

33. See Norrman, *The Insecure World of Henry James's Fiction*, ch. 5.

Usually these 'turning-of-the-tables' inversions are multiple. In James's story 'The Jolly Corner' the protagonist turns the tables on a ghost by deciding to haunt the ghost rather than being haunted by it. But soon this reversal is in turn reversed, and the ghost starts pursuing the man.

For James critics it is important to realize the deep significance of 'turning', and the like, in James's works. Joachim Lang's excellent article 'The Turns in *The Turn of the Screw*', *Jahrbuch für Amerikastudien*, ix (1964) 110–28, was an important milestone. Lang draws attention to the importance and frequency of 'turn' imagery in the novella, beginning with the title itself. An equally important milestone was Hildegard Domaniecki's article 'Complementary Terms in *The Turn of the Screw*: The Straight Turning', *Jahrbuch für Amerikastudien*, x (1965) 206–14. Oxymoronic phrases such as 'straight turning' are perfect vehicles for a description of the psychomorphology of the governess and of James. It is symptomatic that both Butler and James invented the term 'straighteners', though with different meanings. In Butler, 'straighteners' is the name of a half-medical, half-theological profession in Erewhon. In James, the ugly governess Mrs Wix in *What Masie Knew* calls her spectacles 'straighteners': 'She wore glasses which, in humble reference to a divergent obliquity of vision, she called her straighteners ...' – *'What Maisie Knew'; 'In the Cage'; 'The Pupil'* (London: Macmillan, 1922) p. 25.

Lang and Domaniecki are both undoubtedly right, and such works as Shlomith Rimmon's *The Concept of Ambiguity – The Example of James* (Chicago and London: University of Chicago Press, 1977), and my own, can be seen as attempts to show the whole of a picture whose halves have already been well illuminated.

34. Many thematic peculiarities of Henry James become understandable against this background. His curious preoccupation with androgynous characters and hermaphrodites, for instance, as well as fairly numerous stories of 'split personalities', should be seen as consequences of chiasticism.

35. Arthur Koestler, *The Act of Creation* (London: Hutchinson, 1964) p. 33.

36. Samuel Butler, *The Way of All Flesh*, ed. James Cockrane, intro. Richard Hoggart (Harmondsworth: Penguin, 1979) p. 17.

37. Butler's habits of thoughts are reflected in his stylistic habits. Fort comments,

> La phrase s'organise d'ordinaire selon un rythme intérieur qui ne doit rien à un effort de disposition artistique, mais qui naît de la pensée elle-même. Ce rythme est tantôt un balancement, tantôt un renversement. Sa forme la plus simple consiste dans les oppositions élémentaires, 'more or less', 'good or bad', 'for good or ill', 'for better or for worse', ou les groupements de contraires: 'life and death', 'soul and body', 'mind and matter', 'love or hate', 'statical or dynamical', que l'on trouve constamment sous la plume de l'écrivain. Les titres mêmes de ses ouvrages sont souvent frappés en formules de deux termes: *Life and Habit, Evolution Old and New, Alps and Sanctuaries, Luck or Cunning?, God the Known and God the Unknown, Thought and Language.* Il y a là plus qu'une coïncidence. (*Samuel Butler l'écrivain*, p. 71).

38. Cf. Samuel Butler, *Ernest Pontifex or The Way of All Flesh*, ed., with intro. and notes, Daniel F. Howard (London: Methuen, 1965) p. 159.
39. I. A. Richards called this principle 'complementary' and mentions Niels Bohr as one of its advocates. Richards likes to comment on symmetry; he chooses such lines as Keats's 'Beauty is Truth, Truth Beauty' for explication with particular relish.
40. Many critics have noted, and commented on, Butler's inconsistency. See, for instance, Edmund Gosse, 'Samuel Butler', *Aspects and Impressions* (London: Cassell, 1922) pp. 55–76: 'The charm of [Butler's] mind lies in its divagations, its inconsistencies, its puerile and lovable self-revelations ...' (p. 59); 'The Pauli episode is valuable in supplying light on certain defects in Butler's intellectual composition. In measure, it tends to explain the inconsistencies, the irregularities of his mental life, and of his action as a scholar. He was the opposite of those who see life steadily, and see it whole' (p. 69); and 'The amiability, the ruggedness, the nervous instability, the obstinacy as of a rock, the tenderness and the sardonic bitterness which made up so strange an amalgam, are all frankly revealed [in Jones's *Memoir*]. It is for us to arrange them, if we can, into a consistent portrait of a most inconsistent figure' (p. 75).

    I do not think we *can* create a consistent portrait of Butler, except one which, as Butler would have said, is consistent in its inconsistency.
41. Superficially the main theme of *Erewhon Revisited* is the growth of the Sunchild myth in Erewhonian society – a variation on Butler's resurrection-theme. But what comes over most strongly is the sentimental treatment of the parent–offspring theme.
42. Mrs R. S. Garnett, *Samuel Butler: And His Family Relations* (London and Toronto: J. M. Dent; New York: E. P. Dutton, 1926).
43. In *Ex Voto*, ch. 6, Butler uses Melchizedek metaphorically. Referring to a statue called the Vecchietto, he says,

> perhaps the finest figure of all, who looks as if he had dropped straight from the heavens towards which he is steadfastly regarding, and of

whom nothing is known except that, if not by Tabachetti, he must be by a genius in some respect even more commanding, who has left us nothing save this Melchizedek of a figure, without father, mother, or descent. (p. 63)

44. In addition note the equivocation of 'he would be as well cared for as if he were in my own house'. We have had a glimpse of how 'well' that means. 'As–as' constructions, favourites in Butler's style, are relativistic, not absolute, and therefore suitable for use in equivocation.

45. This remarkable ambilateralism even on the questions in which he is himself most deeply involved is far from rare in Butler. In the Preface to the second edition of *Evolution, Old and New,* he is even willing to admit that in the quarrel between himself and Charles Darwin he rather than Darwin may be wrong: 'no man can be judge in his own case, and ... after all Mr Darwin may have been right, and I wrong' (Shrewsbury, v xiii).

46. Cole, *Samuel Butler and 'The Way of All Flesh'*, p. 36. See the whole section pp. 33–6. For another interesting observation by Cole, that Butler was 'ashamed', see pp. 55–6.

47. Martha Garnett's most valuable critical insight is her analysis of the relationship itself, and her insistence on Butler's lack of 'moral robustness', rather than her defence of the family. As she realizes, in Butler's world in order to be able to love one must be allowed to do so by the object of one's affection:

> They [Butler and his father] could never have made a pair. The material was different to begin with, and they were made up quite differently. But it was because Sam wanted to love and be loved, because his father *'would never allow him to feel* towards him as he was always trying to feel', that his intense bitterness was engendered. It was the same towards his sisters; he could not forgive them their distrust; the inevitable distrust of the believer for the sceptic. They, too, *would not let* him feel towards them as he wanted to feel. (*Samuel Butler: And His Family Relations*, pp. 225–6; emphasis added)

She accepts that Butler was 'repulsed and misunderstood': 'Let those who are revolted by the tone he adopts about his home remind themselves that it was the bitterness of pain – the pain of a very loving and sensitive nature repulsed and misunderstood' (p. 221). Given the repulsion and obligatory reciprocity, the development of Butler's relations with his family was more or less inevitable.

Butler's relationship with his family was not one of spontaneous hate; rather the hate came in as a substitute for love: 'Had he really hated his family and wished to break with them, he could at any time have done it; it was easy enough. Difficulty lay, not in turning his back on his home, but in keeping up friendly relations with it; and it was this that he elected to do' (p. 197).

Ruth Gounelas writes that, when Butler attacked the scientific establishment of the day, what he longed for was not really opposition but acceptance:

> Yet in spite of this apparent confidence in his own opinions, Butler's real feelings were far less positive. His consistent attack on the recognized

authorities in the field – their immovable preconceptions, their 'fear-of-giving-themselves-away disease' as he calls it in *Erewhon,* the fact that they were 'destitute of everything that men of honour all the world over have been accustomed to respect', and considered by everyone as invulnerable – only thinly disguised his desperate need for their support. Although he claimed to be writing only for the average man in the street, the sort 'who hang about second hand bookstalls and read nothing but what they are going to take or leave as it may please them', Butler was really yearning for alliance with the professionals.   ('Some Influences', pp. 228–9)

By chiastic definition this has to be so. When hate is love and love hate, asking for hate also means asking for love, just as hating means loving. In addition, since subject is object and object subject, hating the professionals means hating oneself just as much as them – since hating at the same time means being hated, and by both sides.

This is strange 'logic', but in forming a judgement on Butler's relationships and emotional life we must try to stay within this grey area of uncertainty and insecurity, in which nothing means anything and anything everything, even though it tends to make one's head spin.

48. C. E. M. Joad, *Samuel Butler (1835–1902)* (London: Leonard Parsons; Boston: Small, Maynard, 1924) pp. 17–18.
49. Ibid., p. 80.
50. The scholar, like everybody else, is subject to the lure of symmetry, and it is easy to make the mistake of automatically translating the aesthetic pleasure that a symmetric argument affords into a conviction that it represents the truth.
51. Even Higgs's discovery of his son George could be seen in this light. He has been 'mercifully deceived' by fate about the existence of this son for twenty years and fatherhood is sprung upon him as a pleasant surprise. Cf. A. E. Dyson, 'The Honest Sceptic', *The Listener,* 13 Sep 1962, p. 384:

In *Erewhon Revisited* there is an even odder failure to envisage family problems concretely. Mr Higgs returns to Erewhon after an absence of twenty years to discover that he has an illegitimate son called George. The moment the situation becomes clear, he discovers that George, and George's mother, are united in the highest admiration for himself. It is not merely that there are no reproaches: the original sexual act is justified on the plea that anything which brought so admirable a son into the world must have been good. And the son himself turns out to be a model of perfection: more handsome, more courageous, more virtuous than any other man, including the son of Mr Higgs's unhappy marriage to another Erewhonian – the one who went off with him in the balloon. Mr Higgs therefore has the pleasure of conceiving a son, the pleasure of discovering him twenty years later, the pleasure of finding him everything a father could wish, and the pleasure of having not known he even existed in the period between. If this is Butler's formula for getting the best of all possible worlds, one has to admire its thoroughness; but as a serious alternative to the dangers of parental tyranny, one must admit that it is unconvincing.

52. Cf. also Muggeridge, *The Earnest Atheist,* p. 165. Butler was similarly fascinated with some comparable phenomena, such as 'kissing on both cheeks'.

CHAPTER THREE. CHIASTICISM IN SOME OF BUTLER'S WORKS

1. Simultaneously with his chiasticist ideas Butler's chiasticist vocabulary is also beginning to show in this essay; note, for instance, the word 'symmetry' (p. 4).
2. See Gounelas, 'Some Influences', esp. ch. 1, pp. 17–57, and 'Samuel Butler's Cambridge Background, and *Erewhon*', *English Literature in Transition,* XXIV i (1981) 17–39.
3. The passage in question goes as follows:

> sub illis
> Montibus, inquit, erunt & erant sub montibus illis.
> Risit Atlantiades: &, Me mihi, perfide, prodis?
> Me mihi prodis?

The name of the character who speaks first is Battus, cf. βαττολογία. But the commentators apparently do not think that the chiasmus carries any meaning – they ascribe its second half to the narrator, not to Battus – and accordingly I had better let the matter rest.

4. See, for instance, Shrewsbury, I xi, xxxix, and *passim.*
5. Ibid., pp. xxxvii–xxxviii (from ch. 1 of *Unconscious Memory*).
6. Cf., for instance, *Erewhon,* beginning of ch. 22.
7. Shrewsbury, I xxxix; also Jones, I 73.
8. See, for instance, *Erewhon,* ch. 23, p. 177.
9. One reason for the use of permanent double-sided inversion in stylized comedy may be the intelligibility of the code. Permanent inversion is one of the simplest rules of all, and therefore suitable in comedy, which is spoken art, therefore linear and incapable of taking too much obscurity. Riddles please, in comedy as elsewhere, but the key to the riddle must be simple in spoken comedy.
10. See, for instance, Muggeridge, *The Earnest Atheist,* pp. 68–9 and *passim.* On Butler and homoeopathy, see Gounelas, 'Some Influences', pp. 98ff., cf. also her 'Samuel Butler, Homoeopathy and the Unity of Opposing Principles', *Journal of the Australasian Universities Language and Literature Association,* LIII (1980) 25–41.
11. Cf. also *Erewhon,* ch. 10, p. 77.
   Another chiasticist feature of homoeopathy is the doctrine that, if one part of the body is affected by an illness, all of the body will be affected. This matches Butler's 'wedge' philosophy perfectly.
12. See, for instance, *A First Year,* pp. 105 ('crossing and recrossing'), 140 ('cross and recross'), 146 ('crossing and recrossing'); and 'Crossing the Rangitata', p. 183 ('crossed and recrossed'). It is significant that these phrases involve two parts: crossing *and recrossing.* We must not think

that this is dictated merely by the facts of the case. It is dictated by the facts of the case plus chiasticism.

13. Cf. *Erewhon*, ch. 17, p. 134: 'and that even the most blessed rising would be but the disturbing of a still more blessed slumber'. The comment is on the favourite subject of resurrection.

14. Butler then gives a date, thereby making it clear that the chiastic description was put in for its own sake rather than merely to impart information.

15. Butler regarded the 'wh' as a unity and did not invert those two letters. Similarly with the 'th' in 'Thims'. Cf. Jones, I 153.

16. Butler says that it was only in retrospect, when writing *Erewhon Revisited*, that he saw the full implications of the name. Cf. Jones, II 156–7.

17. The name 'Robinson' is suitable in a book of adventure and discovery. 'Jones' is a typically Welsh name, but also very common in England, and may therefore be seen as a symbol of normality – many things in *Erewhon* being normal and average, except inverted. A similar case is 'Thims'.

18. In 'Ydgrun' there is inversion in the order of the syllables and inversion of the sounds or letters in one of the syllables. Presumably Butler departed from 'end-to-beginning' inversion for reasons of euphony.

19. For comments on the other names in *Erewhon*, see, for instance, Joseph Jones, *The Cradle of Erewhon: Samuel Butler in New Zealand* (Austin: University of Texas Press, 1959) pp. 137ff.

20. An alternative early version of the title was *Erewhon: Or Beyond the Range*, see Shrewsbury, II, facing p. xii.

21. When you cross and recross a river you create a pattern of progress which is pleasing to the chiasticist mind. Doubtless this is the reason why Butler is so fascinated with the art of crossing and recrossing rivers. Naturally as is evident from Butler's New Zealand writings, particularly *A First Year in Canterbury Settlement* and 'Crossing the Rangitata', it was necessary for a Canterbury settler to master the art of crossing rivers. But in Butler's case there was also the psychological reason. Going up a river by crossing and recrossing it a number of times produces a zigzagging line. Therefore this activity ate itself deeper and deeper into Butler's consciousness and memory. Again and again in his writings he returns to the idea of crossing and recrossing rivers. In life it may be necessary to cross and recross rivers in order to get to a certain place. Let us therefore disregard Butler's endless reporting of crossings and recrossings in his 'realistic' writings. But in utopian fiction it is not strictly necessary to include crossings and recrossings to the inordinate extent that Butler does (for instance, at the beginning of *Erewhon*) unless there is a special reason. The crossings and recrossings of rivers at the beginning of *Erewhon* (and to a lesser extent in *Erewhon Revisited*) do not exist merely because Butler wanted to draw the geography of the early chapters of *Erewhon* from the Upper Rangitata district. The description fit that part of the world, as critics have pointed out, and as Butler himself confirms in his Preface to the revised edition of Erewhon (1901), but equally important is that they fit a mental landscape as well. The pattern of crossings and recrossings should be seen as a literalization of the abstract idea of 'zigzagging' vacillation in Butler's psyche.

The important feature about river-crossings is their tendency to repeat themselves, i.e. not to involve one crossing but reiterated crossings and recrossings. Testimony of the lack of permanence of direction of any Butlerian move is his tendency automatically to add 'and recrossing' as soon as he has brought in the word 'crossing'. In chapter 3 of *Alps and Sanctuaries* he is not content to let even some ants merely cross a road – they must of necessity cross *and recross* it (Butler then crosses the string of ants in order to reach a meadow, which he crosses, and so on):

> About three or four hundred feet above the river, under some pines, I saw a string of ants crossing and recrossing the road; I have since seen these ants every year in the same place. In one part I almost think the stone is a little worn with the daily passage and repassage of so many thousands of tiny feet, but for the most part it certainly is not. Half an hour or so after crossing the string of ants, one passes from under the pine-trees into a grassy meadow, which in spring is decked with all manner of Alpine flowers; after crossing this, the old St Gothard road is reached, which passed by Prato and Dalpe, so as to avoid the gorge of the Monte Piottino.   (p. 20; see also pp. 260–1)

In chapter 27 Butler writes, 'At the bottom of this huge yawning chasm, rolled the mighty river, and I shuddered at the thought of having to cross and recross it' (p. 242).

2. Cf. Gerold Pestalozzi, *Samuel Butler, der Jüngere 1835–1902: Versuch einer Darstellung seiner Gedankenwelt* (Zürich: J. Rüegg, 1914) p. 25:

> 'Denn das, was Fehr 'Butlerismus' nennt, diese Sucht, jeden Satz umzukehren, ist durchaus nicht ein frivoles Spiel. Er ist gar nicht immer Herr der Situation. Er hat sich zwar dieses Umkehren zum Prinzip gemacht [*Notebooks,* p. 224], um die Möglichkeiten zu erschöpfen, und so vielleicht wichtige Entdeckungen zu machen.

Cf. also Stillman, *Samuel Butler: A Mid-Victorian Modern,* pp. 12, 115; and Harris, *Samuel Butler Author of 'Erewhon'*:

> 'In his own case he made it a practice to view things from a new angle, not for the mere novelty of the process, but because it often led to some new discovery. Always he was 'turning the canvas of his life upside down' in this search for criteria by which to measure it. He knew the inadequacy of so many of the old traditional standards: by thus using his humour he tested them and discovered unsuspected points of view. And such a use of humour, it must always be remembered, was serious and sincere – a voyage of discovery to find new and valuable truth. Mr Desmond MacCarthy put very clearly this aspect of Butler in a *Quarterly Review* article. 'Butler's sense of humour', he says, 'often performed the same service for him that the

dove did for Noah in the Ark. It flew out into the unknown, bringing back to him an indication that he would soon find solid ground beneath his feet.'   (pp. 28–9)

'In the second of the essays [Butler] again resorts to his favourite intellectual exercise of turning familiar propositions or conventional interpretations inside out, on this occasion not so much for the new discoveries he might make about the works in question as for the amount of fun he was going to get out of the process.   (p. 289)

'... complete and well-ordered topsy-turvydom.| ... This logical perversion of ideas in *Erewhon* is, however, particular and selective. ... So his book is paradoxical but never contradictory: it is the creation of a system with this one right granted to the author – a right to twist. As we have seen, it was Butler's delight to be turning things inside out, and examining them from a new point of view, which, though almost an absurd one, may contain valuable guidance in real life.   (p. 75)

'Mr Shaw has spoken of Butler's particular vein of wit which led him to 'take familiar and unquestioned propositions and turn them inside out so neatly as to convince you that they are just as presentable one way as the other, or even that the sides so unexpectedly and quaintly turned out are the right sides. ...'   (p. 96)

23. Or else the chiasticist will pretend that his 'discovery' is valuable, even if it is not; or – finally – he will be blind to any criterion of evaluation that does not regard symmetry as intrinsically valuable.

It is not within the scope of this morphological study to address the question of whether Butler's various theories were true or false. Naturally Butler's love of symmetry does not uniformly make his scholarly and scientific theories true or false. In so far as reality is intrinsically symmetric, an ambilateralist is more likely than others to perceive it correctly. If, on the other hand, it is intrinsically asymmetric, he is more likely than others to make mistakes.

Inversion as a strategy of discovery will be rewarding only in so far as the hitherto-unknown reality that is to be discovered is inherently symmetric. But this is not always so. If the undiscovered reality is intrinsically symmetric, then the habitual inversionist is all set for a great success when he strikes out on his inversionary expedition of discovery. But, if the undiscovered reality is intrinsically asymmetric, he will make a mistake, because he will be blind to what he finds.

The problem for the chiasticist is in evaluating what he finds. His lack of sound judgement on this point is the reason why such a chiasticist as Butler should turn into such a curious mixture of crank and genius. Just as love of symmetry influences the ambilateralist when he goes on his inversionary journey of discovery, so it also, unfortunately, influences him when he tries to evaluate what he finds. His main, and sometimes only, aesthetic criterion is that those things are beautiful which are symmetric or create symmetry. Similarly, his main, and sometimes only criterion of truth is that those hypotheses are true which contribute to the creation of more symmetry. A discovery is real if what has been discovered is symmetry.

Butler's works on evolution cannot really be judged as biology, but must rather be read as something else – philosophy maybe, or theology (as Furbank suggests).

Still, an ambilateralist should not automatically be dismissed or underestimated as a thinker. Although it is so very obvious what leads him to his conclusion, it does not follow from this that he will always be wrong. Because of his habitual questioning of any established symmetry, Butler found it easy to discover, for instance, that contemporary ideas of language had not given sufficient attention to the 'sayee' in the pair of sayer–sayee. Much of Butler's insistence on the importance of the sayee as well as the sayer in the process of communication is in harmony with present-day views.

24. One of Butler's 'palladian' structures in *Erewhon* and *Erewhon Revisited* is 'before-life', life and after-life. Harris comments, 'In *Erewhon Revisited* it is all stated in a symmetrical form, almost like a diagram; the World of the Unborn is thus the perfect counterpart of the World of Vicarious Existence' (*Samuel Butler Author of 'Erewhon'*, p. 267).

25. Self-immolation (like other, milder forms of self-punishment) is also a typical fate of the heroes in the fiction of Henry James. In *The Princess Casamassima*, for instance, the young hero, torn between insincere revolutionaries on the one hand, and equally dislikable upper-class snobs on the other, decides in the end to kill himself. Most of James's works end unhappily, when a hesitating and vacillating hero blames on himself his inability to choose between pest and cholera, and decides to punish himself for not choosing; for staying in the middle – which seems to be forbidden.

26. On Butler's literalism, see Robert E. Shoenberg's excellent article 'The Literal-Mindedness of Samuel Butler', *Studies in English Literature 1500–1900*, IV iv (Autumn 1964) 601–16. Many other critics have also commented on the subject: see, for instance, Hans-Peter Breuer, 'The Source of Morality in Butler's "Erewhon" ', *Victorian Studies*, XVI iii (Mar 1973) 323, and 'A Reconsideration of Samuel Butler's *Shakespeare's Sonnets Reconsidered*', *Dalhousie Review*, LVII (1977) 507–24; De Lange, *Samuel Butler: Critic and Philosopher*, p. 9; Henderson, *Samuel Butler: The Incarnate Bachelor*, p. 162; Kingsmill, *After Puritanism*, pp. 81–2; Muggeridge, *The Earnest Atheist*, pp. 24 ('His mind was intensely, almost pathologically literal') and 64.

27. The chapter opens with some of those passages that Butler added at the turn of the century in order to extend the copyright. I have decided to deal with *Erewhon* in this late and final version, rather than in the original version, because, as we saw above in section I of the present chapter, Butler's chiasticism is in evidence very early, and chronology is therefore not very important. The density of chiasticist material is higher, it is true, in the chapters added later, but that is a difference of degree, not of kind.

28. In Henry James's fiction victims perversely *seek out* their misfortune, and there is usually not a pin to choose between villian and hero. Adam and Maggie Verver in *The Golden Bowl* buy their spouses as if they were goods; but their spouses *offer* themselves precisely *as* goods. In *The Portrait of a Lady* Isabel Archer *goes in search of* the misfortune that – only in a manner of speaking – befalls her, and so on. Those critics who side with one or another party in James's works often cite his 'moral sense', but I am beginning to suspect that this may be mostly something that they read into James's text. Cf. my *The Insecure World of Henry James's Fiction*, ch. 5 and *passim*.

29. '... that his parents have nothing whatever to do with any of these things; and that they have *a right to kill him* at once if they be so minded ...' (*Erewhon*, p. 138; emphasis added).

30. Edmund Wilson, in 'The Satire of Samuel Butler', comments,

> In the chapter on 'The World of the Unborn', there is a magnanimous, an almost tender, insight of a kind very rare in Butler. Here for a moment he is free not to hate; he can understand that parents have not chosen their children any more than their children have chosen them and that the plight in which the situation places us may be equally cruel for both. (*The Triple Thinkers*, p. 213)

Wilson perceptively draws attention to the reciprocity. But otherwise he overstates his case. What can be safely said is not that Butler 'is free not to hate'; only that he is free to hate from two directions, and *in* two directions. And this 'understanding' is not something rare in Butler; on the contrary, if ever there was a variety of insight that came easily to Butler it was precisely this kind of ambilateralist insight.

Wilson's comment on Butler's 'magnanimous' and 'tender' 'insight' is interesting. Though Wilson's example is not one that I should have chosen, I agree with what I take to be Wilson's positive view. The 'tender' side of Butler comes through particularly strongly in *Alps and Sanctuaries*. There is often something particularly appealing about these 'tender' passages, and it is a pity Butler did not cultivate the 'idyllic' more than he did.

31. It should even be remembered that this favourite Butlerian construction of 'as–as', which implies balance, is a perfect vehicle for equivocation. If Arowhena loves Higgs as much as Higgs Arowhena, we do not know how much that is, until we know how much Higgs *does* love Arowhena (which may be more or less). 'As–as' is relativistic. Butler often used 'as–as' for equivocation, and sometimes comments on it explicitly. Jones reports on one such passage of equivocation:

> Butler's lecture 'The Humour of Homer' having appeared in *The Eagle*, he had it printed as a pamphlet in March by Metcalfe of Cambridge, and sent copies to friends, among others, to Garnett, who thanked him for the present of his discourse, 'which', he wrote, 'I shall read with no less pleasure than I heard it'. Butler annotated this with the following explanation and remark:

'*I.e.* "which I hate as much as when I heard the lecture delivered." I have never yet had an opportunity of making this clever euphemism my own – but I may yet have one. – S. B., Mar. 10, 1902.'

This comment is dated about three months before Butler's death; had he not been then seriously out of health he would have remembered that in the opening of the first chapter of 'The Deadlock in Darwinism', which appeared in *The Universal Review* in April 1890 (reprinted in *Essays on Life, Art, and Science* and in *The Humour of Homer and Other Essays*), he had already had an opportunity, and had used it, of making something very like 'this clever euphemism' his own. Speaking of Charles Darwin and Alfred Russel Wallace he wrote, 'Neither can be held as the more profound and conscientious thinker; ... neither is the more ready to welcome criticism and to state his opponent's case in the most telling and pointed way in which it can be put; ... neither is the more genial, generous adversary, or has the profounder horror of anything even approaching literary or scientific want of candour', and so on for nearly a page. Possibly Garnett had this passage in his mind when he wrote his letter of thanks. (Jones, II 131–2).

Harris is greatly in error when he writes (*Samuel Butler Author of 'Erewhon'*, p. 166) that this passage was inserted so as to leave no ambiguity:

It was doubtless in order that no ambiguous flavour might remain in the mouths of those who had read his books on evolution, that he inserted at the beginning of this essay a short and timely tribute to the work of Messrs Wallace and Darwin. We quote this passage, in conclusion, as an instance of the clearness with which a well-understood meaning can be conveyed. ...

On the contrary, the passage was meant to be equivocal, and, far from always trying to avoid equivocation, Butler often went in search of it. Rattray (*Samuel Butler: A Chronicle and an Introduction*, p. 155) quotes an example in which Butler gives his verdict on an American art-collection: 'This collection would vie with any similar one in the old country, or indeed in any part of the world.'

32. Petzold, in *Germanisch-romanische Monatsschrift*, XXVII ii 188–9, makes a similar point about the narrator's conversion of Chowbok – a deed which is meant to compensate for irregularities in the narrator's own life.

33. We realize what a complete reversal of Butler's previous attitudes *Erewhon Revisited* represents when we compare this passage with the one in *Erewhon Revisited* where Professor Hanky claims there had been a reciprocity of affection between him and the Sunchild. In *Erewhon* the worthlessness of reciprocity *per se* makes it a suitable vehicle when you want to sneer at something. In *Erewhon Revisited* the sanctity of reciprocity makes a lie all the worse if the lie claims a mutuality that did not exist.

34. Cf. Edmund Wilson:

'Erewhon', therefore, is not a production which one can compare to 'Candide' or 'Gulliver's Travels'. It is not the definite expression of a satiric point of view based on mature experience: it is simply the brilliant first book of a young man. It does not pretend to either the logic of Swift or the singleness of intention of Voltaire. The narrative is simply a device for uniting an assortment of satirical notions – in some cases, reductions to absurdity of English ideas and institutions; in others, whimsically suggested improvements on them; in others, flights of fantastic reasoning of uncertain application. (*The Triple Thinkers*, pp. 213–14)

This is a good summary. Of the varieties enumerated, the last one, 'flights of fantastic reasoning of uncertain application', is the most important. The anatomy of these 'flights of fantastic reasoning of uncertain application' can be understood when we realize that they become what they are because of chiasticism.

For comments on the nature and function of the irony and satire in *Erewhon*, and some further references, see Henderson, *Samuel Butler: The Incarnate Bachelor*, p. 95 ('He could change from one side to the other several times in a single argument'); E. D. LeMire, 'Irony in *Erewhon*', *Humanities Association Bulletin*, xvi ii (Fall 1965) 27–36; Pestalozzi, *Samuel Butler, der Jüngere*, p. 16; Petzold, in *Germanisch-romanische Monatsschrift*, xxvii ii 185–201; Rattray, *Samuel Butler: A Chronicle and an Introduction*, pp. 39ff.

35. See Martin Gardner, notes to *The Annotated Alice: Alice's Adventures in Wonderland & Through the Looking Glass: by Lewis Carroll: Illustrated by John Tenniel* (London: Thomas Nelson, 1975) pp. 228–44. Cf. also Gardner's *The Ambidextrous Universe*, p. 69.

36. Cf. ibid., pp. 68–9; Corballis and Beale, *The Psychology of Left and Right*, p. 135 and *passim*.

37. Again it is food for thought that the 'two-person' sentence is a typical device in Henry James's dialogues. See my *The Insecure World of Henry James*.

Particularly in James's later works, the distinction between the two individuals taking part in a dialogue has become so blurred – in proportion as James withdrew within his own self – that the dialogues or conversations, although they should by definition presuppose two people, have in reality become the working out of a narcissistic dialectic within one single mind. Very relevant in this context is James's habit of dramatizing, in direct speech and reported within quotation marks, what someone *imagines* an *imagined* partner in an *imagined* dialogue to be saying.

In *The American Scene* James time and again 'quotes', in direct speech and with the use of quotation-marks, what a scene or a view is 'saying' to him. Naturally this is only an extremely developed ambilateralist way of presenting what *he* thinks of the scene or the view.

James's habit of employing this kind of projection of a self as if it were a duality has led to endless controversy among James's critics. It is difficult to blind oneself to the impression that in James's works, particularly his late works, the imagination is slightly diseased, in the sense that the growth of the importance of the self has gone too far. What seems to be a dialogue, because two people are ostensibly engaged in it, is on some other level still a monologue, since the two partners in the dialogue know (or think they know) each other's minds to the extreme extent of being habitually able (or thinking that they are able) to finish each other's sentences – a device which conventionally is reserved in literature for comic twins.

38. The abstract principles of dualism, repetition, inversion, antithesis and reciprocity, which together lead to chiasticist thinking, are not all of the same kind or nature. Dualism, repetition and inversion are primarily purely *structural* principles, where antithesis and reciprocity are principles of a different kind, concerning meaning that is read into the former ones, or extracted from them. Butler tended to equate antitheticality and inversion. Since he needed inversion to create symmetry he accepted antitheticality too, but somewhat uneasily. His attitude to antitheticality is ambivalent. Although he needed it and accepted it he was not entirely blind to its character. Therefore, though he liked to put antithesis into the sentence-structure of his texts, he sometimes attributes these antithetical sayings to dislikable characters, as when the typically Butlerian combination of 'right' and 'wrong' is given to Pryer in chapter 56 of *The Way of All Flesh*: 'Pryer eyed Ernest searchingly, and after a pause said, "I don't know what to make of you, Pontifex; you are at once so very right and so very wrong" ' (p. 251).

With his attitude to antithesis Butler was fond of the word 'but'; nevertheless, in chapter 54 he puts some characteristic 'but' constructions into a letter which is being made fun of. ' "As for you I bid you God speed. Be bold but logical, speculative but cautious, daringly courageous, but properly circumspect withal", etc. etc.' (p. 243).

The numerous cases of reciprocal chiastic constructions in *The Way of All Flesh* reflect Butler's longing for fusion, but while we are on the subject of antithesis let us note that fusion is also openly made fun of – for instance, in chapter 28, in which Dr Skinner tries to bring about a reconciliation with the Church of Rome by attacking it in a pamphlet:

> Then he went on to the matter of these reforms themselves. They opened up a new era in the history of Christendom, and would have such momentous and far-reaching consequences, that they might even lead to a reconciliation between the Churches of England and Rome. Dr Skinner had lately published a pamphlet upon this subject, which had shown great learning, and had attacked the Church of Rome in a way which did not promise much hope of reconciliation. (pp. 118–19)

39. In Henry James's prose such violent revelations are also a regular feature. Most famous are the sudden flashes of insight of the governess in *The Turn of the Screw,* which are described in extraordinarily violent images.

40. Cf. Gounelas, 'Some Influences', p. 29.

41. For a study of this particular aspect see Breuer, in *Victorian Studies,* xvi iii 317–28.

42. One would have expected Butler to bring in Melchizedek here. Even though he is not named, we can take him as being present in spirit. Butler's fascination with Melchizedek should naturally be seen in terms of his uneasy attitude to the problem of initiality. How can one be born

an orphan? How can one envisage an absolute beginning, with nothing preceding it?

43. Cf. Gounelas, 'Some Influences', pp. 110ff.

44. Relativism is of course inherent in chiasticism itself, in the form we find it (chiasticism) in Butler. Cf., for example, De Lange, *Samuel Butler: Critic and Philosopher,* pp. 159–60, and 167 (reference to William James).

45. It was, of course, Streatfeild who chose the title *The Way of All Flesh* rather than *Ernest Pontifex or The Way of All Flesh. A Story of English Domestic Life.*

CHAPTER FOUR. CHIASMUS AND BUTLER'S LIFE

1. For a detailed interpretation based on a similar idea of compensatory asymmetry, see Stillman, *Samuel Butler: A Mid-Victorian Modern,* pp. 181–2.

2. Stillman attributes the phrase 'good hater but bad lover' to Paul Elmer More: 'Paul Elmer More thinks this labour of love *[The Life and Letters of Dr Samuel Butler]* Butler's one dull book because "he was a good hater but a bad lover" ' (ibid., pp. 233–4).

3. Furbank suggests that such changes of opinion show 'Butler's peculiar reaction to the subject of Possession, to the significance, that is, of the words "one's own". (*Samuel Butler (1835–1902),* p. 22). In 1883 Butler had written a favourable note on Titian. But in 1897 he adds a postscript: 'I have changed my mind about Titian. I don't like him.' Furbank comments,

> Now this note and its postscript were clearly not addressed to anyone in particular. Had the question of publication been strongly in Butler's mind, he would naturally have tidied the whole note up. The recording of the simple fact that he had decided upon not liking Titian means plainly that the fact was thought to be important in itself. To have made up his mind upon the subject of a liking or its opposite had a special value for Butler. Everywhere the insistence is that one's opinion shall be one's own, and 'one's own' begins to take on the colour of a valuable possession, another kind of prize or trophy carried off from the world, or, in a different light, a protective good, something to fortify one against attacks or to preserve oneself against mere emptiness or destitution. Likes and dislikes are to be thought a kind of property. (p. 23)

4. Exceptions are the cases in which the solution involves the answer 'both' or 'neither', since these answers are not really proper answers to a 'which-one' question on its own terms, but rather a comment on the nature of the question itself. The answers 'both' or 'neither' preserve symmetry, and therefore Butler not only tolerated them but sought them out, as witness: 'But he said one thing which I shall crib. He said: "Brigands demand your money or your life, but women demand both."

He must have cribbed it from some one, so I shall crib it from him' (Jones, II 272).

5. In Henry James's works there are also many references to reviewing and being reviewed. That some subject–object philosophizing in Butler and James should concern reviewers is not surprising. Reviewers are a class of people that authors are automatically put in an object-relation to.

6. Butler's capacity for splitting the self is put to special uses in his choice of solutions to some problems of narrative technique. In *The Fair Haven* Butler created what is really a single but split personality in the pair of John Pickard Owen and his brother. Overton and Ernest in *The Way of All Flesh* are such another pair, and so perhaps are the narrator and George in *Erewhon Revisited*. Conversely, because of his talent for splitting one personality, Butler was also, as could be expected of an ambilateralist, eager to see two personalities as one. Thus in *The Authoress of the Odyssey* he argues, for instance, that Circe and Penelope are really one and the same woman (two different geographical locations also melt together into one).

On Ernest and Overton, see U. C. Knoepflmacher, ' "Ishmael" or Anti-Hero? The Division of Self: *The Way of All Flesh*', *English Fiction in Transition*, IV iv (1961) 28–35. On relativism and absolutism and the characters of Ernest and Overton, see William H. Marshall, '*The Way of All Flesh*: The Dual Function of Edward Overton', *Texas Studies in Literature and Language*, IV (1963) 583–90. Cf. Muggeridge, *The Earnest Atheist*, pp. 230–1.

7. Cf. Harris, *Samuel Butler Author of 'Erewhon'*, p. 131: 'Often he himself had to create an opponent to criticise his own work, because at that time he had come very near to forfeiting whatever literary reputation he once possessed, his work being treated for the most part with contempt.' See also pp. 132, 149.

8. It does happen in the world of Henry James's characters, and this is one of the reasons why the methods of cognition of the governess in *The Turn of the Screw*, for instance, have attracted such a lot of interest and analysis.

9. It should be remembered, though, that Butler *was* constantly guilty of the misuse of symmetry in logic, in a number of ways. In inventing counter-examples, counter-arguments and refutations, for instance, Butler flitted back and forth between a thesis and its imagined enantiomorph in an unacceptable way. Examples proving the soundness of an imaginary symmetrical twin to the thesis under consideration always counted as refutation of the thesis under consideration, and *vice-versa*, whether there was any justification for seeing a link of symmetry between the two or not. In this respect Butler had a completely distorted idea of what the concepts 'inference' and 'implication' should be allowed to mean, and this uncertainty led to many circular arguments, though it also, paradoxically, led to suspicion of such arguments in others, and attempts, conscious or unconscious, at parody of these.

For some relevant material in this context, see Hans-Peter Breuer, 'Samuel Butler's "The Book of the Machines" and the Argument from Design', *Modern Philology* (Chicago), LXXII iv (May 1975) 365–83.

10. Cf. Joseph Jones, *The Cradle of Erewhon*, pp. 9 and 48.

If Butler wanted separation from his family why did he not stay in New Zealand? The fact that he returned shows that he wanted both separation and union. Many English settlers went to New Zealand with the idea of returning, but Butler's reasons for returning were multiple.

11. Familiarity with Butler's patterns of thought changes one's view of many things in the world drastically. Having seen Butler insist that inversion is a universal method of successful discovery, whether in catching birds (cf. *Erewhon,* ch. 3, p. 13) or in explaining evolution, one can never again see inversion in other authors with such innocent eyes as before. Many philosophers, who are given to inversion and dualism, will never again seem the same. With Butler's bird-catching technique at the back of one's mind, one becomes suspicious of too much reliance on inversion and dualism in any writer and in any system of thought.

It is, for example, difficult not to feel that the branch of literary criticism known as 'deconstruction', which enjoys a degree of popularity at present, relies too heavily on inversion as a method of discovery. John R. Searle, in 'The World Turned Upside Down', *New York Review of Books,* xxx xvi (Oct 27, 1983) 74–9 – a review of Jonathan Culler's *Deconstruction: Theory and Criticism after Structuralism* (Ithaca, NY: Cornell University Press, 1982) – writes,

> And the examples that Culler and Derrida provide are, to say the least, not very convincing. In Culler's book, we get the following examples of knowledge and mastery: speech is a form of writing *(passim),* presence is a certain type of absence (p. 106), the marginal is in fact central (p. 140), the literal is metaphorical (p. 148), truth is a kind of fiction (p. 181), reading is a form of misreading (p. 176), understanding is a form of misunderstanding (p. 176), sanity is a kind of neurosis (p. 160), and a man is a form of woman (p. 171). Some readers may feel that such a list generates not so much feelings of mastery as of monotony.   (p. 77)

See also the subsequent debate: Louis H. Mackey and John Searle, 'An Exchange on Deconstruction', *New York Review of Books,* xxxi i (2 Feb 1980) 47–8.

It is symptomatic, I think, that the undisputable successes of deconstructionist theory applied seem to have been studies on such authors as Henry James, Herman Melville and Friedrich Nietzsche, i.e. authors whose own concern with symmetry, dualism, inversion, and so forth, have ensured that there is something to discover for an investigator to whom inversion is important both as an object of study and a method of study. It is not clear what the value of the methodology will turn out to be with authors less given to dualistic, symmetric and inversionary thought.

12. On Butler and Whitman, see also Gounelas, 'Some Influences', pp. 122ff. and 12: 'Influence was a matter of one extreme or the other – wholesale adoption, or total rejection. The work of another writer was either like Walt Whitman's – deserving unqualified acceptance and praise, or like Goethe's – dull diseased trash.'

13. Ibid., p. ii.
14. Cf. ibid., p. 120.
15. Ibid., p. 6.

List of Works Cited

Aelian, *De natura animalium*.
——, *On the Characteristics of Animals*, trs. A. F. Scholfield, ii (Cambridge, Mass: Harvard University Press, 1959).
Aeschylus, *Agamemnon*.
Aristotle, *De Caelo*.
——, *De incessu animalium*.
——, *De partibus animalium*.
——, *Poetics*.
——, *Politics*.
Babcock, Barbara A. (ed.), *The Reversible World: Symbolic Inversion in Art and Society* (Ithaca, NY, and London: Cornell University Press, 1978).
Bachelard, Gaston, *La philosophie du non: Essai d'une philosophie du nouvel esprit scientifique* (Paris: Presses Universitaires de France, 1973).
Bekker, W. G., *An Historical and Critical Review of Samuel Butler's Literary Works* (Rotterdam: Nijgh & Van Ditmar, 1925).
Bisanz, Adam John, 'Samuel Butler: A Literary Venture into Atheism and Beyond', *Orbis Litterarum*, xxxix iv (1974) 316–37.
——, 'Samuel Butler's "Colleges of Unreason" ', *Orbis Litterarum*, xxviii i (1973) 1–22.
Breuer, Hans-Peter, 'A Reconsideration of Samuel Butler's *Shakespeare's Sonnets Reconsidered*', *Dalhousie Review*, lvii (1977) 507–24.
——, 'Samuel Butler's "The Book of the Machines" and the Argument from Design', *Modern Philology* (Chicago), lxxii iv (May 1975) 365–83.
——, 'The Source of Morality in Butler's "Erewhon" ', *Victorian Studies*, xvi iii (Mar 1973) 317–28.
Iohannis Buridani quaestiones super libris quattuor de caelo et mundo, ed. Ernest Addison Moody, The Mediaeval Academy of America, Publication no. 40 (*Studies and Documents, no. 6*) (Cambridge, 1942).
Butler, Samuel, *Ernest Pontifex or The Way of All Flesh*, ed., with intro. and notes, Daniel F. Howard (London: Methuen, 1965).
——, *Essays on Life, Art and Science*, ed. R. A. Streatfeild (Port Washington, NY, and London: Kennikat Press, 1970; first publ. 1908).
Samuel Butler's Notebooks, ed. Geoffrey Keynes and Brian Hill (London: Jonathan Cape, 1951).
The Shrewsbury Edition of the Works of Samuel Butler, ed. Henry Festing Jones and A. T. Bartholomew, 20 vols (London: Jonathan Cape; and New York: E. P. Dutton, 1923–5).
——, *The Way of All Flesh*, ed. James Cockrane, intro. Richard Hoggart (Harmondsworth: Penguin, 1979).

Cannan, Gilbert, *Samuel Butler: A Critical Study* (London: Martin Secker, 1915).

Chaucer, Geoffrey, *The Parlement of Foulys,* ed. D. S. Brewer (London and Edinburgh: Thomas Nelson, 1960).

Cole, G. D. H., *Samuel Butler and 'The Way of All Flesh'* (London: Home & Van Thal, 1947).

Corballis, Michael C., and Beale, Ivan L., *The Psychology of Left and Right* (Hillsdale, NJ: Lawrence Erlbaum, 1976).

Culler, Jonathan, *Deconstruction: Theory and Criticism after Structuralism* (Ithaca, NY: Cornell University Press, 1982).

De Lange, P. J., *Samuel Butler: Critic and Philosopher* (Zutphen: W. J. Thieme, 1925).

Domaniecki, Hildegard, 'Complementary Terms in *The Turn of the Screw:* The Straight Turning', *Jahrbuch für Amerikastudien,* x (1965) 206–14.

Dyson, A. E., 'The Honest Sceptic', *The Listener,* 13 Sep 1962, pp. 383–4.

Fort, J.-B., *Samuel Butler (1835–1902): étude d'un caractère et d'une intelligence* (Bordeaux: J. Bière, 1935).

——, *Samuel Butler l'écrivain: étude d'un style* (Bordeaux: J. Bière, 1935).

Furbank, P. N., *Samuel Butler (1835–1902),* 2nd edn (Hamden, Conn: Archon Books, 1971).

Gardner, Martin, *The Ambidextrous Universe: Mirror Asymmetry and Time-Reversed Worlds,* illus. John Mackey, 2nd rev., updated edn (New York: Charles Scribner's Sons, 1979).

—— (intro. and notes), *The Annotated Alice: Alice's Adventures in Wonderland & Through the Looking Glass: by Lewis Carroll,* illus. John Tenniel (London: Thomas Nelson, 1975).

Garnett, Mrs R. S., *Samuel Butler: And His Family Relations* (London and Toronto: J. M. Dent, 1926).

Gosse, Edmund, 'Samuel Butler', *Aspects and Impression* (London: Cassell, 1922).

Gounelas, Ruth M., 'Samuel Butler, Homoeopathy and the Unity of Opposing Principles', *Journal of the Australasian Universities Language and Literature Association,* LIII (1980) 25–41.

——, 'Samuel Butler's Cambridge Background, and *Erewhon*', *English Literature in Transition,* XXIV i (1981) 17–39.

——, 'Some Influences on the Work of Samuel Butler (1835–1902)' (Diss., Oxford, 1977).

Greene, Graham, *The Lost Childhood: and Other Essays* (London: Eyre & Spottiswoode, 1951).

Harris, John F., *Samuel Butler Author of 'Erewhon': The Man and His Work* (London: Grant Richards, 1916).

Henderson, Philip, *Samuel Butler: The Incarnate Bachelor* (London: Cohen & West, 1953).

Holt, Lee E., *Samuel Butler* (New York: Twayne, 1964).

Horace, *Epigrams.*

Isidor, *Origines.*

James, Henry, *'What Maisie Knew'; 'In the Cage'; 'The Pupil'* (London: Macmillan, 1922).

Jeffers, Thomas L., *Samuel Butler Revalued* (University Park, Penn., and London: Pennsylvania University Press, 1981).

Joad, C. E. M., *Samuel Butler (1835–1902)* (London: Leonard Parsons; and Boston: Small, Maynard, 1924).

Jones, Henry Festing, *Samuel Butler: Author of Erewhon (1835–1902). A Memoir,* 2 vols (London: Macmillan, 1920).

Jones, Joseph, *The Cradle of Erewhon: Samuel Butler in New Zealand* (Austin: University of Texas Press, 1959).

Kingsmill [Lunn], Hugh, *After Puritanism 1850–1900* (London: Duckworth, 1929).

Knoepflmacher, U. C., ' "Ishmael" or Anti-Hero? The Division of Self: *The Way of All Flesh*', *English Fiction in Transition,* IV iv (1961) 28–35.

Koestler, Arthur, *The Act of Creation* (London: Hutchinson, 1964).

Lang, Joachim, 'The Turns in *The Turn of the Screw*', *Jahrbuch für Amerikastudien,* IX (1964) 110–28.

LeMire, E. D., 'Irony in *Erewhon*', *Humanities Association Bulletin,* XVI ii (Fall 1965) 27–36.

Levin, Gerald, 'Shaw, Butler, and Kant', *Philological Quarterly,* LII i (Jan 1973) 142–56.

Lucan, *Pharsalia.*

Marcellinus, *Res gestae.*

Marshall, William H., '*The Way of All Flesh:* The Dual Function of Edward Overton', *Texas Studies in Literature and Language,* IV (1963) 583–90.

Muggeridge, Malcolm, *The Earnest Atheist: A Study of Samuel Butler* (London: Eyre & Spottiswoode, 1936).

Needham, Rodney (ed.), *Right and Left: Essays on Dual Symbolic Classification* (Chicago and London: University of Chicago Press, 1973).

Nicander, *Theiriaca.*

Norrman, Ralf, *The Insecure World of Henry James's Fiction: Intensity and Ambiguity* (London: Macmillan; and New York: St Martin's Press, 1982).

Orwell, George [Eric Blair], *Animal Farm: A Fairy Story* (London: Longmans, Green, 1964).

Ovid, *Metamorphoses.*

Pestalozzi, Gerold, *Samuel Butler, der Jüngere 1835–1902: Versuch einer Darstellung seiner Gedankenwelt* (Zürich: J. Rüegg, 1914).

Petzold, Dieter, 'This Blessed Inconsistency: Bemerkungen zu den Paradoxien in Samuel Butler's "Erewhon" ', *Germanisch-romanische Monatsschrift* (Heidelberg), XXVII ii (1977) 185–201.

Plato, *Leges.*

Pliny the Elder, *Naturalis historia.*

Pope, Alexander, *The Dunciad,* ed. James Sutherland in *Twickenham Edition of the Poems of Alexander Pope,* V (London: Methuen, 1965).

Quintilian, *Institutio oratoria.*

Rattray, R. F. *Samuel Butler: A Chronicle and an Introduction* (New York: Haskell House, 1974; first publ. 1935).

Rimmon-Kenan, Shlomith, *The Concept of Ambiguity – The Example of James* (Chicago and London: University of Chicago Press, 1977).

Searle, John R., 'The World Turned Upside Down', *New York Review of Books,* XXX xvi (27 Oct 1983) 74–9.

The Works of Bernard Shaw, XI: *'John Bull's Other Island'; 'How He Lied to Her Husband'; 'Major Barbara'* (London: Constable, 1930).

Shoenberg, Robert E., 'The Literal-Mindedness of Samuel Butler', *Studies in English Literature 1500–1900*, IV iv (Autumn 1964) 601–16.

Solinus, *Collectanea rerum memorabilium*.

Stanford, Donald E., 'Robert Bridges on His Poems and Plays: Unpublished Letters by Robert Bridges to Samuel Butler', *Philological Quarterly*, L ii (Apr 1971) 281–91.

Stillman, Clara G., *Samuel Butler: A Mid-Victorian Modern* (New York: Viking, 1932).

Tate, George S., 'Chiasmus as Metaphor: The "Figura Crucis" Tradition and "The Dream of the Rood" ', *Neuphilologische Mitteilungen*, LXXIX ii (1978) 114–25.

Tennyson, Alfred Lord, *'Queen Mary' and 'Harold'*, annot. Alfred Lord Tennyson, ed. Hallam Lord Tennyson (London: Macmillan, 1908).

Weyl, Hermann, *Symmetry* (Princeton, NJ: Princeton University Press, 1952).

Willen, Gerald (ed.), *A Casebook on Henry James's 'The Turn of the Screw'*, 2nd edn (New York: Thomas Y. Crowell, 1971).

Wilson, Edmund, 'The Satire of Samuel Butler', *The Triple Thinkers: Ten Essays on Literature* (London: Oxford University Press, 1938).

Wisenthal, J. L., 'Samuel Butler's Epistle to the Victorians: *The Way of All Flesh* and Unlovely Paul', *Mosaic*, XIII i (1979) 17–29.

Index